OpenMP
Application Programming
Interface

Examples

Version 5.2 – April 2022

Source codes for OpenMP 5.2 Examples are available at github
(https://github.com/OpenMP/Examples/tree/v5.2).

Foreword

The OpenMP Examples document has been updated with new features found in the OpenMP 5.2 Specification. The additional examples and updates are referenced in the Document Revision History of the Appendix on page 529.

Text describing an example with a 5.2 feature specifically states that the feature support begins in the OpenMP 5.2 Specification. Also, an `omp_5.2` keyword is included in the metadata of the source code. These distinctions are presented to remind readers that a 5.2 compliant OpenMP implementation is necessary to use these features in codes.

Examples for most of the 5.2 features are included in this document, and incremental releases will become available as more feature examples and updates are submitted and approved by the OpenMP Examples Subcommittee.

Examples are accepted for this document after discussions, revisions and reviews in the Examples Subcommittee, and two reviews/discussions and two votes in the OpenMP Language Committee. Draft examples are often derived from case studies for new features in the language, and are revised to illustrate the basic application of the features with code comments, and a text description. We are grateful to the numerous members of the Language Committee who took the time to prepare codes and descriptions, and shepherd them through the acceptance process. We sincerely appreciate the Example Subcommittee members, who actively participated and contributed in weekly meetings over the years.

Examples Subcommittee Co-chairs:

Henry Jin (NASA Ames Research Center)
Kent Milfeld (TACC, Texas Advanced Computing Center)

Contents

List of Figures

List of Tables

This page intentionally left blank

1 Introduction

This collection of programming examples supplements the OpenMP API for Shared Memory Parallelization specifications, and is not part of the formal specifications. It assumes familiarity with the OpenMP specifications, and shares the typographical conventions used in that document.

The OpenMP API specification provides a model for parallel programming that is portable across shared memory architectures from different vendors. Compilers from numerous vendors support the OpenMP API.

The directives, library routines, and environment variables demonstrated in this document allow users to create and manage parallel programs while permitting portability. The directives extend the C, C++ and Fortran base languages with single program multiple data (SPMD) constructs, tasking constructs, device constructs, worksharing constructs, and synchronization constructs, and they provide support for sharing and privatizing data. The functionality to control the runtime environment is provided by library routines and environment variables. Compilers that support the OpenMP API often include a command line option to the compiler that activates and allows interpretation of all OpenMP directives.

The documents and source codes for OpenMP Examples can be downloaded from https://github.com/OpenMP/Examples. Each directory holds the contents of a chapter and has a *sources* subdirectory of its codes. The codes for this OpenMP 5.2 Examples document have the tag *v5.2*.

Complete information about the OpenMP API and a list of the compilers that support the OpenMP API can be found at the OpenMP.org web site

```
https://www.openmp.org
```

1.1 Examples Organization

This document includes examples of the OpenMP API directives, constructs, and routines.

Each example is labeled as *ename.seqno.ext*, where *ename* is the example name, *seqno* is the sequence number in a section, and *ext* is the source file extension to indicate the code type and source form. *ext* is one of the following:

- *c*   – C code,
- *cpp* – C++ code,
- *f*   – Fortran code in fixed form, and
- *f90* – Fortran code in free form.

Some of the example labels may include version information (**omp_**verno) to indicate features that are illustrated by an example for a specific OpenMP version, such as "*scan.1.c* (**omp_5.0**)."

———————————————————— C / C++ ————————————————————

A statement following a directive is compound only when necessary, and a non-compound statement is indented with respect to a directive preceding it.

———————————————————— C / C++ ————————————————————

2 OpenMP Directive Syntax

OpenMP *directives* use base-language mechanisms to specify OpenMP program behavior. In C code, the directives are formed exclusively with pragmas, whereas in C++ code, directives are formed from either pragmas or attributes. Fortran directives are formed with comments in free form and fixed form sources (codes). All of these mechanisms allow the compilation to ignore the OpenMP directives if OpenMP is not supported or enabled.

The OpenMP directive is a combination of the base-language mechanism and a *directive-specification*, as shown below. The *directive-specification* consists of the *directive-name* which may seldomly have arguments, followed by optional *clauses*. Full details of the syntax can be found in the OpenMP Specification. Illustrations of the syntax is given in the examples.

The formats for combining a base-language mechanism and a *directive-specification* are:

C/C++ pragmas

    #pragma omp *directive-specification*

C++ attributes

    [[omp :: directive(*directive-specification* **)]]**

    [[using omp : directive(*directive-specification* **)]]**

Fortran comments

    !$omp *directive-specification*

where **c$omp** and ***$omp** may be used in Fortran fixed form sources.

Most OpenMP directives accept clauses that alter the semantics of the directive in some way, and some directives also accept parenthesized arguments that follow the directive name. A clause may just be a keyword (e.g., **untied**) or it may also accept argument lists (e.g., **shared(x,y,z)**) and/or optional modifiers (e.g., **tofrom** in **map(tofrom: x,y,z)**). Clause modifiers may be "simple" or "complex" – a complex modifier consists of a keyword followed by one or more parameters, bracketed by parentheses, while a simple modifier does not. An example of a complex modifier is the **iterator** modifier, as in **map(iterator(i=0:n), tofrom: p[i])**, or the **step** modifier, as in **linear(x: ref, step(4))**. In the preceding examples, **tofrom** and **ref** are simple modifiers.

2.1 C/C++ Pragmas

OpenMP C and C++ directives can be specified with the C/C++ **#pragma** directive. An OpenMP directive begins with **#pragma omp** and is followed by the OpenMP directive name, and required and optional clauses. Lines are continued in the usual manner, and comments may be included at the end. Directives are case sensitive.

The example below illustrates the use of the OpenMP pragma form. The first pragma (PRAG 1) specifies a combined **parallel for** directive, with a **num_threads** clause, and a comment. The second pragma (PRAG 2) shows the same directive split across two lines. The next nested pragmas (PRAG 3 and 4) show the previous combined directive as two separate directives. The executable directives above all apply to the next statement. The **parallel** directive can be applied to a *structured block* as shown in PRAG 5.

─────────────────────────── C / C++ ───────────────────────────

Example directive_syntax_pragma.1.c

```
#include    <omp.h>
#include <stdio.h>
#define NT 4
#define thrd_no omp_get_thread_num

int main(){
    #pragma omp parallel for num_threads(NT)                    // PRAG 1
    for(int i=0; i<NT; i++) printf("thrd no %d\n",thrd_no());

    #pragma omp parallel for \
                num_threads(NT)                                 // PRAG 2
    for(int i=0; i<NT; i++) printf("thrd no %d\n",thrd_no());

    #pragma omp parallel num_threads(NT)                        // PRAG 3-4
    #pragma omp for
    for(int i=0; i<NT; i++) printf("thrd no %d\n",thrd_no());

    #pragma omp parallel num_threads(NT)                        // PRAG 5
    {
        int no = thrd_no();
        if (no%2) { printf("thrd no %d is Odd \n",no); }
        else      { printf("thrd no %d is Even\n",no); }

        #pragma omp for
        for(int i=0; i<NT; i++) printf("thrd no %d\n",thrd_no());
    }
}
/*
        repeated 4 times, any order
        OUTPUT: thrd no 0
```

```
S-31         OUTPUT: thrd no 1
S-32         OUTPUT: thrd no 2
S-33         OUTPUT: thrd no 3
S-34
S-35         any order
S-36         OUTPUT: thrd no 0 is Even
S-37         OUTPUT: thrd no 2 is Even
S-38         OUTPUT: thrd no 1 is Odd
S-39         OUTPUT: thrd no 3 is Odd
S-40    */
```

———————————————— C / C++ ————————————————

2.2 C++ Attributes

OpenMP directives for C++ can also be specified with the **directive** extension for the C++11 standard *attributes*.

The C++ example below shows two ways to parallelize a **for** loop using the **#pragma** syntax. The first pragma uses the combined **parallel for** directive, and the second applies the uncombined closely nested directives, **parallel** and **for**, directly to the same statement. These are labeled PRAG 1-3.

Using the attribute syntax, the same construct in PRAG 1 is applied two different ways in attribute form, as shown in the ATTR 1 and ATTR 2 sections. In ATTR 1 the attribute syntax is used with the **omp : :** namespace form. In ATTR 2 the attribute syntax is used with the **using omp :** namespace form.

Next, parallelization is attempted by applying directives using two different syntaxes. For ATTR 3 and PRAG 4, the loop parallelization will fail to compile because multiple directives that apply to the same statement must all use either the attribute syntax or the pragma syntax. The lines have been commented out and labeled INVALID.

While multiple attributes may be applied to the same statement, compilation may fail if the ordering of the directive matters. For the ATTR 4-5 loop parallelization, the **parallel** directive precedes the **for** directive, but the compiler may reorder consecutive attributes. If the directives are reversed, compilation will fail.

The attribute directive of the ATTR 6 section resolves the previous problem (in ATTR 4-5). Here, the **sequence** attribute is used to apply ordering to the directives of ATTR 4-5, using the **omp : :** namespace qualifier. (The **using omp :** namespace form is not available for the **sequence** attribute.) Note, for the **sequence** attribute a comma must separate the **directive** extensions.

The last 3 pairs of sections (PRAG DECL 1-2, 3-4, and 5-6) show cases where directive ordering does not matter for **declare simd** directives.

In section PRAG DECL 1-2, the two loops use different SIMD forms of the *P* function (one with **simdlen(4)** and the other with **simdlen(8)**), as prescribed by the two different **declare simd** directives applied to the *P* function definitions (at the beginning of the code). The directives use the pragma syntax, and order is not important. For the next set of loops (PRAG DECL 3-4) that use the *Q* function, the attribute syntax is used for the **declare simd** directives. The result is compliant code since directive order is irrelevant. Sections ATTR DECL 5-6 are included for completeness. Here, the attribute form of the **simd** directive is used for loops calling the *Q* function, in combination with the attribute form of the **declare simd** directives declaring the variants for *Q*.

──────────────────────────── C++ ────────────────────────────

Example directive_syntax_attribute.1.cpp (**omp_5.0**)

```
#include <stdio.h>
#include <omp.h>
#define NT 4
#define thrd_no omp_get_thread_num

#pragma omp declare simd linear(i) simdlen(4)
#pragma omp declare simd linear(i) simdlen(8)
double P(int i){ return (double)i * (double)i; }

[[omp::directive(declare simd linear(i) simdlen(4))]]
[[omp::directive(declare simd linear(i) simdlen(8))]]
double Q(int i){ return (double)i * (double)i; }

int main() {

    #pragma omp parallel for num_threads(NT)                  // PRAG 1
    for(int i=0; i<NT; i++) printf("thrd no %d\n",thrd_no());

    #pragma omp parallel num_threads(NT)                      // PRAG 2
    #pragma omp for                                           // PRAG 3
    for(int i=0; i<NT; i++) printf("thrd no %d\n",thrd_no());

                                                              // ATTR 1
    [[omp::directive( parallel for num_threads(NT))]]
    for(int i=0; i<NT; i++) printf("thrd no %d\n",thrd_no());

                                                              // ATTR 2
    [[using omp : directive( parallel for num_threads(NT))]]
    for(int i=0; i<NT; i++) printf("thrd no %d\n",thrd_no());

    // INVALID-- attribute and non-attribute on same statement
    // [[ omp :: directive( parallel num_threads(NT) ) ]]        ATTR 3
    // #pragma omp for                                           PRAG 4
    // for(int i=0; i<NT; i++) printf("thrd no %d\n",thrd_no());
```

```
S-35
S-36
S-37     // INVALID-- directive order not guaranteed
S-38     // [[ omp :: directive( parallel num_threads(NT) ) ]]            ATTR 4
S-39     // [[ omp :: directive( for                        ) ]]            ATTR 5
S-40     // for(int i=0; i<NT; i++) printf("thrd no %d\n",thrd_no());
S-41
S-42                                                          // ATTR 6
S-43     [[omp::sequence(directive(parallel num_threads(NT)),directive(for))]]
S-44     for(int i=0; i<NT; i++) printf("thrd no %d\n",thrd_no());
S-45
S-46     double tmp=0.0f;
S-47     #pragma omp simd reduction(+:tmp) simdlen(4)
S-48     for(int i=0;i<100;i++) tmp += P(i);                   // PRAG DECL 1
S-49     #pragma omp simd reduction(+:tmp) simdlen(8)
S-50     for(int i=0;i<100;i++) tmp += P(i);                   // PRAG DECL 2
S-51     printf("%f\n",tmp);
S-52
S-53     tmp=0.0f;
S-54     #pragma omp simd reduction(+:tmp) simdlen(4)
S-55     for(int i=0;i<100;i++) tmp += Q(i);                   // ATTR DECL 3
S-56     #pragma omp simd reduction(+:tmp) simdlen(8)
S-57     for(int i=0;i<100;i++) tmp += Q(i);                   // ATTR DECL 4
S-58     printf("%f\n",tmp);
S-59
S-60     tmp=0.0f;
S-61     [[ omp :: directive(simd reduction(+:tmp) simdlen(4))]]
S-62     for(int i=0;i<100;i++) tmp += Q(i);                   // ATTR DECL 5
S-63     [[ omp :: directive(simd reduction(+:tmp) simdlen(8))]]
S-64     for(int i=0;i<100;i++) tmp += Q(i);                   // ATTR DECL 6
S-65     printf("%f\n",tmp);
S-66     }
S-67     //    repeated 5 times, any order:
S-68     //    OUTPUT: thrd no  0
S-69     //    OUTPUT: thrd no  1
S-70     //    OUTPUT: thrd no  2
S-71     //    OUTPUT: thrd no  3
S-72
S-73     //    repeated 3 time:
S-74     //    OUTPUT: 656700.000000
S-75
```

C++

2.3 Fortran Comments (Fixed Source Form)

OpenMP directives in Fortran codes with fixed source form are specified as comments with one of the **!$omp**, **c$omp**, and ***$omp** sentinels, followed by a directive name, and required and optional clauses. The sentinel must begin in column 1.

In the example below the first directive (DIR 1) specifies the **parallel do** combined directive, with a **num_threads** clause, and a comment. The second directive (DIR 2) shows the same directive split across two lines. The next nested directives (DIR 3 and 4) show the previous combined directive as two separate directives. Here, an **end** directive (**end parallel**) must be specified to demarcate the range (region) of the **parallel** directive.

──────────────────── Fortran ────────────────────

Example directive_syntax_F_fixed_comment.1.f

```
S-1              program main
S-2              include 'omp_lib.h'
S-3              integer NT
S-4
S-5              NT =4
S-6
S-7        c     sentinel c$omp or *$omp can also be used
S-8
S-9        c$omp parallel do num_threads(NT) !comments allowed here    DIR 1
S-10             do i = 1,NT
S-11                write(*,'("thrd no", i2)') omp_get_thread_num()
S-12             end do
S-13
S-14       !$omp parallel do
S-15       !$omp+ num_threads(NT)                !cont. w. char in col. 6  DIR 2
S-16             do i = 1,NT
S-17                write(*,'("thrd no", i2)') omp_get_thread_num()
S-18             end do
S-19
S-20       *$omp parallel num_threads(NT)    !multi-directive form      DIR 3
S-21       *$omp do                          !                          DIR 4
S-22             do i = 1,NT
S-23                write(*,'("thrd no", i2)') omp_get_thread_num()
S-24             end do
S-25       *$omp end parallel
S-26             end
S-27       !     repeated 3 times, any order
S-28       !     OUTPUT: thrd no   0
S-29       !     OUTPUT: thrd no   1
S-30       !     OUTPUT: thrd no   2
S-31       !     OUTPUT: thrd no   3
```

──────────────────── Fortran ────────────────────

2.4 Fortran Comments (Free Source Form)

OpenMP directives in Fortran codes with free source form are specified as comments that use the `!$omp` sentinel, followed by the directive name, and required and optional clauses. Lines are continued with an ending ampersand (`&`), and the continued line begins with `!$omp` or `!$omp&`. Comments may appear on the same line as the directive. Directives are case insensitive.

In the example below the first directive (DIR 1) specifies the **parallel do** combined directive, with a **num_threads** clause, and a comment. The second directive (DIR 2) shows the same directive split across two lines. The next nested directives (DIR 3 and 4) show the previous combined directive as two separate directives. Here, an **end** directive (**end parallel**) must be specified to demarcate the range (region) of the **parallel** directive.

--------------------------------- Fortran ---------------------------------

Example directive_syntax_F_free_comment.1.f90

```
S-1      program main
S-2         use omp_lib
S-3         integer,parameter :: NT = 4
S-4
S-5         !$omp parallel do num_threads(NT)                    !DIR 1
S-6         do i = 1,NT
S-7           write(*,'("thrd no", i2)') omp_get_thread_num()
S-8         end do
S-9
S-10        !$omp  parallel do  &       !continue line          !DIR 2
S-11        !$omp num_threads(NT)       !or !$omp&
S-12        do i = 1,NT
S-13          write(*,'("thrd no", i2)') omp_get_thread_num()
S-14        end do
S-15
S-16        !$omp parallel num_threads(NT)                       !DIR 3
S-17        !$omp do                                             !DIR 4
S-18        do i = 1,NT
S-19          write(*,'("thrd no", i2)') omp_get_thread_num()
S-20        end do
S-21        !$omp end parallel
S-22
S-23     end program
S-24
S-25   !     repeated 3 times, any order
S-26   !     OUTPUT: thrd no   0
S-27   !     OUTPUT: thrd no   1
S-28   !     OUTPUT: thrd no   2
S-29   !     OUTPUT: thrd no   3
```

--------------------------------- Fortran ---------------------------------

As of OpenMP 5.1, **block** and **end block** statements can be used to designate a structured block for an OpenMP region, and any paired OpenMP **end** directive becomes optional, as shown in the next example. Note, the variables *i* and *thrd_no* are declared within the block structure and are hence private. It was necessary to explicitly declare the *i* variable, due to the **implicit none** statement; it could have also been declared outside the structured block.

──────────────────────────── Fortran ────────────────────────────

Example directive_syntax_F_block.1.f90 (**omp_5.1**)

```
S-1      program main
S-2
S-3        use omp_lib
S-4        implicit none
S-5        integer,parameter :: NT = 2, chunks=3
S-6
S-7        !$omp parallel num_threads(NT)
S-8        block                              ! Fortran 2008 OMP 5.1
S-9          integer :: thrd_no,i
S-10         thrd_no= omp_get_thread_num()
S-11          !$omp do schedule(static,chunks)
S-12          do i = 1,NT*chunks
S-13             write(*,'("ndx=",i0.2," thrd_no=", i0.2)') i,thrd_no
S-14          end do
S-15        end block
S-16     end program
S-17
S-18  ! any order
S-19  ! OUTPUT: ndx=01 thrd_no=00
S-20  ! OUTPUT: ndx=02 thrd_no=00
S-21  ! OUTPUT: ndx=03 thrd_no=00
S-22  ! OUTPUT: ndx=04 thrd_no=01
S-23  ! OUTPUT: ndx=05 thrd_no=01
S-24  ! OUTPUT: ndx=06 thrd_no=01
```

──────────────────────────── Fortran ────────────────────────────

A Fortran BLOCK construct may eliminate the need for a paired **end** directive for an OpenMP construct, as illustrated in the following example.

The first **parallel** construct is specified with an OpenMP loosely structured block (where the first executable construct is not a Fortran 2008 BLOCK construct). A paired **end** directive must end the OpenMP construct. The second **parallel** construct is specified with an OpenMP strictly structured block (consists only of a single Fortran BLOCK construct). The paired **end** directive is optional in this case, and is not used here.

The next two **parallel** directives form an enclosing outer **parallel** construct and a nested inner **parallel** construct. The first **end parallel** directive that subsequently appears terminates the inner **parallel** construct, because a paired **end** directive immediately following a

BLOCK construct that is a strictly structured block of an OpenMP construct is treated as the terminating end directive of that construct. The next **end parallel** directive is required to terminate the outer **parallel** construct.

———————————————— Fortran ————————————————

Example directive_syntax_F_block.2.f90 (**omp_5.1**)

```fortran
program main

  use omp_lib
  implicit none

  !$omp parallel num_threads(2)
    if( omp_get_thread_num() == 0 ) &
      print*, "Loosely  structured block  -- end required."
    block                                ! BLOCK Fortran 2008
      if( omp_get_thread_num() == 0 ) &
          print*, "                            --"
    end block
  !$omp end parallel

  !$omp parallel num_threads(2)
    block
      if( omp_get_thread_num() == 0 ) &
          print*, "Strictly structured block  -- end not required."
    end block
 !!$omp end parallel !is optional for strictly structured block

  print*, "Sequential part"

  !$omp parallel num_threads(2)                        !outer parallel
    if( omp_get_thread_num() == 0 ) &
        print*, "Outer, loosely  structured block."
    !$omp parallel num_threads(2)                      !inner parallel
      block
        if( omp_get_thread_num() == 0 ) &
        print*, "Inner, strictly structured block."
      end block
    !$omp end parallel
  !$omp end parallel
  ! Two end directives are required here.
  ! A single "!$omp end parallel" terminator will fail.
  ! 1st end directive is assumed to be for inner parallel construct.
  ! 2nd end directive applies to outer parallel construct.

end program
```

```
S-41    !OUTPUT, in order:
S-42    ! Loosely  structured block  -- end required.
S-43    !                            --
S-44    ! Strictly structured block  -- end not required.
S-45    ! Sequential part
S-46    ! Outer, loosely  structured block.
S-47    ! Inner, strictly structured block.
S-48    ! Inner, strictly structured block.
```

———————————————— Fortran ————————————————

3 Parallel Execution

A single thread, the *initial thread*, begins sequential execution of an OpenMP enabled program, as if the whole program is in an implicit parallel region consisting of an implicit task executed by the *initial thread*.

A **parallel** construct encloses code, forming a parallel region. An *initial thread* encountering a **parallel** region forks (creates) a team of threads at the beginning of the **parallel** region, and joins them (removes from execution) at the end of the region. The initial thread becomes the primary thread of the team in a **parallel** region with a *thread* number equal to zero, the other threads are numbered from 1 to number of threads minus 1. A team may be comprised of just a single thread.

Each thread of a team is assigned an implicit task consisting of code within the parallel region. The task that creates a parallel region is suspended while the tasks of the team are executed. A thread is tied to its task; that is, only the thread assigned to the task can execute that task. After completion of the **parallel** region, the primary thread resumes execution of the generating task.

Any task within a **parallel** region is allowed to encounter another **parallel** region to form a nested **parallel** region. The parallelism of a nested **parallel** region (whether it forks additional threads, or is executed serially by the encountering task) can be controlled by the **OMP_NESTED** environment variable or the **omp_set_nested()** API routine with arguments indicating true or false.

The number of threads of a **parallel** region can be set by the **OMP_NUM_THREADS** environment variable, the **omp_set_num_threads()** routine, or on the **parallel** directive with the **num_threads** clause. The routine overrides the environment variable, and the clause overrides all. Use the **OMP_DYNAMIC** or the **omp_set_dynamic()** function to specify that the OpenMP implementation dynamically adjust the number of threads for **parallel** regions. The default setting for dynamic adjustment is implementation defined. When dynamic adjustment is on and the number of threads is specified, the number of threads becomes an upper limit for the number of threads to be provided by the OpenMP runtime.

WORKSHARING CONSTRUCTS

A worksharing construct distributes the execution of the associated region among the members of the team that encounter it. There is an implied barrier at the end of the worksharing region (there is no barrier at the beginning). The worksharing constructs are:

- loop constructs: **for** and **do**
- **sections**
- **single**

- `workshare`

The `for` and `do` constructs (loop constructs) create a region consisting of a loop. A loop controlled by a loop construct is called an *associated* loop. Nested loops can form a single region when the `collapse` clause (with an integer argument) designates the number of *associated* loops to be executed in parallel, by forming a "single iteration space" for the specified number of nested loops. The `ordered` clause can also control multiple associated loops.

An associated loop must adhere to a "canonical form" (specified in the *Canonical Loop Form* of the OpenMP Specifications document) which allows the iteration count (of all associated loops) to be computed before the (outermost) loop is executed. Most common loops comply with the canonical form, including C++ iterators.

A `single` construct forms a region in which only one thread (any one of the team) executes the region. The other threads wait at the implied barrier at the end, unless the `nowait` clause is specified.

The `sections` construct forms a region that contains one or more structured blocks. Each block of a `sections` directive is constructed with a `section` construct, and executed once by one of the threads (any one) in the team. (If only one block is formed in the region, the `section` construct, which is used to separate blocks, is not required.) The other threads wait at the implied barrier at the end, unless the `nowait` clause is specified.

The `workshare` construct is a Fortran feature that consists of a region with a single structure block (section of code). Statements in the `workshare` region are divided into units of work, and executed (once) by threads of the team.

MASKED CONSTRUCT

The `masked` construct is not a worksharing construct. The `masked` region is executed only by the primary thread. There is no implicit barrier (and flush) at the end of the `masked` region; hence the other threads of the team continue execution beyond code statements beyond the `masked` region. The `master` construct, which has been deprecated in OpenMP 5.1, has identical semantics to the `masked` construct with no `filter` clause.

3.1 A Simple Parallel Loop

The following example demonstrates how to parallelize a simple loop using the parallel worksharing-loop construct. The loop iteration variable is private by default, so it is not necessary to specify it explicitly in a **private** clause.

―――――――――――――― C / C++ ――――――――――――――

Example ploop.1.c

```
S-1     void simple(int n, float *a, float *b)
S-2     {
S-3         int i;
S-4
S-5     #pragma omp parallel for
S-6         for (i=1; i<n; i++) /* i is private by default */
S-7             b[i] = (a[i] + a[i-1]) / 2.0;
S-8     }
```

―――――――――――――― C / C++ ――――――――――――――
―――――――――――――― Fortran ――――――――――――――

Example ploop.1.f

```
S-1             SUBROUTINE SIMPLE(N, A, B)
S-2
S-3             INTEGER I, N
S-4             REAL B(N), A(N)
S-5
S-6     !$OMP PARALLEL DO   !I is private by default
S-7             DO I=2,N
S-8                 B(I) = (A(I) + A(I-1)) / 2.0
S-9             ENDDO
S-10    !$OMP END PARALLEL DO
S-11
S-12            END SUBROUTINE SIMPLE
```

―――――――――――――― Fortran ――――――――――――――

3.2 `parallel` Construct

The **parallel** construct can be used in coarse-grain parallel programs. In the following example, each thread in the **parallel** region decides what part of the global array *x* to work on, based on the thread number:

——————————————— C / C++ ———————————————

Example parallel.1.c

```
S-1    #include <omp.h>
S-2
S-3    void subdomain(float *x, int istart, int ipoints)
S-4    {
S-5      int i;
S-6
S-7      for (i = 0; i < ipoints; i++)
S-8          x[istart+i] = 123.456;
S-9    }
S-10
S-11   void sub(float *x, int npoints)
S-12   {
S-13       int iam, nt, ipoints, istart;
S-14
S-15   #pragma omp parallel default(shared) private(iam,nt,ipoints,istart)
S-16       {
S-17           iam = omp_get_thread_num();
S-18           nt =  omp_get_num_threads();
S-19           ipoints = npoints / nt;    /* size of partition */
S-20           istart = iam * ipoints;  /* starting array index */
S-21           if (iam == nt-1)     /* last thread may do more */
S-22             ipoints = npoints - istart;
S-23           subdomain(x, istart, ipoints);
S-24       }
S-25   }
S-26
S-27   int main()
S-28   {
S-29       float array[10000];
S-30
S-31       sub(array, 10000);
S-32
S-33       return 0;
S-34   }
```

——————————————— C / C++ ———————————————

— Fortran —

Example parallel.1.f

```
S-1          SUBROUTINE SUBDOMAIN(X, ISTART, IPOINTS)
S-2              INTEGER ISTART, IPOINTS
S-3              REAL X(*)
S-4
S-5              INTEGER I
S-6
S-7              DO 100 I=1,IPOINTS
S-8                  X(ISTART+I) = 123.456
S-9      100     CONTINUE
S-10
S-11         END SUBROUTINE SUBDOMAIN
S-12
S-13         SUBROUTINE SUB(X, NPOINTS)
S-14             INCLUDE "omp_lib.h"      ! or USE OMP_LIB
S-15
S-16             REAL X(*)
S-17             INTEGER NPOINTS
S-18             INTEGER IAM, NT, IPOINTS, ISTART
S-19
S-20     !$OMP PARALLEL DEFAULT(PRIVATE) SHARED(X,NPOINTS)
S-21
S-22             IAM = OMP_GET_THREAD_NUM()
S-23             NT =  OMP_GET_NUM_THREADS()
S-24             IPOINTS = NPOINTS/NT
S-25             ISTART = IAM * IPOINTS
S-26             IF (IAM .EQ. NT-1) THEN
S-27                 IPOINTS = NPOINTS - ISTART
S-28             ENDIF
S-29             CALL SUBDOMAIN(X,ISTART,IPOINTS)
S-30
S-31     !$OMP END PARALLEL
S-32         END SUBROUTINE SUB
S-33
S-34         PROGRAM PAREXAMPLE
S-35             REAL ARRAY(10000)
S-36             CALL SUB(ARRAY, 10000)
S-37         END PROGRAM PAREXAMPLE
```

— Fortran —

3.3 `teams` Construct on Host

Originally the **teams** construct was created for devices (such as GPUs) for independent executions of a structured block by teams within a league (on SMs). It was only available through offloading with the **target** construct, and the execution of a **teams** region could only be directed to host execution by various means such as **if** and **device** clauses, and the **OMP_TARGET_OFFLOAD** environment variable.

In OpenMP 5.0 the **teams** construct was extended to enable the host to execute a **teams** region (without an associated **target** construct), with anticipation of further affinity and threading controls in future OpenMP releases.

In the example below the **teams** construct is used to create two teams, one to execute single precision code, and the other to execute double precision code. Two teams are required, and the thread limit for each team is set to 1/2 of the number of available processors.

―――――――― C / C++ ――――――――

Example host_teams.1.c (**omp_5.0**)

```
#include <stdio.h>
#include <stdlib.h>
#include  <math.h>
#include   <omp.h>
#define    N 1000

int main(){
    int     nteams_required=2, max_thrds, tm_id;
    float   sp_x[N], sp_y[N], sp_a=0.0001e0;
    double  dp_x[N], dp_y[N], dp_a=0.0001e0;

    max_thrds = omp_get_num_procs()/nteams_required;

    // Create 2 teams, each team works in a different precision
    #pragma omp teams num_teams(nteams_required) \
                      thread_limit(max_thrds)   private(tm_id)
    {
       tm_id = omp_get_team_num();

       if( omp_get_num_teams() != 2 )   //if only getting 1, quit
       { printf("error: Insufficient teams on host, 2 required\n");
         exit(0);
       }

       if(tm_id == 0)   // Do Single Precision Work (SAXPY) with this team
       {
          #pragma omp parallel
          {
```

```
S-29              #pragma omp for                                  //init
S-30              for(int i=0; i<N; i++){sp_x[i] = i*0.0001;   sp_y[i]=i; }
S-31
S-32              #pragma omp for simd simdlen(8)
S-33              for(int i=0; i<N; i++){sp_x[i] = sp_a*sp_x[i] + sp_y[i];}
S-34          }
S-35       }
S-36
S-37       if(tm_id == 1)   // Do Double Precision Work (DAXPY) with this team
S-38       {
S-39          #pragma omp parallel
S-40          {
S-41             #pragma omp for                               //init
S-42             for(int i=0; i<N; i++){dp_x[i] = i*0.0001;   dp_y[i]=i; }
S-43
S-44             #pragma omp for simd simdlen(4)
S-45             for(int i=0; i<N; i++){dp_x[i] = dp_a*dp_x[i] + dp_y[i];}
S-46          }
S-47       }
S-48     }
S-49
S-50   printf("i=%d  sp|dp   %f %f \n",N-1, sp_x[N-1], dp_x[N-1]);
S-51   printf("i=%d  sp|dp   %f %f \n",N/2, sp_x[N/2], dp_x[N/2]);
S-52 //OUTPUT1:i=999   sp|dp   999.000000 999.000010
S-53 //OUTPUT2:i=500   sp|dp   500.000000 500.000005
S-54
S-55   return 0;
S-56 }
```

———————————————————— C / C++ ————————————————————
———————————————————— Fortran ————————————————————

1   *Example host_teams.1.f90* (`omp_5.0`)

```
S-1
S-2   program main
S-3      use omp_lib
S-4      integer            :: nteams_required=2, max_thrds, tm_id
S-5      integer,parameter :: N=1000
S 6      real               :: sp_x(N), sp_y(N), sp_a=0.0001e0
S-7      double precision  :: dp_x(N), dp_y(N), dp_a=0.0001d0
S-8
S-9      max_thrds = omp_get_num_procs()/nteams_required
S-10
S-11     !! Create 2 teams, each team works in a different precision
S-12     !$omp teams num_teams(nteams_required) thread_limit(max_thrds) \
S-13              private(tm_id)
S-14
```

```
S-15              tm_id = omp_get_team_num()
S-16
S-17              if( omp_get_num_teams() /= 2 ) then    !! if only getting 1, quit
S-18                 stop "error: Insufficient teams on host, 2 required."
S-19              endif
S-20
S-21              !! Do Single Precision Work (SAXPY) with this team
S-22              if(tm_id == 0) then
S-23
S-24                 !$omp parallel
S-25                   !$omp do            !! init
S-26                   do i = 1,N
S-27                      sp_x(i) = i*0.0001e0
S-28                      sp_y(i) = i
S-29                   end do
S-30
S-31                   !$omp do simd simdlen(8)
S-32                   do i = 1,N
S-33                      sp_x(i) = sp_a*sp_x(i) + sp_y(i)
S-34                   end do
S-35                 !$omp end parallel
S-36
S-37              endif
S-38
S-39              !! Do Double Precision Work (DAXPY) with this team
S-40              if(tm_id == 1) then
S-41
S-42                 !$omp parallel
S-43                   !$omp do            !! init
S-44                   do i = 1,N
S-45                      dp_x(i) = i*0.0001d0
S-46                      dp_y(i) = i
S-47                   end do
S-48
S-49                   !$omp do simd simdlen(4)
S-50                   do i = 1,N
S-51                      dp_x(i) = dp_a*dp_x(i) + dp_y(i)
S-52                   end do
S-53                 !$omp end parallel
S-54
S-55              endif
S-56           !$omp end teams
S-57
S-58           write(*,'( "i=",i4," sp|dp= ", e15.7, d25.16  )') &
S-59                   N, sp_x(N), dp_x(N)
S-60           write(*,'( "i=",i4," sp|dp= ", e15.7, d25.16  )') &
S-61                   N/2, sp_x(N/2), dp_x(N/2)
```

```
S-62                !! i=1000 sp|dp=     0.1000000E+04      0.1000000010000000D+04
S-63                !! i= 500 sp|dp=     0.5000000E+03      0.5000000050000000D+03
S-64    end program
```

———————————————— Fortran ————————————————

3.4 Controlling the Number of Threads
on Multiple Nesting Levels

The following examples demonstrate how to use the **OMP_NUM_THREADS** environment variable to
control the number of threads on multiple nesting levels:

———————————————————— C / C++ ————————————————————

Example nthrs_nesting.1.c

```
S-1     #include <stdio.h>
S-2     #include <omp.h>
S-3     int main (void)
S-4     {
S-5       omp_set_nested(1);
S-6       omp_set_dynamic(0);
S-7       #pragma omp parallel
S-8       {
S-9         #pragma omp parallel
S-10        {
S-11          #pragma omp single
S-12          {
S-13          /*
S-14          * If OMP_NUM_THREADS=2,3 was set, the following should print:
S-15          * Inner: num_thds=3
S-16          * Inner: num_thds=3
S-17          *
S-18          * If nesting is not supported, the following should print:
S-19          * Inner: num_thds=1
S-20          * Inner: num_thds=1
S-21          */
S-22              printf ("Inner: num_thds=%d\n", omp_get_num_threads());
S-23          }
S-24        }
S-25        #pragma omp barrier
S-26        omp_set_nested(0);
S-27        #pragma omp parallel
S-28        {
S-29          #pragma omp single
S-30          {
S-31          /*
S-32          * Even if OMP_NUM_THREADS=2,3 was set, the following should
S-33          * print, because nesting is disabled:
S-34          * Inner: num_thds=1
S-35          * Inner: num_thds=1
S-36          */
S-37              printf ("Inner: num_thds=%d\n", omp_get_num_threads());
S-38          }
```

```
S-39                }
S-40            #pragma omp barrier
S-41            #pragma omp single
S-42            {
S-43                /*
S-44                 * If OMP_NUM_THREADS=2,3 was set, the following should print:
S-45                 * Outer: num_thds=2
S-46                 */
S-47                printf ("Outer: num_thds=%d\n", omp_get_num_threads());
S-48            }
S-49        }
S-50    return 0;
S-51 }
```

———————————————— C / C++ ————————————————

———————————————— Fortran ————————————————

1   *Example nthrs_nesting.1.f*

```
S-1             program icv
S-2             use omp_lib
S-3             call omp_set_nested(.true.)
S-4             call omp_set_dynamic(.false.)
S-5  !$omp parallel
S-6  !$omp parallel
S-7  !$omp single
S-8             ! If OMP_NUM_THREADS=2,3 was set, the following should print:
S-9             ! Inner: num_thds= 3
S-10            ! Inner: num_thds= 3
S-11            ! If nesting is not supported, the following should print:
S-12            ! Inner: num_thds= 1
S-13            ! Inner: num_thds= 1
S-14            print *, "Inner: num_thds=", omp_get_num_threads()
S-15 !$omp end single
S-16 !$omp end parallel
S-17 !$omp barrier
S-18            call omp_set_nested(.false.)
S-19 !$omp parallel
S-20 !$omp single
S-21            ! Even if OMP_NUM_THREADS=2,3 was set, the following should print,
S-22            ! because nesting is disabled:
S-23            ! Inner: num_thds= 1
S-24            ! Inner: num_thds= 1
S-25            print *, "Inner: num_thds=", omp_get_num_threads()
S-26 !$omp end single
S-27 !$omp end parallel
S-28 !$omp barrier
S-29 !$omp single
```

```
S-30              ! If OMP_NUM_THREADS=2,3 was set, the following should print:
S-31              ! Outer: num_thds= 2
S-32              print *, "Outer: num_thds=", omp_get_num_threads()
S-33      !$omp end single
S-34      !$omp end parallel
S-35              end
```

─────────────── Fortran ───────────────

3.5 Interaction Between the `num_threads` Clause and `omp_set_dynamic`

The following example demonstrates the **num_threads** clause and the effect of the **omp_set_dynamic** routine on it.

The call to the **omp_set_dynamic** routine with argument **0** in C/C++, or **.FALSE.** in Fortran, disables the dynamic adjustment of the number of threads in OpenMP implementations that support it. In this case, 10 threads are provided. Note that in case of an error the OpenMP implementation is free to abort the program or to supply any number of threads available.

─────────────────── C / C++ ───────────────────

Example nthrs_dynamic.1.c

```
S-1    #include <omp.h>
S-2    int main()
S-3    {
S-4      omp_set_dynamic(0);
S-5      #pragma omp parallel num_threads(10)
S-6      {
S-7        /* do work here */
S-8      }
S-9      return 0;
S-10   }
```

─────────────────── C / C++ ───────────────────

─────────────────── Fortran ───────────────────

Example nthrs_dynamic.1.f

```
S-1          PROGRAM EXAMPLE
S-2            INCLUDE "omp_lib.h"        ! or USE OMP_LIB
S-3            CALL OMP_SET_DYNAMIC(.FALSE.)
S-4   !$OMP     PARALLEL NUM_THREADS(10)
S-5               ! do work here
S-6   !$OMP     END PARALLEL
S-7          END PROGRAM EXAMPLE
```

─────────────────── Fortran ───────────────────

The call to the **omp_set_dynamic** routine with a non-zero argument in C/C++, or **.TRUE.** in Fortran, allows the OpenMP implementation to choose any number of threads between 1 and 10.

──────────────────────────────── C / C++ ────────────────────────────────

Example nthrs_dynamic.2.c

```
S-1     #include <omp.h>
S-2     int main()
S-3     {
S-4       omp_set_dynamic(1);
S-5       #pragma omp parallel num_threads(10)
S-6       {
S-7         /* do work here */
S-8       }
S-9       return 0;
S-10    }
```

──────────────────────────────── C / C++ ────────────────────────────────
──────────────────────────────── Fortran ────────────────────────────────

Example nthrs_dynamic.2.f

```
S-1             PROGRAM EXAMPLE
S-2               INCLUDE "omp_lib.h"        ! or USE OMP_LIB
S-3               CALL OMP_SET_DYNAMIC(.TRUE.)
S-4     !$OMP       PARALLEL NUM_THREADS(10)
S-5                   ! do work here
S-6     !$OMP       END PARALLEL
S-7             END PROGRAM EXAMPLE
```

──────────────────────────────── Fortran ────────────────────────────────

It is good practice to set the *dyn-var* ICV explicitly by calling the **omp_set_dynamic** routine, as its default setting is implementation defined.

3.6 Fortran Restrictions on the do Construct

If an **end do** directive follows a *do-construct* in which several **DO** statements share a **DO** termination statement, then a **do** directive can only be specified for the outermost of these **DO** statements. The following example contains correct usages of loop constructs:

Example fort_do.1.f

```
S-1         SUBROUTINE WORK(I, J)
S-2         INTEGER I,J
S-3         END SUBROUTINE WORK
S-4
S-5         SUBROUTINE DO_GOOD()
S-6           INTEGER I, J
S-7           REAL A(1000)
S-8
S-9           DO 100 I = 1,10
S-10  !$OMP     DO
S-11            DO 100 J = 1,10
S-12              CALL WORK(I,J)
S-13  100       CONTINUE       !   !$OMP ENDDO implied here
S-14
S-15  !$OMP     DO
S-16            DO 200 J = 1,10
S-17  200         A(I) = I + 1
S-18  !$OMP     ENDDO
S-19
S-20  !$OMP     DO
S-21            DO 300 I = 1,10
S-22              DO 300 J = 1,10
S-23                CALL WORK(I,J)
S-24  300       CONTINUE
S-25  !$OMP     ENDDO
S-26          END SUBROUTINE DO_GOOD
```

The following example is non-conforming because the matching **do** directive for the **end do** does not precede the outermost loop:

Example fort_do.2.f

```
S-1         SUBROUTINE WORK(I, J)
S-2         INTEGER I,J
S-3         END SUBROUTINE WORK
S-4
S-5         SUBROUTINE DO_WRONG
S-6           INTEGER I, J
S-7
```

```
S-8              DO 100 I = 1,10
S-9     !$OMP      DO
S-10             DO 100 J = 1,10
S-11               CALL WORK(I,J)
S-12    100      CONTINUE
S-13    !$OMP    ENDDO
S-14             END SUBROUTINE DO_WRONG
```

———————————————————————— Fortran ————————————————————————

3.7 `nowait` Clause

If there are multiple independent loops within a **parallel** region, you can use the **nowait** clause to avoid the implied barrier at the end of the loop construct, as follows:

C / C++

Example nowait.1.c

```
S-1     #include <math.h>
S-2
S-3     void nowait_example(int n, int m, float *a, float *b, float *y, float *z)
S-4     {
S-5       int i;
S-6       #pragma omp parallel
S-7       {
S-8         #pragma omp for nowait
S-9           for (i=1; i<n; i++)
S-10            b[i] = (a[i] + a[i-1]) / 2.0;
S-11
S-12        #pragma omp for nowait
S-13          for (i=0; i<m; i++)
S-14            y[i] = sqrt(z[i]);
S-15      }
S-16    }
```

C / C++

Fortran

Example nowait.1.f

```
S-1             SUBROUTINE NOWAIT_EXAMPLE(N, M, A, B, Y, Z)
S-2
S-3             INTEGER N, M
S-4             REAL A(*), B(*), Y(*), Z(*)
S-5
S-6             INTEGER I
S-7
S-8     !$OMP PARALLEL
S-9
S-10    !$OMP DO
S-11            DO I=2,N
S-12              B(I) = (A(I) + A(I-1)) / 2.0
S-13            ENDDO
S-14    !$OMP END DO NOWAIT
S-15
S-16    !$OMP DO
S-17            DO I=1,M
S-18              Y(I) = SQRT(Z(I))
```

```
S-19              ENDDO
S-20      !$OMP END DO NOWAIT
S-21
S-22      !$OMP END PARALLEL
S-23
S-24              END SUBROUTINE NOWAIT_EXAMPLE
```

—————————————— Fortran ——————————————

1   In the following example, static scheduling distributes the same logical iteration numbers to the
2   threads that execute the three loop regions. This allows the **nowait** clause to be used, even though
3   there is a data dependence between the loops. The dependence is satisfied as long the same thread
4   executes the same logical iteration numbers in each loop.

5   Note that the iteration count of the loops must be the same. The example satisfies this requirement,
6   since the iteration space of the first two loops is from **0** to **n−1** (from **1** to **N** in the Fortran version),
7   while the iteration space of the last loop is from **1** to **n** (**2** to **N+1** in the Fortran version).

—————————————— C / C++ ——————————————

8   *Example nowait.2.c*

```
S-1
S-2     #include <math.h>
S-3     void nowait_example2(int n, float *a, float *b, float *c, float *y, float
S-4     *z)
S-5     {
S-6         int i;
S-7     #pragma omp parallel
S-8         {
S-9     #pragma omp for schedule(static) nowait
S-10        for (i=0; i<n; i++)
S-11           c[i] = (a[i] + b[i]) / 2.0f;
S-12    #pragma omp for schedule(static) nowait
S-13        for (i=0; i<n; i++)
S-14           z[i] = sqrtf(c[i]);
S-15    #pragma omp for schedule(static) nowait
S-16        for (i=1; i<=n; i++)
S-17           y[i] = z[i-1] + a[i];
S-18        }
S-19    }
```

—————————————— C / C++ ——————————————

1   *Example nowait.2.f90*

```
S-1        SUBROUTINE NOWAIT_EXAMPLE2(N, A, B, C, Y, Z)
S-2        INTEGER N
S-3        REAL A(*), B(*), C(*), Y(*), Z(*)
S-4        INTEGER I
S-5  !$OMP PARALLEL
S-6  !$OMP DO SCHEDULE(STATIC)
S-7        DO I=1,N
S-8           C(I) = (A(I) + B(I)) / 2.0
S-9        ENDDO
S-10 !$OMP END DO NOWAIT
S-11 !$OMP DO SCHEDULE(STATIC)
S-12       DO I=1,N
S-13          Z(I) = SQRT(C(I))
S-14       ENDDO
S-15 !$OMP END DO NOWAIT
S-16 !$OMP DO SCHEDULE(STATIC)
S-17       DO I=2,N+1
S-18          Y(I) = Z(I-1) + A(I)
S-19       ENDDO
S-20 !$OMP END DO NOWAIT
S-21 !$OMP END PARALLEL
S-22       END SUBROUTINE NOWAIT_EXAMPLE2
```

3.8 `collapse` Clause

In the following example, the **k** and **j** loops are associated with the loop construct. So the iterations of the **k** and **j** loops are collapsed into one loop with a larger iteration space, and that loop is then divided among the threads in the current team. Since the **i** loop is not associated with the loop construct, it is not collapsed, and the **i** loop is executed sequentially in its entirety in every iteration of the collapsed **k** and **j** loop.

The variable **j** can be omitted from the **private** clause when the **collapse** clause is used since it is implicitly private. However, if the **collapse** clause is omitted then **j** will be shared if it is omitted from the **private** clause. In either case, **k** is implicitly private and could be omitted from the **private** clause.

───────────────────────────── C / C++ ─────────────────────────────

Example collapse.1.c (**omp_3.0**)

```
void bar(float *a, int i, int j, int k);

int kl, ku, ks, jl, ju, js, il, iu,is;

void sub(float *a)
{
    int i, j, k;

    #pragma omp for collapse(2) private(i, k, j)
    for (k=kl; k<=ku; k+=ks)
        for (j=jl; j<=ju; j+=js)
            for (i=il; i<=iu; i+=is)
                bar(a,i,j,k);
}
```

───────────────────────────── C / C++ ─────────────────────────────
───────────────────────────── Fortran ─────────────────────────────

Example collapse.1.f (**omp_3.0**)

```
      subroutine sub(a)

      real a(*)
      integer kl, ku, ks, jl, ju, js, il, iu, is
      common /csub/ kl, ku, ks, jl, ju, js, il, iu, is
      integer i, j, k

!$omp do collapse(2) private(i,j,k)
      do k = kl, ku, ks
         do j = jl, ju, js
```

```
S-12              do i = il, iu, is
S-13                  call bar(a,i,j,k)
S-14              enddo
S-15           enddo
S-16        enddo
S-17    !$omp end do
S-18
S-19        end subroutine
```

—————————————————————— Fortran ——————————————————————

In the next example, the **k** and **j** loops are associated with the loop construct. So the iterations of the **k** and **j** loops are collapsed into one loop with a larger iteration space, and that loop is then divided among the threads in the current team.

The sequential execution of the iterations in the **k** and **j** loops determines the order of the iterations in the collapsed iteration space. This implies that in the sequentially last iteration of the collapsed iteration space, **k** will have the value **2** and **j** will have the value **3**. Since **klast** and **jlast** are **lastprivate**, their values are assigned by the sequentially last iteration of the collapsed **k** and **j** loop. This example prints: **2 3**.

—————————————————————— C / C++ ——————————————————————

Example collapse.2.c (**omp_3.0**)

```
S-1
S-2     #include <stdio.h>
S-3     void test()
S-4     {
S-5        int j, k, jlast, klast;
S-6        #pragma omp parallel
S-7        {
S-8           #pragma omp for collapse(2) lastprivate(jlast, klast)
S-9           for (k=1; k<=2; k++)
S-10             for (j=1; j<=3; j++)
S-11             {
S-12                jlast=j;
S-13                klast=k;
S-14             }
S-15          #pragma omp single
S-16          printf("%d %d\n", klast, jlast);
S-17       }
S-18    }
```

—————————————————————— C / C++ ——————————————————————

Example collapse.2.f (**omp_3.0**)

```
S-1
S-2          program test
S-3   !$omp parallel
S-4   !$omp do private(j,k) collapse(2) lastprivate(jlast, klast)
S-5          do k = 1,2
S-6            do j = 1,3
S-7              jlast=j
S-8              klast=k
S-9            enddo
S-10         enddo
S-11  !$omp end do
S-12  !$omp single
S-13         print *, klast, jlast
S-14  !$omp end single
S-15  !$omp end parallel
S-16         end program test
```

The next example illustrates the interaction of the **collapse** and **ordered** clauses.

In the example, the loop construct has both a **collapse** clause and an **ordered** clause. The **collapse** clause causes the iterations of the **k** and **j** loops to be collapsed into one loop with a larger iteration space, and that loop is divided among the threads in the current team. An **ordered** clause is added to the loop construct because an ordered region binds to the loop region arising from the loop construct.

According to Section 2.12.8 of the OpenMP 4.0 specification, a thread must not execute more than one ordered region that binds to the same loop region. So the **collapse** clause is required for the example to be conforming. With the **collapse** clause, the iterations of the **k** and **j** loops are collapsed into one loop, and therefore only one ordered region will bind to the collapsed **k** and **j** loop. Without the **collapse** clause, there would be two ordered regions that bind to each iteration of the **k** loop (one arising from the first iteration of the **j** loop, and the other arising from the second iteration of the **j** loop).

The code prints

```
0 1 1
0 1 2
0 2 1
1 2 2
1 3 1
1 3 2
```

1   *Example collapse.3.c* (`omp_3.0`)

```
S-1    #include <omp.h>
S-2    #include <stdio.h>
S-3    void work(int a, int j, int k);
S-4    void sub()
S-5    {
S-6       int j, k, a;
S-7       #pragma omp parallel num_threads(2)
S-8       {
S-9          #pragma omp for collapse(2) ordered private(j,k) schedule(static,3)
S-10         for (k=1; k<=3; k++)
S-11            for (j=1; j<=2; j++)
S-12            {
S-13               #pragma omp ordered
S-14               printf("%d %d %d\n", omp_get_thread_num(), k, j);
S-15               /* end ordered */
S-16               work(a,j,k);
S-17            }
S-18      }
S-19   }
```

2   *Example collapse.3.f* (`omp_3.0`)

```
S-1          program test
S-2          include 'omp_lib.h'
S-3    !$omp parallel num_threads(2)
S-4    !$omp do collapse(2) ordered private(j,k) schedule(static,3)
S-5          do k = 1,3
S-6             do j = 1,2
S-7    !$omp ordered
S-8             print *, omp_get_thread_num(), k, j
S-9    !$omp end ordered
S-10            call work(a,j,k)
S-11            enddo
S-12         enddo
S-13   !$omp end do
S-14   !$omp end parallel
S-15         end program test
```

The following example illustrates the collapse of a non-rectangular loop nest, a new feature in
OpenMP 5.0. In a loop nest, a non-rectangular loop has a loop bound that references the iteration
variable of an enclosing loop.

The motivation for this feature is illustrated in the example below that creates a symmetric
correlation matrix for a set of variables. Note that the initial value of the second loop depends on
the index variable of the first loop for the loops to be collapsed. Here the data are represented by a
2D array, each row corresponds to a variable and each column corresponds to a sample of the
variable – the last two columns are the sample mean and standard deviation (for Fortran, rows and
columns are swapped).

——————————————————— C / C++ ———————————————————

Example collapse.4.c (**omp_5.0**)

```c
#include <stdio.h>
#define N 20
#define M 10

// routine to calculate a
// For variable a[i]:
// a[i][0],...,a[i][n-1]    contains the n samples
// a[i][n]                  contains the sample mean
// a[i][n+1]                contains the standard deviation
extern void calc_a(int n,int m, float a[][N+2]);

int main(){
  float a[M][N+2], b[M][M];

  calc_a(N,M,a);

  #pragma omp parallel for collapse(2)
  for (int i = 0; i < M; i++)
    for (int j = i; j < M; j++)
    {
        float temp = 0.0f;
        for (int k = 0; k < N; k++)
          temp += (a[i][k]-a[i][N])*(a[j][k]-a[j][N]);

        b[i][j] = temp / (a[i][N+1] * a[j][N+1] * (N - 1));
        b[j][i] = b[i][j];
    }

  printf("b[0][0] = %f, b[M-1][M-1] = %f\n", b[0][0], b[M-1][M-1]);

  return 0;
}
```

——————————————————— C / C++ ———————————————————

1   *Example collapse.4.f90* (`omp_5.0`)

```fortran
S-1    module calc_m
S-2      interface
S-3      subroutine calc_a(n, m, a)
S-4      integer n, m
S-5      real a(n+2,m)
S-6      ! routine to calculate a
S-7      ! For variable a(*,j):
S-8      ! a(1,j),...,a(n,j)   contains the n samples
S-9      ! a(n+1,j)            contains the sample mean
S-10     ! a(n+2,j)            contains the standard deviation
S-11     end subroutine
S-12     end interface
S-13   end module
S-14
S-15   program main
S-16     use calc_m
S-17     integer, parameter :: N=20, M=10
S-18     real a(N+2,M), b(M,M)
S-19     real temp
S-20     integer i, j, k
S-21
S-22     call calc_a(N,M,a)
S-23
S-24     !$omp parallel do collapse(2) private(k,temp)
S-25     do i = 1, M
S-26        do j = i, M
S-27           temp = 0.0
S-28           do k = 1, N
S-29              temp = temp + (a(k,i)-a(N+1,i))*(a(k,j)-a(N+1,j))
S-30           end do
S-31
S-32           b(i,j) = temp / (a(N+2,i) * a(N+2,j) * (N - 1))
S-33           b(j,i) = b(i,j)
S-34        end do
S-35     end do
S-36
S-37     print *,"b(1,1) = ",b(1,1),", b(M,M) = ",b(M,M)
S-38
S-39   end program
```

3.9 `linear` Clause in Loop Constructs

The following example shows the use of the **linear** clause in a loop construct to allow the proper parallelization of a loop that contains an induction variable (*j*). At the end of the execution of the loop construct, the original variable *j* is updated with the value *N/2* from the last iteration of the loop.

―――――――――――――――――――― C / C++ ――――――――――――――――――――

Example linear_in_loop.1.c (**omp_4.5**)

```
S-1    #include <stdio.h>
S-2
S-3    #define N 100
S-4    int main(void)
S-5    {
S-6        float a[N], b[N/2];
S-7        int i, j;
S-8
S-9        for ( i = 0; i < N; i++ )
S-10           a[i] = i + 1;
S-11
S-12       j = 0;
S-13       #pragma omp parallel
S-14       #pragma omp for linear(j:1)
S-15       for ( i = 0; i < N; i += 2 ) {
S-16           b[j] = a[i] * 2.0f;
S-17           j++;
S-18       }
S-19
S-20       printf( "%d %f %f\n", j, b[0], b[j-1] );
S-21       /* print out: 50 2.0 198.0 */
S-22
S-23       return 0;
S-24   }
```

―――――――――――――――――――― C / C++ ――――――――――――――――――――

1   *Example linear_in_loop.1.f90* (**omp_4**.5)

```fortran
S-1    program linear_loop
S-2       implicit none
S-3       integer, parameter :: N = 100
S-4       real :: a(N), b(N/2)
S-5       integer :: i, j
S-6
S-7       do i = 1, N
S-8          a(i) = i
S-9       end do
S-10
S-11      j = 0
S-12      !$omp parallel
S-13      !$omp do linear(j:1)
S-14      do i = 1, N, 2
S-15         j = j + 1
S-16         b(j) = a(i) * 2.0
S-17      end do
S-18      !$omp end parallel
S-19
S-20      print *, j, b(1), b(j)
S-21      ! print out: 50 2.0 198.0
S-22
S-23   end program
```

3.10 `parallel sections` Construct

In the following example routines **XAXIS**, **YAXIS**, and **ZAXIS** can be executed concurrently. The first **section** directive is optional. Note that all **section** directives need to appear in the **parallel sections** construct.

──────────────────────── C / C++ ────────────────────────

Example psections.1.c

```
S-1    void XAXIS();
S-2    void YAXIS();
S-3    void ZAXIS();
S-4
S-5    void sect_example()
S-6    {
S-7      #pragma omp parallel sections
S-8      {
S-9        #pragma omp section
S-10         XAXIS();
S-11
S-12       #pragma omp section
S-13         YAXIS();
S-14
S-15       #pragma omp section
S-16         ZAXIS();
S-17     }
S-18   }
```

──────────────────────── C / C++ ────────────────────────
──────────────────────── Fortran ────────────────────────

Example psections.1.f

```
S-1          SUBROUTINE SECT_EXAMPLE()
S-2    !$OMP PARALLEL SECTIONS
S-3    !$OMP SECTION
S-4          CALL XAXIS()
S-5    !$OMP SECTION
S-6          CALL YAXIS()
S-7
S-8    !$OMP SECTION
S-9          CALL ZAXIS()
S-10
S-11   !$OMP END PARALLEL SECTIONS
S-12         END SUBROUTINE SECT_EXAMPLE
```

──────────────────────── Fortran ────────────────────────

3.11 `firstprivate` Clause and `sections` Construct

In the following example of the **sections** construct the **firstprivate** clause is used to initialize the private copy of **section_count** of each thread. The problem is that the **section** constructs modify **section_count**, which breaks the independence of the **section** constructs. When different threads execute each section, both sections will print the value 1. When the same thread executes the two sections, one section will print the value 1 and the other will print the value 2. Since the order of execution of the two sections in this case is unspecified, it is unspecified which section prints which value.

──────────────── C / C++ ────────────────

Example fpriv_sections.1.c

```
S-1     #include <omp.h>
S-2     #include <stdio.h>
S-3     #define NT 4
S-4     int main( ) {
S-5         int section_count = 0;
S-6         omp_set_dynamic(0);
S-7         omp_set_num_threads(NT);
S-8     #pragma omp parallel
S-9     #pragma omp sections firstprivate( section_count )
S-10    {
S-11    #pragma omp section
S-12        {
S-13            section_count++;
S-14            /* may print the number one or two */
S-15            printf( "section_count %d\n", section_count );
S-16        }
S-17    #pragma omp section
S-18        {
S-19            section_count++;
S-20            /* may print the number one or two */
S-21            printf( "section_count %d\n", section_count );
S-22        }
S-23    }
S-24        return 0;
S-25    }
```

──────────────── C / C++ ────────────────

1   *Example fpriv_sections.1.f90*

```
S-1    program section
S-2        use omp_lib
S-3        integer :: section_count = 0
S-4        integer, parameter :: NT = 4
S-5        call omp_set_dynamic(.false.)
S-6        call omp_set_num_threads(NT)
S-7    !$omp parallel
S-8    !$omp sections firstprivate ( section_count )
S-9    !$omp section
S-10       section_count = section_count + 1
S-11   ! may print the number one or two
S-12       print *, 'section_count', section_count
S-13   !$omp section
S-14       section_count = section_count + 1
S-15   ! may print the number one or two
S-16       print *, 'section_count', section_count
S-17   !$omp end sections
S-18   !$omp end parallel
S-19   end program section
```

3.12 `single` Construct

The following example demonstrates the **single** construct. In the example, only one thread prints each of the progress messages. All other threads will skip the **single** region and stop at the barrier at the end of the **single** construct until all threads in the team have reached the barrier. If other threads can proceed without waiting for the thread executing the **single** region, a **nowait** clause can be specified, as is done in the third **single** construct in this example. The user must not make any assumptions as to which thread will execute a **single** region.

———————————————— C / C++ ————————————————

Example single.1.c

```
S-1     #include <stdio.h>
S-2
S-3     void work1() {}
S-4     void work2() {}
S-5
S-6     void single_example()
S-7     {
S-8       #pragma omp parallel
S-9       {
S-10        #pragma omp single
S-11          printf("Beginning work1.\n");
S-12
S-13        work1();
S-14
S-15        #pragma omp single
S-16          printf("Finishing work1.\n");
S-17
S-18        #pragma omp single nowait
S-19          printf("Finished work1 and beginning work2.\n");
S-20
S-21        work2();
S-22      }
S-23    }
```

———————————————— C / C++ ————————————————

1   *Example single.1.f*

```
S-1              SUBROUTINE WORK1()
S-2              END SUBROUTINE WORK1
S-3
S-4              SUBROUTINE WORK2()
S-5              END SUBROUTINE WORK2
S-6
S-7              PROGRAM SINGLE_EXAMPLE
S-8      !$OMP PARALLEL
S-9
S-10     !$OMP SINGLE
S-11             print *, "Beginning work1."
S-12     !$OMP END SINGLE
S-13
S-14             CALL WORK1()
S-15
S-16     !$OMP SINGLE
S-17             print *, "Finishing work1."
S-18     !$OMP END SINGLE
S-19
S-20     !$OMP SINGLE
S-21             print *, "Finished work1 and beginning work2."
S-22     !$OMP END SINGLE NOWAIT
S-23
S-24             CALL WORK2()
S-25
S-26     !$OMP END PARALLEL
S-27
S-28             END PROGRAM SINGLE_EXAMPLE
```

3.13 workshare Construct

The following are examples of the **workshare** construct.

In the following example, **workshare** spreads work across the threads executing the **parallel** region, and there is a barrier after the last statement. Implementations must enforce Fortran execution rules inside of the **workshare** block.

Example workshare.1.f

```
S-1          SUBROUTINE WSHARE1(AA, BB, CC, DD, EE, FF, N)
S-2          INTEGER N
S-3          REAL AA(N,N), BB(N,N), CC(N,N), DD(N,N), EE(N,N), FF(N,N)
S-4
S-5   !$OMP     PARALLEL
S-6   !$OMP      WORKSHARE
S-7               AA = BB
S-8               CC = DD
S-9               EE = FF
S-10  !$OMP      END WORKSHARE
S-11  !$OMP     END PARALLEL
S-12
S-13         END SUBROUTINE WSHARE1
```

In the following example, the barrier at the end of the first **workshare** region is eliminated with a **nowait** clause. Threads doing **CC = DD** immediately begin work on **EE = FF** when they are done with **CC = DD**.

Example workshare.2.f

```
S-1          SUBROUTINE WSHARE2(AA, BB, CC, DD, EE, FF, N)
S-2          INTEGER N
S-3          REAL AA(N,N), BB(N,N), CC(N,N)
S-4          REAL DD(N,N), EE(N,N), FF(N,N)
S-5
S-6   !$OMP     PARALLEL
S-7   !$OMP      WORKSHARE
S-8               AA = BB
S-9               CC = DD
S-10  !$OMP      END WORKSHARE NOWAIT
S-11  !$OMP      WORKSHARE
S-12              EE = FF
S-13  !$OMP      END WORKSHARE
S-14  !$OMP     END PARALLEL
S-15         END SUBROUTINE WSHARE2
```

1   The following example shows the use of an **atomic** directive inside a **workshare** construct. The
2   computation of **SUM(AA)** is workshared, but the update to **R** is atomic.

3   *Example workshare.3.f*

```
S-1          SUBROUTINE WSHARE3(AA, BB, CC, DD, N)
S-2          INTEGER N
S-3          REAL AA(N,N), BB(N,N), CC(N,N), DD(N,N)
S-4          REAL R
S-5            R=0
S-6    !$OMP    PARALLEL
S-7    !$OMP      WORKSHARE
S-8                AA = BB
S-9    !$OMP        ATOMIC UPDATE
S-10                 R = R + SUM(AA)
S-11                CC = DD
S-12   !$OMP      END WORKSHARE
S-13   !$OMP    END PARALLEL
S-14          END SUBROUTINE WSHARE3
```

4   Fortran **WHERE** and **FORALL** statements are *compound statements*, made up of a *control* part and a
5   *statement* part. When **workshare** is applied to one of these compound statements, both the
6   control and the statement parts are workshared. The following example shows the use of a **WHERE**
7   statement in a **workshare** construct.

8   Each task gets worked on in order by the threads:

9   **AA = BB** then
10   **CC = DD** then
11   **EE .ne. 0** then
12   **FF = 1 / EE** then
13   **GG = HH**

14   *Example workshare.4.f*

```
S-1          SUBROUTINE WSHARE4(AA, BB, CC, DD, EE, FF, GG, HH, N)
S-2          INTEGER N
S-3          REAL AA(N,N), BB(N,N), CC(N,N)
S-4          REAL DD(N,N), EE(N,N), FF(N,N)
S-5          REAL GG(N,N), HH(N,N)
S-6
S-7    !$OMP    PARALLEL
S-8    !$OMP      WORKSHARE
S-9                AA = BB
S-10               CC = DD
S-11               WHERE (EE .ne. 0) FF = 1 / EE
```

```
S-12                 GG = HH
S-13   !$OMP     END WORKSHARE
S-14   !$OMP   END PARALLEL
S-15
S-16           END SUBROUTINE WSHARE4
```

1   In the following example, an assignment to a shared scalar variable is performed by one thread in a
2   **workshare** while all other threads in the team wait.

3   *Example workshare.5.f*

```
S-1            SUBROUTINE WSHARE5(AA, BB, CC, DD, N)
S-2            INTEGER N
S-3            REAL AA(N,N), BB(N,N), CC(N,N), DD(N,N)
S-4
S-5              INTEGER SHR
S-6
S-7    !$OMP   PARALLEL SHARED(SHR)
S-8    !$OMP     WORKSHARE
S-9                AA = BB
S-10               SHR = 1
S-11               CC = DD * SHR
S-12   !$OMP     END WORKSHARE
S-13   !$OMP   END PARALLEL
S-14
S-15           END SUBROUTINE WSHARE5
```

4   The following example contains an assignment to a private scalar variable, which is performed by
5   one thread in a **workshare** while all other threads wait. It is non-conforming because the private
6   scalar variable is undefined after the assignment statement.

7   *Example workshare.6.f*

```
S-1            SUBROUTINE WSHARE6_WRONG(AA, BB, CC, DD, N)
S-2            INTEGER N
S-3            REAL AA(N,N), BB(N,N), CC(N,N), DD(N,N)
S-4
S-5              INTEGER PRI
S-6
S-7    !$OMP   PARALLEL PRIVATE(PRI)
S-8    !$OMP     WORKSHARE
S-9                AA = BB
S-10               PRI = 1
S-11               CC = DD * PRI
S-12   !$OMP     END WORKSHARE
S-13   !$OMP   END PARALLEL
```

```
S-14
S-15        END SUBROUTINE WSHARE6_WRONG
```

Fortran execution rules must be enforced inside a **workshare** construct. In the following
example, the same result is produced in the following program fragment regardless of whether the
code is executed sequentially or inside an OpenMP program with multiple threads:

Example workshare.7.f

```
S-1         SUBROUTINE WSHARE7(AA, BB, CC, N)
S-2         INTEGER N
S-3         REAL AA(N), BB(N), CC(N)
S-4
S-5   !$OMP     PARALLEL
S-6   !$OMP         WORKSHARE
S-7             AA(1:50)   = BB(11:60)
S-8             CC(11:20) = AA(1:10)
S-9   !$OMP         END WORKSHARE
S-10  !$OMP     END PARALLEL
S-11
S-12        END SUBROUTINE WSHARE7
```

────────────────────────── Fortran ──────────────────────────

3.14 `masked` Construct

The following example demonstrates the **masked** construct. In the example, the primary thread (thread number 0) keeps track of how many iterations have been executed and prints out a progress report in the iteration loop. The other threads skip the **masked** region without waiting. The **filter** clause can be used to specify a thread number other than the primary thread to execute a structured block, as illustrated by the second **masked** construct after the iteration loop. If the thread specified in a **filter** clause does not exist in the team then the structured block is not executed by any thread.

―――――――――――――――――― C / C++ ――――――――――――――――――

Example masked.1.c (**omp_5.1**)

```
S-1    #include <stdio.h>
S-2
S-3    extern float average(float,float,float);
S-4
S-5    void masked_example( float* x, float* xold, int n, float tol )
S-6    {
S-7      int c, i, toobig;
S-8      float error, y;
S-9      c = 0;
S-10     #pragma omp parallel
S-11     {
S-12       do {
S-13         #pragma omp for private(i)
S-14         for( i = 1; i < n-1; ++i ){
S-15           xold[i] = x[i];
S-16         }
S-17         #pragma omp single
S-18         {
S-19           toobig = 0;
S-20         }
S-21         #pragma omp for private(i,y,error) reduction(+:toobig)
S-22         for( i = 1; i < n-1; ++i ){
S-23           y = x[i];
S-24           x[i] = average( xold[i-1], x[i], xold[i+1] );
S-25           error = y - x[i];
S-26           if( error > tol || error < -tol ) ++toobig;
S-27         }
S-28         #pragma omp masked            // primary thread (thread 0)
S-29         {
S-30           ++c;
S-31           printf( "iteration %d, toobig=%d\n", c, toobig );
S-32         }
S-33       } while( toobig > 0 );
S-34       #pragma omp barrier
```

```
S-35        #pragma omp masked filter(1)   // thread 1
S-36        {
S-37          // The printf statement will not be executed
S-38          // if the number of threads is less than 2.
S-39          printf( "total number of iterations = %d\n", c );
S-40        }
S-41      }
S-42    }
```

———————————————————— C / C++ ————————————————————
———————————————————— Fortran ————————————————————

1   *Example masked.1.f* (**omp_5.1**)

```
S-1         SUBROUTINE MASKED_EXAMPLE( X, XOLD, N, TOL )
S-2         REAL X(*), XOLD(*), TOL
S-3         INTEGER N
S-4         INTEGER C, I, TOOBIG
S-5         REAL ERROR, Y, AVERAGE
S-6         EXTERNAL AVERAGE
S-7         C = 0
S-8         TOOBIG = 1
S-9   !$OMP PARALLEL
S-10          DO WHILE( TOOBIG > 0 )
S-11  !$OMP      DO PRIVATE(I)
S-12               DO I = 2, N-1
S-13                 XOLD(I) = X(I)
S-14               ENDDO
S-15  !$OMP      SINGLE
S-16             TOOBIG = 0
S-17  !$OMP      END SINGLE
S-18  !$OMP      DO PRIVATE(I,Y,ERROR), REDUCTION(+:TOOBIG)
S-19             DO I = 2, N-1
S-20               Y = X(I)
S-21               X(I) = AVERAGE( XOLD(I-1), X(I), XOLD(I+1) )
S-22               ERROR = Y-X(I)
S-23               IF( ERROR > TOL .OR. ERROR < -TOL ) TOOBIG = TOOBIG+1
S-24             ENDDO
S-25  !$OMP      MASKED              ! primary thread (thread 0)
S-26             C = C + 1
S-27             PRINT *, 'Iteration ', C, 'TOOBIG=', TOOBIG
S-28  !$OMP      END MASKED
S-29          ENDDO
S-30  !$OMP   BARRIER
S-31  !$OMP   MASKED FILTER(1)      ! thread 1
S-32          ! The print statement will not be executed
S-33          ! if the number of threads is less than 2.
S-34          PRINT *, 'Total number of iterations =', C
```

```
S-35    !$OMP    END MASKED
S-36    !$OMP  END PARALLEL
S-37          END SUBROUTINE MASKED_EXAMPLE
```
──────────────────────────── Fortran ────────────────────────────

3.15 `loop` Construct

The following example illustrates the use of the OpenMP 5.0 `loop` construct for the execution of a loop. The `loop` construct asserts to the compiler that the iterations of the loop are free of data dependencies and may be executed concurrently. It allows the compiler to use heuristics to select the parallelization scheme and compiler-level optimizations for the concurrency.

───────────────────────────── C / C++ ─────────────────────────────

Example loop.1.c (`omp_5.0`)

```
S-1     #include  <stdio.h>
S-2     #define N 100
S-3     int main()
S-4     {
S-5       float x[N], y[N];
S-6       float a = 2.0;
S-7       for(int i=0;i<N;i++){ x[i]=i; y[i]=0;}   // initialize
S-8
S-9       #pragma omp parallel
S-10      {
S-11        #pragma omp loop
S-12        for(int i = 0; i < N; ++i) y[i] = a*x[i] + y[i];
S-13      }
S-14      if(y[N-1] != (N-1)*2.0) printf("Error: 2*(N-1) != y[N-1]=%f",y[N-1]);
S-15    }
```

───────────────────────────── C / C++ ─────────────────────────────
───────────────────────────── Fortran ─────────────────────────────

Example loop.1.f90 (`omp_5.0`)

```
S-1
S-2     program main
S-3       integer, parameter :: N=100
S-4       real :: x(N), y(N)
S-5       real :: a = 2.0e0
S-6
S-7       x=(/ (i,i=1,N) /); y=1.0e0                        !! initialize
S-8
S-9       !$omp parallel
S-10        !$omp loop
S-11          do i=1,N; y(i) = a*x(i) + y(i); enddo
S-12        !$omp end parallel
S-13
S-14      if(y(N) /= N*2.0e0) print*,"Error: 2*N /= y(N); y(N)=",y(N)
S-15    end program
```
───────────────────────────── Fortran ─────────────────────────────

3.16 Parallel Random Access Iterator Loop

--------------------------------- C++ ---------------------------------

The following example shows a parallel random access iterator loop.

Example pra_iterator.1.cpp (`omp_3.0`)

```cpp
S-1    #include <vector>
S-2    void iterator_example()
S-3    {
S-4      std::vector<int> vec(23);
S-5      std::vector<int>::iterator it;
S-6    #pragma omp parallel for default(none) shared(vec)
S-7      for (it = vec.begin(); it < vec.end(); it++)
S-8      {
S-9        // do work with *it //
S-10     }
S-11   }
```

--------------------------------- C++ ---------------------------------

3.17 `omp_set_dynamic` and `omp_set_num_threads` Routines

Some programs rely on a fixed, prespecified number of threads to execute correctly. Because the default setting for the dynamic adjustment of the number of threads is implementation defined, such programs can choose to turn off the dynamic threads capability and set the number of threads explicitly to ensure portability. The following example shows how to do this using `omp_set_dynamic`, and `omp_set_num_threads`.

In this example, the program executes correctly only if it is executed by 16 threads. If the implementation is not capable of supporting 16 threads, the behavior of this example is implementation defined. Note that the number of threads executing a **parallel** region remains constant during the region, regardless of the dynamic threads setting. The dynamic threads mechanism determines the number of threads to use at the start of the **parallel** region and keeps it constant for the duration of the region.

C / C++

Example set_dynamic_nthrs.1.c

```
#include <omp.h>
#include <stdlib.h>

void do_by_16(float *x, int iam, int ipoints) {}

void dynthreads(float *x, int npoints)
{
  int iam, ipoints;

  omp_set_dynamic(0);
  omp_set_num_threads(16);

  #pragma omp parallel shared(x, npoints) private(iam, ipoints)
  {
    if (omp_get_num_threads() != 16)
      abort();

    iam = omp_get_thread_num();
    ipoints = npoints/16;
    do_by_16(x, iam, ipoints);
  }
}
```

C / C++
---

1   *Example set_dynamic_nthrs.1.f*

```
S-1          SUBROUTINE DO_BY_16(X, IAM, IPOINTS)
S-2            REAL X(*)
S-3            INTEGER IAM, IPOINTS
S-4          END SUBROUTINE DO_BY_16
S-5
S-6          SUBROUTINE DYNTHREADS(X, NPOINTS)
S-7
S-8            INCLUDE "omp_lib.h"         ! or USE OMP_LIB
S-9
S-10           INTEGER NPOINTS
S-11           REAL X(NPOINTS)
S-12
S-13           INTEGER IAM, IPOINTS
S-14
S-15           CALL OMP_SET_DYNAMIC(.FALSE.)
S-16           CALL OMP_SET_NUM_THREADS(16)
S-17
S-18   !$OMP    PARALLEL SHARED(X,NPOINTS) PRIVATE(IAM, IPOINTS)
S-19
S-20             IF (OMP_GET_NUM_THREADS() .NE. 16) THEN
S-21               STOP
S-22             ENDIF
S-23
S-24             IAM = OMP_GET_THREAD_NUM()
S-25             IPOINTS = NPOINTS/16
S-26             CALL DO_BY_16(X,IAM,IPOINTS)
S-27
S-28   !$OMP    END PARALLEL
S-29
S-30          END SUBROUTINE DYNTHREADS
```

3.18 `omp_get_num_threads` Routine

In the following example, the **`omp_get_num_threads`** call returns 1 in the sequential part of the code, so **np** will always be equal to 1. To determine the number of threads that will be deployed for the **parallel** region, the call should be inside the **parallel** region.

─────────────────────────── C / C++ ───────────────────────────

Example get_nthrs.1.c

```
S-1    #include <omp.h>
S-2    void work(int i);
S-3
S-4    void incorrect() {
S-5      int np, i;
S-6
S-7      np = omp_get_num_threads();  /* misplaced */
S-8
S-9      #pragma omp parallel for schedule(static)
S-10     for (i=0; i < np; i++)
S-11       work(i);
S-12   }
```

─────────────────────────── C / C++ ───────────────────────────
─────────────────────────── Fortran ───────────────────────────

Example get_nthrs.1.f

```
S-1            SUBROUTINE WORK(I)
S-2            INTEGER I
S-3              I = I + 1
S-4            END SUBROUTINE WORK
S-5
S-6            SUBROUTINE INCORRECT()
S-7              INCLUDE "omp_lib.h"        ! or USE OMP_LIB
S-8              INTEGER I, NP
S-9
S-10             NP = OMP_GET_NUM_THREADS()    !misplaced: will return 1
S-11   !$OMP     PARALLEL DO SCHEDULE(STATIC)
S-12               DO I = 0, NP-1
S-13                 CALL WORK(I)
S-14               ENDDO
S-15   !$OMP     END PARALLEL DO
S-16           END SUBROUTINE INCORRECT
```

─────────────────────────── Fortran ───────────────────────────

The following example shows how to rewrite this program without including a query for the
number of threads:

C / C++

Example get_nthrs.2.c

```
S-1    #include <omp.h>
S-2    void work(int i);
S-3
S-4    void correct()
S-5    {
S-6      int i;
S-7
S-8      #pragma omp parallel private(i)
S-9      {
S-10       i = omp_get_thread_num();
S-11       work(i);
S-12     }
S-13   }
```

C / C++

Fortran

Example get_nthrs.2.f

```
S-1          SUBROUTINE WORK(I)
S-2            INTEGER I
S-3
S-4            I = I + 1
S-5
S-6          END SUBROUTINE WORK
S-7
S-8          SUBROUTINE CORRECT()
S-9            INCLUDE "omp_lib.h"        ! or USE OMP_LIB
S-10           INTEGER I
S-11
S-12   !$OMP    PARALLEL PRIVATE(I)
S-13           I = OMP_GET_THREAD_NUM()
S-14           CALL WORK(I)
S-15   !$OMP    END PARALLEL
S-16
S-17         END SUBROUTINE CORRECT
```

Fortran

This page intentionally left blank

4 OpenMP Affinity

OpenMP Affinity consists of a **proc_bind** policy (thread affinity policy) and a specification of places ("location units" or *processors* that may be cores, hardware threads, sockets, etc.). OpenMP Affinity enables users to bind computations on specific places. The placement will hold for the duration of the parallel region. However, the runtime is free to migrate the OpenMP threads to different cores (hardware threads, sockets, etc.) prescribed within a given place, if two or more cores (hardware threads, sockets, etc.) have been assigned to a given place.

Often the binding can be managed without resorting to explicitly setting places. Without the specification of places in the **OMP_PLACES** variable, the OpenMP runtime will distribute and bind threads using the entire range of processors for the OpenMP program, according to the **OMP_PROC_BIND** environment variable or the **proc_bind** clause. When places are specified, the OMP runtime binds threads to the places according to a default distribution policy, or those specified in the **OMP_PROC_BIND** environment variable or the **proc_bind** clause.

In the OpenMP Specifications document a processor refers to an execution unit that is enabled for an OpenMP thread to use. A processor is a core when there is no SMT (Simultaneous Multi-Threading) support or SMT is disabled. When SMT is enabled, a processor is a hardware thread (HW-thread). (This is the usual case; but actually, the execution unit is implementation defined.) Processor numbers are numbered sequentially from 0 to the number of cores less one (without SMT), or 0 to the number HW-threads less one (with SMT). OpenMP places use the processor number to designate binding locations (unless an "abstract name" is used.)

The processors available to a process may be a subset of the system's processors. This restriction may be the result of a wrapper process controlling the execution (such as **numactl** on Linux systems), compiler options, library-specific environment variables, or default kernel settings. For instance, the execution of multiple MPI processes, launched on a single compute node, will each have a subset of processors as determined by the MPI launcher or set by MPI affinity environment variables for the MPI library.

Threads of a team are positioned onto places in a compact manner, a scattered distribution, or onto the primary thread's place, by setting the **OMP_PROC_BIND** environment variable or the **proc_bind** clause to **close**, **spread**, or **primary** (**master** has been deprecated), respectively. When **OMP_PROC_BIND** is set to FALSE no binding is enforced; and when the value is TRUE, the binding is implementation defined to a set of places in the **OMP_PLACES** variable or to places defined by the implementation if the **OMP_PLACES** variable is not set.

The **OMP_PLACES** variable can also be set to an abstract name (**threads**, **cores**, **sockets**) to specify that a place is either a single hardware thread, a core, or a socket, respectively. This description of the **OMP_PLACES** is most useful when the number of threads is equal to the number of hardware thread, cores or sockets. It can also be used with a **close** or **spread** distribution policy when the equality doesn't hold.

4.1 `proc_bind` Clause

The following examples demonstrate how to use the **proc_bind** clause to control the thread binding for a team of threads in a **parallel** region. The machine architecture is depicted in Figure 4.1. It consists of two sockets, each equipped with a quad-core processor and configured to execute two hardware threads simultaneously on each core. These examples assume a contiguous core numbering starting from 0, such that the hardware threads 0,1 form the first physical core.

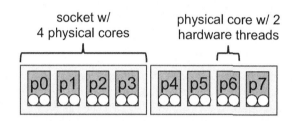

FIGURE 4.1: A machine architecture with two quad-core processors

The following equivalent place list declarations consist of eight places (which we designate as p0 to p7):

```
OMP_PLACES="{0,1},{2,3},{4,5},{6,7},{8,9},{10,11},{12,13},{14,15}"
```

or

```
OMP_PLACES="{0:2}:8:2"
```

4.1.1 Spread Affinity Policy

The following example shows the result of the **spread** affinity policy on the partition list when the number of threads is less than or equal to the number of places in the parent's place partition, for the machine architecture depicted above. Note that the threads are bound to the first place of each subpartition.

─────────────────── C / C++ ───────────────────

Example affinity.1.c (**omp_4.0**)

```
S-1
S-2   void work();
S-3
S-4   int main()
S-5   {
S-6
S-7   #pragma omp parallel proc_bind(spread) num_threads(4)
S-8      {
```

```
S-9          work();
S-10       }
S-11
S-12       return 0;
S-13
S-14   }
```

———————————— C / C++ ————————————
———————————— Fortran ————————————

1   *Example affinity.1.f* (`omp_4.0`)

```
S-1          PROGRAM EXAMPLE
S-2   !$OMP PARALLEL PROC_BIND(SPREAD) NUM_THREADS(4)
S-3          CALL WORK()
S-4   !$OMP END PARALLEL
S-5          END PROGRAM EXAMPLE
```

———————————— Fortran ————————————

2   It is unspecified on which place the primary thread is initially started. If the primary thread is
3   initially started on p0, the following placement of threads will be applied in the parallel region:

4   • thread 0 executes on p0 with the place partition p0,p1
5   • thread 1 executes on p2 with the place partition p2,p3
6   • thread 2 executes on p4 with the place partition p4,p5
7   • thread 3 executes on p6 with the place partition p6,p7

8   If the primary thread would initially be started on p2, the placement of threads and distribution of
9   the place partition would be as follows:

10 • thread 0 executes on p2 with the place partition p2,p3
11 • thread 1 executes on p4 with the place partition p4,p5
12 • thread 2 executes on p6 with the place partition p6,p7
13 • thread 3 executes on p0 with the place partition p0,p1

14 The following example illustrates the **spread** thread affinity policy when the number of threads is
15 greater than the number of places in the parent's place partition.

16 Let T be the number of threads in the team, and P be the number of places in the parent's place
17 partition. The first T/P threads of the team (including the primary thread) execute on the parent's
18 place. The next T/P threads execute on the next place in the place partition, and so on, with wrap
19 around.

1   *Example affinity.2.c* (**omp_4.0**)

```
S-1    void work();
S-2    void foo()
S-3    {
S-4      #pragma omp parallel num_threads(16) proc_bind(spread)
S-5      {
S-6        work();
S-7      }
S-8    }
```

2   *Example affinity.2.f90* (**omp_4.0**)

```
S-1    subroutine foo
S-2    !$omp parallel num_threads(16) proc_bind(spread)
S-3           call work()
S-4    !$omp end parallel
S-5    end subroutine
```

3   It is unspecified on which place the primary thread is initially started. If the primary thread is
4   initially started on p0, the following placement of threads will be applied in the parallel region:

5   • threads 0,1 execute on p0 with the place partition p0
6   • threads 2,3 execute on p1 with the place partition p1
7   • threads 4,5 execute on p2 with the place partition p2
8   • threads 6,7 execute on p3 with the place partition p3
9   • threads 8,9 execute on p4 with the place partition p4
10   • threads 10,11 execute on p5 with the place partition p5
11   • threads 12,13 execute on p6 with the place partition p6
12   • threads 14,15 execute on p7 with the place partition p7

13   If the primary thread would initially be started on p2, the placement of threads and distribution of
14   the place partition would be as follows:

15   • threads 0,1 execute on p2 with the place partition p2
16   • threads 2,3 execute on p3 with the place partition p3
17   • threads 4,5 execute on p4 with the place partition p4
18   • threads 6,7 execute on p5 with the place partition p5
19   • threads 8,9 execute on p6 with the place partition p6
20   • threads 10,11 execute on p7 with the place partition p7
21   • threads 12,13 execute on p0 with the place partition p0
22   • threads 14,15 execute on p1 with the place partition p1

4.1.2 Close Affinity Policy

The following example shows the result of the **close** affinity policy on the partition list when the number of threads is less than or equal to the number of places in parent's place partition, for the machine architecture depicted above. The place partition is not changed by the **close** policy.

─────────────────────── C / C++ ───────────────────────

Example affinity.3.c (**omp_4.0**)

```
S-1    void work();
S-2    int main()
S-3    {
S-4    #pragma omp parallel proc_bind(close) num_threads(4)
S-5       {
S-6          work();
S-7       }
S-8       return 0;
S-9    }
```

─────────────────────── C / C++ ───────────────────────
─────────────────────── Fortran ───────────────────────

Example affinity.3.f (**omp_4.0**)

```
S-1          PROGRAM EXAMPLE
S-2    !$OMP PARALLEL PROC_BIND(CLOSE) NUM_THREADS(4)
S-3          CALL WORK()
S-4    !$OMP END PARALLEL
S-5          END PROGRAM EXAMPLE
```

─────────────────────── Fortran ───────────────────────

It is unspecified on which place the primary thread is initially started. If the primary thread is initially started on p0, the following placement of threads will be applied in the **parallel** region:

- thread 0 executes on p0 with the place partition p0-p7
- thread 1 executes on p1 with the place partition p0-p7
- thread 2 executes on p2 with the place partition p0-p7
- thread 3 executes on p3 with the place partition p0-p7

If the primary thread would initially be started on p2, the placement of threads and distribution of the place partition would be as follows:

- thread 0 executes on p2 with the place partition p0-p7
- thread 1 executes on p3 with the place partition p0-p7
- thread 2 executes on p4 with the place partition p0-p7
- thread 3 executes on p5 with the place partition p0-p7

The following example illustrates the **close** thread affinity policy when the number of threads is greater than the number of places in the parent's place partition.

Let *T* be the number of threads in the team, and *P* be the number of places in the parent's place partition. The first *T/P* threads of the team (including the primary thread) execute on the parent's place. The next *T/P* threads execute on the next place in the place partition, and so on, with wrap around. The place partition is not changed by the **close** policy.

───────────────────────────── C / C++ ─────────────────────────────

Example affinity.4.c (**omp_4.0**)

```
S-1    void work();
S-2    void foo()
S-3    {
S-4      #pragma omp parallel num_threads(16) proc_bind(close)
S-5      {
S-6        work();
S-7      }
S-8    }
```

───────────────────────────── C / C++ ─────────────────────────────

───────────────────────────── Fortran ─────────────────────────────

Example affinity.4.f90 (**omp_4.0**)

```
S-1    subroutine foo
S-2    !$omp parallel num_threads(16) proc_bind(close)
S-3          call work()
S-4    !$omp end parallel
S-5    end subroutine
```

───────────────────────────── Fortran ─────────────────────────────

It is unspecified on which place the primary thread is initially started. If the primary thread is initially running on p0, the following placement of threads will be applied in the parallel region:

- threads 0,1 execute on p0 with the place partition p0-p7
- threads 2,3 execute on p1 with the place partition p0-p7
- threads 4,5 execute on p2 with the place partition p0-p7
- threads 6,7 execute on p3 with the place partition p0-p7
- threads 8,9 execute on p4 with the place partition p0-p7
- threads 10,11 execute on p5 with the place partition p0-p7
- threads 12,13 execute on p6 with the place partition p0-p7
- threads 14,15 execute on p7 with the place partition p0-p7

If the primary thread would initially be started on p2, the placement of threads and distribution of the place partition would be as follows:

- threads 0,1 execute on p2 with the place partition p0-p7

1   • threads 2,3 execute on p3 with the place partition p0-p7
2   • threads 4,5 execute on p4 with the place partition p0-p7
3   • threads 6,7 execute on p5 with the place partition p0-p7
4   • threads 8,9 execute on p6 with the place partition p0-p7
5   • threads 10,11 execute on p7 with the place partition p0-p7
6   • threads 12,13 execute on p0 with the place partition p0-p7
7   • threads 14,15 execute on p1 with the place partition p0-p7

4.1.3 Primary Affinity Policy

The following example shows the result of the **primary** affinity policy on the partition list for the machine architecture depicted above. The place partition is not changed by the primary policy.

— C / C++ —

Example affinity.5.c (**omp_4.0**)

```
S-1    void work();
S-2    int main()
S-3    {
S-4    #pragma omp parallel proc_bind(primary) num_threads(4)
S-5       {
S-6          work();
S-7       }
S-8       return 0;
S-9    }
```

— C / C++ —

— Fortran —

Example affinity.5.f (**omp_4.0**)

```
S-1          PROGRAM EXAMPLE
S-2    !$OMP PARALLEL PROC_BIND(primary) NUM_THREADS(4)
S-3          CALL WORK()
S-4    !$OMP END PARALLEL
S-5          END PROGRAM EXAMPLE
```

— Fortran —

1 It is unspecified on which place the primary thread is initially started. If the primary thread is
2 initially running on p0, the following placement of threads will be applied in the parallel region:

3 • threads 0-3 execute on p0 with the place partition p0-p7

4 If the primary thread would initially be started on p2, the placement of threads and distribution of
5 the place partition would be as follows:

6 • threads 0-3 execute on p2 with the place partition p0-p7

4.2 Task Affinity

8   The next example illustrates the use of the **affinity** clause with a **task** construct. The variables
9   in the **affinity** clause provide a hint to the runtime that the task should execute "close" to the
10 physical storage location of the variables. For example, on a two-socket platform with a local
11 memory component close to each processor socket, the runtime will attempt to schedule the task
12 execution on the socket where the storage is located.

13 Because the C/C++ code employs a pointer, an array section is used in the **affinity** clause.
14 Fortran code can use an array reference to specify the storage, as shown here.

15 Note, in the second task of the C/C++ code the *B* pointer is declared shared. Otherwise, by default,
16 it would be firstprivate since it is a local variable, and would probably be saved for the second task
17 before being assigned a storage address by the first task. Also, one might think it reasonable to use
18 the **affinity** clause *affinity(B[:N])* on the second **task** construct. However, the storage behind
19 *B* is created in the first task, and the array section reference may not be valid when the second task
20 is generated. The use of the *A* array is sufficient for this case, because one would expect the storage
21 for *A* and *B* would be physically "close" (as provided by the hint in the first task).

─────────────────────────── C / C++ ───────────────────────────

22 *Example affinity.6.c* (**omp_5.0**)

```
S-1    double * alloc_init_B(double *A, int N);
S-2    void      compute_on_B(double *B, int N);
S-3
S-4    void task_affinity(double *A, int N)
S-5    {
S-6       double * B;
S-7       #pragma omp task depend(out:B) shared(B) affinity(A[0:N])
S-8       {
S-9         B = alloc_init_B(A,N);
S-10      }
S-11
S-12      #pragma omp task depend( in:B) shared(B) affinity(A[0:N])
S-13      {
S-14        compute_on_B(B,N);
```

```
S-15          }
S-16
S-17      #pragma omp taskwait
S-18  }
S-19
```

──────────────────────── C / C++ ────────────────────────
──────────────────────── Fortran ────────────────────────

1   *Example affinity.6.f90* (**omp_5.0**)

```
S-1   subroutine task_affinity(A, N)
S-2
S-3     external alloc_init_B
S-4     external compute_on_B
S-5     double precision, allocatable :: B(:)
S-6
S-7     !$omp task depend(out:B) shared(B) affinity(A)
S-8       call alloc_init_B(B,A)
S-9     !$omp end task
S-10
S-11    !$omp task depend(in:B) shared(B) affinity(A)
S-12      call compute_on_B(B)
S-13    !$omp end task
S-14
S-15    !$omp taskwait
S-16
S-17  end subroutine
S-18
```

──────────────────────── Fortran ────────────────────────

4.3 Affinity Display

The following examples illustrate ways to display thread affinity. Automatic display of affinity can be invoked by setting the **OMP_DISPLAY_AFFINITY** environment variable to **TRUE**. The format of the output can be customized by setting the **OMP_AFFINITY_FORMAT** environment variable to an appropriate string. Also, there are API calls for the user to display thread affinity at selected locations within code.

For the first example the environment variable **OMP_DISPLAY_AFFINITY** has been set to **TRUE**, and execution occurs on an 8-core system with **OMP_NUM_THREADS** set to 8.

The affinity for the primary thread is reported through a call to the API **omp_display_affinity()** routine. For default affinity settings the report shows that the primary thread can execute on any of the cores. In the following parallel region the affinity for each of the team threads is reported automatically since the **OMP_DISPLAY_AFFINITY** environment variable has been set to **TRUE**.

These two reports are often useful (as in hybrid codes using both MPI and OpenMP) to observe the affinity (for an MPI task) before the parallel region, and during an OpenMP parallel region. Note: the next parallel region uses the same number of threads as in the previous parallel region and affinities are not changed, so affinity is NOT reported.

In the last parallel region, the thread affinities are reported because the thread affinity has changed.

C / C++

Example affinity_display.1.c (**omp_5.0**)

```
#include <stdio.h>
#include <omp.h>

int main(void) {                      //MAX threads = 8, single socket system

    //API call-- Displays Affinity of Primary Thread
    omp_display_affinity(NULL);

    // API CALL OUTPUT (default format):
    // team_num= 0, nesting_level= 0, thread_num= 0,
    // thread_affinity= 0,1,2,3,4,5,6,7

    // OMP_DISPLAY_AFFINITY=TRUE, OMP_NUM_THREADS=8
    #pragma omp parallel num_threads(omp_get_num_procs())
    {
      if(omp_get_thread_num()==0)
         printf("1st Parallel Region -- Affinity Reported \n");

    // DISPLAY OUTPUT (default format) has been sorted:
    // team_num= 0, nesting_level= 1, thread_num= 0, thread_affinity= 0
    // team_num= 0, nesting_level= 1, thread_num= 1, thread_affinity= 1
```

```
S-22        // ...
S-23        // team_num= 0, nesting_level= 1, thread_num= 7, thread_affinity= 7
S-24
S-25           // doing work here
S-26        }
S-27
S-28        #pragma omp parallel num_threads( omp_get_num_procs() )
S-29        {
S-30           if(omp_get_thread_num()==0)
S-31              printf("%s%s\n","Same Affinity as in Previous Parallel Region",
S-32                             " -- no Affinity Reported\n");
S-33
S-34        // NO AFFINITY OUTPUT:
S-35        //(output in 1st parallel region only for OMP_DISPLAY_AFFINITY=TRUE)
S-36
S-37           // doing more work here
S-38        }
S-39
S-40        // Report Affinity for 1/2 number of threads
S-41        #pragma omp parallel num_threads( omp_get_num_procs()/2 )
S-42        {
S-43          if(omp_get_thread_num()==0)
S-44             printf("Report Affinity for using 1/2 of max threads.\n");
S-45
S-46        // DISPLAY OUTPUT (default format) has been sorted:
S-47        // team_num= 0, nesting_level= 1, thread_num= 0, thread_affinity= 0,1
S-48        // team_num= 0, nesting_level= 1, thread_num= 1, thread_affinity= 2,3
S-49        // team_num= 0, nesting_level= 1, thread_num= 2, thread_affinity= 4,5
S-50        // team_num= 0, nesting_level= 1, thread_num= 3, thread_affinity= 6,7
S-51
S-52          // do work
S-53        }
S-54
S-55        return 0;
S-56     }
```

───────────────────────────── C / C++ ─────────────────────────────
───────────────────────────── Fortran ─────────────────────────────

1   *Example affinity_display.1.f90* (omp_5.0)

```
S-1     program affinity_display            ! MAX threads = 8, single socket system
S-2
S-3        use omp_lib
S-4        implicit none
S-5        character(len=0) :: null
S-6
S-7        ! API call - Displays Affinity of Primary Thread
```

```
S-8          call omp_display_affinity(null)
S-9
S-10         ! API CALL OUTPUT (default format):
S-11         ! team_num= 0, nesting_level= 0, thread_num= 0, &
S-12         !   thread_affinity= 0,1,2,3,4,5,6,7
S-13
S-14
S-15         ! OMP_DISPLAY_AFFINITY=TRUE, OMP_NUM_THREADS=8
S-16
S-17      !$omp parallel num_threads(omp_get_num_procs())
S-18
S-19        if(omp_get_thread_num()==0) then
S-20           print*, "1st Parallel Region  -- Affinity Reported"
S-21        endif
S-22
S-23         ! DISPLAY OUTPUT (default format) has been sorted:
S-24         ! team_num= 0, nesting_level= 1, thread_num= 0, thread_affinity= 0
S-25         ! team_num= 0, nesting_level= 1, thread_num= 1, thread_affinity= 1
S-26         ! ...
S-27         ! team_num= 0, nesting_level= 1, thread_num= 7, thread_affinity= 7
S-28
S-29          ! doing work here
S-30
S-31      !$omp end parallel
S-32
S-33      !$omp parallel num_threads( omp_get_num_procs() )
S-34
S-35        if(omp_get_thread_num()==0) then
S-36           print*, "Same Affinity in Parallel Region -- no Affinity Reported"
S-37        endif
S-38
S-39         ! NO AFFINITY OUTPUT:
S-40         ! (output in 1st parallel region only for
S-41         !   OMP_DISPLAY_AFFINITY=TRUE)
S-42
S-43          ! doing more work here
S-44
S-45      !$omp end parallel
S-46
S-47      ! Report Affinity for 1/2 number of threads
S-48      !$omp parallel num_threads( omp_get_num_procs()/2 )
S-49
S-50        if(omp_get_thread_num()==0) then
S-51           print*, "Altered Affinity in Parallel Region -- Affinity Reported"
S-52        endif
S-53
S-54         ! DISPLAY OUTPUT (default format) has been sorted:
```

```
S-55        ! team_num= 0, nesting_level= 1, thread_num= 0, &
S-56        !   thread_affinity= 0,1
S-57        ! team_num= 0, nesting_level= 1, thread_num= 1, &
S-58        !   thread_affinity= 2,3
S-59        ! team_num= 0, nesting_level= 1, thread_num= 2, &
S-60        !   thread_affinity= 4,5
S-61        ! team_num= 0, nesting_level= 1, thread_num= 3, &
S-62        !   thread_affinity= 6,7
S-63
S-64         ! do work
S-65
S-66        !$omp end parallel
S-67
S-68     end program
```

———————————————— Fortran ————————————————

In the following example 2 threads are forked, and each executes on a socket. Next, a nested parallel region runs half of the available threads on each socket.

These OpenMP environment variables have been set:

- **OMP_PROC_BIND**="TRUE"
- **OMP_NUM_THREADS**="2,4"
- **OMP_PLACES**="{0,2,4,6},{1,3,5,7}"
- **OMP_AFFINITY_FORMAT**="nest_level= %L, parent_thrd_num= %a, thrd_num= %n, thrd_affinity= %A"

where the numbers correspond to core ids for the system. Note, **OMP_DISPLAY_AFFINITY** is not set and is **FALSE** by default. This example shows how to use API routines to perform affinity display operations.

For each of the two first-level threads the **OMP_PLACES** variable specifies a place with all the core-ids of the socket ({0,2,4,6} for one thread and {1,3,5,7} for the other). (As is sometimes the case in 2-socket systems, one socket may consist of the even id numbers, while the other may have the odd id numbers.) The affinities are printed according to the **OMP_AFFINITY_FORMAT** format: providing the parallel nesting level (%L), the ancestor thread number (%a), the thread number (%n) and the thread affinity (%A). In the nested parallel region within the *socket_work* routine the affinities for the threads on each socket are printed according to this format.

────────────────────── C / C++ ──────────────────────

1   *Example affinity_display.2.c* (**omp_5.0**)

```
S-1    #include <stdio.h>
S-2    #include <stdlib.h>
S-3    #include <omp.h>
S-4
S-5    void socket_work(int socket_num, int n_thrds);
S-6
S-7    int main(void)
S-8    {
S-9       int n_sockets, socket_num, n_thrds_on_socket;
S-10
S-11      omp_set_nested(1);              // or env var= OMP_NESTED=true
S-12      omp_set_max_active_levels(2); // or env var= OMP_MAX_ACTIVE_LEVELS=2
S-13
S-14      n_sockets          = omp_get_num_places();
S-15      n_thrds_on_socket = omp_get_place_num_procs(0);
S-16
S-17  // OMP_NUM_THREADS=2,4
S-18  // OMP_PLACES="{0,2,4,6},{1,3,5,7}"  #2 sockets; even/odd proc-ids
S-19  // OMP_AFFINITY_FORMAT=\
S-20  // "nest_level= %L, parent_thrd_num= %a, thrd_num= %n, thrd_affinity= %A"
S-21
S-22      #pragma omp parallel num_threads(n_sockets) private(socket_num)
S-23      {
S-24         socket_num = omp_get_place_num();
S-25
S-26         if(socket_num==0)
S-27            printf(" LEVEL 1 AFFINITIES 1 thread/socket, %d sockets:\n\n",
S-28                    n_sockets);
S-29
S-30         // not needed if OMP_DISPLAY_AFFINITY=TRUE
S-31         omp_display_affinity(NULL);
S-32
S-33  // OUTPUT:
S-34  // LEVEL 1 AFFINITIES 1 thread/socket, 2 sockets:
S-35  // nest_level= 1, parent_thrd_num= 0, thrd_num= 0, thrd_affinity= 0,2,4,6
S-36  // nest_level= 1, parent_thrd_num= 0, thrd_num= 1, thrd_affinity= 1,3,5,7
S-37
S-38         socket_work(socket_num, n_thrds_on_socket);
S-39      }
S-40
S-41    return 0;
S-42    }
S-43
S-44   void socket_work(int socket_num, int n_thrds)
```

```
S-45     {
S-46        #pragma omp parallel num_threads(n_thrds)
S-47        {
S-48           if(omp_get_thread_num()==0)
S-49              printf(" LEVEL 2 AFFINITIES, %d threads on socket %d\n",
S-50                     n_thrds, socket_num);
S-51
S-52              // not needed if OMP_DISPLAY_AFFINITY=TRUE
S-53              omp_display_affinity(NULL);
S-54
S-55     // OUTPUT:
S-56     // LEVEL 2 AFFINITIES, 4 threads on socket 0
S-57     // nest_level= 2, parent_thrd_num= 0, thrd_num= 0, thrd_affinity= 0
S-58     // nest_level= 2, parent_thrd_num= 0, thrd_num= 1, thrd_affinity= 2
S-59     // nest_level= 2, parent_thrd_num= 0, thrd_num= 2, thrd_affinity= 4
S-60     // nest_level= 2, parent_thrd_num= 0, thrd_num= 3, thrd_affinity= 6
S-61
S-62     // LEVEL 2 AFFINITIES, 4 threads on socket 1
S-63     // nest_level= 2, parent_thrd_num= 1, thrd_num= 0, thrd_affinity= 1
S-64     // nest_level= 2, parent_thrd_num= 1, thrd_num= 1, thrd_affinity= 3
S-65     // nest_level= 2, parent_thrd_num= 1, thrd_num= 2, thrd_affinity= 5
S-66     // nest_level= 2, parent_thrd_num= 1, thrd_num= 3, thrd_affinity= 7
S-67
S-68           // ... Do Some work on Socket
S-69        }
S-70     }
```

──────────────────── C / C++ ────────────────────
──────────────────── Fortran ────────────────────

1   *Example affinity_display.2.f90* (**omp_5.0**)

```
S-1      program affinity_display
S-2
S-3         use omp_lib
S-4         implicit none
S-5         character(len=0) :: null
S-6         integer          :: n_sockets, socket_num, n_thrds_on_socket;
S-7
S-8         call omp_set_nested(.true.)          ! or env var= OMP_NESTED=true
S-9         call omp_set_max_active_levels(2)    ! or env var= OMP_MAX_ACTIVE_LEVELS=2
S-10
S-11        n_sockets        = omp_get_num_places()
S-12        n_thrds_on_socket = omp_get_place_num_procs(0)
S-13
S-14        ! OMP_NUM_THREADS=2,4
S-15        ! OMP_PLACES="{0,2,4,6},{1,3,5,7}"  #2 sockets; even/odd proc-ids
S-16        ! OMP_AFFINITY_FORMAT=\
```

```
S-17            !"nest_level= %L, parent_thrd_num= %a, thrd_num= %n, thrd_affinity= %A"
S-18
S-19        !$omp parallel num_threads(n_sockets) private(socket_num)
S-20
S-21          socket_num = omp_get_place_num()
S-22
S-23          if(socket_num==0) then
S-24            write(*,'("LEVEL 1 AFFINITIES 1 thread/socket ",i0," sockets")') &
S-25                    n_sockets
S-26          endif
S-27
S-28          call omp_display_affinity(null)    ! not needed
S-29                                             ! if OMP_DISPLAY_AFFINITY=TRUE
S-30
S-31            ! OUTPUT:
S-32            ! LEVEL 1 AFFINITIES 1 thread/socket, 2 sockets:
S-33            ! nest_level= 1, parent_thrd_num= 0, thrd_num= 0, &
S-34            !   thrd_affinity= 0,2,4,6
S-35            ! nest_level= 1, parent_thrd_num= 0, thrd_num= 1, &
S-36            !   thrd_affinity= 1,3,5,7
S-37
S-38          call socket_work(socket_num, n_thrds_on_socket)
S-39
S-40        !$omp end parallel
S-41
S-42     end program
S-43
S-44     subroutine socket_work(socket_num, n_thrds)
S-45        use omp_lib
S-46        implicit none
S-47        integer :: socket_num, n_thrds
S-48        character(len=0) :: null
S-49
S-50        !$omp parallel num_threads(n_thrds)
S-51
S-52            if(omp_get_thread_num()==0) then
S-53            write(*,'("LEVEL 2 AFFINITIES, ",i0," threads on socket ",i0)') &
S-54                    n_thrds,socket_num
S-55            endif
S-56
S-57          call omp_display_affinity(null)   ! not needed
S-58                                            ! if OMP_DISPLAY_AFFINITY=TRUE
S-59
S-60          ! OUTPUT:
S-61          ! LEVEL 2 AFFINITIES, 4 threads on socket 0
S-62          ! nest_level= 2, parent_thrd_num= 0, thrd_num= 0, thrd_affinity= 0
S-63          ! nest_level= 2, parent_thrd_num= 0, thrd_num= 1, thrd_affinity= 2
```

```
S-64              ! nest_level= 2, parent_thrd_num= 0, thrd_num= 2, thrd_affinity= 4
S-65              ! nest_level= 2, parent_thrd_num= 0, thrd_num= 3, thrd_affinity= 6
S-66
S-67              ! LEVEL 2 AFFINITIES, 4 thrds on socket 1
S-68              ! nest_level= 2, parent_thrd_num= 1, thrd_num= 0, thrd_affinity= 1
S-69              ! nest_level= 2, parent_thrd_num= 1, thrd_num= 1, thrd_affinity= 3
S-70              ! nest_level= 2, parent_thrd_num= 1, thrd_num= 2, thrd_affinity= 5
S-71              ! nest_level= 2, parent_thrd_num= 1, thrd_num= 3, thrd_affinity= 7
S-72
S-73              ! ... Do Some work on Socket
S-74
S-75          !$omp end parallel
S-76
S-77      end subroutine
```

---------------------------- Fortran ----------------------------

The next example illustrates more details about affinity formatting. First, the
omp_get_affinity_format() API routine is used to obtain the default format. The code
checks to make sure the storage provides enough space to hold the format. Next, the
omp_set_affinity_format() API routine sets a user-defined format: *host=%20H*
thrd_num=%0.4n binds_to=%A.

The host, thread number and affinity fields are specified by *%20H*, *%0.4n* and *%A*: *H*, *n* and *A* are
single character "short names" for the host, thread_num and thread_affinity data to be printed, with
format sizes of *20*, *4*, and "size as needed". The period (.) indicates that the field is displayed
right-justified (default is left-justified) and the "0" indicates that any unused space is to be prefixed
with zeros (e.g. instead of "1", "0001" is displayed for the field size of 4).

Within the parallel region the affinity for each thread is captured by
omp_capture_affinity() into a buffer array with elements indexed by the thread number
(*thrd_num*). After the parallel region, the thread affinities are printed in thread-number order.

If the storage area in buffer is inadequate for holding the affinity data, the stored affinity data is
truncated. The maximum value for the number of characters (*nchars*) returned by
omp_capture_affinity is captured by the **reduction(max:max_req_store)** clause
and the *if(nchars >= max_req_store) max_req_store=nchars* statement. It is used to report possible
truncation (if *max_req_store* > *buffer_store*).

1   *Example affinity_display.3.c* (**omp_5.0**)

```
S-1     #include <stdio.h>
S-2     #include <stdlib.h>  // also null is in <stddef.h>
S-3     #include <stddef.h>
S-4     #include <string.h>
S-5     #include <omp.h>
S-6
S-7     #define FORMAT_STORE    80
S-8     #define BUFFER_STORE    80
S-9
S-10    int main(void){
S-11
S-12       int i, n, thrd_num, max_req_store;
S-13       size_t nchars;
S-14
S-15       char default_format[FORMAT_STORE];
S-16       char my_format[]   = "host=%20H thrd_num=%0.4n binds_to=%A";
S-17       char **buffer;
S-18
S-19
S-20       // CODE SEGMENT 1           AFFINITY FORMAT
S-21
S-22       // Get and Display Default Affinity Format
S-23
S-24       nchars = omp_get_affinity_format(default_format,(size_t)FORMAT_STORE);
S-25       printf("Default Affinity Format is: %s\n",default_format);
S-26
S-27       if(nchars >= FORMAT_STORE){
S-28          printf("Caution: Reported Format is truncated.  Increase\n");
S-29          printf("         FORMAT_STORE to %d.\n", nchars+1);
S-30       }
S-31
S-32       // Set Affinity Format
S-33
S-34       omp_set_affinity_format(my_format);
S-35       printf("Affinity Format set to: %s\n",my_format);
S-36
S-37
S-38       // CODE SEGMENT 2            CAPTURE AFFINITY
S-39
S-40       // Set up buffer for affinity of n threads
S-41
S-42       n = omp_get_num_procs();
S-43       buffer = (char **)malloc( sizeof(char *) * n );
S-44       for(i=0;i<n;i++){
```

```
S-45              buffer[i]=(char *)malloc( sizeof(char) * BUFFER_STORE);
S-46          }
S-47
S-48          // Capture Affinity using Affinity Format set above.
S-49          // Use max reduction to check size of buffer areas
S-50          max_req_store = 0;
S-51          #pragma omp parallel private(thrd_num,nchars) \
S-52                              reduction(max:max_req_store)
S-53          {
S-54             //safety: don't exceed # of buffers
S-55             if(omp_get_num_threads()>n) exit(1);
S-56
S-57             thrd_num=omp_get_thread_num();
S-58             nchars=omp_capture_affinity(buffer[thrd_num],
S-59                                  (size_t)BUFFER_STORE,NULL);
S-60             if(nchars > max_req_store) max_req_store=nchars;
S-61
S-62             // ...
S-63          }
S-64
S-65          for(i=0;i<n;i++){
S-66             printf("thrd_num= %d, affinity: %s\n", i,buffer[i]);
S-67          }
S-68          // For 4 threads with OMP_PLACES='{0,1},{2,3},{4,5},{6,7}'
S-69          // Format     host=%20H thrd_num=%0.4n binds_to=%A
S-70
S-71          // affinity: host=hpc.cn567          thrd_num=0000 binds_to=0,1
S-72          // affinity: host=hpc.cn567          thrd_num=0001 binds_to=2,3
S-73          // affinity: host=hpc.cn567          thrd_num=0002 binds_to=4,5
S-74          // affinity: host=hpc.cn567          thrd_num=0003 binds_to=6,7
S-75
S-76
S-77          if(max_req_store>=BUFFER_STORE){
S-78             printf("Caution: Affinity string truncated.  Increase\n");
S-79             printf("         BUFFER_STORE to %d\n",max_req_store+1);
S-80          }
S-81
S-82          for(i=0;i<n;i++) free(buffer[i]);
S-83          free (buffer);
S-84
S-85          return 0;
S-86      }
```

—————————————————————— C / C++ ——————————————————————

1   *Example affinity_display.3.f90* (`omp_5.0`)

```fortran
program affinity_display
   use omp_lib
   implicit none
   integer, parameter :: FORMAT_STORE=80
   integer, parameter :: BUFFER_STORE=80

   integer            :: i, n, thrd_num, nchars, max_req_store

   character(FORMAT_STORE)     :: default_format
   character(*), parameter     :: my_format = &
                                  "host=%20H thrd_num=%0.4n binds_to=%A"
   character(:), allocatable   :: buffer(:)
   character(len=0)            :: null


!  CODE SEGMENT 1          AFFINITY FORMAT

!                                 Get and Display Default Affinity Format

   nchars = omp_get_affinity_format(default_format)
   print*,"Default Affinity Format: ", trim(default_format)

   if( nchars > FORMAT_STORE) then
      print*,"Caution: Reported Format is truncated.  Increase"
      print*,"         FORMAT_STORE to ", nchars
   endif

!                          Set Affinity Format

   call omp_set_affinity_format(my_format)
   print*,"Affinity Format set to: ", my_format



!  CODE SEGMENT 2          CAPTURE AFFINITY

!                                 Set up buffer for affinity of n threads

   n = omp_get_num_procs()
   allocate( character(len=BUFFER_STORE)::buffer(0:n-1) )

!                                 Capture Affinity using Affinity Format set above.
!                                 Use max reduction to check size of buffer areas
   max_req_store = 0
   !$omp parallel private(thrd_num,nchars) reduction(max:max_req_store)
```

```
S-45
S-46        if(omp_get_num_threads()>n) stop "ERROR: increase buffer lines"
S-47
S-48        thrd_num=omp_get_thread_num()
S-49        nchars=omp_capture_affinity(buffer(thrd_num),null)
S-50        if(nchars>max_req_store) max_req_store=nchars
S-51        !  ...
S-52
S-53     !$omp end parallel
S-54
S-55     do i = 0, n-1
S-56        print*, "thrd_num= ",i,"   affinity:", trim(buffer(i))
S-57     end do
S-58            !  For 4 threads with OMP_PLACES='{0,1},{2,3},{4,5},{6,7}'
S-59            !  Format:   host=%20H thrd_num=%0.4n binds_to=%A
S-60
S-61            !  affinity: host=hpc.cn567            thrd_num=0000 binds_to=0,1
S-62            !  affinity: host=hpc.cn567            thrd_num=0001 binds_to=2,3
S-63            !  affinity: host=hpc.cn567            thrd_num=0002 binds_to=4,5
S-64            !  affinity: host=hpc.cn567            thrd_num=0003 binds_to=6,7
S-65
S-66     if(max_req_store > BUFFER_STORE) then
S-67        print*,  "Caution: Affinity string truncated.  Increase"
S-68        print*,  "            BUFFER_STORE to ",max_req_store
S-69     endif
S-70
S-71     deallocate(buffer)
S-72  end program
```
———————————————————— Fortran ————————————————————

4.4 Affinity Query Functions

In the example below a team of threads is generated on each socket of the system, using nested parallelism. Several query functions are used to gather information to support the creation of the teams and to obtain socket and thread numbers.

For proper execution of the code, the user must create a place partition, such that each place is a listing of the core numbers for a socket. For example, in a 2 socket system with 8 cores in each socket, and sequential numbering in the socket for the core numbers, the **OMP_PLACES** variable would be set to "{0:8},{8:8}", using the place syntax {*lower_bound*:*length*:*stride*}, and the default stride of 1.

The code determines the number of sockets (*n_sockets*) using the **omp_get_num_places()** query function. In this example each place is constructed with a list of each socket's core numbers, hence the number of places is equal to the number of sockets.

The outer parallel region forms a team of threads, and each thread executes on a socket (place) because the **proc_bind** clause uses **spread** in the outer **parallel** construct. Next, in the *socket_init* function, an inner parallel region creates a team of threads equal to the number of elements (core numbers) from the place of the parent thread. Because the outer **parallel** construct uses a **spread** affinity policy, each of its threads inherits a subpartition of the original partition. Hence, the **omp_get_place_num_procs** query function returns the number of elements (here procs = cores) in the subpartition of the thread. After each parent thread creates its nested parallel region on the section, the socket number and thread number are reported.

Note: Portable tools like hwloc (Portable HardWare LOCality package), which support many common operating systems, can be used to determine the configuration of a system. On some systems there are utilities, files or user guides that provide configuration information. For instance, the socket number and proc_id's for a socket can be found in the /proc/cpuinfo text file on Linux systems.

———————————————— C / C++ ————————————————

Example affinity_query.1.c (**omp_4.5**)

```
#include <stdio.h>
#include <omp.h>

void socket_init(int socket_num)
{
   int n_procs;

   n_procs = omp_get_place_num_procs(socket_num);
   #pragma omp parallel num_threads(n_procs) proc_bind(close)
   {
      printf("Reporting in from socket num, thread num:  %d %d\n",
                             socket_num, omp_get_thread_num() );
   }
}

int main()
{
   int n_sockets, socket_num;

   omp_set_nested(1);                 // or export OMP_NESTED=true
   omp_set_max_active_levels(2);      // or export OMP_MAX_ACTIVE_LEVELS=2

   n_sockets = omp_get_num_places();
   #pragma omp parallel num_threads(n_sockets) private(socket_num) \
                        proc_bind(spread)
   {
      socket_num = omp_get_place_num();
      socket_init(socket_num);
   }
```

```
S-30
S-31      return 0;
S-32    }
```

──────────────────────── C / C++ ────────────────────────
──────────────────────── Fortran ────────────────────────

1   *Example affinity_query.1.f90* (omp_4.5)

```
S-1    subroutine socket_init(socket_num)
S-2       use omp_lib
S-3       integer  :: socket_num, n_procs
S-4
S-5       n_procs = omp_get_place_num_procs(socket_num)
S-6       !$omp parallel num_threads(n_procs) proc_bind(close)
S-7
S-8          print*,"Reporting in from socket num, thread num: ",  &
S-9                                   socket_num,omp_get_thread_num()
S-10      !$omp end parallel
S-11   end subroutine
S-12
S-13   program numa_teams
S-14      use omp_lib
S-15      integer :: n_sockets, socket_num
S-16
S-17      call omp_set_nested(.true.)              ! or export OMP_NESTED=true
S-18      call omp_set_max_active_levels(2) ! or export OMP_MAX_ACTIVE_LEVELS=2
S-19
S-20      n_sockets = omp_get_num_places()
S-21      !$omp parallel num_threads(n_sockets) private(socket_num) &
S-22      !$omp&           proc_bind(spread)
S-23
S-24         socket_num = omp_get_place_num()
S-25         call socket_init(socket_num)
S-26
S-27      !$omp end parallel
S-28   end program
```

──────────────────────── Fortran ────────────────────────

This page intentionally left blank

5 Tasking

Tasking constructs provide units of work to a thread for execution. Worksharing constructs do this, too (e.g. **for**, **do**, **sections**, and **singles** constructs); but the work units are tightly controlled by an iteration limit and limited scheduling, or a limited number of **sections** or **single** regions. Worksharing was designed with "data parallel" computing in mind. Tasking was designed for "task parallel" computing and often involves non-locality or irregularity in memory access.

The **task** construct can be used to execute work chunks: in a while loop; while traversing nodes in a list; at nodes in a tree graph; or in a normal loop (with a **taskloop** construct). Unlike the statically scheduled loop iterations of worksharing, a task is often enqueued, and then dequeued for execution by any of the threads of the team within a parallel region. The generation of tasks can be from a single generating thread (creating sibling tasks), or from multiple generators in a recursive graph tree traversals. A **taskloop** construct bundles iterations of an associated loop into tasks, and provides similar controls found in the **task** construct.

Sibling tasks are synchronized by the **taskwait** construct, and tasks and their descendent tasks can be synchronized by containing them in a **taskgroup** region. Ordered execution is accomplished by specifying dependences with a **depend** clause. Also, priorities can be specified as hints to the scheduler through a **priority** clause.

Various clauses can be used to manage and optimize task generation, as well as reduce the overhead of execution and to relinquish control of threads for work balance and forward progress.

Once a thread starts executing a task, it is the designated thread for executing the task to completion, even though it may leave the execution at a scheduling point and return later. The thread is tied to the task. Scheduling points can be introduced with the **taskyield** construct. With an **untied** clause any other thread is allowed to continue the task. An **if** clause with an expression that evaluates to *false* results in an *undeferred* task, which instructs the runtime to suspend the generating task until the undeferred task completes its execution. By including the data environment of the generating task into the generated task with the **mergeable** and **final** clauses, task generation overhead can be reduced.

A complete list of the tasking constructs and details of their clauses can be found in the *Tasking Constructs* chapter of the OpenMP Specifications, in the *OpenMP Application Programming Interface* section.

5.1 `task` and `taskwait` Constructs

The following example shows how to traverse a tree-like structure using explicit tasks. Note that the **`traverse`** function should be called from within a parallel region for the different specified tasks to be executed in parallel. Also note that the tasks will be executed in no specified order because there are no synchronization directives. Thus, assuming that the traversal will be done in post order, as in the sequential code, is wrong.

-- C / C++ --

Example tasking.1.c (`omp_3.0`)

```
S-1
S-2    struct node {
S-3      struct node *left;
S-4      struct node *right;
S-5    };
S-6
S-7    extern void process(struct node *);
S-8
S-9    void traverse( struct node *p )
S-10   {
S-11     if (p->left)
S-12   #pragma omp task    // p is firstprivate by default
S-13         traverse(p->left);
S-14     if (p->right)
S-15   #pragma omp task      // p is firstprivate by default
S-16         traverse(p->right);
S-17     process(p);
S-18   }
```

-- C / C++ --
-- Fortran --

Example tasking.1.f90 (`omp_3.0`)

```
S-1
S-2            RECURSIVE SUBROUTINE traverse ( P )
S-3              TYPE Node
S-4                 TYPE(Node), POINTER :: left, right
S-5              END TYPE Node
S-6              TYPE(Node) :: P
S-7
S-8              IF (associated(P%left)) THEN
S-9                !$OMP TASK      ! P is firstprivate by default
S-10                  CALL traverse(P%left)
S-11                !$OMP END TASK
S-12              ENDIF
S-13              IF (associated(P%right)) THEN
```

```
S-14             !$OMP TASK       ! P is firstprivate by default
S-15                 CALL traverse(P%right)
S-16             !$OMP END TASK
S-17           ENDIF
S-18           CALL process ( P )
S-19
S-20       END SUBROUTINE
```

———————————————————————— Fortran ————————————————————————

In the next example, we force a postorder traversal of the tree by adding a **taskwait** directive.
Now, we can safely assume that the left and right sons have been executed before we process the
current node.

———————————————————————— C / C++ ————————————————————————

Example tasking.2.c (**omp_3.0**)

```
S-1   struct node {
S-2     struct node *left;
S-3     struct node *right;
S-4   };
S-5   extern void process(struct node *);
S-6   void postorder_traverse( struct node *p ) {
S-7       if (p->left)
S-8           #pragma omp task     // p is firstprivate by default
S-9               postorder_traverse(p->left);
S-10      if (p->right)
S-11          #pragma omp task     // p is firstprivate by default
S-12              postorder_traverse(p->right);
S-13      #pragma omp taskwait
S-14      process(p);
S-15  }
```

———————————————————————— C / C++ ————————————————————————

1   *Example tasking.2.f90* (`omp_3.0`)

```
S-1          RECURSIVE SUBROUTINE traverse ( P )
S-2            TYPE Node
S-3                TYPE(Node), POINTER :: left, right
S-4            END TYPE Node
S-5            TYPE(Node) :: P
S-6            IF (associated(P%left)) THEN
S-7                !$OMP TASK     ! P is firstprivate by default
S-8                    CALL traverse(P%left)
S-9                !$OMP END TASK
S-10           ENDIF
S-11           IF (associated(P%right)) THEN
S-12               !$OMP TASK     ! P is firstprivate by default
S-13                   CALL traverse(P%right)
S-14               !$OMP END TASK
S-15           ENDIF
S-16           !$OMP TASKWAIT
S-17           CALL process ( P )
S-18         END SUBROUTINE
```

2   The following example demonstrates how to use the **task** construct to process elements of a linked
3   list in parallel. The thread executing the **single** region generates all of the explicit tasks, which
4   are then executed by the threads in the current team. The pointer *p* is **firstprivate** by default
5   on the **task** construct so it is not necessary to specify it in a **firstprivate** clause.

6   *Example tasking.3.c* (`omp_3.0`)

```
S-1
S-2    typedef struct node node;
S-3    struct node {
S-4        int data;
S-5        node * next;
S-6    };
S-7
S-8    void process(node * p)
S-9    {
S-10       /* do work here */
S-11   }
S-12
S-13   void increment_list_items(node * head)
S-14   {
S-15       #pragma omp parallel
S-16       {
```

```
S-17            #pragma omp single
S-18                {
S-19                    node * p = head;
S-20                    while (p) {
S-21                        #pragma omp task
S-22                        // p is firstprivate by default
S-23                            process(p);
S-24                        p = p->next;
S-25                    }
S-26                }
S-27            }
S-28     }
```

———————————————— C / C++ ————————————————
———————————————— Fortran ————————————————

1   *Example tasking.3.f90* (**omp_3.0**)

```
S-1
S-2         MODULE LIST
S-3             TYPE NODE
S-4                 INTEGER :: PAYLOAD
S-5                 TYPE (NODE), POINTER :: NEXT
S-6             END TYPE NODE
S-7         CONTAINS
S-8
S-9             SUBROUTINE PROCESS(p)
S-10                TYPE (NODE), POINTER :: P
S-11                    ! do work here
S-12            END SUBROUTINE
S-13
S-14            SUBROUTINE INCREMENT_LIST_ITEMS (HEAD)
S-15
S-16                TYPE (NODE), POINTER :: HEAD
S-17                TYPE (NODE), POINTER :: P
S-18                !$OMP PARALLEL PRIVATE(P)
S-19                    !$OMP SINGLE
S-20                        P => HEAD
S-21                        DO
S-22                            !$OMP TASK
S-23                                ! P is firstprivate by default
S-24                                CALL PROCESS(P)
S-25                            !$OMP END TASK
S-26                            P => P%NEXT
S-27                            IF ( .NOT. ASSOCIATED (P) ) EXIT
S-28                        END DO
S-29                    !$OMP END SINGLE
S-30                !$OMP END PARALLEL
```

```
S-31
S-32            END SUBROUTINE
S-33
S-34          END MODULE
```

———————————————————— Fortran ————————————————————

1   The **fib()** function should be called from within a **parallel** region for the different specified
2   tasks to be executed in parallel. Also, only one thread of the **parallel** region should call **fib()**
3   unless multiple concurrent Fibonacci computations are desired.

———————————————————— C / C++ ————————————————————

4   *Example tasking.4.c* (**omp_3.0**)

```
S-1       int fib(int n) {
S-2          int i, j;
S-3          if (n<2)
S-4            return n;
S-5          else {
S-6            #pragma omp task shared(i)
S-7                i=fib(n-1);
S-8            #pragma omp task shared(j)
S-9                j=fib(n-2);
S-10           #pragma omp taskwait
S-11               return i+j;
S-12          }
S-13       }
```

———————————————————— C / C++ ————————————————————
———————————————————— Fortran ————————————————————

5   *Example tasking.4.f* (**omp_3.0**)

```
S-1         RECURSIVE INTEGER FUNCTION fib(n) RESULT(res)
S-2         INTEGER n, i, j
S-3         IF ( n .LT. 2) THEN
S-4           res = n
S-5         ELSE
S-6   !$OMP TASK SHARED(i)
S-7             i = fib( n-1 )
S-8   !$OMP END TASK
S-9   !$OMP TASK SHARED(j)
S-10            j = fib( n-2 )
S-11  !$OMP END TASK
S-12  !$OMP TASKWAIT
S-13            res = i+j
S-14         END IF
S-15         END FUNCTION
```

———————————————————— Fortran ————————————————————

Note: There are more efficient algorithms for computing Fibonacci numbers. This classic recursion algorithm is for illustrative purposes.

The following example demonstrates a way to generate a large number of tasks with one thread and execute them with the threads in the team. While generating these tasks, the implementation may reach its limit on unassigned tasks. If it does, the implementation is allowed to cause the thread executing the task generating loop to suspend its task at the task scheduling point in the **task** directive, and start executing unassigned tasks. Once the number of unassigned tasks is sufficiently low, the thread may resume execution of the task generating loop.

—————————————————— C / C++ ——————————————————

Example tasking.5.c (**omp_3.0**)

```
#define LARGE_NUMBER 10000000
double item[LARGE_NUMBER];
extern void process(double);

int main()
{
#pragma omp parallel
  {
    #pragma omp single
    {
      int i;
      for (i=0; i<LARGE_NUMBER; i++)
            #pragma omp task    // i is firstprivate, item is shared
                process(item[i]);
    }
  }
}
```

—————————————————— C / C++ ——————————————————
—————————————————— Fortran ——————————————————

Example tasking.5.f (**omp_3.0**)

```
        real*8 item(10000000)
        integer i

!$omp parallel
!$omp single ! loop iteration variable i is private
        do i=1,10000000
!$omp task
            ! i is firstprivate, item is shared
            call process(item(i))
!$omp end task
        end do
!$omp end single
```

```
S-13    !$omp end parallel
S-14
S-15          end
```

———————————————————— Fortran ————————————————————

The following example is the same as the previous one, except that the tasks are generated in an
untied task. While generating the tasks, the implementation may reach its limit on unassigned tasks.
If it does, the implementation is allowed to cause the thread executing the task generating loop to
suspend its task at the task scheduling point in the **task** directive, and start executing unassigned
tasks. If that thread begins execution of a task that takes a long time to complete, the other threads
may complete all the other tasks before it is finished.

In this case, since the loop is in an untied task, any other thread is eligible to resume the task
generating loop. In the previous examples, the other threads would be forced to idle until the
generating thread finishes its long task, since the task generating loop was in a tied task.

———————————————————— C / C++ ————————————————————

Example tasking.6.c (`omp_3.0`)

```
S-1     #define LARGE_NUMBER 10000000
S-2     double item[LARGE_NUMBER];
S-3     extern void process(double);
S-4     int main() {
S-5     #pragma omp parallel
S-6       {
S-7         #pragma omp single
S-8         {
S-9           int i;
S-10          #pragma omp task untied
S-11          // i is firstprivate, item is shared
S-12          {
S-13              for (i=0; i<LARGE_NUMBER; i++)
S-14                  #pragma omp task
S-15                      process(item[i]);
S-16          }
S-17        }
S-18      }
S-19      return 0;
S-20    }
```

———————————————————— C / C++ ————————————————————

1   *Example tasking.6.f* (**omp_3.0**)

```
S-1          real*8 item(10000000)
S-2    !$omp parallel
S-3    !$omp single
S-4    !$omp task untied
S-5          ! loop iteration variable i is private
S-6          do i=1,10000000
S-7    !$omp task ! i is firstprivate, item is shared
S-8             call process(item(i))
S-9    !$omp end task
S-10         end do
S-11   !$omp end task
S-12   !$omp end single
S-13   !$omp end parallel
S-14         end
```

2   The following two examples demonstrate how the scheduling rules illustrated in Section 2.11.3 of
3   the OpenMP 4.0 specification affect the usage of **threadprivate** variables in tasks. A
4   **threadprivate** variable can be modified by another task that is executed by the same thread.
5   Thus, the value of a **threadprivate** variable cannot be assumed to be unchanged across a task
6   scheduling point. In untied tasks, task scheduling points may be added in any place by the
7   implementation.

8   A task switch may occur at a task scheduling point. A single thread may execute both of the task
9   regions that modify **tp**. The parts of these task regions in which **tp** is modified may be executed in
10   any order so the resulting value of **var** can be either 1 or 2.

11   *Example tasking.7.c* (**omp_3.0**)

```
S-1
S-2    int tp;
S-3    #pragma omp threadprivate(tp)
S-4    int var;
S-5    void work()
S-6    {
S-7    #pragma omp task
S-8        {
S-9            /* do work here */
S-10   #pragma omp task
S-11           {
S-12               tp = 1;
S-13               /* do work here */
S-14   #pragma omp task
```

```
S-15                {
S-16                    /* no modification of tp */
S-17                }
S-18                var = tp; //value of tp can be 1 or 2
S-19            }
S-20        tp = 2;
S-21    }
S-22 }
```

———————————————————— C / C++ ————————————————————
———————————————————— Fortran ————————————————————

Example tasking.7.f (`omp_3.0`)

```
S-1        module example
S-2        integer tp
S-3 !$omp threadprivate(tp)
S-4        integer var
S-5        contains
S-6        subroutine work
S-7 !$omp task
S-8            ! do work here
S-9 !$omp task
S-10            tp = 1
S-11            ! do work here
S-12 !$omp task
S-13            ! no modification of tp
S-14 !$omp end task
S-15            var = tp     ! value of var can be 1 or 2
S-16 !$omp end task
S-17            tp = 2
S-18 !$omp end task
S-19        end subroutine
S-20        end module
```

———————————————————— Fortran ————————————————————

In this example, scheduling constraints prohibit a thread in the team from executing a new task that modifies **tp** while another such task region tied to the same thread is suspended. Therefore, the value written will persist across the task scheduling point.

1   *Example tasking.8.c* (**omp_3.0**)

```
S-1
S-2     int tp;
S-3     #pragma omp threadprivate(tp)
S-4     int var;
S-5     void work()
S-6     {
S-7     #pragma omp parallel
S-8         {
S-9             /* do work here */
S-10    #pragma omp task
S-11            {
S-12                tp++;
S-13                /* do work here */
S-14    #pragma omp task
S-15                {
S-16                    /* do work here but don't modify tp */
S-17                }
S-18                var = tp; //Value does not change after write above
S-19            }
S-20        }
S-21    }
```

2   *Example tasking.8.f* (**omp_3.0**)

```
S-1             module example
S-2             integer tp
S-3     !$omp threadprivate(tp)
S-4             integer var
S-5             contains
S-6             subroutine work
S-7     !$omp parallel
S-8                 ! do work here
S-9     !$omp task
S-10                tp = tp + 1
S-11                ! do work here
S-12    !$omp task
S-13                    ! do work here but don't modify tp
S-14    !$omp end task
S-15                var = tp     ! value does not change after write above
S-16    !$omp end task
S-17    !$omp end parallel
```

```
S-18          end subroutine
S-19          end module
```
———————————————————— Fortran ————————————————————

The following two examples demonstrate how the scheduling rules illustrated in Section 2.11.3 of
the OpenMP 4.0 specification affect the usage of locks and critical sections in tasks. If a lock is
held across a task scheduling point, no attempt should be made to acquire the same lock in any code
that may be interleaved. Otherwise, a deadlock is possible.

In the example below, suppose the thread executing task 1 defers task 2. When it encounters the
task scheduling point at task 3, it could suspend task 1 and begin task 2 which will result in a
deadlock when it tries to enter critical region 1.

———————————————————— C / C++ ————————————————————

Example tasking.9.c (`omp_3.0`)

```
S-1     void work()
S-2     {
S-3        #pragma omp task
S-4        { //Task 1
S-5           #pragma omp task
S-6           { //Task 2
S-7               #pragma omp critical //Critical region 1
S-8               {/*do work here */ }
S-9           }
S-10          #pragma omp critical //Critical Region 2
S-11          {
S-12              //Capture data for the following task
S-13              #pragma omp task
S-14              { /* do work here */ } //Task 3
S-15          }
S-16       }
S-17    }
```
———————————————————— C / C++ ————————————————————

1   *Example tasking.9.f* (`omp_3.0`)

```
S-1              module example
S-2              contains
S-3              subroutine work
S-4      !$omp task
S-5              ! Task 1
S-6      !$omp task
S-7              ! Task 2
S-8      !$omp critical
S-9              ! Critical region 1
S-10             ! do work here
S-11     !$omp end critical
S-12     !$omp end task
S-13     !$omp critical
S-14             ! Critical region 2
S-15             ! Capture data for the following task
S-16     !$omp task
S-17             !Task 3
S-18             ! do work here
S-19     !$omp end task
S-20     !$omp end critical
S-21     !$omp end task
S-22             end subroutine
S-23             end module
```

2   In the following example, **lock** is held across a task scheduling point. However, according to the
3   scheduling restrictions, the executing thread can't begin executing one of the non-descendant tasks
4   that also acquires **lock** before the task region is complete. Therefore, no deadlock is possible.

5   *Example tasking.10.c* (`omp_3.0`)

```
S-1      #include <omp.h>
S-2      void work() {
S-3          omp_lock_t lock;
S-4          omp_init_lock(&lock);
S-5      #pragma omp parallel
S-6          {
S-7              int i;
S-8      #pragma omp for
S-9              for (i = 0; i < 100; i++) {
S-10     #pragma omp task
S-11                 {
S-12             // lock is shared by default in the task
```

```
S-13            omp_set_lock(&lock);
S-14                    // Capture data for the following task
S-15    #pragma omp task
S-16            // Task Scheduling Point 1
S-17                    { /* do work here */ }
S-18                    omp_unset_lock(&lock);
S-19            }
S-20        }
S-21    }
S-22    omp_destroy_lock(&lock);
S-23    }
```

———————————————————— C / C++ ————————————————————

———————————————————— Fortran ————————————————————

1   *Example tasking.10.f90* (`omp_3.0`)

```
S-1         module example
S-2         include 'omp_lib.h'
S-3         integer (kind=omp_lock_kind) lock
S-4         integer i
S-5
S-6         contains
S-7
S-8         subroutine work
S-9         call omp_init_lock(lock)
S-10    !$omp parallel
S-11        !$omp do
S-12        do i=1,100
S-13            !$omp task
S-14                ! Outer task
S-15                call omp_set_lock(lock)        ! lock is shared by
S-16                                               ! default in the task
S-17                        ! Capture data for the following task
S-18                        !$omp task     ! Task Scheduling Point 1
S-19                            ! do work here
S-20                        !$omp end task
S-21                call omp_unset_lock(lock)
S-22            !$omp end task
S-23        end do
S-24    !$omp end parallel
S-25        call omp_destroy_lock(lock)
S-26        end subroutine
S-27
S-28        end module
```

———————————————————— Fortran ————————————————————

The following examples illustrate the use of the **mergeable** clause in the **task** construct. In this first example, the **task** construct has been annotated with the **mergeable** clause. The addition of this clause allows the implementation to reuse the data environment (including the ICVs) of the parent task for the task inside **foo** if the task is included or undeferred. Thus, the result of the execution may differ depending on whether the task is merged or not. Therefore the mergeable clause needs to be used with caution. In this example, the use of the mergeable clause is safe. As **x** is a shared variable the outcome does not depend on whether or not the task is merged (that is, the task will always increment the same variable and will always compute the same value for **x**).

─────────────────────────────── C / C++ ───────────────────────────────

Example tasking.11.c (**omp_3.1**)

```
#include <stdio.h>
void foo ( )
{
    int x = 2;
    #pragma omp task shared(x) mergeable
    {
        x++;
    }
    #pragma omp taskwait
    printf("%d\n",x);  // prints 3
}
```

─────────────────────────────── C / C++ ───────────────────────────────
─────────────────────────────── Fortran ───────────────────────────────

Example tasking.11.f90 (**omp_3.1**)

```
subroutine foo()
  integer :: x
  x = 2
!$omp task shared(x) mergeable
  x = x + 1
!$omp end task
!$omp taskwait
  print *, x       ! prints 3
end subroutine
```

─────────────────────────────── Fortran ───────────────────────────────

This second example shows an incorrect use of the **mergeable** clause. In this example, the created task will access different instances of the variable **x** if the task is not merged, as **x** is **firstprivate**, but it will access the same variable **x** if the task is merged. As a result, the behavior of the program is unspecified, and it can print two different values for **x** depending on the decisions taken by the implementation.

1 *Example tasking.12.c* (`omp_3.1`)

```
S-1    #include <stdio.h>
S-2    void foo ( )
S-3    {
S-4       int x = 2;
S-5       #pragma omp task mergeable
S-6       {
S-7          x++;
S-8       }
S-9       #pragma omp taskwait
S-10      printf("%d\n",x);   // prints 2 or 3
S-11   }
```

2 *Example tasking.12.f90* (`omp_3.1`)

```
S-1    subroutine foo()
S-2       integer :: x
S-3       x = 2
S-4    !$omp task mergeable
S-5       x = x + 1
S-6    !$omp end task
S-7    !$omp taskwait
S-8       print *, x    ! prints 2 or 3
S-9    end subroutine
```

The following example shows the use of the **final** clause and the **omp_in_final** API call in a recursive binary search program. To reduce overhead, once a certain depth of recursion is reached the program uses the **final** clause to create only included tasks, which allow additional optimizations.

The use of the **omp_in_final** API call allows programmers to optimize their code by specifying which parts of the program are not necessary when a task can create only included tasks (that is, the code is inside a **final** task). In this example, the use of a different state variable is not necessary so once the program reaches the part of the computation that is finalized and copying from the parent state to the new state is eliminated. The allocation of **new_state** in the stack could also be avoided but it would make this example less clear. The **final** clause is most effective when used in conjunction with the **mergeable** clause since all tasks created in a **final** task region are included tasks that can be merged if the **mergeable** clause is present.

1   *Example tasking.13.c* (**omp_3.1**)

```
S-1    #include <string.h>
S-2    #include <omp.h>
S-3    #define LIMIT  3 /* arbitrary limit on recursion depth */
S-4    void check_solution(char *);
S-5    void bin_search (int pos, int n, char *state)
S-6    {
S-7       if ( pos == n ) {
S-8          check_solution(state);
S-9          return;
S-10      }
S-11      #pragma omp task final( pos > LIMIT ) mergeable
S-12      {
S-13         char new_state[n];
S-14         if (!omp_in_final() ) {
S-15           memcpy(new_state, state, pos );
S-16            state = new_state;
S-17         }
S-18         state[pos] = 0;
S-19         bin_search(pos+1, n, state );
S-20      }
S-21      #pragma omp task final( pos > LIMIT ) mergeable
S-22      {
S-23         char new_state[n];
S-24         if (! omp_in_final() ) {
S-25           memcpy(new_state, state, pos );
S-26            state = new_state;
S-27         }
S-28         state[pos] = 1;
S-29         bin_search(pos+1, n, state );
S-30      }
S-31      #pragma omp taskwait
S-32   }
```

Example tasking.13.f90 (**omp_3.1**)

```fortran
recursive subroutine bin_search(pos, n, state)
  use omp_lib
  integer :: pos, n
  character, pointer :: state(:)
  character, target, dimension(n) :: new_state1, new_state2
  integer, parameter :: LIMIT = 3
  if (pos .eq. n) then
    call check_solution(state)
    return
  endif
!$omp task final(pos > LIMIT) mergeable
  if (.not. omp_in_final()) then
    new_state1(1:pos) = state(1:pos)
    state => new_state1
  endif
  state(pos+1) = 'z'
  call bin_search(pos+1, n, state)
!$omp end task
!$omp task final(pos > LIMIT) mergeable
  if (.not. omp_in_final()) then
    new_state2(1:pos) = state(1:pos)
    state => new_state2
  endif
  state(pos+1) = 'y'
  call bin_search(pos+1, n, state)
!$omp end task
!$omp taskwait
end subroutine
```

The following example illustrates the difference between the **if** and the **final** clauses. The **if** clause has a local effect. In the first nest of tasks, the one that has the **if** clause will be undeferred but the task nested inside that task will not be affected by the **if** clause and will be created as usual. Alternatively, the **final** clause affects all **task** constructs in the **final** task region but not the **final** task itself. In the second nest of tasks, the nested tasks will be created as included tasks. Note also that the conditions for the **if** and **final** clauses are usually the opposite.

1   *Example tasking.14.c* (`omp_3.1`)

```
S-1     void bar(void);
S-2
S-3     void foo ( )
S-4     {
S-5        int i;
S-6        #pragma omp task if(0)   // This task is undeferred
S-7        {
S-8           #pragma omp task      // This task is a regular task
S-9           for (i = 0; i < 3; i++) {
S-10              #pragma omp task      // This task is a regular task
S-11              bar();
S-12          }
S-13       }
S-14       #pragma omp task final(1) // This task is a regular task
S-15       {
S-16          #pragma omp task  // This task is included
S-17          for (i = 0; i < 3; i++) {
S-18              #pragma omp task      // This task is also included
S-19              bar();
S-20          }
S-21       }
S-22    }
```

2   *Example tasking.14.f90* (`omp_3.1`)

```
S-1     subroutine foo()
S-2     integer i
S-3     !$omp task if(.FALSE.) ! This task is undeferred
S-4     !$omp task              ! This task is a regular task
S-5        do i = 1, 3
S-6          !$omp task               ! This task is a regular task
S-7            call bar()
S-8          !$omp end task
S-9        enddo
S-10    !$omp end task
S-11    !$omp end task
S-12    !$omp task final(.TRUE.) ! This task is a regular task
S-13    !$omp task              ! This task is included
S-14        do i = 1, 3
S-15          !$omp task               ! This task is also included
S-16          call bar()
S-17          !$omp end task
```

```
S-18        enddo
S-19    !$omp end task
S-20    !$omp end task
S-21    end subroutine
```

———————————————— Fortran ————————————————

1

5.2 Task Priority

2 In this example we compute arrays in a matrix through a *compute_array* routine. Each task has a
3 priority value equal to the value of the loop variable *i* at the moment of its creation. A higher
4 priority on a task means that a task is a candidate to run sooner.

5 The creation of tasks occurs in ascending order (according to the iteration space of the loop) but a
6 hint, by means of the **priority** clause, is provided to reverse the execution order.

─────────────── C / C++ ───────────────

7 *Example task_priority.1.c* (**omp_4.5**)

```
S-1    void compute_array (float *node, int M);
S-2
S-3    void compute_matrix (float *array, int N, int M)
S-4    {
S-5       int i;
S-6       #pragma omp parallel private(i)
S-7       #pragma omp single
S-8       {
S-9          for (i=0;i<N; i++) {
S-10             #pragma omp task priority(i)
S-11             compute_array (&array[i*M], M);
S-12          }
S-13       }
S-14    }
```

─────────────── C / C++ ───────────────
─────────────── Fortran ───────────────

8 *Example task_priority.1.f90* (**omp_4.5**)

```
S-1    subroutine compute_matrix(matrix, M, N)
S-2       implicit none
S-3       integer :: M, N
S-4       real :: matrix(M, N)
S-5       integer :: i
S-6       interface
S-7          subroutine compute_array(node, M)
S-8          implicit none
S-9          integer :: M
S-10         real :: node(M)
S-11         end subroutine
S-12      end interface
S-13      !$omp parallel private(i)
S-14      !$omp single
S-15      do i=1,N
S-16         !$omp task priority(i)
```

```
S-17              call compute_array(matrix(:, i), M)
S-18            !$omp end task
S-19          enddo
S-20        !$omp end single
S-21        !$omp end parallel
S-22    end subroutine compute_matrix
```

Fortran

5.3 Task Dependences

5.3.1 Flow Dependence

This example shows a simple flow dependence using a **depend** clause on the **task** construct.

———————————————— C / C++ ————————————————

Example task_dep.1.c (**omp_4.0**)

```
S-1    #include <stdio.h>
S-2    int main() {
S-3       int x = 1;
S-4       #pragma omp parallel
S-5       #pragma omp single
S-6       {
S-7          #pragma omp task shared(x) depend(out: x)
S-8             x = 2;
S-9          #pragma omp task shared(x) depend(in: x)
S-10            printf("x = %d\n", x);
S-11      }
S-12      return 0;
S-13   }
```

———————————————— C / C++ ————————————————
———————————————— Fortran ————————————————

Example task_dep.1.f90 (**omp_4.0**)

```
S-1    program example
S-2       integer :: x
S-3       x = 1
S-4       !$omp parallel
S-5       !$omp single
S-6          !$omp task shared(x) depend(out: x)
S-7             x = 2
S-8          !$omp end task
S-9          !$omp task shared(x) depend(in: x)
S-10            print*, "x = ", x
S-11         !$omp end task
S-12      !$omp end single
S-13      !$omp end parallel
S-14   end program
```

———————————————— Fortran ————————————————

The program will always print "x = 2", because the **depend** clauses enforce the ordering of the tasks. If the **depend** clauses had been omitted, then the tasks could execute in any order and the program and the program would have a race condition.

5.3.2 Anti-dependence

2 This example shows an anti-dependence using the **depend** clause on the **task** construct.

──────────────────────── C / C++ ────────────────────────

3 *Example task_dep.2.c* (**omp_4.0**)

```
S-1    #include <stdio.h>
S-2    int main()
S-3    {
S-4        int x = 1;
S-5        #pragma omp parallel
S-6        #pragma omp single
S-7        {
S-8            #pragma omp task shared(x) depend(in: x)
S-9                printf("x = %d\n", x);
S-10           #pragma omp task shared(x) depend(out: x)
S-11               x = 2;
S-12       }
S-13       return 0;
S-14   }
```

──────────────────────── C / C++ ────────────────────────
──────────────────────── Fortran ────────────────────────

4 *Example task_dep.2.f90* (**omp_4.0**)

```
S-1    program example
S-2        integer :: x
S-3        x = 1
S-4        !$omp parallel
S-5        !$omp single
S-6            !$omp task shared(x) depend(in: x)
S-7                print*, "x = ", x
S-8            !$omp end task
S-9            !$omp task shared(x) depend(out: x)
S-10               x = 2
S-11           !$omp end task
S-12       !$omp end single
S-13       !$omp end parallel
S-14   end program
```

──────────────────────── Fortran ────────────────────────

5
6
7
The program will always print "x = 1", because the **depend** clauses enforce the ordering of the tasks. If the **depend** clauses had been omitted, then the tasks could execute in any order and the program would have a race condition.

5.3.3 Output Dependence

This example shows an output dependence using the **depend** clause on the **task** construct.

――――――――――――――――――― C / C++ ―――――――――――――――――――

Example task_dep.3.c (**omp_4.0**)

```
S-1    #include <stdio.h>
S-2    int main() {
S-3       int x;
S-4       #pragma omp parallel
S-5       #pragma omp single
S-6       {
S-7          #pragma omp task shared(x) depend(out: x)
S-8             x = 1;
S-9          #pragma omp task shared(x) depend(out: x)
S-10            x = 2;
S-11         #pragma omp taskwait
S-12         printf("x = %d\n", x);
S-13      }
S-14      return 0;
S-15   }
```

――――――――――――――――――― C / C++ ―――――――――――――――――――
――――――――――――――――――― Fortran ―――――――――――――――――――

Example task_dep.3.f90 (**omp_4.0**)

```
S-1    program example
S-2       integer :: x
S-3       !$omp parallel
S-4       !$omp single
S-5          !$omp task shared(x) depend(out: x)
S-6             x = 1
S-7          !$omp end task
S-8          !$omp task shared(x) depend(out: x)
S-9             x = 2
S-10         !$omp end task
S-11         !$omp taskwait
S-12         print*, "x = ", x
S-13      !$omp end single
S-14      !$omp end parallel
S-15   end program
```

――――――――――――――――――― Fortran ―――――――――――――――――――

The program will always print "x = 2", because the **depend** clauses enforce the ordering of the tasks. If the **depend** clauses had been omitted, then the tasks could execute in any order and the program would have a race condition.

5.3.4 Concurrent Execution with Dependences

In this example we show potentially concurrent execution of tasks using multiple flow dependences expressed using the **depend** clause on the **task** construct.

— C / C++ —

Example task_dep.4.c (**omp_4.0**)

```
S-1     #include <stdio.h>
S-2     int main() {
S-3        int x = 1;
S-4        #pragma omp parallel
S-5        #pragma omp single
S-6        {
S-7           #pragma omp task shared(x) depend(out: x)
S-8              x = 2;
S-9           #pragma omp task shared(x) depend(in: x)
S-10             printf("x + 1 = %d. ", x+1);
S-11          #pragma omp task shared(x) depend(in: x)
S-12             printf("x + 2 = %d\n", x+2);
S-13       }
S-14       return 0;
S-15    }
```

— C / C++ —

— Fortran —

Example task_dep.4.f90 (**omp_4.0**)

```
S-1
S-2     program example
S-3        integer :: x
S-4
S-5        x = 1
S-6
S-7        !$omp parallel
S-8        !$omp single
S-9
S-10          !$omp task shared(x) depend(out: x)
S-11             x = 2
S-12          !$omp end task
S-13
S-14          !$omp task shared(x) depend(in: x)
S-15             print*, "x + 1 = ", x+1, "."
S-16          !$omp end task
S-17
S-18          !$omp task shared(x) depend(in: x)
S-19             print*, "x + 2 = ", x+2, "."
```

```
S-20          !$omp end task
S-21
S-22       !$omp end single
S-23       !$omp end parallel
S-24    end program
```

———————————————————— Fortran ————————————————————

The last two tasks are dependent on the first task. However, there is no dependence between the last
two tasks, which may execute in any order (or concurrently if more than one thread is available).
Thus, the possible outputs are "x + 1 = 3. x + 2 = 4. " and "x + 2 = 4. x + 1 = 3. ". If the **depend**
clauses had been omitted, then all of the tasks could execute in any order and the program would
have a race condition.

5.3.5 Matrix multiplication

This example shows a task-based blocked matrix multiplication. Matrices are of NxN elements, and
the multiplication is implemented using blocks of BSxBS elements.

———————————————————— C / C++ ————————————————————

Example task_dep.5.c (**omp_4.0**)

```
S-1   // Assume BS divides N perfectly
S-2   void matmul_depend(int N, int BS, float A[N][N], float B[N][N], float
S-3   C[N][N] )
S-4   {
S-5      int i, j, k, ii, jj, kk;
S-6      for (i = 0; i < N; i+=BS) {
S-7         for (j = 0; j < N; j+=BS) {
S-8            for (k = 0; k < N; k+=BS) {
S-9   // Note 1: i, j, k, A, B, C are firstprivate by default
S-10  // Note 2: A, B and C are just pointers
S-11  #pragma omp task private(ii, jj, kk) \
S-12              depend ( in: A[i:BS][k:BS], B[k:BS][j:BS] ) \
S-13              depend ( inout: C[i:BS][j:BS] )
S-14              for (ii = i; ii < i+BS; ii++ )
S-15                 for (jj = j; jj < j+BS; jj++ )
S-16                    for (kk = k; kk < k+BS; kk++ )
S-17                       C[ii][jj] = C[ii][jj] + A[ii][kk] * B[kk][jj];
S-18            }
S-19         }
S-20      }
S-21  }
```

———————————————————— C / C++ ————————————————————

1 *Example task_dep.5.f90* (**omp_4.0**)

```fortran
S-1    ! Assume BS divides N perfectly
S-2    subroutine matmul_depend (N, BS, A, B, C)
S-3       implicit none
S-4       integer :: N, BS, BM
S-5       real, dimension(N, N) :: A, B, C
S-6       integer :: i, j, k, ii, jj, kk
S-7       BM = BS - 1
S-8       do i = 1, N, BS
S-9          do j = 1, N, BS
S-10            do k = 1, N, BS
S-11   !$omp task shared(A,B,C) private(ii,jj,kk) &
S-12   !$omp depend ( in: A(i:i+BM, k:k+BM), B(k:k+BM, j:j+BM) ) &
S-13   !$omp depend ( inout: C(i:i+BM, j:j+BM) )
S-14   !   I,J,K are firstprivate by default
S-15               do ii = i, i+BM
S-16                  do jj = j, j+BM
S-17                     do kk = k, k+BM
S-18                        C(jj,ii) = C(jj,ii) + A(kk,ii) * B(jj,kk)
S-19                     end do
S-20                  end do
S-21               end do
S-22   !$omp end task
S-23            end do
S-24         end do
S-25      end do
S-26   end subroutine
```

5.3.6 `taskwait` with Dependences

In this subsection three examples illustrate how the **depend** clause can be applied to a **taskwait** construct to make the generating task wait for specific child tasks to complete. This is an OpenMP 5.0 feature. In the same manner that dependences can order executions among child tasks with **depend** clauses on **task** constructs, the generating task can be scheduled to wait on child tasks at a **taskwait** before it can proceed.

Note: Since the **depend** clause on a **taskwait** construct relaxes the default synchronization behavior (waiting for all children to finish), it is important to realize that child tasks that are not predecessor tasks, as determined by the **depend** clause of the **taskwait** construct, may be running concurrently while the generating task is executing after the taskwait.

In the first example the generating task waits at the **taskwait** construct for the completion of the first child task because a dependence on the first task is produced by *x* with an **in** dependence type within the **depend** clause of the **taskwait** construct. Immediately after the first **taskwait** construct it is safe to access the *x* variable by the generating task, as shown in the print statement. There is no completion restraint on the second child task. Hence, immediately after the first **taskwait** it is unsafe to access the *y* variable since the second child task may still be executing. The second **taskwait** ensures that the second child task has completed; hence it is safe to access the *y* variable in the following print statement.

─────────────────────── C / C++ ───────────────────────

Example task_dep.6.c (**omp_5.0**)

```
#include<stdio.h>

void foo()
{
    int x = 0, y = 2;

    #pragma omp task depend(inout: x) shared(x)
    x++;                                        // 1st child task

    #pragma omp task shared(y)
    y--;                                        // 2nd child task

    #pragma omp taskwait depend(in: x)          // 1st taskwait

    printf("x=%d\n",x);

    // Second task may not be finished.
    // Accessing y here will create a race condition.

    #pragma omp taskwait                        // 2nd taskwait

    printf("y=%d\n",y);
}

int main()
{
    #pragma omp parallel
    #pragma omp single
    foo();

    return 0;
}
```

─────────────────────── C / C++ ───────────────────────

1   *Example task_dep.6.f90* (**omp_5.0**)

```fortran
S-1     subroutine foo()
S-2         implicit none
S-3         integer :: x, y
S-4
S-5         x = 0
S-6         y = 2
S-7
S-8         !$omp task depend(inout: x) shared(x)
S-9             x = x + 1                         !! 1st child task
S-10        !$omp end task
S-11
S-12        !$omp task shared(y)
S-13            y = y - 1                         !! 2nd child task
S-14        !$omp end task
S-15
S-16        !$omp taskwait depend(in: x)         !! 1st taskwait
S-17
S-18        print*, "x=", x
S-19
S-20        !! Second task may not be finished.
S-21        !! Accessing y here will create a race condition.
S-22
S-23        !$omp taskwait                       !! 2nd taskwait
S-24
S-25        print*, "y=", y
S-26
S-27    end subroutine foo
S-28
S-29    program p
S-30        implicit none
S-31        !$omp parallel
S-32        !$omp single
S-33            call foo()
S-34        !$omp end single
S-35        !$omp end parallel
S-36    end program p
```

2   In this example the first two tasks are serialized, because a dependence on the first child is produced
3   by x with the **in** dependence type in the **depend** clause of the second task. However, the
4   generating task at the first **taskwait** waits only on the first child task to complete, because a
5   dependence on only the first child task is produced by x with an **in** dependence type within the
6   **depend** clause of the **taskwait** construct. The second **taskwait** (without a **depend** clause)

is included to guarantee completion of the second task before *y* is accessed. (While unnecessary, the **depend(inout: y)** clause on the 2nd child task is included to illustrate how the child task dependences can be completely annotated in a data-flow model.)

─────────────────────── C / C++ ───────────────────────

Example task_dep.7.c (**omp_5.0**)

```
#include<stdio.h>

void foo()
{
    int x = 0, y = 2;

    #pragma omp task depend(inout: x) shared(x)
    x++;                                           // 1st child task

    #pragma omp task depend(in: x) depend(inout: y) shared(x, y)
    y -= x;                                        // 2nd child task

    #pragma omp taskwait depend(in: x)             // 1st taskwait

    printf("x=%d\n",x);

    // Second task may not be finished.
    // Accessing y here would create a race condition.

    #pragma omp taskwait                           // 2nd taskwait

    printf("y=%d\n",y);

}

int main()
{
    #pragma omp parallel
    #pragma omp single
    foo();

    return 0;
}
```

─────────────────────── C / C++ ───────────────────────

1   *Example task_dep.7.f90* (**omp_5.0**)

```
S-1    subroutine foo()
S-2    implicit none
S-3    integer :: x, y
S-4
S-5        x = 0
S-6        y = 2
S-7
S-8        !$omp task depend(inout: x) shared(x)
S-9            x = x + 1                          !! 1st child task
S-10       !$omp end task
S-11
S-12       !$omp task depend(in: x) depend(inout: y) shared(x, y)
S-13           y = y - x                          !! 2nd child task
S-14       !$omp end task
S-15
S-16       !$omp taskwait depend(in: x)           !! 1st taskwait
S-17
S-18       print*, "x=", x
S-19
S-20       !! Second task may not be finished.
S-21       !! Accessing y here would create a race condition.
S-22
S-23       !$omp taskwait                         !! 2nd taskwait
S-24
S-25       print*, "y=", y
S-26
S-27   end subroutine foo
S-28
S-29   program p
S-30   implicit none
S-31       !$omp parallel
S-32       !$omp single
S-33           call foo()
S-34       !$omp end single
S-35       !$omp end parallel
S-36   end program p
```

2   This example is similar to the previous one, except the generating task is directed to also wait for
3   completion of the second task.

4   The **depend** clause of the **taskwait** construct now includes an **in** dependence type for *y*.
5   Hence the generating task must now wait on completion of any child task having *y* with an **out**
6   (here **inout**) dependence type in its **depend** clause. So, the **depend** clause of the **taskwait**

construct now constrains the second task to complete at the **taskwait**, too. (This change makes the second **taskwait** of the previous example unnecessary– it has been removed in this example.)

Note: While a taskwait construct ensures that all child tasks have completed; a depend clause on a taskwait construct only waits for specific child tasks (prescribed by the dependence type and list items in the **taskwait**'s **depend** clause). This and the previous example illustrate the need to carefully determine the dependence type of variables in the **taskwait depend** clause when selecting child tasks that the generating task must wait on, so that its execution after the taskwait does not produce race conditions on variables accessed by non-completed child tasks.

———————————————————— C / C++ ————————————————————

Example task_dep.8.c (**omp_5.0**)

```
#include<stdio.h>

void foo()
{
    int x = 0, y = 2;

    #pragma omp task depend(inout: x) shared(x)
    x++;                                          // 1st child task

    #pragma omp task depend(in: x) depend(inout: y) shared(x, y)
    y -= x;                                       // 2st child task

    #pragma omp taskwait depend(in: x,y)

    printf("x=%d\n",x);
    printf("y=%d\n",y);

}

int main()
{
    #pragma omp parallel
    #pragma omp single
    foo();

    return 0;
}
```

———————————————————— C / C++ ————————————————————

1   *Example task_dep.8.f90* (**omp_5.0**)

```fortran
S-1     subroutine foo()
S-2     implicit nonE
S-3     integer :: x, y
S-4
S-5         x = 0
S-6         y = 2
S-7
S-8         !$omp task depend(inout: x) shared(x)
S-9             x = x + 1                          !! 1st child task
S-10        !$omp end task
S-11
S-12        !$omp task depend(in: x) depend(inout: y) shared(x, y)
S-13            y = y - x                          !! 2nd child task
S-14        !$omp end task
S-15
S-16        !$omp taskwait depend(in: x,y)
S-17
S-18        print*, "x=", x
S-19        print*, "y=", y
S-20
S-21    end subroutine foo
S-22
S-23    program p
S-24    implicit none
S-25        !$omp parallel
S-26        !$omp single
S-27            call foo()
S-28        !$omp end single
S-29        !$omp end parallel
S-30    end program p
```

5.3.7 Mutually Exclusive Execution with Dependences

In this example we show a series of tasks, including mutually exclusive tasks, expressing dependences using the **depend** clause on the **task** construct.

The program will always print 6. Tasks T1, T2 and T3 will be scheduled first, in any order. Task T4 will be scheduled after tasks T1 and T2 are completed. T5 will be scheduled after tasks T1 and T3 are completed. Due to the **mutexinoutset** dependence type on **c**, T4 and T5 may be scheduled in any order with respect to each other, but not at the same time. Tasks T6 will be scheduled after both T4 and T5 are completed.

——————————————— C / C++ ———————————————

Example task_dep.9.c (**omp_5.0**)

```
#include <stdio.h>
int main()
{
   int a, b, c, d;
   #pragma omp parallel
   #pragma omp single
   {
      #pragma omp task depend(out: c)
         c = 1;   /* Task T1 */
      #pragma omp task depend(out: a)
         a = 2;   /* Task T2 */
      #pragma omp task depend(out: b)
         b = 3;   /* Task T3 */
      #pragma omp task depend(in: a) depend(mutexinoutset: c)
         c += a;  /* Task T4 */
      #pragma omp task depend(in: b) depend(mutexinoutset: c)
         c += b;  /* Task T5 */
      #pragma omp task depend(in: c)
         d = c;   /* Task T6 */
   }
   printf("%d\n", d);
   return 0;
}
```

——————————————— C / C++ ———————————————

1   *Example task_dep.9.f90* (**omp_5.0**)

```fortran
S-1    program example
S-2      integer :: a, b, c, d
S-3      !$omp parallel
S-4      !$omp single
S-5        !$omp task depend(out: c)
S-6        c = 1        ! Task T1
S-7        !$omp end task
S-8        !$omp task depend(out: a)
S-9        a = 2        ! Task T2
S-10       !$omp end task
S-11       !$omp task depend(out: b)
S-12       b = 3        ! Task T3
S-13       !$omp end task
S-14       !$omp task depend(in: a) depend(mutexinoutset: c)
S-15       c = c + a  ! Task T4
S-16       !$omp end task
S-17       !$omp task depend(in: b) depend(mutexinoutset: c)
S-18       c = c + b  ! Task T5
S-19       !$omp end task
S-20       !$omp task depend(in: c)
S-21       d = c        ! Task T6
S-22       !$omp end task
S-23     !$omp end single
S-24     !$omp end parallel
S-25     print *, d
S-26   end program
```

2   The following example demonstrates a situation where the **mutexinoutset** dependence type is
3   advantageous. If **shortTaskB** completes before **longTaskA**, the runtime can take advantage of
4   this by scheduling **longTaskBC** before **shortTaskAC**.

5   *Example task_dep.10.c* (**omp_5.0**)

```c
S-1    extern int longTaskA(), shortTaskB();
S-2    extern int shortTaskAC(int,int), longTaskBC(int,int);
S-3    void foo (void)
S-4    {
S-5      int a, b, c;
S-6      c = 0;
S-7      #pragma omp parallel
S-8      #pragma omp single
S-9      {
```

```
S-10        #pragma omp task depend(out: a)
S-11            a = longTaskA();
S-12        #pragma omp task depend(out: b)
S-13            b = shortTaskB();
S-14        #pragma omp task depend(in: a) depend(mutexinoutset: c)
S-15            c = shortTaskAC(a,c);
S-16        #pragma omp task depend(in: b) depend(mutexinoutset: c)
S-17            c = longTaskBC(b,c);
S-18    }
S-19  }
```

——————————————————— C / C++ ———————————————————
——————————————————— Fortran ———————————————————

1   *Example task_dep.10.f90* (omp_5.0)

```
S-1   subroutine foo
S-2      integer :: a,b,c
S-3      c = 0
S-4      !$omp parallel
S-5      !$omp single
S-6        !$omp task depend(out: a)
S-7            a = longTaskA()
S-8        !$omp end task
S-9        !$omp task depend(out: b)
S-10           b = shortTaskB()
S-11       !$omp end task
S-12       !$omp task depend(in: a) depend(mutexinoutset: c)
S-13           c = shortTaskAC(a,c)
S-14       !$omp end task
S-15       !$omp task depend(in: b) depend(mutexinoutset: c)
S-16           c = longTaskBC(b,c)
S-17       !$omp end task
S-18     !$omp end single
S-19     !$omp end parallel
S-20  end subroutine foo
```

——————————————————— Fortran ———————————————————

5.3.8 Multidependences Using Iterators

The following example uses an iterator to define a dynamic number of dependences.

In the **single** construct of a parallel region a loop generates n tasks and each task has an **out** dependence specified through an element of the *v* array. This is followed by a single task that defines an **in** dependence on each element of the array. This is accomplished by using the **iterator** modifier in the **depend** clause, supporting a dynamic number of dependences (*n* here).

The task for the *print_all_elements* function is not executed until all dependences prescribed (or registered) by the iterator are fulfilled; that is, after all the tasks generated by the loop have completed.

Note, one cannot simply use an array section in the **depend** clause of the second task construct because this would violate the **depend** clause restriction:

"List items used in **depend** clauses of the same task or sibling tasks must indicate identical storage locations or disjoint storage locations".

In this case each of the loop tasks use a single disjoint (different storage) element in their **depend** clause; however, the array-section storage area prescribed in the commented directive is neither identical nor disjoint to the storage prescribed by the elements of the loop tasks. The iterator overcomes this restriction by effectively creating n disjoint storage areas.

───────────────────────── C / C++ ─────────────────────────

Example task_dep.11.c (**omp_5.0**)

```
#include<stdio.h>

void set_an_element(int *p, int val) {
    *p = val;
}

void print_all_elements(int *v, int n) {
    int i;
    for (i = 0; i < n; ++i) {
        printf("%d, ", v[i]);
    }
    printf("\n");
}

void parallel_computation(int n) {
    int v[n];
    #pragma omp parallel
    #pragma omp single
    {
        int i;
        for (i = 0; i < n; ++i)
            #pragma omp task depend(out: v[i])
```

```
S-23                    set_an_element(&v[i], i);
S-24
S-25                #pragma omp task depend(iterator(it = 0:n), in: v[it])
S-26            // The following violates array-section restriction:
S-27            // #pragma omp task depend(in: v[0:n])
S-28                print_all_elements(v, n);
S-29            }
S-30        }
S-31
```

―――――――――――――――――――――――――――― C / C++ ――――――――――――――――――――――――――
―――――――――――――――――――――――――――― Fortran ―――――――――――――――――――――――――

Example task_dep.11.f90 (**omp_5.0**)

```
S-1     subroutine set_an_element(e, val)
S-2         implicit none
S-3         integer :: e, val
S-4
S-5         e = val
S-6
S-7     end subroutine
S-8
S-9     subroutine print_all_elements(v, n)
S-10        implicit none
S-11        integer :: n, v(n)
S-12
S-13        print *, v
S-14
S-15    end subroutine
S-16
S-17    subroutine parallel_computation(n)
S-18        implicit none
S-19        integer :: n
S-20        integer :: i, v(n)
S-21
S-22        !$omp parallel
S-23        !$omp single
S-24            do i=1, n
S-25                !$omp task depend(out: v(i))
S-26                    call set_an_element(v(i), i)
S-27                !$omp end task
S-28            enddo
S-29
S-30            !$omp task depend(iterator(it = 1:n), in: v(it))
S-31            !!$omp task depend(in: v(1:n)) Violates Array section restriction.
S-32                call print_all_elements(v, n)
S-33            !$omp end task
```

S-34
S-35   `!$omp end single`
S-36   `!$omp end parallel`
S-37   `end subroutine`

——————————————— Fortran ———————————————

5.3.9 Dependence for Undeferred Tasks

In the following example, we show that even if a task is undeferred as specified by an **if** clause that evaluates to *false*, task dependences are still honored.

The **depend** clauses of the first and second explicit tasks specify that the first task is completed before the second task.

The second explicit task has an **if** clause that evaluates to *false*. This means that the execution of the generating task (the implicit task of the **single** region) must be suspended until the second explicit task is completed. But, because of the dependence, the first explicit task must complete first, then the second explicit task can execute and complete, and only then the generating task can resume to the print statement. Thus, the program will always print "x = 2".

——————————————— C / C++ ———————————————

Example task_dep.12.c (**omp_4.0**)

```
#include <stdio.h>
int main (int argc, char *argv[])
{
  int x = 0;
  #pragma omp parallel
  #pragma omp single
  {
    /* first explicit task */
    #pragma omp task shared(x) depend(out: x)
      x = 1;

    /* second explicit task */
    #pragma omp task shared(x) depend(inout: x) if(0)
      x = 2;

    /* statement executed by parent implicit task
       prints: x = 2 */
    printf("x = %d\n", x);
  }
  return 0;
}
```

——————————————— C / C++ ———————————————

1   *Example task_dep.12.f90* (`omp_4.0`)

```fortran
S-1   program example
S-2      integer :: x
S-3      x = 0
S-4      !$omp parallel
S-5      !$omp single
S-6        !... first explicit task
S-7        !$omp task shared(x) depend(out: x)
S-8           x = 1
S-9        !$omp end task
S-10
S-11       !... second explicit task
S-12       !$omp task shared(x) depend(inout: x) if(.false.)
S-13          x = 2
S-14       !$omp end task
S-15
S-16       !... statement executed by parent implicit task
S-17       ! prints: x = 2
S-18        print*, "x = ", x
S-19     !$omp end single
S-20     !$omp end parallel
S-21   end program
```

2   In OpenMP 5.1 the **omp_all_memory** *reserved locator* was introduced to specify storage of all
3   objects in memory. In the following example, it is used in Task 4 as a convenient way to specify that
4   the locator (list item) denotes the storage of all objects (locations) in memory, and will therefore
5   match the *a* and *d* locators of Task 2, Task 3 and Task 6. The dependences guarantee the ordered
6   execution of Tasks 2 and 3 before 4, and Task 4 before Task 6. Since there are no dependences
7   imposed on Task 1 and Task 5, they can be scheduled to execute at any time, with no ordering.

8   *Example task_dep.13.c* (`omp_5.1`)

```c
S-1   #include <stdio.h>
S-2
S-3   int main(){
S-4      int a=1, d=1;
S-5
S-6      #pragma omp parallel masked num_threads(5)
S-7      {
S-8         #pragma omp task                                    // Task 1
S-9         { printf("T1\n"); }
S-10
```

```
S-11            #pragma omp task depend(out: a)                  // Task 2
S-12            { a++;
S-13              printf("T2 a=%i\n", a); }
S-14
S-15            #pragma omp task depend(out: d)                  // Task 3
S-16            { d++;
S-17              printf("T3 d=%i\n", d); }
S-18
S-19            #pragma omp task depend(inout: omp_all_memory) // Task 4
S-20            { a++; d++;
S-21              printf("T4 a=%i d=%i\n",    a,d);}
S-22
S-23            #pragma omp task                                 // Task 5
S-24            { printf("T5\n"); }
S-25
S-26            #pragma omp task depend(in: a,d)                 // Task 6
S-27            { a++; d++;
S-28              printf("T6 a=%i d=%i\n", a,d); }
S-29        }
S-30    }
S-31
S-32    /* OUTPUT: ordered {T2,T3 any order}, {T4}, {T6}
S-33        T2 a=2
S-34        T3 d=2
S-35        T4 a=3 d=3
S-36        T6 a=4 d=4
S-37
S-38      OUTPUT: unordered (can appear interspersed in ordered output)
S-39        T1
S-40        T5
S-41    */
```

———————————————————— C / C++ ————————————————————
———————————————————— Fortran ————————————————————

1   *Example task_dep.13.f90* (`omp_5.1`)

```
S-1     program main
S-2       integer :: a=1, d=1
S-3
S-4       !$omp parallel masked  num_threads(5)
S-5
S-6         !$omp task                                  !! Task 1
S-7            write(*,'("T1")')
S-8         !$omp end task
S-9
S-10        !$omp task depend(out: a)                   !! Task 2
S-11           a=a+1
```

```
S-12          write(*,'("T2 a=",i1)') a
S-13      !$omp end task
S-14
S-15      !$omp task depend(out: d)                    !! Task 3
S-16          d=d+1
S-17          write(*,'("T3 d=",i1)') d
S-18      !$omp end task
S-19
S-20
S-21      !$omp task depend(inout: omp_all_memory)     !! Task 4
S-22          a=a+1; d=d+1
S-23          write(*,'("T4 a=",i1," d=",i1)') a, d
S-24      !$omp end task
S-25
S-26      !$omp task                                   !! Task 5
S-27          write(*,'("T5")')
S-28      !$omp end task
S-29
S-30      !$omp task depend(in: a,d)                   !! Task 6
S-31          a=a+1; d=d+1
S-32          write(*,'("T6 a=",i1," d=",i1)') a, d
S-33      !$omp end task
S-34
S-35    !$omp end parallel masked
S-36
S-37  end program
S-38
S-39  ! OUTPUT: ordered  {T2,T3 any order}, {T4}, {T6}
S-40  ! T2 a=2
S-41  ! T3 d=2
S-42  ! T4 a=3 d=3
S-43  ! T6 a=4 d=4
S-44  ! OUTPUT: unordered (can appear interspersed in ordered output)
S-45  ! T1
S-46  ! T5
```

5.4 Task Detachment

The **detach** clause on a **task** construct provides a mechanism for an asynchronous routine to be called within a task block, and for the routine's callback to signal completion to the OpenMP runtime, through an event fulfillment, triggered by a call to the **omp_fulfill_event** routine. When a **detach** clause is used on a task construct, completion of the *detachable* task occurs when the task's structured block is completed AND an *allow-completion* event is fulfilled by a call to the **omp_fulfill_event** routine with the *event-handle* argument.

The first example illustrates the basic components used in a detachable task. The second example is a program that executes asynchronous IO, and illustrates methods that are also inherent in asynchronous messaging within MPI and asynchronous commands in streams within GPU codes. Interfaces to asynchronous operations found in IO, MPI and GPU parallel computing platforms and their programming models are not standardized.

The first example creates a detachable task that executes the asynchronous *async_work* routine, passing the *omp_fulfill_event* function and the (firstprivate) event handle to the function. Here, the **omp_fulfill_event** function is the "callback" function to be executed at the end of the *async_work* function's asynchronous operations, with the associated data, *event*.

──────────────────────── C / C++ ────────────────────────

Example task_detach.1.c (**omp_5.0**)

```
#include <omp.h>

void async_work(void (*)(void*), void*);
void work();

int main() {
  int async=1;
  #pragma omp parallel
  #pragma omp masked
  {

    omp_event_handle_t event;
    #pragma omp task detach(event)
    {
      if(async) {
        async_work( (void (*)(void*)) omp_fulfill_event, (void*) event );
      } else {
        work();
        omp_fulfill_event(event);
      }
    }
                    // Other work
```

```
S-23        #pragma omp taskwait
S-24      }
S-25      return 0;
S-26    }
```

———————————————————— C / C++ ————————————————————
———————————————————— Fortran ————————————————————

Example task_detach.1.f90 (omp_5.0)

```
S-1   program main
S-2     use omp_lib
S-3     implicit none
S-4
S-5     external :: async_work, work
S-6
S-7     logical :: async=.true.
S-8     integer(omp_event_handle_kind) :: event
S-9
S-10    !$omp parallel
S-11    !$omp masked
S-12
S-13      !$omp task detach(event)
S-14
S-15        if(async) then
S-16          call async_work(omp_fulfill_event, event)
S-17        else
S-18          call work()
S-19          call omp_fulfill_event(event)
S-20        endif
S-21
S-22      !$omp end task
S-23                      !! Other work
S-24
S-25      !$omp taskwait
S-26
S-27    !$omp end masked
S-28    !$omp end parallel
S-29
S-30  end program
```

———————————————————— Fortran ————————————————————

In the following example, text data is written asynchronously to the file *async_data*, using POSIX asynchronous IO (aio). An aio "control block", *cb*, is set up to send a signal when IO is complete, and the *sigaction* function registers the signal action, a callback to *callback_aioSigHandler*.

The first task (TASK1) starts the asynchronous IO and runs as a detachable task. The second and third tasks (TASK2 and TASK3) perform synchronous IO to stdout with print statements. The difference between the two types of tasks is that the thread for TASK1 is freed for other execution within the parallel region, while the threads for TASK2 and TASK3 wait on the (synchronous) IO to complete, and cannot perform other work while the operating system is performing the synchronous IO. The **if** clause ensures that the detachable task is launched and the call to the *aio_write* function returns before TASK2 and TASK3 are generated (while the async IO occurs in the "background" and eventually executes the callback function). The barrier at the end of the parallel region ensures that the detachable task has completed.

C / C++

Example task_detach.2.c (**omp_5.0**)

```
// use -lrt on loader line
#include   <stdio.h>
#include <unistd.h>
#include   <fcntl.h>
#include     <aio.h>
#include   <errno.h>
#include <signal.h>

#include     <omp.h>

#define IO_SIGNAL SIGUSR1          // Signal used to notify I/O completion

                                   // Handler for I/O completion signal
static void callback_aioSigHandler(int sig, siginfo_t *si,
                                   void *ucontext) {
   if (si->si_code == SI_ASYNCIO){
      printf( "OUT: I/O completion signal received.\n");
      omp_fulfill_event( (omp_event_handle_t)(si->si_value.sival_ptr) );
   }
}

void work(int i){ printf("OUT: Executing work(%d)\n", i);}

int main() {
   // Write "Written Asynchronously." to file data, using POSIX
   // asynchronous IO. Error checking not included for clarity
   // and simplicity.

   char      data[] = "Written Asynchronously.";
```

```
S-31
S-32        struct      aiocb cb;
S-33        struct sigaction sa;
S-34
S-35        omp_event_handle_t event;
S-36
S-37        int fd = open(  "async_data", O_CREAT|O_RDWR|O_TRUNC,0664);
S-38
S-39        // Setup async io (aio) control block (cb)
S-40        cb.aio_nbytes  = sizeof(data)-1;
S-41        cb.aio_fildes  = fd;
S-42        cb.aio_buf     = data;
S-43        cb.aio_reqprio = 0;
S-44        cb.aio_offset  = 0;
S-45        cb.aio_sigevent.sigev_notify = SIGEV_SIGNAL;
S-46        cb.aio_sigevent.sigev_signo  = IO_SIGNAL;
S-47
S-48        // Setup Signal Handler  Callback
S-49        sigemptyset(&sa.sa_mask);
S-50        sa.sa_flags = SA_RESTART | SA_SIGINFO;
S-51        sa.sa_sigaction = callback_aioSigHandler;    //callback
S-52        sigaction(IO_SIGNAL, &sa, NULL);
S-53
S-54        #pragma omp parallel num_threads(2)
S-55        #pragma omp masked
S-56        {
S-57
S-58           #pragma omp task detach(event) if(0)                  // TASK1
S-59           {
S-60              cb.aio_sigevent.sigev_value.sival_ptr = (void *) event;
S-61              aio_write(&cb);
S-62           }
S-63
S-64           #pragma omp task                                      // TASK2
S-65              work(1);
S-66           #pragma omp task                                      // TASK3
S-67              work(2);
S-68
S-69        } // Parallel region barrier ensures completion of detachable task.
S-70
S-71        // Making sure the aio operation completed.
S-72        // With OpenMP detachable task the condition will always be false:
S-73        while(aio_error(&cb) == EINPROGRESS) {
S-74        printf(" INPROGRESS\n");} //Safeguard
S-75
S-76        close(fd);
S-77        return 0;
```

```
S-78    }
S-79    /* Any Order:
S-80    OUT: I/O completion signal received.
S-81    OUT: Executing work(1)
S-82    OUT: Executing work(2)
S-83    */
```

——————————————— C / C++ ———————————————

5.5 `taskgroup` Construct

In this example, tasks are grouped and synchronized using the **taskgroup** construct.

Initially, one task (the task executing the **start_background_work()** call) is created in the **parallel** region, and later a parallel tree traversal is started (the task executing the root of the recursive **compute_tree()** calls). While synchronizing tasks at the end of each tree traversal, using the **taskgroup** construct ensures that the formerly started background task does not participate in the synchronization and is left free to execute in parallel. This is opposed to the behavior of the **taskwait** construct, which would include the background tasks in the synchronization.

—————————————————— C / C++ ——————————————————

Example taskgroup.1.c (**omp_4.0**)

```
S-1    extern void start_background_work(void);
S-2    extern void check_step(void);
S-3    extern void print_results(void);
S-4    struct tree_node
S-5    {
S-6       struct tree_node *left;
S-7       struct tree_node *right;
S-8    };
S-9    typedef struct tree_node* tree_type;
S-10   extern void init_tree(tree_type);
S-11   #define max_steps 100
S-12   void compute_something(tree_type tree)
S-13   {
S-14      // some computation
S-15   }
S-16   void compute_tree(tree_type tree)
S-17   {
S-18      if (tree->left)
S-19      {
S-20        #pragma omp task
S-21          compute_tree(tree->left);
S-22      }
S-23      if (tree->right)
S-24      {
S-25        #pragma omp task
S-26          compute_tree(tree->right);
S-27      }
S-28      #pragma omp task
S-29      compute_something(tree);
S-30   }
S-31   int main()
S-32   {
```

```
S-33      int i;
S-34      tree_type tree;
S-35      init_tree(tree);
S-36      #pragma omp parallel
S-37      #pragma omp single
S-38      {
S-39        #pragma omp task
S-40          start_background_work();
S-41        for (i = 0; i < max_steps; i++)
S-42        {
S-43            #pragma omp taskgroup
S-44            {
S-45                #pragma omp task
S-46                  compute_tree(tree);
S-47            } // wait on tree traversal in this step
S-48            check_step();
S-49        }
S-50      } // only now is background work required to be complete
S-51      print_results();
S-52      return 0;
S-53    }
```

—————————————————— C / C++ ——————————————————
—————————————————— Fortran ——————————————————

1   *Example taskgroup.1.f90* (`omp_4.0`)

```
S-1     module tree_type_mod
S-2       integer, parameter :: max_steps=100
S-3       type tree_type
S-4         type(tree_type), pointer :: left, right
S-5       end type
S-6       contains
S-7         subroutine compute_something(tree)
S-8           type(tree_type), pointer :: tree
S-9   ! some computation
S-10        end subroutine
S-11        recursive subroutine compute_tree(tree)
S-12          type(tree_type), pointer :: tree
S-13          if (associated(tree%left)) then
S-14  !$omp task
S-15            call compute_tree(tree%left)
S-16  !$omp end task
S-17          endif
S-18          if (associated(tree%right)) then
S-19  !$omp task
S-20            call compute_tree(tree%right)
S-21  !$omp end task
```

```
S-22          endif
S-23    !$omp task
S-24          call compute_something(tree)
S-25    !$omp end task
S-26        end subroutine
S-27    end module
S-28    program main
S-29      use tree_type_mod
S-30      type(tree_type), pointer :: tree
S-31      call init_tree(tree);
S-32    !$omp parallel
S-33    !$omp single
S-34    !$omp task
S-35      call start_background_work()
S-36    !$omp end task
S-37      do i=1, max_steps
S-38    !$omp taskgroup
S-39    !$omp task
S-40          call compute_tree(tree)
S-41    !$omp end task
S-42    !$omp end taskgroup ! wait on tree traversal in this step
S-43          call check_step()
S-44        enddo
S-45    !$omp end single
S-46    !$omp end parallel    ! only now is background work required to be complete
S-47      call print_results()
S-48    end program
```

Fortran

5.6 `taskyield` Construct

The following example illustrates the use of the **taskyield** directive. The tasks in the example compute something useful and then do some computation that must be done in a critical region. By using **taskyield** when a task cannot get access to the **critical** region the implementation can suspend the current task and schedule some other task that can do something useful.

——————————————————————— C / C++ ———————————————————————

Example taskyield.1.c (**omp_3.1**)

```
S-1    #include <omp.h>
S-2
S-3    void something_useful ( void );
S-4    void something_critical ( void );
S-5    void foo ( omp_lock_t * lock, int n )
S-6    {
S-7        int i;
S-8
S-9        for ( i = 0; i < n; i++ )
S-10          #pragma omp task
S-11          {
S-12              something_useful();
S-13              while ( !omp_test_lock(lock) ) {
S-14                  #pragma omp taskyield
S-15              }
S-16              something_critical();
S-17              omp_unset_lock(lock);
S-18          }
S-19   }
```

——————————————————————— C / C++ ———————————————————————
——————————————————————— Fortran ———————————————————————

Example taskyield.1.f90 (**omp_3.1**)

```
S-1    subroutine foo ( lock, n )
S-2        use omp_lib
S-3        integer (kind=omp_lock_kind) :: lock
S-4        integer n
S-5        integer i
S-6
S-7        do i = 1, n
S-8          !$omp task
S-9            call something_useful()
S-10           do while ( .not. omp_test_lock(lock) )
S-11             !$omp taskyield
S-12           end do
S-13           call something_critical()
```

```
S-14            call omp_unset_lock(lock)
S-15        !$omp end task
S-16      end do
S-17
S-18  end subroutine
```

————————————— Fortran —————————————

5.7 `taskloop` Construct

The following example illustrates how to execute a long running task concurrently with tasks created with a **taskloop** directive for a loop having unbalanced amounts of work for its iterations.

The **grainsize** clause specifies that each task is to execute at least 500 iterations of the loop.

The **nogroup** clause removes the implicit taskgroup of the **taskloop** construct; the explicit **taskgroup** construct in the example ensures that the function is not exited before the long-running task and the loops have finished execution.

──────────────────── C / C++ ────────────────────

Example taskloop.1.c (**omp_4.5**)

```
S-1    void long_running_task(void);
S-2    void loop_body(int i, int j);
S-3
S-4    void parallel_work(void) {
S-5       int i, j;
S-6    #pragma omp taskgroup
S-7       {
S-8    #pragma omp task
S-9          long_running_task(); // can execute concurrently
S-10
S-11   #pragma omp taskloop private(j) grainsize(500) nogroup
S-12         for (i = 0; i < 10000; i++) { // can execute concurrently
S-13            for (j = 0; j < i; j++) {
S-14               loop_body(i, j);
S-15            }
S-16         }
S-17      }
S-18   }
```

──────────────────── C / C++ ────────────────────

1 *Example taskloop.1.f90* (omp_4.5)

```
S-1    subroutine parallel_work
S-2      integer i
S-3      integer j
S-4    !$omp taskgroup
S-5
S-6    !$omp task
S-7      call long_running_task()
S-8    !$omp end task
S-9
S-10   !$omp taskloop private(j) grainsize(500) nogroup
S-11     do i=1,10000
S-12       do j=1,i
S-13         call loop_body(i, j)
S-14       end do
S-15     end do
S-16   !$omp end taskloop
S-17
S-18   !$omp end taskgroup
S-19   end subroutine
```

2
3 Because a **taskloop** construct encloses a loop, it is often incorrectly perceived as a worksharing construct (when it is directly nested in a **parallel** region).

4
5 While a worksharing construct distributes the loop iterations across all threads in a team, the entire loop of a **taskloop** construct is executed by every thread of the team.

6
7 In the example below the first taskloop occurs closely nested within a **parallel** region and the entire loop is executed by each of the T threads; hence the reduction sum is executed $T*N$ times.

8
9
10 The loop of the second taskloop is within a **single** region and is executed by a single thread so that only N reduction sums occur. (The other N-1 threads of the **parallel** region will participate in executing the tasks. This is the common use case for the **taskloop** construct.)

11 In the example, the code thus prints **x1 = 16384** ($T*N$) and **x2 = 1024** (N).

1   *Example taskloop.2.c* (omp_4.5)

```
S-1     #include <stdio.h>
S-2
S-3     #define T 16
S-4     #define N 1024
S-5
S-6     void parallel_work() {
S-7         int x1 = 0, x2 = 0;
S-8
S-9         #pragma omp parallel shared(x1,x2) num_threads(T)
S-10        {
S-11            #pragma omp taskloop
S-12            for (int i = 0; i < N; ++i) {
S-13                #pragma omp atomic
S-14                x1++;              // executed T*N times
S-15            }
S-16
S-17            #pragma omp single
S-18            #pragma omp taskloop
S-19            for (int i = 0; i < N; ++i) {
S-20                #pragma omp atomic
S-21                x2++;              // executed N times
S-22            }
S-23        }
S-24
S-25        printf("x1 = %d, x2 = %d\n", x1, x2);
S-26    }
```

2   *Example taskloop.2.f90* (omp_4.5)

```
S-1     subroutine parallel_work
S-2         implicit none
S-3         integer :: x1, x2
S-4         integer :: i
S-5         integer, parameter :: T = 16
S-6         integer, parameter :: N = 1024
S-7
S-8         x1 = 0
S-9         x2 = 0
S-10        !$omp parallel shared(x1,x2) num_threads(T)
S-11        !$omp taskloop
S-12        do i = 1,N
S-13            !$omp atomic
```

```
S-14              x1 = x1 + 1        ! executed T*N times
S-15          !$omp end atomic
S-16      end do
S-17      !$omp end taskloop
S-18
S-19      !$omp single
S-20      !$omp taskloop
S-21      do i = 1,N
S-22          !$omp atomic
S-23          x2 = x2 + 1        ! executed N times
S-24          !$omp end atomic
S-25      end do
S-26      !$omp end taskloop
S-27      !$omp end single
S-28      !$omp end parallel
S-29
S-30      write (*,'(A,I0,A,I0)') 'x1 = ', x1, ', x2 = ',x2
S-31  end subroutine
```

—————————————— Fortran ——————————————

5.8 Combined `parallel masked` and `taskloop` Constructs

Just as the **for** and **do** constructs were combined with the **parallel** construct for convenience, so too, the combined **parallel masked taskloop** and **parallel masked taskloop simd** constructs have been created for convenience when using the **taskloop** construct.

In the following example the first **taskloop** construct is enclosed by the usual **parallel** and **masked** constructs to form a team of threads, and a single task generator (primary thread) for the **taskloop** construct.

The same OpenMP operations for the first taskloop are accomplished by the second taskloop with the **parallel masked taskloop** combined construct. The third taskloop uses the combined **parallel masked taskloop simd** construct to accomplish the same behavior as closely nested **parallel masked**, and **taskloop simd** constructs.

As with any combined construct the clauses of the components may be used with appropriate restrictions. The combination of the **parallel masked** construct with the **taskloop** or **taskloop simd** construct produces no additional restrictions.

───────────────────────── C / C++ ─────────────────────────

Example parallel_masked_taskloop.1.c (**omp_5.1**)

```
#include <stdio.h>
#define N 100

int main()
{
   int i, a[N],b[N],c[N];

   for(int i=0; i<N; i++){ b[i]=i; c[i]=i; }  //init

   #pragma omp parallel
   #pragma omp masked
   #pragma omp taskloop                     // taskloop 1
   for(i=0;i<N;i++){ a[i] = b[i] + c[i]; }

   #pragma omp parallel masked taskloop     // taskloop 2
   for(i=0;i<N;i++){ b[i] = a[i] + c[i]; }

   #pragma omp parallel masked taskloop simd // taskloop 3
   for(i=0;i<N;i++){ c[i] = a[i] + b[i]; }

   printf(" %d %d\n",c[0],c[N-1]);   // 0 and 495
}
```

───────────────────────── C / C++ ─────────────────────────

1   *Example parallel_masked_taskloop.1.f90* (**omp_5.1**)

```fortran
S-1    program main
S-2
S-3       integer, parameter :: N=100
S-4       integer :: i, a(N),b(N),c(N)
S-5
S-6       do i=1,N                              !! initialize
S-7          b(i) = i
S-8          c(i) = i
S-9       enddo
S-10
S-11      !$omp parallel
S-12      !$omp masked
S-13      !$omp taskloop                        !! taskloop 1
S-14      do i=1,N
S-15         a(i) = b(i) + c(i)
S-16      enddo
S-17      !$omp end taskloop
S-18      !$omp end masked
S-19      !$omp end parallel
S-20
S-21      !$omp parallel masked taskloop        !! taskloop 2
S-22      do i=1,N
S-23         b(i) = a(i) + c(i)
S-24      enddo
S-25      !$omp end parallel masked taskloop
S-26
S-27      !$omp parallel masked taskloop simd !! taskloop 3
S-28      do i=1,N
S-29         c(i) = a(i) + b(i)
S-30      enddo
S-31      !$omp end parallel masked taskloop simd
S-32
S-33      print*,c(1),c(N)   !! 5 and 500
S-34
S-35   end program
```

This page intentionally left blank

6 Devices

The **target** construct consists of a **target** directive and an execution region. The **target** region is executed on the default device or the device specified in the **device** clause.

In OpenMP version 4.0, by default, all variables within the lexical scope of the construct are copied *to* and *from* the device, unless the device is the host, or the data exists on the device from a previously executed data-type construct that has created space on the device and possibly copied host data to the device storage.

The constructs that explicitly create storage, transfer data, and free storage on the device are categorized as structured and unstructured. The **target data** construct is structured. It creates a data region around **target** constructs, and is convenient for providing persistent data throughout multiple **target** regions. The **target enter data** and **target exit data** constructs are unstructured, because they can occur anywhere and do not support a "structure" (a region) for enclosing **target** constructs, as does the **target data** construct.

The **map** clause is used on **target** constructs and the data-type constructs to map host data. It specifies the device storage and data movement **to** and **from** the device, and controls on the storage duration.

There is an important change in the OpenMP 4.5 specification that alters the data model for scalar variables and C/C++ pointer variables. The default behavior for scalar variables and C/C++ pointer variables in a 4.5 compliant code is **firstprivate**. Example codes that have been updated to reflect this new behavior are annotated with a description that describes changes required for correct execution. Often it is a simple matter of mapping the variable as **tofrom** to obtain the intended 4.0 behavior.

In OpenMP version 4.5 the mechanism for target execution is specified as occurring through a *target task*. When the **target** construct is encountered a new *target task* is generated. The *target task* completes after the **target** region has executed and all data transfers have finished.

This new specification does not affect the execution of pre-4.5 code; it is a necessary element for asynchronous execution of the **target** region when using the new **nowait** clause introduced in OpenMP 4.5.

6.1 `target` Construct

6.1.1 `target` Construct on `parallel` Construct

This following example shows how the **target** construct offloads a code region to a target device. The variables *p*, *v1*, *v2*, and *N* are implicitly mapped to the target device.

─────────────────── C / C++ ───────────────────

Example target.1.c (**omp_4.0**)

```
S-1    extern void init(float*, float*, int);
S-2    extern void output(float*, int);
S-3    void vec_mult(int N)
S-4    {
S-5       int i;
S-6       float p[N], v1[N], v2[N];
S-7       init(v1, v2, N);
S-8       #pragma omp target
S-9       #pragma omp parallel for private(i)
S-10      for (i=0; i<N; i++)
S-11        p[i] = v1[i] * v2[i];
S-12      output(p, N);
S-13   }
```

─────────────────── C / C++ ───────────────────

─────────────────── Fortran ───────────────────

Example target.1.f90 (**omp_4.0**)

```
S-1    subroutine vec_mult(N)
S-2       integer ::  i,N
S-3       real     ::  p(N), v1(N), v2(N)
S-4       call init(v1, v2, N)
S-5       !$omp target
S-6       !$omp parallel do
S-7       do i=1,N
S-8          p(i) = v1(i) * v2(i)
S-9       end do
S-10      !$omp end target
S-11      call output(p, N)
S-12   end subroutine
```

─────────────────── Fortran ───────────────────

6.1.2 `target` Construct with `map` Clause

This following example shows how the **target** construct offloads a code region to a target device. The variables *p*, *v1* and *v2* are explicitly mapped to the target device using the **map** clause. The variable *N* is implicitly mapped to the target device.

———————————————————————— C / C++ ————————————————————————

Example target.2.c (**omp_4.0**)

```
S-1    extern void init(float*, float*, int);
S-2    extern void output(float*, int);
S-3    void vec_mult(int N)
S-4    {
S-5       int i;
S-6       float p[N], v1[N], v2[N];
S-7       init(v1, v2, N);
S-8       #pragma omp target map(v1, v2, p)
S-9       #pragma omp parallel for
S-10      for (i=0; i<N; i++)
S-11        p[i] = v1[i] * v2[i];
S-12      output(p, N);
S-13   }
```

———————————————————————— C / C++ ————————————————————————

———————————————————————— Fortran ————————————————————————

Example target.2.f90 (**omp_4.0**)

```
S-1    subroutine vec_mult(N)
S-2       integer ::   i,N
S-3       real     ::  p(N), v1(N), v2(N)
S-4       call init(v1, v2, N)
S-5       !$omp target map(v1,v2,p)
S-6       !$omp parallel do
S-7       do i=1,N
S-8          p(i) = v1(i) * v2(i)
S-9       end do
S-10      !$omp end target
S-11      call output(p, N)
S-12   end subroutine
```

———————————————————————— Fortran ————————————————————————

6.1.3 `map` Clause with `to`/`from` map-types

The following example shows how the `target` construct offloads a code region to a target device. In the `map` clause, the `to` and `from` map-types define the mapping between the original (host) data and the target (device) data. The `to` map-type specifies that the data will only be read on the device, and the `from` map-type specifies that the data will only be written to on the device. By specifying a guaranteed access on the device, data transfers can be reduced for the `target` region.

The `to` map-type indicates that at the start of the `target` region the variables *v1* and *v2* are initialized with the values of the corresponding variables on the host device, and at the end of the `target` region the variables *v1* and *v2* are not assigned to their corresponding variables on the host device.

The `from` map-type indicates that at the start of the `target` region the variable *p* is not initialized with the value of the corresponding variable on the host device, and at the end of the `target` region the variable *p* is assigned to the corresponding variable on the host device.

─────────────────────────── C / C++ ───────────────────────────

Example target.3.c (`omp_4.0`)

```
extern void init(float*, float*, int);
extern void output(float*, int);
void vec_mult(int N)
{
   int i;
   float p[N], v1[N], v2[N];
   init(v1, v2, N);
   #pragma omp target map(to: v1, v2) map(from: p)
   #pragma omp parallel for
   for (i=0; i<N; i++)
     p[i] = v1[i] * v2[i];
   output(p, N);
}
```

─────────────────────────── C / C++ ───────────────────────────

The `to` and `from` map-types allow programmers to optimize data motion. Since data for the *v* arrays are not returned, and data for the *p* array are not transferred to the device, only one-half of the data is moved, compared to the default behavior of an implicit mapping.

1   *Example target.3.f90* (**omp_4.0**)

```
S-1    subroutine vec_mult(N)
S-2       integer :: i,N
S-3       real    :: p(N), v1(N), v2(N)
S-4       call init(v1, v2, N)
S-5       !$omp target map(to: v1,v2) map(from: p)
S-6       !$omp parallel do
S-7       do i=1,N
S-8          p(i) = v1(i) * v2(i)
S-9       end do
S-10      !$omp end target
S-11      call output(p, N)
S-12   end subroutine
```

2   6.1.4 map **Clause with Array Sections**

3   The following example shows how the **target** construct offloads a code region to a target device.
4   In the **map** clause, map-types are used to optimize the mapping of variables to the target device.
5   Because variables *p*, *v1* and *v2* are pointers, array section notation must be used to map the arrays.
6   The notation **:N** is equivalent to **0:N**.

7   *Example target.4.c* (**omp_4.0**)

```
S-1    extern void init(float*, float*, int);
S-2    extern void output(float*, int);
S-3    void vec_mult(float *p, float *v1, float *v2, int N)
S-4    {
S-5       int i;
S-6       init(v1, v2, N);
S-7       #pragma omp target map(to: v1[0:N], v2[:N]) map(from: p[0:N])
S-8       #pragma omp parallel for
S-9       for (i=0; i<N; i++)
S-10        p[i] = v1[i] * v2[i];
S-11      output(p, N);
S-12   }
```

In C, the length of the pointed-to array must be specified. In Fortran the extent of the array is known and the length need not be specified. A section of the array can be specified with the usual Fortran syntax, as shown in the following example. The value 1 is assumed for the lower bound for array section *v2(:N)*.

───────────────────────────── Fortran ─────────────────────────────

Example target.4.f90 (**omp_4.0**)

```
S-1    module mults
S-2    contains
S-3    subroutine vec_mult(p,v1,v2,N)
S-4       real,pointer,dimension(:) :: p, v1, v2
S-5       integer                   :: N,i
S-6       call init(v1, v2, N)
S-7       !$omp target map(to: v1(1:N), v2(:N)) map(from: p(1:N))
S-8       !$omp parallel do
S-9       do i=1,N
S-10         p(i) = v1(i) * v2(i)
S-11      end do
S-12      !$omp end target
S-13      call output(p, N)
S-14   end subroutine
S-15   end module
```

───────────────────────────── Fortran ─────────────────────────────

A more realistic situation in which an assumed-size array is passed to **vec_mult** requires that the length of the arrays be specified, because the compiler does not know the size of the storage. A section of the array must be specified with the usual Fortran syntax, as shown in the following example. The value 1 is assumed for the lower bound for array section *v2(:N)*.

───────────────────────────── Fortran ─────────────────────────────

Example target.4b.f90 (**omp_4.0**)

```
S-1    module mults
S-2    contains
S-3    subroutine vec_mult(p,v1,v2,N)
S-4       real,dimension(*) :: p, v1, v2
S-5       integer           :: N,i
S-6       call init(v1, v2, N)
S-7       !$omp target map(to: v1(1:N), v2(:N)) map(from: p(1:N))
S-8       !$omp parallel do
S-9       do i=1,N
S-10         p(i) = v1(i) * v2(i)
S-11      end do
S-12      !$omp end target
S-13      call output(p, N)
```

```
S-14    end subroutine
S-15    end module
```

──────────────────── Fortran ────────────────────

6.1.5 `target` Construct with `if` Clause

The following example shows how the **target** construct offloads a code region to a target device.

The **if** clause on the **target** construct indicates that if the variable N is smaller than a given threshold, then the **target** region will be executed by the host device.

The **if** clause on the **parallel** construct indicates that if the variable N is smaller than a second threshold then the **parallel** region is inactive.

──────────────────── C / C++ ────────────────────

Example target.5.c (**omp_4.0**)

```
S-1     #define THRESHOLD1 1000000
S-2     #define THRESHOLD2 1000
S-3
S-4     extern void init(float*, float*, int);
S-5     extern void output(float*, int);
S-6
S-7     void vec_mult(float *p, float *v1, float *v2, int N)
S-8     {
S-9        int i;
S-10
S-11       init(v1, v2, N);
S-12
S-13       #pragma omp target if(N>THRESHOLD1) map(to: v1[0:N], v2[:N])\
S-14           map(from: p[0:N])
S-15       #pragma omp parallel for if(N>THRESHOLD2)
S-16       for (i=0; i<N; i++)
S-17         p[i] = v1[i] * v2[i];
S-18
S-19       output(p, N);
S-20    }
```

──────────────────── C / C++ ────────────────────

1   *Example target.5.f90* (**omp_4.0**)

```
S-1     module params
S-2     integer,parameter :: THRESHOLD1=1000000, THRESHHOLD2=1000
S-3     end module
S-4
S-5     subroutine vec_mult(p, v1, v2, N)
S-6        use params
S-7        real    ::  p(N), v1(N), v2(N)
S-8        integer ::  i
S-9
S-10       call init(v1, v2, N)
S-11
S-12       !$omp target if(N>THRESHHOLD1) map(to: v1, v2 ) map(from: p)
S-13         !$omp parallel do if(N>THRESHOLD2)
S-14         do i=1,N
S-15            p(i) = v1(i) * v2(i)
S-16         end do
S-17       !$omp end target
S-18
S-19       call output(p, N)
S-20    end subroutine
```

2   The following example is a modification of the above *target.5* code to show the combined **target**
3   and parallel loop directives. It uses the *directive-name* modifier in multiple **if** clauses to specify
4   the component directive to which it applies.

5   The **if** clause with the **target** modifier applies to the **target** component of the combined
6   directive, and the **if** clause with the **parallel** modifier applies to the **parallel** component of
7   the combined directive.

8   *Example target.6.c* (**omp_4.5**)

```
S-1     #define THRESHOLD1 1000000
S-2     #define THRESHOLD2 1000
S-3
S-4     extern void init(float*, float*, int);
S-5     extern void output(float*, int);
S-6
S-7     void vec_mult(float *p, float *v1, float *v2, int N)
S-8     {
S-9        int i;
S-10
S-11       init(v1, v2, N);
```

```
S-12
S-13        #pragma omp target parallel for \
S-14             if(target: N>THRESHOLD1) if(parallel: N>THRESHOLD2) \
S-15             map(to: v1[0:N], v2[:N]) map(from: p[0:N])
S-16        for (i=0; i<N; i++)
S-17          p[i] = v1[i] * v2[i];
S-18
S-19        output(p, N);
S-20      }
```

———————————————————— C / C++ ————————————————————
———————————————————— Fortran ————————————————————

1   *Example target.6.f90* (omp_4.5)

```
S-1     module params
S-2     integer,parameter :: THRESHOLD1=1000000, THRESHHOLD2=1000
S-3     end module
S-4
S-5     subroutine vec_mult(p, v1, v2, N)
S-6        use params
S-7        real    :: p(N), v1(N), v2(N)
S-8        integer :: i
S-9
S-10       call init(v1, v2, N)
S-11
S-12       !$omp target parallel do  &
S-13       !$omp&   if(target: N>THRESHHOLD1) if(parallel: N>THRESHOLD2) &
S-14       !$omp&   map(to: v1, v2 ) map(from: p)
S-15         do i=1,N
S-16            p(i) = v1(i) * v2(i)
S-17         end do
S-18       !$omp end target parallel do
S-19
S-20       call output(p, N)
S-21    end subroutine
```

———————————————————— Fortran ————————————————————

6.1.6 Target Reverse Offload

Beginning with OpenMP 5.0, implementations are allowed to offload back to the host (reverse offload).

In the example below the *error_handler* function is executed back on the host, if an erroneous value is detected in the *A* array on the device.

This is accomplished by specifying the *device-modifier* **ancestor** modifier, along with a device number of **1**, to indicate that the execution is to be performed on the immediate parent (*1st ancestor*)– the host.

The **requires** directive (another 5.0 feature) uses the **reverse_offload** clause to guarantee that the reverse offload is implemented.

Note that the **declare target** directive uses the **device_type** clause (another 5.0 feature) to specify that the *error_handler* function is compiled to execute on the *host* only. This ensures that no attempt will be made to create a device version of the function. This feature may be necessary if the function exists in another compile unit.

——————————————— C / C++ ———————————————

Example target_reverse_offload.7.c (**omp_5.2**)

```
#include <stdio.h>
#include <stdlib.h>

#define N 100

#pragma omp requires reverse_offload

void error_handler(int wrong_value, int index)
{
    printf(" Error in offload: A[%d]=%d\n", index,wrong_value);
    printf("          Expecting: A[i ]=i\n");
    exit(1);
// output:   Error in offload: A[99]=-1
//                   Expecting: A[i ]=i

}
#pragma omp declare target device_type(host) enter(error_handler)

int main()
{
    int A[N];

    for (int i=0; i<N; i++) A[i] = i;

```

```
S-26        A[N-1]=-1;
S-27
S-28        #pragma omp target map(A)
S-29        {
S-30           for (int i=0; i<N; i++)
S-31           {
S-32              if (A[i] != i)
S-33              {
S-34                 #pragma omp target device(ancestor: 1) map(always,to: A[i:1])
S-35                    error_handler(A[i], i);
S-36              }
S-37           }
S-38        }
S-39        return 0;
S-40     }
```

—————————————————————— C / C++ ——————————————————————
—————————————————————— Fortran ——————————————————————

Example target_reverse_offload.7.f90 (**omp_5.0**)

```
S-1
S-2     !$omp requires reverse_offload
S-3
S-4     subroutine error_handler(wrong_value, index)
S-5       integer :: wrong_value,index
S-6       !$omp declare target device_type(host)
S-7
S-8       write( *,'("Error in offload: A(",i3,")=",i3)' ) index,wrong_value
S-9       write( *,'("        Expecting: A( i)= i")'     )
S-10      stop
S-11        !!output: Error in offload: A( 99)= -1
S-12        !!                Expecting: A( i)= i
S-13    end subroutine
S-14
S-15    program rev_off
S-16      use omp_lib
S-17      integer, parameter :: N=100
S-18      integer            :: A(N) = (/ (i, i=1,100) /)
S-19
S-20      A(N-1)=-1
S-21
S-22      !$omp target map(A)
S-23        do i=1,N
S-24          if (A(i) /= i)  then
S-25            !$omp target device(ancestor: 1) map(always,to :A(i))
S-26              call error_handler(A(i), i)
S-27            !$omp end target
```

```
S-28              endif
S-29           end do
S-30        !$omp end target
S-31
S-32    end program
```
————————————————————————— Fortran ——————————————————————————

6.2 `defaultmap` Clause

The implicitly-determined, data-mapping and data-sharing attribute rules of variables referenced in a **target** construct can be changed by the **defaultmap** clause introduced in OpenMP 5.0. The implicit behavior is specified as **alloc**, **to**, **from**, **tofrom**, **firstprivate**, **none**, **default** or **present**, and is applied to a variable-category, where **scalar**, **aggregate**, **allocatable**, and **pointer** are the variable categories.

In OpenMP, a "category" has a common data-mapping and data-sharing behavior for variable types within the category. In C/C++, **scalar** refers to base-language scalar variables, except pointers. In Fortran it refers to a scalar variable, as defined by the base language, with intrinsic type, and excludes character type.

Also, **aggregate** refers to arrays and structures (C/C++) and derived types (Fortran). Fortran has the additional category of **allocatable**.

In the example below, the first **target** construct uses **defaultmap** clauses to set data-mapping and possibly data-sharing attributes that reproduce the default implicit mapping (data-mapping and data-sharing attributes). That is, if the **defaultmap** clauses were removed, the results would be identical.

In the second **target** construct all implicit behavior is removed by specifying the **none** implicit behavior in the **defaultmap** clause. Hence, all variables must be explicitly mapped. In the C/C++ code a scalar (s), an array (A) and a structure (S) are explicitly mapped **tofrom**. The Fortran code uses a derived type (D) in lieu of structure.

The third **target** construct shows another usual case for using the **defaultmap** clause. The default mapping for (non-pointer) scalar variables is specified as **tofrom**. Here, the default implicit mapping for s3 is **tofrom** as specified in the **defaultmap** clause, and s1 and s2 are explicitly mapped with the **firstprivate** data-sharing attribute.

In the fourth **target** construct all arrays, structures (C/C++) and derived types (Fortran) are mapped with **firstprivate** data-sharing behavior by a **defaultmap** clause with an **aggregate** variable category. For the H allocated array in the Fortran code, the **allocable** category must be used in a separate **defaultmap** clause to acquire **firsprivate** data-sharing behavior (H has the Fortran allocatable attribute).

——————————————— C / C++ ———————————————

Example target_defaultmap.1.c (**omp_5.0**)

```
#include <stdlib.h>
#include <stdio.h>
#define N 2

int main(){
  typedef struct S_struct { int s; int A[N]; } S_struct_t;


```

```
S-9      int          s;          //scalar int variable (scalar)
S-10     int          A[N];       //aggregate variable  (array)
S-11     S_struct_t   S;          //aggregate variable  (structure)
S-12     int          *ptr;       //scalar, pointer variable (pointer)
S-13
S-14     int          s1, s2, s3;
S-15
S-16  // Initialize everything to zero;
S-17     s=2; s1=s2=s3=0;
S-18     A[0]=0; A[1]=0;
S-19     S.s=0; S.A[0]=0; S.A[1]=0;
S-20
S-21  // Target Region 1
S-22                     // Uses defaultmap to set scalars, aggregates &
S-23                     // pointers to normal defaults.
S-24     #pragma omp target \
S-25            defaultmap(firstprivate: scalar)   //could also be default \
S-26            defaultmap(tofrom:       aggregate)//could also be default \
S-27            defaultmap(default:      pointer)  //must be default        \
S-28            map(ptr2m[:N])
S-29     {
S-30         s      = 3;              //SCALAR firstprivate, value not returned
S-31
S-32         A[0]   = 3;  A[1] = 3; //AGGREGATE array, default map tofrom
S-33
S-34                                 //AGGREGATE structure, default tofrom
S-35         S.s    = 2;
S-36         S.A[0] = 2;  S.A[1] = 2;
S-37
S-38         ptr = &A[0];            //POINTER is private
S-39         ptr[0] = 2;   ptr[1] = 2;
S-40
S-41     }
S-42     if(s==2 && A[0]==2 && S.s==2 && S.A[0]==2)
S-43       printf(" PASSED 1 of 4\n");
S-44
S-45
S-46  // Target Region 2
S-47                     // no implicit mapping allowed.
S-48     #pragma omp target defaultmap(none) map(tofrom: s, A, S)
S-49     {
S-50         s      +=5;             // All variables must be explicitly mapped
S-51         A[0]   +=5; A[1]+=5;
S-52         S.s    +=5;
S-53         S.A[0]+=5; S.A[1]+=5;
S-54     }
S-55     if(s==7 && A[0]==7 && S.s==7 && S.A[0]==7)
```

```
S-56            printf(" PASSED 2 of 4\n");
S-57
S-58
S-59    // Target Region 3
S-60            // defaultmap & explicit map with variables in same category
S-61        s1=s2=s3=1;
S-62        #pragma  omp defaultmap(tofrom: scalar) map(firstprivate: s1,s2)
S-63        {
S-64            s1 += 5;            // firstprivate (s1 value not returned to host)
S-65            s2 += 5;            // firstprivate (s2 value not returned to host)
S-66            s3 += s1 + s2;   // mapped as tofrom
S-67        }
S-68        if(s1==1 && s2==1 && s3==13 ) printf(" PASSED 3 of 4\n");
S-69
S-70
S-71    // Target Region 4
S-72        A[0]=0;  A[1]=0;
S-73        S.A[0]=0;  S.A[1]=0;
S-74
S-75        // arrays and structure are firstprivate, and scalars are from
S-76        #pragma omp target defaultmap(firstprivate: aggregate) \
S-77                        map(from: s1, s2)
S-78        {
S-79
S-80            A[0]+=1;  S.A[0]+=1;  //Aggregate changes not returned to host
S-81            A[1]+=1;  S.A[1]+=1;  //Aggregate changes not returned to host
S-82            s1 = A[0]+S.A[0]; //s1 value returned to host
S-83            s2 = A[1]+S.A[1]; //s1 value returned to host
S-84        }
S-85        if( A[0]==0 && S.A[0]==0 && s1==2 ) printf(" PASSED 4 of 4\n");
S-86
S-87    }
```

———————————————— C / C++ ————————————————
———————————————— Fortran ————————————————

1   *Example target_defaultmap.1.f90* (**omp_5.0**)

```
S-1     program defaultmap
S-2       integer, parameter :: N=2
S-3
S-4       type DDT_sA
S-5         integer  :: s
S-6         integer  :: A(N)
S-7       end type
S-8
S-9       integer                   :: s,s1,s2,s3 !! SCALAR: variable (integer)
S-10
```

```
S-11        integer,target     :: A(N)          !! AGGREGATE: Array
S-12        type(DDT_sA)       :: D             !! AGGREGATE: Derived Data Type (D)
S-13
S-14        integer,allocatable :: H(:)         !! ALLOCATABLE: Heap allocated array
S-15
S-16        integer,pointer    :: ptrA(:)      !! POINTER: points to Array
S-17
S-18     ! Assign vaues to scalar, Array, Allocatable, and Pointers
S-19
S-20       s=2;
S-21       s1=0;    s2=0;       s3=0
S-22       D%s=0;   D%A(1)=0; D%A(2)=0
S-23       A(1)=0;  A(2)=0
S-24
S-25       allocate( H(2) )
S-26       H(1)=0;  H(2)=0
S-27
S-28    !! Target Region 1
S-29                        !! Using defaultmap to set scalars, aggregates &
S-30                        !! pointers and allocatables to normal defaults.
S-31       !$omp target                                       &
S-32       !$omp&         defaultmap( firstprivate: scalar)      &
S-33       !$omp&         defaultmap( tofrom:      aggregate)    &
S-34       !$omp&         defaultmap( tofrom:      allocatable) &
S-35       !$omp&         defaultmap( default:     pointer)
S-36
S-37          s = 3                         !! SCALAR firstprivate, val not returned
S-38
S-39          A(1) = 3                      !! AGGREGATE array, default map tofrom
S-40          A(2) = 3
S-41
S-42          D%s = 2                       !! AGGR. Derived Type, default map tofrom
S-43          D%A(1) = 2;  D%A(2) = 2
S-44
S-45          H(1) = 2;     H(2) = 2        !! ALLOCATABLE, default map tofrom
S-46
S-47          ptrA=>A                       !! POINTER is private
S-48          ptrA(1) = 2; ptrA(2) = 2
S-49
S-50       !$omp end target
S-51
S-52       if(s==2 .and. A(1)==2 .and. D%s==2 .and. D%A(1)==2 .and. H(1) == 2) &
S-53          print*," PASSED 1 of 4"
S-54
S-55    !! Target Region 2
S-56                     !! no implicit mapping allowed
S-57       !$omp target defaultmap(none) map(tofrom: s, A, D)
```

```
S-58
S-59          s=s+5                     !! All variables must be explicitly mapped
S-60          A(1)=A(1)+5;          A(2)=A(2)+5
S-61          D%s=D%s+5
S-62          D%A(1)=D%A(1)+5; D%A(2)=D%A(2)+5
S-63
S-64      !$omp end target
S-65      if(s==7 .and. A(1)==7 .and. D%s==7 .and. D%A(1)==7) &
S-66          print*," PASSED 2 of 4"
S-67
S-68  !! Target Region 3
S-69              !!defaultmap & explicit map with variables in same category
S-70      s1=1; s2=1; s3=1
S-71      !$omp defaultmap(tofrom: scalar) map(firstprivate: s1,s2)
S-72
S-73          s1 = s1+5;          !! firstprivate (s1 value not returned to host)
S-74          s2 = s2+5;          !! firstprivate (s2 value not returned to host)
S-75          s3 = s3 +s1 + s2;   !! mapped as tofrom
S-76
S-77      !$omp end target
S-78      if(s1==1 .and. s2==1 .and. s3==13) print*," PASSED 3 of 4"
S-79
S-80  !! Target Region 4
S-81      A(1)=0;   A(2)=0
S-82      D%A(1)=0; D%A(2)=0
S-83      H(1)=0;   H(2)=0
S-84              !! non-allocated arrays & derived types are in AGGREGATE cat.
S-85              !! Allocatable Arrays are in ALLOCATABLE category
S-86              !! Scalars are explicitly mapped from
S-87      !$omp target defaultmap(firstprivate: aggregate ) &
S-88      !$omp&       defaultmap(firstprivate: allocatable) &
S-89      !$omp&       map(from: s1, s2)
S-90
S-91          A(1)=A(1)+1; D%A(1)=D%A(1)+1; H(1)=H(1)+1 !! changes to A, D%A, H
S-92          A(2)=A(2)+1; D%A(2)=D%A(2)+1; H(2)=H(2)+1 !!   not returned to host
S-93          s1 = A(1)+D%A(1)+H(1)                     !! s1 returned to host
S-94          s2 = A(2)+D%A(2)+H(1)                     !! s2 returned to host
S-95
S-96      !$omp end target
S-97      if(A(1)==0 .and. D%A(1)==0 .and. H(1)==0 .and. s1==3) &
S-98          print*," PASSED 4 of 4"
S-99
S-100     deallocate(H)
S-101
S-102 end program
```

Fortran

6.3 Pointer Mapping

Pointers that contain host addresses require that those addresses are translated to device addresses for them to be useful in the context of a device data environment. Broadly speaking, there are two scenarios where this is important.

The first scenario is where the pointer is mapped to the device data environment, such that references to the pointer inside a **target** region are to the corresponding pointer. Pointer attachment ensures that the corresponding pointer will contain a device address when all of the following conditions are true:

- the pointer is mapped by directive A to a device;
- a list item that uses the pointer as its base pointer (call it the *pointee*) is mapped, to the same device, by directive B, which may be the same as A;
- the effect of directive B is to create either the corresponding pointer or pointee in the device data environment of the device.

Given the above conditions, pointer attachment is initiated as a result of directive B and subsequent references to the pointee list item in a target region that use the pointer will access the corresponding pointee. The corresponding pointer remains in this *attached* state until it is removed from the device data environment.

The second scenario, which is only applicable for C/C++, is where the pointer is implicitly privatized inside a **target** construct when it appears as the base pointer to a list item on the construct and does not appear explicitly as a list item in a **map** clause, **is_device_ptr** clause, or data-sharing attribute clause. This scenario can be further split into two cases: the list item is a zero-length array section (e.g., *p[:0]*) or it is not.

If it is a zero-length array section, this will trigger a runtime check on entry to the **target** region for a previously mapped list item where the value of the pointer falls within the range of its base address and ending address. If such a match is found the private pointer is initialized to the device address corresponding to the value of the original pointer, and otherwise it is initialized to NULL (or retains its original value if the **unified_address** requirement is specified for that compilation unit).

If the list item (again, call it the *pointee*) is not a zero-length array section, the private pointer will be initialized such that references in the **target** region to the pointee list item that use the pointer will access the corresponding pointee.

The following example shows the basics of mapping pointers with and without associated storage on the host.

Storage for pointers *ptr1* and *ptr2* is created on the host. To map storage that is associated with a pointer on the host, the data can be explicitly mapped as an array section so that the compiler knows the amount of data to be assigned in the device (to the "corresponding" data storage area). On the **target** construct array sections are mapped; however, the pointer *ptr1* is mapped, while *ptr2* is not. Since *ptr2* is not explicitly mapped, it is firstprivate. This creates a subtle difference in the way these pointers can be used.

As a firstprivate pointer, *ptr2* can be manipulated on the device; however, as an explicitly mapped pointer, *ptr1* becomes an *attached* pointer and cannot be manipulated. In both cases the host pointer is not updated with the device pointer address—as one would expect for distributed memory. The storage data on the host is updated from the corresponding device data at the end of the **target** region.

As a comparison, note that the *aray* array is automatically mapped, since the compiler knows the extent of the array.

The pointer *ptr3* is used inside the **target** construct, but it does not appear in a data-mapping or data-sharing clause. Nor is there a **defaultmap** clause on the construct to indicate what its implicit data-mapping or data-sharing attribute should be. For such a case, *ptr3* will be implicitly privatized within the construct and there will be a runtime check to see if the host memory to which it is pointing has corresponding memory in the device data environment. If this runtime check passes, the private *ptr3* would be initialized to point to the corresponding memory. But in this case the check does not pass and so it is initialized to null. Since *ptr3* is private, the value to which it is assigned in the **target** region is not returned into the original *ptr3* on the host.

――――――――――――――――― C / C++ ―――――――――――――――――

Example target_ptr_map.1.c (**omp_5.0**)

```
#include <stdio.h>
#include <stdlib.h>
#define N 100

int main()
{
  int *ptr1;
  int *ptr2;
  int *ptr3;
  int aray[N];

  ptr1 = (int *)malloc(sizeof(int)*N);
  ptr2 = (int *)malloc(sizeof(int)*N);

  #pragma omp target map(ptr1, ptr1[:N]) map(ptr2[:N] )
  {
    for (int i=0; i<N; i++)
    {
        ptr1[i] = i;
        ptr2[i] = i;
        aray[i] = i;
    }

```

```
S-24        //*(++ptr1) = 9;   //NOT ALLOWED since ptr1 is an attached pointer
S-25          *(++ptr2) = 9;   //     allowed since ptr2 is firstprivate
S-26
S-27        ptr3=(int *)malloc(sizeof(int)*N); // ptr3 is firstprivate
S-28                                           // ptr3 value not returned
S-29        for (int i=0; i<N; i++) ptr3[i] = 5;
S-30
S-31        for (int i=0; i<N; i++) ptr1[i] += ptr3[i];
S-32
S-33        free(ptr3);      // explicitly free allocated storage on device
S-34      }
S-35
S-36      printf(" %d %d\n",ptr1[1],ptr2[1]);
S-37      //         6  9
S-38
S-39      free(ptr1);
S-40      free(ptr2);
S-41      return 0;
S-42    }
```

———————————————————— C / C++ ————————————————————

In the following example the global pointer *p* appears in a declare target directive. Hence, the pointer *p* will persist on the device throughout executions in all **target** regions.

The pointer is also used in an array section of a **map** clause on a **target** construct. When the pointer of storage associated with a declare target directive is mapped, as for the array section *p[:N]* in the **target** construct, the array section on the device is *attached* to the device pointer *p* on entry to the construct, and the value of the device pointer *p* becomes undefined on exit. (Of course, storage allocation for the array section on the device will occur before the pointer on the device is *attached*.)

———————————————————— C / C++ ————————————————————

Example target_ptr_map.2.c (**omp_5.1**)

```
S-1     #include <stdio.h>
S-2     #include <stdlib.h>
S-3     #define N 100
S-4
S-5     #pragma omp begin declare target
S-6       int *p;
S-7       extern void use_arg_p(int *p, int n);
S-8       extern void use_global_p(    int n);
S-9     #pragma omp end declare target
S-10
S-11    int main()
S-12    {
S-13      int i;
```

```
S-14        p = (int *)malloc(sizeof(int)*N);
S-15
S-16        #pragma omp target map(p[:N])   // device p attached to array section
S-17        {
S-18          for (i=0; i<N; i++) p[i] = i;
S-19          use_arg_p(p, N);
S-20          use_global_p(N);
S-21        }                               // value of host p is preserved
S-22
S-23        printf(" %3.3d %3.3d\n", p[1], p[N-1]);
S-24               // 003   297   <- output
S-25
S-26        free(p);
S-27        return 0;
S-28      }
S-29
S-30      // A #pragma omp begin declare target is optional here
S-31      // because of prototype spec
S-32      void use_arg_p(int *q, int n)
S-33      {
S-34        int i;
S-35        for (i=0; i<n; i++)
S-36          q[i] *= 2;
S-37      }
S-38
S-39      void use_global_p(int n)
S-40      {
S-41        int i;
S-42        for (i=0; i<n; i++)
S-43          p[i] += i;     // valid since p is in declare target and called from
S-44                         // inside target region where p was attached to
S-45                         // valid memory
S-46      }
S-47      // A #pragma omp end declare target is optional here
S-48      // because of prototype spec
```

───────────────── C / C++ ─────────────────

The following two examples illustrate subtle differences in pointer attachment to device address because of the order of data mapping.

In example *target_ptr_map.3a* the global pointer *p1* points to array *x* and *p2* points to array *y* on the host. The array section *x[:N]* is mapped by the **target enter data** directive while array *y* is mapped on the **target** construct. Since the **begin declare target** directive is applied to the declaration of *p1*, *p1* is a treated like a mapped variable on the **target** construct and references to *p1* inside the construct will be to the corresponding *p1* that exists on the device. However, the corresponding *p1* will be undefined since there is no pointer attachment for it. Pointer attachment for *p1* would require that (1) *p1* (or an lvalue expression that refers to the same storage as *p1*) appears as a base pointer to a list item in a **map** clause, and (2) the construct that has the **map** clause causes the list item to transition from *not mapped* to *mapped*. The conditions are clearly not satisfied for this example.

The problem for *p2* in this example is also subtle. It will be privatized inside the **target** construct, with a runtime check for whether the memory to which it is pointing has corresponding memory that is accessible on the device. If this check is successful, then the *p2* inside the construct would be appropriately initialized to point to that corresponding memory. Unfortunately, despite there being an implicit map of the array *y* (to which *p2* is pointing) on the construct, the order of this map relative to the initialization of *p2* is unspecified. Therefore, the initial value of *p2* will also be undefined.

Thus, referencing values via either *p1* or *p2* inside the **target** region would be invalid.

———————————————————————— C / C++ ————————————————————————

Example target_ptr_map.3a.c (**omp_5.1**)

```
#define N 100

int x[N], y[N];
#pragma omp begin declare target
int *p1;
#pragma omp end declare target
int *p2;

int foo()
{
  p1 = &x[0];
  p2 = &y[0];

  // Explicitly map array section x[:N]
  #pragma omp target enter data map(x[:N])

  #pragma omp target  // as if .. map(p1) map(p1[:0]) map(p2[:0]) map(y)
  {
    // Accessing the mapped arrays x,y is OK here.
    x[0] = 1;
    y[1] = 2;

    // Pointer attachment for p1 does not occur here
    //   because p1[:0] does not allocate a new array section and
    //   array x is present on the target construct as it was mapped
    //   before by the target enter data directive.
    p1[0] = 3;      // accessing p1 is undefined

    // The initial value of p2 in the target region is undefined
    //   because map(y) may occur after map(p2[:0]).
```

```
S-31        p2[1] = 4;        // accessing p2 is undefined
S-32    }
S-33
S-34    return 0;
S-35 }
```

──────────────── C / C++ ────────────────

In example *target_ptr_map.3b* the mapping orders for arrays *x* and *y* were rearranged to allow
proper pointer attachments. On the **target** construct, the **map(x)** clause triggers pointer
attachment for *p1* to the device address of *x*. Pointer *p2* is assigned the device address of the
previously mapped array *y*. Referencing values via either *p1* or *p2* inside the **target** region is
now valid.

──────────────── C / C++ ────────────────

Example target_ptr_map.3b.c (**omp_5.1**)

```
S-1   #define N 100
S-2
S-3   int x[N], y[N];
S-4   #pragma omp begin declare target
S-5   int *p1;
S-6   #pragma omp end declare target
S-7   int *p2;
S-8
S-9   int foo()
S-10  {
S-11    p1 = &x[0];
S-12    p2 = &y[0];
S-13
S-14    // Explicitly map array section y[:N]
S-15    #pragma omp target enter data map(y[:N])
S-16
S-17    #pragma omp target map(x[:N]) map(p1[:N]) map(p2[:0])
S-18    {
S-19      // Accessing the mapped arrays x,y is OK here.
S-20      x[0] = 1;
S-21      y[1] = 2;
S-22
S-23      // Pointer attachment for p1 occurs here when array x is mapped
S-24      //   on the target construct (as p1 = &x[0] on the device)
S-25      p1[0] = 3;        // accessing p1 is OK
S-26
S-27      // p2 in the target region is initialized to &y[0]
S-28      p2[1] = 4;        // accessing p2 is OK
S-29    }
S-30
```

```
S-31      return 0;
S-32    }
```

──────────────────────────── C / C++ ────────────────────────────

In the following example, storage allocated on the host is not mapped in a **target** region if it is
determined that the host memory is accessible from the device. On platforms that support host
memory access from a target device, it may be more efficient to omit map clauses and avoid the
potential memory allocation and data transfers that may result from the map. The
omp_target_is_accessible API routine is used to determine if the host storage of size
buf_size is accessible on the device, and a metadirective is used to select the directive variant (a
target with/without a **map** clause).

The **omp_target_is_accessible** routine will return true if the storage indicated by the first
and second arguments is accessible on the target device. In this case, the host pointer *ptr* may be
directly dereferenced in the subsequent **target** region to access this storage, rather than mapping
an array section based off the pointer. By explicitly specifying the host pointer in a
firstprivate clause on the construct, its original value will be used directly in the **target**
region. In OpenMP 5.1, removing the **firstprivate** clause will result in an implicit presence
check of the storage to which *ptr* points, and since this storage is not mapped by the program, *ptr*
will be NULL-initialized in the **target** region. In the next version of the OpenMP Specification,
a false presence check without the **firstprivate** clause will cause the pointer to retain its
original value.

──────────────────────────── C / C++ ────────────────────────────

Example target_ptr_map.4.c (**omp_5.2**)

```
S-1    #include <stdio.h>
S-2    #include <stdlib.h>
S-3    #include <omp.h>
S-4
S-5    void do_work(int *ptr, const int size);
S-6
S-7    int main()
S-8    {
S-9       const int n = 1000;
S-10      const int buf_size = sizeof(int) * n;
S-11      const int dev = omp_get_default_device();
S-12
S-13      int *ptr = (int *) malloc(buf_size); // possibly compiled on
S-14                                           // Unified Shared Memory system
S-15      const int accessible = omp_target_is_accessible(ptr, buf_size, dev);
S-16
S-17      #pragma omp metadirective \
S-18         when(user={condition(accessible)}): target firstprivate(ptr) ) \
S-19         otherwise(                          target map(ptr[:n])        )
S-20      {
```

```
S-21            do_work(ptr, n);
S-22        }
S-23
S-24        free(ptr);
S-25        return 0;
S-26    }
```

──────────────────── C / C++ ────────────────────

Similar to the previous example, the **omp_target_is_accessible** routine is used to discover
if a deep copy is required for the platform. Here, the *deep_copy* map, defined in the
declare mapper directive, is used if the host storage referenced by *s.ptr* (or *s%ptr* in Fortran) is
not accessible from the device.

──────────────────── C / C++ ────────────────────

Example target_ptr_map.5.c (**omp_5.2**)

```
S-1     #include <stdio.h>
S-2     #include <stdlib.h>
S-3     #include <omp.h>
S-4
S-5     typedef struct {
S-6         int *ptr;
S-7         int buf_size;
S-8     } T;
S-9
S-10    #pragma omp declare mapper(deep_copy: T s) map(s, s.ptr[:s.buf_size])
S-11
S-12    void do_work(int *ptr, const int size);
S-13
S-14    int main()
S-15    {
S-16        const int n = 1000;
S-17        const int buf_size = sizeof(int) * n;
S-18        T s = { 0, buf_size };
S-19        const int dev = omp_get_default_device();
S-20        s.ptr = (int *)malloc(buf_size);
S-21        const int accessible =
S-22            omp_target_is_accessible(s.ptr, s.buf_size, dev);
S-23
S-24        #pragma omp metadirective \
S-25            when(user={condition(accessible)}: target) \
S-26            otherwise(target map(mapper(deep_copy),tofrom:s) )
S-27        {
S-28            do_work(s.ptr, n);
S-29        }
S-30
S-31        free(s.ptr);
```

```
S-32        return 0;
S-33    }
```

———————————————————— C / C++ ————————————————————
———————————————————— Fortran ————————————————————

1   *Example target_ptr_map.5.f90* (**omp_5.2**)

```
S-1     program main
S-2         use omp_lib
S-3
S-4         use, intrinsic :: iso_c_binding, only : c_loc, c_size_t, c_sizeof, c_int
S-5         implicit none
S-6         external :: do_work
S-7
S-8         type T
S-9             integer,pointer :: ptr(:)
S-10            integer         :: buf_size
S-11        end type
S-12
S-13        !$omp declare mapper(deep_copy: T :: s) map(s, s%ptr(:s%buf_size))
S-14
S-15        integer,parameter :: n = 1000
S-16        integer(c_int)    :: dev, accessible
S-17        integer(c_size_t) :: buf_size
S-18
S-19        type(T) s
S-20
S-21        allocate(s%ptr(n))
S-22
S-23        buf_size = c_sizeof(s%ptr(1))*n
S-24        dev = omp_get_default_device()
S-25
S-26        accessible = omp_target_is_accessible(c_loc(s%ptr(1)), buf_size, dev)
S-27
S-28        !$omp  begin metadirective                              &
S-29        !$omp&        when(user={condition(accessible)}: target) &
S-30        !$omp&        otherwise( target map(mapper(deep_copy),tofrom:s) )
S-31
S-32            call do_work(s, n)
S-33
S-34        !$omp  end    metadirective
S-35
S-36        deallocate(s%ptr)
S-37
S-38    end program
```

———————————————————— Fortran ————————————————————

6.4 Structure Mapping

In the example below, only structure elements *S.a*, *S.b* and *S.p* of the *S* structure appear in **map** clauses of a **target** construct. Only these components have corresponding variables and storage on the device. Hence, the large arrays, *S.buffera* and *S.bufferb*, and the *S.x* component have no storage on the device and cannot be accessed.

Also, since the pointer member *S.p* is used in an array section of a **map** clause, the array storage of the array section on the device, *S.p[:N]*, is *attached* to the pointer member *S.p* on the device. Explicitly mapping the pointer member *S.p* is optional in this case.

Note: The buffer arrays and the *x* variable have been grouped together, so that the components that will reside on the device are all together (without gaps). This allows the runtime to optimize the transfer and the storage footprint on the device.

C / C++

Example target_struct_map.1.c (**omp_5.1**)

```
#include <stdio.h>
#include <stdlib.h>
#define N 100
#define BAZILLION 2000000

struct foo {
  char buffera[BAZILLION];
  char bufferb[BAZILLION];
  float x;
  float a, b;
  float *p;
};

#pragma omp begin declare target
void saxpyfun(struct foo *S)
{
  int i;
  for(i=0; i<N; i++)
    S->p[i] = S->p[i]*S->a + S->b;
}
#pragma omp end declare target

int main()
{
  struct foo S;
  int i;

  S.a = 2.0;
  S.b = 4.0;
```

```
S-30        S.p = (float *)malloc(sizeof(float)*N);
S-31        for(i=0; i<N; i++) S.p[i] = i;
S-32
S-33        #pragma omp target map(alloc:S.p) map(S.p[:N]) map(to:S.a, S.b)
S-34        saxpyfun(&S);
S-35
S-36        printf(" %4.0f %4.0f\n", S.p[0], S.p[N-1]);
S-37               //     4   202   <- output
S-38
S-39        free(S.p);
S-40        return 0;
S-41    }
```

──────────────────────────── C / C++ ────────────────────────────

1   The following example is a slight modification of the above example for a C++ class. In the member
2   function *SAXPY::driver* the array section *p[:N]* is *attached* to the pointer member *p* on the device.

──────────────────────────── C++ ────────────────────────────

3   *Example target_struct_map.2.cpp* (**omp_5.1**)

```
S-1     #include <cstdio>
S-2     #include <cstdlib>
S-3     #define N 100
S-4
S-5     class SAXPY {
S-6       private:
S-7         float a, b, *p;
S-8       public:
S-9         float buffer[N];
S-10
S-11        SAXPY(float arg_a, float arg_b){ a=arg_a; b=arg_b; }
S-12        void driver();
S-13        void saxpyfun(float *p);
S-14    };
S-15
S-16    #pragma omp begin declare target
S-17    void SAXPY::saxpyfun(float *q)
S-18    {
S-19      for(int i=0; i<N; i++)
S-20        buffer[i] = q[i]*a + b;
S-21    }
S-22    #pragma omp end declare target
S-23
S-24    void SAXPY::driver()
S-25    {
S-26      p = (float *) malloc(N*sizeof(float));
S-27      for(int i=0; i<N; i++) p[i]=i;
```

```
S-28
S-29       #pragma omp target map(alloc:p) map(to:p[:N]) map(to:a,b) \
S-30                   map(from:buffer[:N])    // attach(p) to device_malloc()
S-31       {
S-32         saxpyfun(p);
S-33       }
S-34
S-35       free(p);
S-36     }
S-37
S-38     int main()
S-39     {
S-40       SAXPY my_saxpy(2.0,4.0);
S-41
S-42       my_saxpy.driver();
S-43
S-44       printf(" %4.0f %4.0f\n", my_saxpy.buffer[0], my_saxpy.buffer[N-1]);
S-45             //    4    202      <- output
S-46
S-47       return 0;
S-48     }
```

──────────────────────────── C++ ────────────────────────────

The next example shows two ways in which the structure may be *incorrectly* mapped.

In Case 1, the array section *S1.p[:N]* is first mapped in an enclosing **target data** construct, and the **target** construct then implicitly maps the structure *S1*. The initial map of the array section does not map the base pointer *S1.p* – it only maps the elements of the array section. Furthermore, the implicit map is not sufficient to ensure pointer attachment for the structure member *S1.p* (refer to the conditions for pointer attachment described in Section 6.3). Consequentially, the dereference operation *S1.p[i]* in the call to *saxpyfun* will probably fail because *S1.p* contains a host address.

In Case 2, again an array section is mapped on an enclosing **target data** construct. This time, the nested **target** construct explicitly maps *S2.p*, *S2.a*, and *S2.b*. But as in Case 1, this does not satisfy the conditions for pointer attachment since the construct must map a list item for which *S2.p* is a base pointer, and it must do so when the *S2.p* is already present on the device or will be created on the device as a result of the same construct.

──────────────────────────── C / C++ ────────────────────────────

Example target_struct_map.3.c (**omp_5.1**)

```
S-1     #include <stdio.h>
S-2     #include <stdlib.h>
S-3     #define N 100
S-4     #define BAZILLION 2000000
S-5
S-6     struct foo {
```

```
S-7        char buffera[BAZILLION];
S-8        char bufferb[BAZILLION];
S-9        float x;
S-10       float a, b;
S-11       float *p;
S-12     };
S-13
S-14     #pragma omp begin declare target
S-15     void saxpyfun(struct foo *S)
S-16     {
S-17       int i;
S-18       for(i=0; i<N; i++)
S-19         S->p[i] = S->p[i] * S->a + S->b; // S->p[i] invalid
S-20     }
S-21     #pragma omp end declare target
S-22
S-23     int main()
S-24     {
S-25       struct foo S1, S2;
S-26       int i;
S-27
S-28       // Case 1
S-29
S-30       S1.a = 2.0;
S-31       S1.b = 4.0;
S-32       S1.p = (float *)malloc(sizeof(float)*N);
S-33       for(i=0; i<N; i++) S1.p[i] = i;
S-34
S-35       // No pointer attachment for S1.p here
S-36       #pragma omp target data map(S1.p[:N])
S-37       #pragma omp target // implicit map of S1
S-38       saxpyfun(&S1);
S-39
S-40       // Case 2
S-41
S-42       S2.a = 2.0;
S-43       S2.b = 4.0;
S-44       S2.p = (float *)malloc(sizeof(float)*N);
S-45       for(i=0; i<N; i++) S2.p[i] = i;
S-46
S-47       // No pointer attachment for S2.p here either
S-48       #pragma omp target data map(S2.p[:N])
S-49       #pragma omp target map(S2.p, S2.a, S2.b) // implicit map of S2
S-50       saxpyfun(&S2);
S-51
S-52       // These print statement may not execute because the
S-53       // above code is invalid
```

```
S-54        printf(" %4.0f %4.0f\n", S1.p[0], S1.p[N-1]);
S-55        printf(" %4.0f %4.0f\n", S2.p[0], S2.p[N-1]);
S-56
S-57        free(S1.p);
S-58        free(S2.p);
S-59        return 0;
S-60      }
```

—————————————————— C / C++ ——————————————————

1 The following example correctly implements pointer attachment cases that involve implicit
2 structure maps.

3 In Case 1, members *p*, *a*, and *b* of the structure *S1* are explicitly mapped by the **target data**
4 construct, to avoid mapping parts of *S1* that aren't required on the device. The mapped *S1.p* is
5 attached to the array section *S1.p[:N]*, and remains attached while it exists on the device (for the
6 duration of **target data** region). Due to the *S1* reference inside the nested **target** construct,
7 the construct implicitly maps *S1* so that the reference refers to the corresponding storage created by
8 the enclosing **target data** region. Note that only the members *a*, *b*, and *p* may be accessed from
9 this storage.

10 In Case 2, only the storage for the array section *S2.p[:N]* is mapped by the **target data**
11 construct. The nested **target** construct explicitly maps *S2.a* and *S2.b* and explicitly maps an array
12 section for which *S2.p* is a base pointer. This satisfies the conditions for *S2.p* becoming an attached
13 pointer. The array section in this case is zero-length, but the effect would be the same if the length
14 was a positive integer less than or equal to *N*. There is also an implicit map of the containing
15 structure *S2*, again due to the reference to *S2* inside the construct. The effect of this implicit map
16 permits access only to members *a*, *b*, and *p*, as for Case 1.

17 In Case 3, there is no **target data** construct. The **target** construct explicitly maps *S3.a* and
18 *S3.b* and explicitly maps an array section for which *S3.p* is a base pointer. Again, there is an
19 implicit map of the structure referenced in the construct, *S3*. This implicit map also causes *S3.p* to
20 be implicitly mapped, because no other part of *S3* is present prior to the construct being
21 encountered. The result is an attached pointer *S3.p* on the device. As for Cases 1 and 2, this implicit
22 map only ensures that storage for the members *a*, *b*, and *p* are accessible within the corresponding
23 *S3* that is created on the device.

—————————————————— C / C++ ——————————————————

24 *Example target_struct_map.4.c* (**omp_5.1**)

```
S-1    #include <stdio.h>
S-2    #include <stdlib.h>
S-3    #define N 100
S-4    #define BAZILLION 2000000
S-5
S-6    struct foo {
S-7      char buffera[BAZILLION];
S-8      char bufferb[BAZILLION];
```

```
S-9       float x;
S-10      float a, b;
S-11      float *p;
S-12    };
S-13
S-14    #pragma omp begin declare target
S-15    void saxpyfun(struct foo *S)
S-16    {
S-17      int i;
S-18      for(i=0; i<N; i++)
S-19        S->p[i] = S->p[i]*S->a + S->b;
S-20    }
S-21    #pragma omp end declare target
S-22
S-23    int main()
S-24    {
S-25      struct foo S1, S2, S3;
S-26      int i;
S-27
S-28      // Case 1
S-29
S-30      S1.a = 2.0;
S-31      S1.b = 4.0;
S-32      S1.p = (float *)malloc(sizeof(float)*N);
S-33      for(i=0; i<N; i++) S1.p[i] = i;
S-34
S-35      // The target data construct results in pointer attachment for S1.p.
S-36      // Explicitly mapping S1.p, S1.a, and S1.b rather than S1 avoids
S-37      // mapping the entire structure (including members buffera, bufferb,
S-38      // and x).
S-39      #pragma omp target data map(S1.p[:N],S1.p,S1.a,S1.b)
S-40      #pragma omp target //implicit map of S1
S-41      saxpyfun(&S1);
S-42
S-43
S-44      // Case 2
S-45
S-46      S2.a = 2.0;
S-47      S2.b = 4.0;
S-48      S2.p = (float *)malloc(sizeof(float)*N);
S-49      for(i=0; i<N; i++) S2.p[i] = i;
S-50
S-51      // The target construct results in pointer attachment for S2.p.
S-52      #pragma omp target data map(S2.p[:N])
S-53      #pragma omp target map(S2.p[:0], S2.a, S2.b) // implicit map of S2
S-54      saxpyfun(&S2);
S-55
```

```
S-56        // Case 3
S-57
S-58        S3.a = 2.0;
S-59        S3.b = 4.0;
S-60        S3.p = (float *)malloc(sizeof(float)*N);
S-61        for(i=0; i<N; i++) S3.p[i] = i;
S-62
S-63        // The target construct results in pointer attachment for S3.p.
S-64        // Note that S3.p is implicitly mapped due to the implicit map of S3
S-65        // (but corresponding storage is NOT created for members buffera,
S-66        // bufferb, and x).
S-67        #pragma omp target map(S3.p[:N], S3.a, S3.b)  // implicit map of S3
S-68        saxpyfun(&S3);
S-69
S-70        printf(" %4.0f %4.0f\n", S1.p[0], S1.p[N-1]);  //OUT1 4 202
S-71        printf(" %4.0f %4.0f\n", S2.p[0], S2.p[N-1]);  //OUT2 4 202
S-72        printf(" %4.0f %4.0f\n", S3.p[0], S3.p[N-1]);  //OUT3 4 202
S-73
S-74        free(S1.p);
S-75        free(S2.p);
S-76        free(S3.p);
S-77        return 0;
S-78    }
S-79
```

C / C++

6.5 Fortran Allocatable Array Mapping

The following examples illustrate the use of Fortran allocatable arrays in **target** regions.

In the first example, allocatable variables (*a* and *b*) are first allocated on the host, and then mapped onto a device in the Target 1 and 2 sections, respectively. For *a* the map is implicit and for *b* an explicit map is used. Both are mapped with the default **tofrom** map type. The user-level behavior is similar to non-allocatable arrays. However, the mapping operations include creation of the allocatable variable, creation of the allocated storage, setting the allocation status to allocated, and making sure the allocatable variable references the storage.

In Target 3 and 4 sections, allocatable variables are mapped in two different ways before they are allocated on the host and subsequently used on the device. In one case, a **target data** construct creates an enclosing region for the allocatable variable to persist, and in the other case a **declare target** directive maps the allocation variable for all device executions. In both cases the new array storage is mapped **tofrom** with the **always** modifier. An explicit map is used here with an **always** modifier to ensure that the allocatable variable status is updated on the device.

Note: OpenMP 5.1 specifies that an **always** map modifier guarantees the allocation status update for an existing allocatable variable on the device. In OpenMP 6.0, this restriction may be relaxed to also guarantee updates without the **always** modifier.

In Target 3 and 4 sections, the behavior of an allocatable variable is very much like a Fortran pointer, in which a pointer can be mapped to a device with an associated or disassociated status, and associated storage can be mapped and attached as needed. For allocatable variables, the update of the allocation status to allocated (allowing reference to allocated storage) on the device, is similar to pointer attachment.

------- Fortran -------

Example target_fort_allocatable_map.1.f90 (**omp_5.1**)

```
program main
  implicit none
  integer :: i

  integer, save, allocatable :: d(:)
  !$omp    declare target(d)

  integer, allocatable :: a(:)
  integer, allocatable :: b(:)
  integer, allocatable :: c(:)

  allocate(a(4))
  !$omp target                          ! Target 1
    a(:) = 4
  !$omp end target
  print *, a ! prints 4*4
```

```
S-17
S-18         allocate(b(4))
S-19         !$omp target map(b)                    ! Target 2
S-20           b(:) = 4
S-21         !$omp end target
S-22         print *, b ! prints 4*4
S-23
S-24         !$omp target data map(c)
S-25
S-26           allocate(c(4), source=[1,2,3,4])
S-27           !$omp target map(always,tofrom:c) ! Target 3
S-28             c(:) = 4
S-29           !$omp end target
S-30           print *, c ! prints 4*4
S-31
S-32           deallocate(c)
S-33
S-34         !$omp end target data
S-35
S-36         allocate(d(4), source=[1,2,3,4])
S-37         !$omp target map(always,tofrom:d) ! Target 4
S-38           d(:) = d(:) + [ ( i,i=size(d),1,-1) ]
S-39         !$omp end target
S-40         print *, d ! prints 4*5
S-41
S-42         deallocate(a, b, d)
S-43
S-44     end program
```
————————————————————— Fortran —————————————————————

Once an allocatable variable has been allocated on the host, its allocation status may not be changed
in a **target** region, either explicitly or implicitly. The following example illustrates typical
operations on allocatable variables that violate this restriction. Note, an assignment that reshapes or
reassigns (causing a deallocation and allocation) in a **target** region is not conforming. Also, an
initial intrinsic assignment of an allocatable variable requires deallocation before the **target**
region ends.

————————————————————— Fortran —————————————————————

Example target_fort_allocatable_map.2.f90 (**omp_5.1**)

```
S-1      program main
S-2        implicit none
S-3
S-4        integer, allocatable :: a(:,:), b(:), c(:)
S-5        integer              :: x(10,2)
S-6
S-7        allocate(a(2,10))
```

```
S-8
S-9        !$omp target
S-10         a = x                    ! Reshape (or resize) NOT ALLOWED (implicit change)
S-11
S-12         deallocate(a)       ! Allocation status change of "a" NOT ALLOWED.
S-13
S-14         allocate(b(20))     ! Allocation of  b *
S-15
S-16         c = 10                   ! Intrinsic assignment allocates c *
S-17
S-18         ! * Since an explicit deallocation for b and c does not occur before
S-19         ! the end of the target region, the PROGRAM BEHAVIOR IS UNSPECIFIED.
S-20       !$omp end target
S-21
S-22   end program
```

———————————————————————— Fortran ————————————————————————

The next example illustrates a corner case of this restriction (allocatable status change in a **target**
region). Two allocatable arrays are passed to a subroutine within a **target** region. The
dummy-variable arrays are declared allocatable. Also, the *ain* variable has the *intent(in)* attribute,
and *bout* has the *intent(out)* attribute. For the dummy argument with the attributes *allocatable* and
intent(out), the compiler will deallocate the associated actual argument when the subroutine is
invoked. (However, the allocation on procedure entry can be avoided by specifying the intent as
intent(inout), making the intended use conforming.)

———————————————————————— Fortran ————————————————————————

Example target_fort_allocatable_map.3.f90 (**omp_5.1**)

```
S-1   module corfu
S-2   contains
S-3     subroutine foo(ain,bout)
S-4       implicit none
S-5       integer, allocatable, intent( in) :: ain(:)
S-6       integer, allocatable, intent(out) :: bout(:) !"out" causes de/realloc
S-7       !$omp declare target
S-8       bout = ain
S-9     end subroutine
S-10   end module
S-11
S-12   program  main
S-13     use corfu
S-14     implicit none
S-15
S-16     integer, allocatable :: a(:)
S-17     integer, allocatable :: b(:)
S-18     allocate(a(10),b(10))
S-19     a(:)=10
```

```
S-20        b(:)=10
S-21
S-22        !$omp target
S-23
S-24        call foo(a,b)  !ERROR: b deallocation/reallocation not allowed
S-25                       !  in target region
S-26
S-27        !$omp end target
S-28
S-29    end program
```

Fortran

6.6 Array Sections in Device Constructs

The following examples show the usage of array sections in **map** clauses on **target** and **target data** constructs.

This example shows the invalid usage of two separate sections of the same array inside of a **target** construct.

─────────────────────────── C / C++ ───────────────────────────

Example array_sections.1.c (**omp_4.0**)

```
S-1    void foo ()
S-2    {
S-3       int A[30];
S-4    #pragma omp target data map( A[0:4] )
S-5    {
S-6       /* Cannot map distinct parts of the same array */
S-7       #pragma omp target map( A[7:20] )
S-8       {
S-9          A[2] = 0;
S-10      }
S-11   }
S-12   }
```

─────────────────────────── C / C++ ───────────────────────────

─────────────────────────── Fortran ───────────────────────────

Example array_sections.1.f90 (**omp_4.0**)

```
S-1    subroutine foo()
S-2    integer :: A(30)
S-3       A = 1
S-4       !$omp target data map( A(1:4) )
S-5          ! Cannot map distinct parts of the same array
S-6          !$omp target map( A(8:27) )
S-7             A(3) = 0
S-8          !$omp end target
S-9       !$omp end target data
S-10   end subroutine
```

─────────────────────────── Fortran ───────────────────────────

This example shows the invalid usage of two separate sections of the same array inside of a **target** construct.

──────────────────────── C / C++ ────────────────────────

Example array_sections.2.c (**omp_4.0**)

```
S-1    void foo ()
S-2    {
S-3        int A[30], *p;
S-4    #pragma omp target data map( A[0:4] )
S-5    {
S-6        p = &A[0];
S-7        /* invalid because p[3] and A[3] are the same
S-8         * location on the host but the array section
S-9         * specified via p[...] is not a subset of A[0:4] */
S-10       #pragma omp target map( p[3:20] )
S-11       {
S-12          A[2] = 0;
S-13          p[8] = 0;
S-14       }
S-15    }
S-16    }
```

──────────────────────── C / C++ ────────────────────────

──────────────────────── Fortran ────────────────────────

Example array_sections.2.f90 (**omp_4.0**)

```
S-1    subroutine foo()
S-2    integer,target  :: A(30)
S-3    integer,pointer :: p(:)
S-4        A=1
S-5        !$omp target data map( A(1:4) )
S-6         p=>A
S-7          ! invalid because p(4) and A(4) are the same
S-8          ! location on the host but the array section
S-9          ! specified via p(...) is not a subset of A(1:4)
S-10        !$omp target map( p(4:23) )
S-11           A(3) = 0
S-12           p(9) = 0
S-13        !$omp end target
S-14      !$omp end target data
S-15    end subroutine
```

──────────────────────── Fortran ────────────────────────

This example shows the valid usage of two separate sections of the same array inside of a **target** construct.

———————————————————————— C / C++ ————————————————————————

Example array_sections.3.c (**omp_4.0**)

```
S-1   void foo ()
S-2   {
S-3      int A[30], *p;
S-4   #pragma omp target data map( A[0:4] )
S-5   {
S-6      p = &A[0];
S-7      #pragma omp target map( p[7:20] )
S-8      {
S-9         A[2] = 0;
S-10        p[8] = 0;
S-11     }
S-12  }
S-13  }
```

———————————————————————— C / C++ ————————————————————————

———————————————————————— Fortran ————————————————————————

Example array_sections.3.f90 (**omp_4.0**)

```
S-1   subroutine foo()
S-2   integer,target  :: A(30)
S-3   integer,pointer :: p(:)
S-4      !$omp target data map( A(1:4) )
S-5        p=>A
S-6        !$omp target map( p(8:27) )
S-7           A(3) = 0
S-8           p(9) = 0
S-9        !$omp end target
S-10     !$omp end target data
S-11  end subroutine
```

———————————————————————— Fortran ————————————————————————

This example shows the valid usage of a wholly contained array section of an already mapped array section inside of a **target** construct.

───────────────────────── C / C++ ─────────────────────────

Example array_sections.4.c (**omp_4.0**)

```
S-1   void foo ()
S-2   {
S-3      int A[30], *p;
S-4   #pragma omp target data map( A[0:10] )
S-5   {
S-6      p = &A[0];
S-7      #pragma omp target map( p[3:7] )
S-8      {
S-9         A[2] = 0;
S-10        p[8] = 0;
S-11        A[8] = 1;
S-12     }
S-13  }
S-14  }
```

───────────────────────── C / C++ ─────────────────────────
───────────────────────── Fortran ─────────────────────────

Example array_sections.4.f90 (**omp_4.0**)

```
S-1   subroutine foo()
S-2   integer,target  :: A(30)
S-3   integer,pointer :: p(:)
S-4      !$omp target data map( A(1:10) )
S-5        p=>A
S-6        !$omp target map( p(4:10) )
S-7           A(3) = 0
S-8           p(9) = 0
S-9           A(9) = 1
S-10       !$omp end target
S-11     !$omp end target data
S-12  end subroutine
```

───────────────────────── Fortran ─────────────────────────

6.7 C++ Virtual Functions

The 5.2 OpenMP Specification clarified restrictions on the use of polymorphic classes and virtual functions when used within **target** regions. The following example identifies problem cases in which the restrictions are not followed (for Unified Shared Memory, as prescribed by the **requires** directive).

The first section illustrates the restriction that when mapping an object for the first time, the static and dynamic types must match.

For the first target region the behavior of the implicit map of *ar* is not specified– its static type (A) doesn't match its dynamic type (D). Hence access to the virtual functions is undefined. However, the second target region can access *D::vf()* since the object to which *ap* points is not mapped and therefore the restriction does not apply.

The second section illustrates the restriction:

"Invoking a virtual member function of an object on a device other than the device on which the object was constructed results in unspecified behavior, unless the object is accessible and was constructed on the host device."

An instantiation of a polymorphic class (*A*) occurs in the **target** region, and access of its virtual function is incorrectly attempted on the host (another device). However, once the object is deleted on the target device and instantiated on the host, access within the next **target** region is permitted.

─────────────────────────── C++ ───────────────────────────

Example virtual_functions.1.cpp (**omp_5.2**)

```
S-1    #include <iostream>
S-2    #pragma omp requires unified_shared_memory
S-3
S-4    #pragma omp begin declare target
S-5    class A {
S-6      public:
S-7        virtual void vf()  { std::cout << "In A\n"; }
S-8    };
S-9
S-10   class D: public A {
S-11     public:
S-12       void vf() override { std::cout << "In D\n"; }
S-13   };
S-14   #pragma omp end declare target
S-15
S-16   int main(){
S-17
S-18       // Section 1 ----------------------------------------------------
S-19       D d;                   // D derives from A, and A::vf() is virtual
S-20       A &ar = d;             // reference to Derived object d
```

```
S-22      #pragma omp target // implicit map of ar is illegal here
S-23      {
S-24          ar.vf();           // unspecified whether A::vf() or D::vf() is called
S-25      }
S-26
S-27      A *ap = &d;         // pointer to derived object d
S-28      #pragma omp target // No need for mapping with Unified Share Memory
S-29      {                  // implicit ap[:0] map is fine
S-30          ap->vf();      // calls D::vf()
S-31      }
S-32
S-33      // Section 2 ------------------------------------------------
S-34      ap = nullptr;
S-35      #pragma omp target map(ap)
S-36      {
S-37          ap = new A();
S-38      }
S-39
S-40      ap->vf();       // illegal
S-41
S-42      #pragma omp target
S-43      {
S-44          delete ap;
S-45      }
S-46      ap = new A();
S-47      #pragma omp target  // No need for mapping with Unified Share Memory
S-48      {
S-49          ap->vf();   // ok
S-50      }
S-51
S-52      return 0;
S-53  }
```

— C++ —

6.8 Array Shaping

— C / C++ —

A pointer variable can be shaped to a multi-dimensional array to facilitate data access. This is achieved by a *shape-operator* casted in front of a pointer (lvalue expression):

$$([s_1] [s_2] \ldots [s_n]) \, pointer$$

where each s_i is an integral-type expression of positive value. The shape-operator can appear in either the *motion-clause* of the **target update** directive or the **depend** clause.

The following example shows the use of the shape-operator in the **target update** directive. The shape-operator (**[nx][ny+2]**) casts pointer variable a to a 2-dimentional array of size $nx \times (ny+2)$. The resulting array is then accessed as array sections (such as **[0:nx][1]** and **[0:nx][ny]**) in the **from** or **to** clause for transferring two columns of noncontiguous boundary data from or to the device. Note the use of additional parentheses around the shape-operator and a to ensure the correct precedence over array-section operations.

Example array_shaping.1.c (**omp_5.1**)

```
S-1     #pragma omp begin declare target
S-2       int do_work(double *a, int nx, int ny);
S-3       int other_work(double *a, int nx, int ny);
S-4     #pragma omp end declare target
S-5
S-6     void exch_data(double *a, int nx, int ny);
S-7
S-8     void array_shaping(double *a, int nx, int ny)
S-9     {
S-10        // map data to device and do work
S-11        #pragma omp target data map(a[0:nx*(ny+2)])
S-12        {
S-13           // do work on the device
S-14           #pragma omp target  // map(a[0:nx*(ny+2)]) is optional here
S-15           do_work(a, nx, ny);
S-16
S-17           // update boundary points (two columns of 2D array) on the host
S-18           // pointer is shaped to 2D array using the shape-operator
S-19           #pragma omp target update from( (([nx][ny+2])a)[0:nx][1], \
S-20                                            (([nx][ny+2])a)[0:nx][ny] )
S-21
S-22           // exchange ghost points with neighbors
S-23           exch_data(a, nx, ny);
S-24
S-25           // update ghost points (two columns of 2D array) on the device
S-26           // pointer is shaped to 2D array using the shape-operator
S-27           #pragma omp target update to( (([nx][ny+2])a)[0:nx][0], \
S-28                                          (([nx][ny+2])a)[0:nx][ny+1] )
S-29
S-30           // perform other work on the device
S-31           #pragma omp target  // map(a[0:nx*(ny+2)]) is optional here
S-32           other_work(a, nx, ny);
S-33        }
S-34     }
```

———————————————————— C / C++ ————————————————————

The shape operator is not defined for Fortran. Explicit array shaping of procedure arguments can be used instead to achieve a similar goal. Below is the Fortran-equivalent of the above example that illustrates the support of transferring two rows of noncontiguous boundary data in the **target update** directive.

---------------------------------- Fortran ----------------------------------

Example array_shaping.1.f90 (**omp_5.2**)

```
S-1
S-2     module m
S-3        interface
S-4           subroutine do_work(a, nx, ny)
S-5              !$omp declare target enter(do_work)
S-6              integer, intent(in) :: nx, ny
S-7              double precision a(0:nx+1,ny)
S-8           end subroutine do_work
S-9
S-10          subroutine other_work(a, nx, ny)
S-11             !$omp declare target enter(other_work)
S-12             integer, intent(in) :: nx, ny
S-13             double precision a(0:nx+1,ny)
S-14          end subroutine other_work
S-15
S-16          subroutine exch_data(a, nx, ny)
S-17             integer, intent(in) :: nx, ny
S-18             double precision a(0:nx+1,ny)
S-19          end subroutine exch_data
S-20       end interface
S-21    end module m
S-22
S-23    subroutine array_shaping(a, nx, ny)
S-24       use m
S-25       implicit none
S-26       integer, intent(in) :: nx, ny
S-27       double precision a(0:nx+1,ny)
S-28
S-29       ! map data to device and do work
S-30       !$omp target data map(a)
S-31
S-32          ! do work on the device
S-33          !$omp target       ! map(a) is optional here
S-34          call do_work(a, nx, ny)
S-35          !$omp end target
S-36
S-37          ! update boundary points (two rows of 2D array) on the host.
S-38          ! data transferred are noncontiguous
S-39          !$omp target update from( a(1,1:ny), a(nx,1:ny) )
```

```
S-40
S-41            ! exchange ghost points with neighbors
S-42            call exch_data(a, nx, ny)
S-43
S-44            ! update ghost points (two rows of 2D array) on the device.
S-45            ! data transferred are noncontiguous
S-46            !$omp target update to( a(0,1:ny), a(nx+1,1:ny) )
S-47
S-48            ! perform other work on the device
S-49            !$omp target       ! map(a) is optional here
S-50            call other_work(a, nx, ny)
S-51            !$omp end target
S-52
S-53        !$omp end target data
S-54
S-55    end subroutine
```

▲——————————————————————— Fortran ————————————————————————▲

6.9 `declare mapper` Directive

The following examples show how to use the **declare mapper** directive to prescribe a map for later use. It is also quite useful for pre-defining partitioned and nested structure elements.

In the first example the **declare mapper** directive specifies that any structure of type *myvec_t* for which implicit data-mapping rules apply will be mapped according to its **map** clause. The variable *v* is used for referencing the structure and its elements within the **map** clause. Within the **map** clause the *v* variable specifies that all elements of the structure are to be mapped. Additionally, the array section *v.data[0:v.len]* specifies that the dynamic storage for data is to be mapped.

Within the main program the *s* variable is typed as *myvec_t*. Since the variable is found within the target region and the type has a mapping prescribed by a **declare mapper** directive, it will be automatically mapped according to its prescription: full structure, plus the dynamic storage of the *data* element.

───────────────────── C / C++ ─────────────────────

Example target_mapper.1.c (**omp_5.0**)

```
#include    <stdlib.h>
#include    <stdio.h>
#define N 100

typedef struct myvec{
    size_t len;
    double *data;
} myvec_t;

#pragma omp declare mapper(myvec_t v) \
                    map(v, v.data[0:v.len])
void init(myvec_t *s);

int main(){
    myvec_t s;

    s.data = (double *)calloc(N,sizeof(double));
    s.len  = N;

    #pragma omp target
    init(&s);

    printf("s.data[%d]=%lf\n",N-1,s.data[N-1]);   //s.data[99]=99.000000
}

void init(myvec_t *s)
{ for(int i=0; i<s->len; i++) s->data[i]=i; }
```

───────────────────── C / C++ ─────────────────────

1   *Example target_mapper.1.f90* (`omp_5.0`)

```fortran
S-1
S-2    module my_structures
S-3      type myvec_t
S-4        integer                      :: len
S-5        double precision, pointer    :: data(:)
S-6      end type
S-7    end module
S-8
S-9    program main
S-10     use my_structures
S-11     integer, parameter :: N=100
S-12
S-13     !$omp   declare mapper(myvec_t :: v) &
S-14     !$omp&             map(v, v%data(1:v%len))
S-15
S-16     type(myvec_t) :: s
S-17
S-18     allocate(s%data(N))
S-19     s%data(1:N) = 0.0d0
S-20     s%len = N
S-21
S-22     !$omp target
S-23     call init(s)
S-24     !$omp end target
S-25
S-26     print*,"s%data(",N,")=",s%data(N)   !! s%data( 100 )=100.000000000000
S-27   end program
S-28
S-29   subroutine init(s)
S-30     use my_structures
S-31     type(myvec_t) :: s
S-32
S-33     s%data = [ (i, i=1,s%len) ]
S-34   end subroutine
```

2   The next example illustrates the use of the *mapper-identifier* and deep copy within a structure. The
3   structure, *dzmat_t*, represents a complex matrix, with separate real (*r_m*) and imaginary (*i_m*)
4   elements. Two map identifiers are created for partitioning the *dzmat_t* structure.

5   For the C/C++ code the first identifier is named *top_id* and maps the top half of two matrices of
6   type *dzmat_t*; while the second identifier, *bottom_id*, maps the lower half of two matrices. Each
7   identifier is applied to a different **target** construct, as **map(mapper(top_id), tofrom:**

1

1   `a,b)` and `map(mapper(bottom_id), tofrom:   a,b)`. Each target offload is allowed to
2   execute concurrently on two different devices (*0* and *1*) through the **nowait** clause.

3   The Fortran code uses the *left_id* and *right_id* map identifiers in the
4   `map(mapper(left_id),tofrom:   a,b)` and `map(mapper(right_id),tofrom:`
5   `a,b)` map clauses. The array sections for these left and right contiguous portions of the matrices
6   were defined previously in the **declare mapper** directive.

7   Note, the *is* and *ie* scalars are firstprivate by default for a target region, but are declared firstprivate
8   anyway to remind the user of important firstprivate data-sharing properties required here.

––––––––––––––––––––– C / C++ –––––––––––––––––––––

9   *Example target_mapper.2.c* (`omp_5.1`)

```
S-1     #include <stdio.h>
S-2     //                     N MUST BE EVEN
S-3     #define N   100
S-4
S-5       typedef struct dzmat
S-6       {
S-7          double r_m[N][N];
S-8          double i_m[N][N];
S-9       } dzmat_t;
S-10
S-11      #pragma omp declare mapper( top_id: dzmat_t v) \
S-12                      map(v.r_m[0:N/2][0:N],      \
S-13                          v.i_m[0:N/2][0:N]        )
S-14
S-15      #pragma omp declare mapper(bottom_id: dzmat_t v) \
S-16                      map(v.r_m[N/2:N/2][0:N],      \
S-17                          v.i_m[N/2:N/2][0:N]        )
S-18    //initialization
S-19    void dzmat_init(dzmat_t *z, int is, int ie, int n);
S-20    //matrix add: c=a+b
S-21    void host_add(  dzmat_t *a, dzmat_t *b, dzmat_t *c, int n);
S-22
S-23
S-24    int main()
S-25    {
S-26      dzmat_t a,b,c;
S-27      int     is,ie;
S-28
S-29      is=0; ie=N/2-1;        //top N/2 rows on device 0
S-30      #pragma omp target map(mapper(top_id), tofrom: a,b) device(0) \
S-31                      firstprivate(is,ie) nowait
S-32      {
S-33        dzmat_init(&a,is,ie,N);
S-34        dzmat_init(&b,is,ie,N);
```

```
S-35        }
S-36
S-37        is=N/2; ie=N-1;          //bottom N/2 rows on device 1
S-38        #pragma omp target map(mapper(bottom_id), tofrom: a,b) device(1) \
S-39                        firstprivate(is,ie) nowait
S-40        {
S-41          dzmat_init(&a,is,ie,N);
S-42          dzmat_init(&b,is,ie,N);
S-43        }
S-44
S-45        #pragma omp taskwait
S-46
S-47        host_add(&a,&b,&c,N);
S-48    }
```

───────────────────────── C / C++ ─────────────────────────
───────────────────────── Fortran ─────────────────────────

1   *Example target_mapper.2.f90* (omp_5.1)

```
S-1     module complex_mats
S-2
S-3       integer, parameter :: N=100      !N must be even
S-4       type dzmat_t
S-5         double precision ::   r_m(N,N),  i_m(N,N)
S-6       end type
S-7
S-8       !$omp  declare mapper( left_id: dzmat_t :: v) map( v%r_m(N,   1:N/2), &
S-9       !$omp&                                       v%i_m(N,   1:N/2))
S-10
S-11      !$omp  declare mapper(right_id: dzmat_t :: v) map( v%r_m(N,N/2+1:N), &
S-12      !$omp&                                       v%i_m(N,N/2+1:N))
S-13
S-14    end module
S-15
S-16
S-17    program main
S-18      use   complex_mats
S-19      type(dzmat_t) :: a,b,c
S-20      external dzmat_init, host_add  !initialization and matrix add: a=b+c
S-21
S-22      integer :: is,ie
S-23
S-24
S-25      is=1; ie=N/2              !left N/2 columns on device 0
S-26      !$omp target map(mapper( left_id), tofrom: a,b) device(0) &
S-27      !$omp&           firstprivate(is,ie) nowait
S-28        call dzmat_init(a,is,ie)
```

```
S-29          call dzmat_init(b,is,ie)
S-30       !$omp end target
S-31
S-32       is=N/2+1; ie=N            !right N/2 columns on device 1
S-33       !$omp target map(mapper(right_id), tofrom: a,b) device(1) &
S-34       !$omp&           firstprivate(is,ie) nowait
S-35         call dzmat_init(a,is,ie)
S-36         call dzmat_init(b,is,ie)
S-37       !$omp end target
S-38
S-39       !$omp taskwait
S-40
S-41       call host_add(a,b,c)
S-42
S-43    end program main
```

—————————————————————————————— Fortran ——————————————————————————————

In the third example *myvec* structures are nested within a *mypoints* structure. The *myvec_t* type is
mapped as in the first example. Following the *mypoints* structure declaration, the *mypoints_t* type is
mapped by a **declare mapper** directive. For this structure the *hostonly_data* element will not
be mapped; also the array section of *x* (*v.x[:1]*) and *x* will be mapped; and *scratch* will be allocated
and used as scratch storage on the device. The default map-type mapping, **tofrom**, applies to the *x*
array section, but not to *scratch* which is explicitly mapped with the **alloc** map-type. Note: the
variable *v* is not included in the map list (otherwise the *hostonly_data* would be mapped)– just the
elements to be mapped are listed.

The two mappers are combined when a *mypoints_t* structure type is mapped, because the mapper
myvec_t structure type is used within a *mypoints_t* type structure.

—————————————————————————————— C / C++ ——————————————————————————————

Example target_mapper.3.c (**omp_5.0**)

```
S-1
S-2    #include <stdlib.h>
S-3    #include  <stdio.h>
S-4
S-5    #define N 100
S-6
S-7    typedef struct myvec {
S-8        size_t len;
S-9        double *data;
S-10   } myvec_t;
S-11
S-12   #pragma omp declare mapper(myvec_t v) \
S-13                       map(v, v.data[0:v.len])
S-14
S-15   typedef struct mypoints {
```

```
S-16          struct myvec scratch;
S-17          struct myvec *x;
S-18          double hostonly_data[500000];
S-19    } mypoints_t;
S-20
S-21    #pragma omp declare mapper(mypoints_t v)   \
S-22                      map(v.x, v.x[0] ) map(alloc:v.scratch)
S-23
S-24    void init_mypts_array(mypoints_t *P, int n);
S-25    void eval_mypts_array(mypoints_t *P, int n);
S-26
S-27    int main(){
S-28
S-29        mypoints_t P;
S-30
S-31        init_mypts_array(&P, N);
S-32
S-33        #pragma omp target map(P)
S-34        eval_mypts_array(&P, N);
S-35
S-36    }
```

———————————————————— C / C++ ————————————————————
———————————————————— Fortran ————————————————————

Example target_mapper.3.f90 (**omp_5.0**)

```
S-1
S-2     module my_structures
S-3       type myvec_t
S-4         integer                    :: len
S-5         double precision, pointer :: data(:)
S-6       end type
S-7       !$omp  declare mapper(myvec_t :: v) &
S-8       !$omp&          map(v)
S-9
S-10      type mypoints_t
S-11        type(myvec_t)              :: scratch
S-12        type(myvec_t), pointer    :: x(:)
S-13        double precision           :: hostonly_data(500000)
S-14      end  type
S-15      !$omp  declare mapper(mypoints_t :: v)  &
S-16      !$omp&          map(v%x, v%x(1)) map(alloc:v%scratch)
S-17
S-18     end module
S-19
S-20
S-21     program main
```

```
S-22      use my_structures
S-23      external  init_mypts_array, eval_mypts_array
S-24
S-25      type(mypoints_t) :: P
S-26
S-27       call init_mypts_array(P)
S-28
S-29       !$omp target map(P)
S-30       call eval_mypts_array(P)
S-31
S-32   end program
S-33
```

Fortran

6.10 `target data` Construct

6.10.1 Simple `target data` Construct

This example shows how the **target data** construct maps variables to a device data environment. The **target data** construct creates a new device data environment and maps the variables *v1*, *v2*, and *p* to the new device data environment. The **target** construct enclosed in the **target data** region creates a new device data environment, which inherits the variables *v1*, *v2*, and *p* from the enclosing device data environment. The variable *N* is mapped into the new device data environment from the encountering task's data environment.

─────────────────── C / C++ ───────────────────

Example target_data.1.c (**omp_4.0**)

```
S-1     extern void init(float*, float*, int);
S-2     extern void output(float*, int);
S-3     void vec_mult(float *p, float *v1, float *v2, int N)
S-4     {
S-5         int i;
S-6         init(v1, v2, N);
S-7         #pragma omp target data map(to: v1[0:N], v2[:N]) map(from: p[0:N])
S-8         {
S-9             #pragma omp target
S-10            #pragma omp parallel for
S-11            for (i=0; i<N; i++)
S-12              p[i] = v1[i] * v2[i];
S-13        }
S-14        output(p, N);
S-15    }
```

─────────────────── C / C++ ───────────────────

The Fortran code passes a reference and specifies the extent of the arrays in the declaration. No length information is necessary in the map clause, as is required with C/C++ pointers.

───────────────────────── Fortran ─────────────────────────

Example target_data.1.f90 (**omp_4.0**)

```
S-1    subroutine vec_mult(p, v1, v2, N)
S-2       real     ::  p(N), v1(N), v2(N)
S-3       integer ::  i
S-4       call init(v1, v2, N)
S-5       !$omp target data map(to: v1, v2) map(from: p)
S-6       !$omp target
S-7       !$omp parallel do
S-8          do i=1,N
S-9             p(i) = v1(i) * v2(i)
S-10         end do
S-11      !$omp end target
S-12      !$omp end target data
S-13      call output(p, N)
S-14   end subroutine
```

───────────────────────── Fortran ─────────────────────────

6.10.2 `target data` Region Enclosing Multiple `target` Regions

The following examples show how the **target data** construct maps variables to a device data environment of a **target** region. The **target data** construct creates a device data environment and encloses **target** regions, which have their own device data environments. The device data environment of the **target data** region is inherited by the device data environment of an enclosed **target** region. The **target data** construct is used to create variables that will persist throughout the **target data** region.

In the following example the variables *v1* and *v2* are mapped at each **target** construct. Instead of mapping the variable *p* twice, once at each **target** construct, *p* is mapped once by the **target data** construct.

1   *Example target_data.2.c* (**omp_4.0**)

```
S-1     extern void init(float*, float*, int);
S-2     extern void init_again(float*, float*, int);
S-3     extern void output(float*, int);
S-4     void vec_mult(float *p, float *v1, float *v2, int N)
S-5     {
S-6        int i;
S-7        init(v1, v2, N);
S-8        #pragma omp target data map(from: p[0:N])
S-9        {
S-10          #pragma omp target map(to: v1[:N], v2[:N])
S-11          #pragma omp parallel for
S-12          for (i=0; i<N; i++)
S-13            p[i] = v1[i] * v2[i];
S-14          init_again(v1, v2, N);
S-15          #pragma omp target map(to: v1[:N], v2[:N])
S-16          #pragma omp parallel for
S-17          for (i=0; i<N; i++)
S-18            p[i] = p[i] + (v1[i] * v2[i]);
S-19       }
S-20       output(p, N);
S-21    }
```

2   The Fortran code uses reference and specifies the extent of the *p*, *v1* and *v2* arrays. No length
3   information is necessary in the **map** clause, as is required with C/C++ pointers. The arrays *v1* and
4   *v2* are mapped at each **target** construct. Instead of mapping the array *p* twice, once at each target
5   construct, *p* is mapped once by the **target data** construct.

6   *Example target_data.2.f90* (**omp_4.0**)

```
S-1     subroutine vec_mult(p, v1, v2, N)
S-2        real    ::  p(N), v1(N), v2(N)
S-3        integer ::  i
S-4        call init(v1, v2, N)
S-5        !$omp target data map(from: p)
S-6           !$omp target map(to: v1, v2 )
S-7              !$omp parallel do
S-8              do i=1,N
S-9                 p(i) = v1(i) * v2(i)
S-10             end do
S-11          !$omp end target
S-12          call init_again(v1, v2, N)
```

```
S-13          !$omp target map(to: v1, v2 )
S-14            !$omp parallel do
S-15            do i=1,N
S-16               p(i) = p(i) + v1(i) * v2(i)
S-17            end do
S-18          !$omp end target
S-19        !$omp end target data
S-20      call output(p, N)
S-21   end subroutine
```

———————————————————————— Fortran ————————————————————————

1   In the following example, the array *Q* is mapped once at the enclosing **target data** region
2   instead of at each **target** construct. In OpenMP 4.0, a scalar variable is implicitly mapped with
3   the **tofrom** map-type. But since OpenMP 4.5, a scalar variable, such as the *tmp* variable, has to be
4   explicitly mapped with the **tofrom** map-type at the first **target** construct in order to return its
5   reduced value from the parallel loop construct to the host. The variable defaults to firstprivate at the
6   second **target** construct.

———————————————————————— C / C++ ————————————————————————

7   *Example target_data.3.c* (**omp_4.0**)

```
S-1
S-2    #include <math.h>
S-3    #define COLS 100
S-4
S-5    void gramSchmidt(float Q[][COLS], const int rows)
S-6    {
S-7        int cols = COLS;
S-8        #pragma omp target data map(Q[0:rows][0:cols])
S-9        for(int k=0; k < cols; k++)
S-10       {
S-11           double tmp = 0.0;
S-12
S-13           #pragma omp target map(tofrom: tmp)
S-14           #pragma omp parallel for reduction(+:tmp)
S-15           for(int i=0; i < rows; i++)
S-16               tmp += (Q[i][k] * Q[i][k]);
S-17
S-18           tmp = 1/sqrt(tmp);
S-19
S-20           #pragma omp target
S-21           #pragma omp parallel for
S-22           for(int i=0; i < rows; i++)
S-23               Q[i][k] *= tmp;
S-24       }
S-25   }
S-26
```

```
S-27   /* Note:    The variable tmp is now mapped with tofrom, for correct
S-28             execution with 4.5 (and pre-4.5) compliant compilers.
S-29             See Devices Intro.
S-30   */
```

———————————————————————— C / C++ ————————————————————————

———————————————————————— Fortran ————————————————————————

1   *Example target_data.3.f90* (omp_4.0)

```
S-1    subroutine gramSchmidt(Q,rows,cols)
S-2    integer              ::   rows,cols,  i,k
S-3    double precision     :: Q(rows,cols), tmp
S-4         !$omp target data map(Q)
S-5         do k=1,cols
S-6            tmp = 0.0d0
S-7            !$omp target map(tofrom: tmp)
S-8               !$omp parallel do reduction(+:tmp)
S-9               do i=1,rows
S-10                 tmp = tmp + (Q(i,k) * Q(i,k))
S-11              end do
S-12           !$omp end target
S-13
S-14            tmp = 1.0d0/sqrt(tmp)
S-15
S-16           !$omp target
S-17              !$omp parallel do
S-18              do i=1,rows
S-19                  Q(i,k) = Q(i,k)*tmp
S-20              enddo
S-21           !$omp end target
S-22        end do
S-23        !$omp end target data
S-24    end subroutine
S-25
S-26    ! Note:   The variable tmp is now mapped with tofrom, for correct
S-27    ! execution with 4.5 (and pre-4.5) compliant compilers. See Devices Intro.
```

———————————————————————— Fortran ————————————————————————

6.10.3 `target data` Construct with Orphaned Call

The following two examples show how the **target data** construct maps variables to a device data environment. The **target data** construct's device data environment encloses the **target** construct's device data environment in the function **vec_mult()**.

When the type of the variable appearing in an array section is pointer, the pointer variable and the storage location of the corresponding array section are mapped to the device data environment. The pointer variable is treated as if it had appeared in a **map** clause with a map-type of **alloc**. The array section's storage location is mapped according to the map-type in the **map** clause (the default map-type is **tofrom**).

The **target** construct's device data environment inherits the storage locations of the array sections *v1[0:N]*, *v2[:n]*, and *p0[0:N]* from the enclosing **target data** construct's device data environment. Neither initialization nor assignment is performed for the array sections in the new device data environment.

The pointer variables *p1*, *v3*, and *v4* are mapped into the **target** construct's device data environment with an implicit map-type of alloc and they are assigned the address of the storage location associated with their corresponding array sections. Note that the following pairs of array section storage locations are equivalent (*p0[:N]*, *p1[:N]*), (*v1[:N]*,*v3[:N]*), and (*v2[:N]*,*v4[:N]*).

——————————————————— C / C++ ———————————————————

Example target_data.4.c (**omp_4.0**)

```
S-1    void vec_mult(float*, float*, float*, int);
S-2
S-3    extern void init(float*, float*, int);
S-4    extern void output(float*, int);
S-5
S-6
S-7    void foo(float *p0, float *v1, float *v2, int N)
S-8    {
S-9       init(v1, v2, N);
S-10
S-11      #pragma omp target data map(to: v1[0:N], v2[:N]) map(from: p0[0:N])
S-12      {
S-13         vec_mult(p0, v1, v2, N);
S-14      }
S-15
S-16      output(p0, N);
S-17   }
S-18
S-19
S-20   void vec_mult(float *p1, float *v3, float *v4, int N)
S-21   {
```

```
S-22          int i;
S-23          #pragma omp target map(to: v3[0:N], v4[:N]) map(from: p1[0:N])
S-24          #pragma omp parallel for
S-25          for (i=0; i<N; i++)
S-26          {
S-27            p1[i] = v3[i] * v4[i];
S-28          }
S-29      }
```

─────────────────────── C / C++ ───────────────────────

The Fortran code maps the pointers and storage in an identical manner (same extent, but uses indices from 1 to *N*).

The **target** construct's device data environment inherits the storage locations of the arrays *v1*, *v2* and *p0* from the enclosing **target data** constructs's device data environment. However, in Fortran the associated data of the pointer is known, and the shape is not required.

The pointer variables *p1*, *v3*, and *v4* are mapped into the **target** construct's device data environment with an implicit map-type of **alloc** and they are assigned the address of the storage location associated with their corresponding array sections. Note that the following pair of array storage locations are equivalent (*p0*,*p1*), (*v1*,*v3*), and (*v2*,*v4*).

─────────────────────── Fortran ───────────────────────

Example target_data.4.f90 (**omp_4.0**)

```
S-1       module mults
S-2       contains
S-3       subroutine foo(p0,v1,v2,N)
S-4       real,pointer,dimension(:) :: p0, v1, v2
S-5       integer                   :: N,i
S-6
S-7          call init(v1, v2, N)
S-8
S-9          !$omp target data map(to: v1, v2) map(from: p0)
S-10          call vec_mult(p0,v1,v2,N)
S-11         !$omp end target data
S-12
S-13         call output(p0, N)
S-14
S-15      end subroutine
S-16
S-17      subroutine vec_mult(p1,v3,v4,N)
S-18      real,pointer,dimension(:) :: p1, v3, v4
S-19      integer                   :: N,i
S-20
S-21         !$omp target map(to: v3, v4) map(from: p1)
S-22         !$omp parallel do
```

```
S-23        do i=1,N
S-24           p1(i) = v3(i) * v4(i)
S-25        end do
S-26        !$omp end target
S-27
S-28     end subroutine
S-29     end module
```
———————————————————— Fortran ————————————————————

In the following example, the variables *p1*, *v3*, and *v4* are references to the pointer variables *p0*, *v1* and *v2* respectively. The **target** construct's device data environment inherits the pointer variables *p0*, *v1*, and *v2* from the enclosing **target data** construct's device data environment. Thus, *p1*, *v3*, and *v4* are already present in the device data environment.

———————————————————— C++ ————————————————————

Example target_data.5.cpp (**omp_4.0**)

```
S-1      void vec_mult(float* &, float* &, float* &, int &);
S-2      extern void init(float*, float*, int);
S-3      extern void output(float*, int);
S-4      void foo(float *p0, float *v1, float *v2, int N)
S-5      {
S-6         init(v1, v2, N);
S-7         #pragma omp target data map(to: v1[0:N], v2[:N]) map(from: p0[0:N])
S-8         {
S-9            vec_mult(p0, v1, v2, N);
S-10        }
S-11        output(p0, N);
S-12     }
S-13     void vec_mult(float* &p1, float* &v3, float* &v4, int &N)
S-14     {
S-15        int i;
S-16        #pragma omp target map(to: v3[0:N], v4[:N]) map(from: p1[0:N])
S-17        #pragma omp parallel for
S-18        for (i=0; i<N; i++)
S-19          p1[i] = v3[i] * v4[i];
S-20     }
```
———————————————————— C++ ————————————————————

In the following example, the usual Fortran approach is used for dynamic memory. The *p0*, *v1*, and *v2* arrays are allocated in the main program and passed as references from one routine to another. In **vec_mult**, *p1*, *v3* and *v4* are references to the *p0*, *v1*, and *v2* arrays, respectively. The **target** construct's device data environment inherits the arrays *p0*, *v1*, and *v2* from the enclosing target data construct's device data environment. Thus, *p1*, *v3*, and *v4* are already present in the device data environment.

Example target_data.5.f90 (`omp_4.0`)

```fortran
S-1     module my_mult
S-2     contains
S-3     subroutine foo(p0,v1,v2,N)
S-4     real,dimension(:) :: p0, v1, v2
S-5     integer           :: N,i
S-6        call init(v1, v2, N)
S-7        !$omp target data map(to: v1, v2) map(from: p0)
S-8         call vec_mult(p0,v1,v2,N)
S-9        !$omp end target data
S-10       call output(p0, N)
S-11    end subroutine
S-12    subroutine vec_mult(p1,v3,v4,N)
S-13    real,dimension(:) :: p1, v3, v4
S-14    integer           :: N,i
S-15       !$omp target map(to: v3, v4) map(from: p1)
S-16       !$omp parallel do
S-17       do i=1,N
S-18          p1(i) = v3(i) * v4(i)
S-19       end do
S-20       !$omp end target
S-21    end subroutine
S-22    end module
S-23    program main
S-24    use my_mult
S-25    integer, parameter :: N=1024
S-26    real,allocatable, dimension(:) :: p, v1, v2
S-27       allocate( p(N), v1(N), v2(N) )
S-28       call foo(p,v1,v2,N)
S-29       deallocate( p, v1, v2 )
S-30    end program
```

6.10.4 `target data` Construct with `if` Clause

The following two examples show how the **target data** construct maps variables to a device data environment.

In the following example, the if clause on the **target data** construct indicates that if the variable *N* is smaller than a given threshold, then the **target data** construct will not create a device data environment.

The **target** constructs enclosed in the **target data** region must also use an **if** clause on the same condition, otherwise the pointer variable *p* is implicitly mapped with a map-type of **tofrom**, but the storage location for the array section *p[0:N]* will not be mapped in the device data environments of the **target** constructs.

———————————————————— C / C++ ————————————————————

Example target_data.6.c (**omp_4.0**)

```
#define THRESHOLD 1000000
extern void init(float*, float*, int);
extern void init_again(float*, float*, int);
extern void output(float*, int);
void vec_mult(float *p, float *v1, float *v2, int N)
{
    int i;
    init(v1, v2, N);
    #pragma omp target data if(N>THRESHOLD) map(from: p[0:N])
    {
        #pragma omp target if (N>THRESHOLD) map(to: v1[:N], v2[:N])
        #pragma omp parallel for
        for (i=0; i<N; i++)
          p[i] = v1[i] * v2[i];
        init_again(v1, v2, N);
        #pragma omp target if (N>THRESHOLD) map(to: v1[:N], v2[:N])
        #pragma omp parallel for
        for (i=0; i<N; i++)
          p[i] = p[i] + (v1[i] * v2[i]);
    }
    output(p, N);
}
```

———————————————————— C / C++ ————————————————————

The `if` clauses work the same way for the following Fortran code. The **target** constructs enclosed in the **target data** region should also use an `if` clause with the same condition, so that the **target data** region and the **target** region are either both created for the device, or are both ignored.

───────────────────────────────── Fortran ─────────────────────────────────

Example target_data.6.f90 (**omp_4.0**)

```fortran
module params
integer,parameter :: THRESHOLD=1000000
end module
subroutine vec_mult(p, v1, v2, N)
   use params
   real     ::  p(N), v1(N), v2(N)
   integer ::  i
   call init(v1, v2, N)
   !$omp target data if(N>THRESHOLD) map(from: p)
      !$omp target if(N>THRESHOLD) map(to: v1, v2)
         !$omp parallel do
         do i=1,N
             p(i) = v1(i) * v2(i)
         end do
      !$omp end target
      call init_again(v1, v2, N)
      !$omp target if(N>THRESHOLD) map(to: v1, v2)
         !$omp parallel do
         do i=1,N
             p(i) = p(i) + v1(i) * v2(i)
         end do
      !$omp end target
   !$omp end target data
   call output(p, N)
end subroutine
```

───────────────────────────────── Fortran ─────────────────────────────────

In the following example, when the **if** clause conditional expression on the **target** construct evaluates to *false*, the target region will execute on the host device. However, the **target data** construct created an enclosing device data environment that mapped *p[0:N]* to a device data environment on the default device. At the end of the **target data** region the array section *p[0:N]* will be assigned from the device data environment to the corresponding variable in the data environment of the task that encountered the **target data** construct, resulting in undefined values in *p[0:N]*.

———————————————————— C / C++ ————————————————————

Example target_data.7.c (**omp_4.0**)

```
S-1     #define THRESHOLD 1000000
S-2     extern void init(float*, float*, int);
S-3     extern void output(float*, int);
S-4     void vec_mult(float *p, float *v1, float *v2, int N)
S-5     {
S-6         int i;
S-7         init(v1, v2, N);
S-8         #pragma omp target data map(from: p[0:N])
S-9         {
S-10            #pragma omp target if (N>THRESHOLD) map(to: v1[:N], v2[:N])
S-11            #pragma omp parallel for
S-12            for (i=0; i<N; i++)
S-13                p[i] = v1[i] * v2[i];
S-14        } /* UNDEFINED behavior if N<=THRESHOLD */
S-15        output(p, N);
S-16    }
```

———————————————————— C / C++ ————————————————————

The **if** clauses work the same way for the following Fortran code. When the **if** clause conditional expression on the **target** construct evaluates to *false*, the **target** region will execute on the host device. However, the **target data** construct created an enclosing device data environment that mapped the *p* array (and *v1* and *v2*) to a device data environment on the default target device. At the end of the **target data** region the *p* array will be assigned from the device data environment to the corresponding variable in the data environment of the task that encountered the **target data** construct, resulting in undefined values in *p*.

———————————————— Fortran ————————————————

Example target_data.7.f90 (**omp_4.0**)

```
S-1    module params
S-2    integer, parameter :: THRESHOLD=1000000
S-3    end module
S-4    subroutine vec_mult(p, v1, v2, N)
S-5       use params
S-6       real     :: p(N), v1(N), v2(N)
S-7       integer :: i
S-8       call init(v1, v2, N)
S-9       !$omp target data map(from: p)
S-10         !$omp target if(N>THRESHOLD) map(to: v1, v2)
S-11            !$omp parallel do
S-12            do i=1,N
S-13               p(i) = v1(i) * v2(i)
S-14            end do
S-15         !$omp end target
S-16      !$omp end target data
S-17      call output(p, N)   !*** UNDEFINED behavior if N<=THRESHOLD
S-18   end subroutine
```

———————————————— Fortran ————————————————

6.11 `target enter data` and `target exit data` Constructs

The structured data construct (**`target data`**) provides persistent data on a device for subsequent **`target`** constructs as shown in the **`target data`** examples above. This is accomplished by creating a single **`target data`** region containing **`target`** constructs.

The unstructured data constructs allow the creation and deletion of data on the device at any appropriate point within the host code, as shown below with the **`target enter data`** and **`target exit data`** constructs.

The following C++ code creates/deletes a vector in a constructor/destructor of a class. The constructor creates a vector with **`target enter data`** and uses an **`alloc`** modifier in the **`map`** clause to avoid copying values to the device. The destructor deletes the data (**`target exit data`**) and uses the **`delete`** modifier in the **`map`** clause to avoid copying data back to the host. Note, the stand-alone **`target enter data`** occurs after the host vector is created, and the **`target exit data`** construct occurs before the host data is deleted.

-- C++ --

Example target_unstructured_data.1.cpp (**`omp_4.5`**)

```
class Matrix
{

  Matrix(int n) {
    len = n;
    v = new double[len];
    #pragma omp target enter data map(alloc:v[0:len])
  }

  ~Matrix() {
    // NOTE: delete map type should be used, since the corresponding
    // host data will cease to exist after the deconstructor is called.

    #pragma omp target exit data map(delete:v[0:len])
    delete[] v;
  }

  private:
  double* v;
  int len;

};
```

-- C++ --

The following C code allocates and frees the data member of a Matrix structure. The **init_matrix** function allocates the memory used in the structure and uses the **target enter data** directive to map it to the target device. The **free_matrix** function removes the mapped array from the target device and then frees the memory on the host. Note, the stand-alone **target enter data** occurs after the host memory is allocated, and the **target exit data** construct occurs before the host data is freed.

─────────────────────────── C / C++ ───────────────────────────

Example target_unstructured_data.1.c (**omp_4.5**)

```
S-1    #include <stdlib.h>
S-2    typedef struct {
S-3      double *A;
S-4      int N;
S-5    } Matrix;
S-6
S-7    void init_matrix(Matrix *mat, int n)
S-8    {
S-9      mat->A = (double *)malloc(n*sizeof(double));
S-10     mat->N = n;
S-11     #pragma omp target enter data map(alloc:mat->A[:n])
S-12   }
S-13
S-14   void free_matrix(Matrix *mat)
S-15   {
S-16     #pragma omp target exit data map(delete:mat->A[:mat->N])
S-17     mat->N = 0;
S-18     free(mat->A);
S-19     mat->A = NULL;
S-20   }
```

─────────────────────────── C / C++ ───────────────────────────

The following Fortran code allocates and deallocates a module array. The **initialize** subroutine allocates the module array and uses the **target enter data** directive to map it to the target device. The **finalize** subroutine removes the mapped array from the target device and then deallocates the array on the host. Note, the stand-alone **target enter data** occurs after the host memory is allocated, and the **target exit data** construct occurs before the host data is deallocated.

———————————————————— Fortran ————————————————————

Example target_unstructured_data.1.f90 (**omp_4.5**)

```
S-1    module example
S-2      real(8), allocatable :: A(:)
S-3
S-4      contains
S-5        subroutine initialize(N)
S-6          integer :: N
S-7
S-8          allocate(A(N))
S-9          !$omp target enter data map(alloc:A)
S-10
S-11        end subroutine initialize
S-12
S-13        subroutine finalize()
S-14
S-15          !$omp target exit data map(delete:A)
S-16          deallocate(A)
S-17
S-18        end subroutine finalize
S-19    end module example
```

———————————————————— Fortran ————————————————————

6.12 `target update` Construct

6.12.1 Simple `target data` and `target update` Constructs

The following example shows how the **target update** construct updates variables in a device data environment.

The **target data** construct maps array sections *v1[:N]* and *v2[:N]* (arrays *v1* and *v2* in the Fortran code) into a device data environment.

The task executing on the host device encounters the first **target** region and waits for the completion of the region.

After the execution of the first **target** region, the task executing on the host device then assigns new values to *v1[:N]* and *v2[:N]* (*v1* and *v2* arrays in Fortran code) in the task's data environment by calling the function **init_again()**.

The **target update** construct assigns the new values of *v1* and *v2* from the task's data environment to the corresponding mapped array sections in the device data environment of the **target data** construct.

The task executing on the host device then encounters the second **target** region and waits for the completion of the region.

The second **target** region uses the updated values of *v1[:N]* and *v2[:N]*.

---------------------------------- C / C++ ----------------------------------

Example target_update.1.c (**omp_4.0**)

```
S-1    extern void init(float *, float *, int);
S-2    extern void init_again(float *, float *, int);
S-3    extern void output(float *, int);
S-4    void vec_mult(float *p, float *v1, float *v2, int N)
S-5    {
S-6       int i;
S-7       init(v1, v2, N);
S-8       #pragma omp target data map(to: v1[:N], v2[:N]) map(from: p[0:N])
S-9       {
S-10         #pragma omp target
S-11         #pragma omp parallel for
S-12         for (i=0; i<N; i++)
S-13           p[i] = v1[i] * v2[i];
S-14         init_again(v1, v2, N);
S-15         #pragma omp target update to(v1[:N], v2[:N])
S-16         #pragma omp target
S-17         #pragma omp parallel for
S-18         for (i=0; i<N; i++)
```

```
S-19                p[i] = p[i] + (v1[i] * v2[i]);
S-20            }
S-21        output(p, N);
S-22    }
```

———————————————————— C / C++ ————————————————————
———————————————————— Fortran ————————————————————

1   *Example target_update.1.f90* (**omp_4.0**)

```
S-1     subroutine vec_mult(p, v1, v2, N)
S-2        real    ::  p(N), v1(N), v2(N)
S-3        integer ::  i
S-4        call init(v1, v2, N)
S-5        !$omp target data map(to: v1, v2) map(from: p)
S-6           !$omp target
S-7           !$omp parallel do
S-8              do i=1,N
S-9                  p(i) = v1(i) * v2(i)
S-10             end do
S-11          !$omp end target
S-12          call init_again(v1, v2, N)
S-13          !$omp target update to(v1, v2)
S-14          !$omp target
S-15          !$omp parallel do
S-16             do i=1,N
S-17                 p(i) = p(i) + v1(i) * v2(i)
S-18             end do
S-19          !$omp end target
S-20       !$omp end target data
S-21       call output(p, N)
S-22    end subroutine
```

———————————————————— Fortran ————————————————————

6.12.2 `target update` Construct with `if` Clause

The following example shows how the **target update** construct updates variables in a device data environment.

The **target data** construct maps array sections *v1[:N]* and *v2[:N]* (arrays *v1* and *v2* in the Fortran code) into a device data environment. In between the two **target** regions, the task executing on the host device conditionally assigns new values to *v1* and *v2* in the task's data environment. The function **maybe_init_again()** returns *true* if new data is written.

When the conditional expression (the return value of **maybe_init_again()**) in the **if** clause is *true*, the **target update** construct assigns the new values of *v1* and *v2* from the task's data environment to the corresponding mapped array sections in the **target data** construct's device data environment.

─────────────── C / C++ ───────────────

Example target_update.2.c (**omp_4.0**)

```
S-1   extern void init(float *, float *, int);
S-2   extern int maybe_init_again(float *, int);
S-3   extern void output(float *, int);
S-4   void vec_mult(float *p, float *v1, float *v2, int N)
S-5   {
S-6      int i;
S-7      init(v1, v2, N);
S-8      #pragma omp target data map(to: v1[:N], v2[:N]) map(from: p[0:N])
S-9      {
S-10        int changed;
S-11        #pragma omp target
S-12        #pragma omp parallel for
S-13        for (i=0; i<N; i++)
S-14          p[i] = v1[i] * v2[i];
S-15        changed = maybe_init_again(v1,  N);
S-16        #pragma omp target update if (changed) to(v1[:N])
S-17        changed = maybe_init_again(v2,  N);
S-18        #pragma omp target update if (changed) to(v2[:N])
S-19        #pragma omp target
S-20        #pragma omp parallel for
S-21        for (i=0; i<N; i++)
S-22          p[i] = p[i] + (v1[i] * v2[i]);
S-23      }
S-24      output(p, N);
S-25   }
```

─────────────── C / C++ ───────────────

1   *Example target_update.2.f90* (**omp_4.0**)

```fortran
S-1     subroutine vec_mult(p, v1, v2, N)
S-2        interface
S-3           logical function maybe_init_again (v1, N)
S-4           real :: v1(N)
S-5           integer :: N
S-6           end function
S-7        end interface
S-8        real    ::  p(N), v1(N), v2(N)
S-9        integer :: i
S-10       logical :: changed
S-11       call init(v1, v2, N)
S-12       !$omp target data map(to: v1, v2) map(from: p)
S-13          !$omp target
S-14             !$omp parallel do
S-15             do i=1, N
S-16                p(i) = v1(i) * v2(i)
S-17             end do
S-18          !$omp end target
S-19          changed = maybe_init_again(v1, N)
S-20          !$omp target update if(changed) to(v1(:N))
S-21          changed = maybe_init_again(v2, N)
S-22          !$omp target update if(changed) to(v2(:N))
S-23          !$omp target
S-24             !$omp parallel do
S-25             do i=1, N
S-26                p(i) = p(i) + v1(i) * v2(i)
S-27             end do
S-28          !$omp end target
S-29       !$omp end target data
S-30       call output(p, N)
S-31    end subroutine
```

6.13 Declare Target Directive

6.13.1 Declare Target Directive for a Procedure

The following example shows how the declare target directive is used to indicate that the corresponding call inside a **target** region is to a **fib** function that can execute on the default target device.

A version of the function is also available on the host device. When the **if** clause conditional expression on the **target** construct evaluates to *false*, the **target** region (thus **fib**) will execute on the host device.

For the following C/C++ code the declaration of the function **fib** appears between the **begin declare target** and **end declare target** directives. In the corresponding Fortran code, the **declare target** directive appears at the end of the specification part of the subroutine.

─────────────────────── C / C++ ───────────────────────

Example declare_target.1.c (**omp_5.1**)

```
#pragma omp begin declare target
extern void fib(int N);
#pragma omp end declare target

#define THRESHOLD 1000000
void fib_wrapper(int n)
{
   #pragma omp target if(n > THRESHOLD)
   {
      fib(n);
   }
}
```

─────────────────────── C / C++ ───────────────────────

The Fortran **fib** subroutine contains a **declare target** declaration to indicate to the compiler to create an device executable version of the procedure. The subroutine name has not been included on the **declare target** directive and is, therefore, implicitly assumed.

The program uses the **module_fib** module, which presents an explicit interface to the compiler with the **declare target** declarations for processing the **fib** call.

1   *Example declare_target.1.f90* (**omp_4.0**)

```
S-1     module module_fib
S-2     contains
S-3       subroutine fib(N)
S-4         integer :: N
S-5         !$omp declare target
S-6         !...
S-7       end subroutine
S-8     end module
S-9     module params
S-10    integer :: THRESHOLD=1000000
S-11    end module
S-12    program my_fib
S-13    use params
S-14    use module_fib
S-15      !$omp target if( N > THRESHOLD )
S-16        call fib(N)
S-17      !$omp end target
S-18    end program
```

2   The next Fortran example shows the use of an external subroutine. As the subroutine is neither use
3   associated nor an internal procedure, the **declare target** declarations within a external
4   subroutine are unknown to the main program unit; therefore, a **declare target** must be
5   provided within the program scope for the compiler to determine that a target binary should be
6   available.

7   *Example declare_target.2.f90* (**omp_4.0**)

```
S-1     program my_fib
S-2     integer :: N = 8
S-3     interface
S-4       subroutine fib(N)
S-5         !$omp declare target
S-6         integer :: N
S-7       end subroutine fib
S-8     end interface
S-9       !$omp target
S-10        call fib(N)
S-11      !$omp end target
S-12    end program
S-13    subroutine fib(N)
S-14    integer :: N
S-15    !$omp declare target
```

```
S-16        print*,"hello from fib"
S-17        !...
S-18    end subroutine
```

───────────────────────────── Fortran ─────────────────────────────

6.13.2 Declare Target Directive for Class Type

The following example shows the use of the **begin declare target** and
end declare target pair to designate the beginning and end of the affected declarations, as
introduced in OpenMP 5.1. The **begin declare target** directive was defined to
symmetrically complement the terminating ("end") directive.

───────────────────────────── C++ ─────────────────────────────

The example also shows 3 different ways to use a declare target directive for a class and an external
member-function definition (for the *XOR1*, *XOR2*, and *XOR3* classes and definitions for their
corresponding *foo* member functions).

For *XOR1*, a **begin declare target** and **end declare target** directive enclose both the
class and its member function definition. The compiler immediately knows to create a device
version of the function for execution in a **target** region.

For *XOR2*, the class member function definition is not specified with a declare target directive. An
implicit declare target is created for the member function definition. The same applies if this
declaration arrangement for the class and function are included through a header file.

For *XOR3*, the class and its member function are not enclosed by **begin declare target** and
end declare target directives, but there is an implicit declare target since the class, its
function and the **target** construct are in the same file scope. That is, the class and its function are
treated as if delimited by a declare target directive. The same applies if the class and function are
included through a header file.

Example declare_target.2a.cpp (**omp_5.1**)

```
S-1    #include <iostream>
S-2    using namespace std;
S-3
S-4      #pragma omp begin declare target // declare target--class and function
S-5      class XOR1
S-6      {
S-7         int a;
S-8       public:
S-9         XOR1(int arg): a(arg) {};
S-10        int foo();
S-11     }
S-12     int XOR1::foo() { return a^0x01; }
S-13     #pragma omp end declare target
```

```
S-14
S-15      #pragma omp begin declare target // declare target--class, not function
S-16      class XOR2
S-17      {
S-18          int a;
S-19        public:
S-20          XOR2(int arg): a(arg) {};
S-21          int foo();
S-22      };
S-23      #pragma omp end declare target
S-24
S-25      int XOR2::foo() { return a^0x01;}
S-26
S-27      class XOR3                    // declare target--neither class nor function
S-28      {
S-29          int a;
S-30        public:
S-31          XOR3(int arg): a(arg) {};
S-32          int foo();
S-33      };
S-34      int XOR3::foo() { return a^0x01;}
S-35
S-36   int main (){
S-37
S-38      XOR1 my_XOR1(3);
S-39      XOR2 my_XOR2(3);
S-40      XOR3 my_XOR3(3);
S-41      int res1, res2, res3;
S-42
S-43      #pragma omp target map(tofrom:res1)
S-44      res1=my_XOR1.foo();
S-45
S-46      #pragma omp target map(tofrom:res2)
S-47      res2=my_XOR2.foo();
S-48
S-49      #pragma omp target map(tofrom:res3)
S-50      res3=my_XOR3.foo();
S-51
S-52      cout << res1 << endl;   // OUT1: 2
S-53      cout << res2 << endl;   // OUT2: 2
S-54      cout << res3 << endl;   // OUT3: 2
S-55   }
```

1   Often class definitions and their function definitions are included in separate files, as shown in
2   *declare_target.2b_classes.hpp* and *declare_target.2b_functions.cpp* below. In this case, it is

1   necessary to specify in a declare target directive for the classes. However, as long as the
2   *2b_functions.cpp* file includes the corresponding declare target classes, there is no need to specify
3   the functions with a declare target directive. The functions are treated as if they are specified with a
4   declare target directive. Compiling the *declare_target.2b_functions.cpp* and
5   *declare_target.2b_main.cpp* files separately and linking them, will create appropriate executable
6   device functions for the target device.

7   *Example declare_target.2b_classes.hpp* (**omp_5.1**)

```
S-1   #pragma omp begin declare target
S-2   class XOR1
S-3   {
S-4       int a;
S-5     public:
S-6       XOR1(int arg): a(arg) {};
S-7       int foo();
S-8   };
S-9   #pragma omp end declare target
```

8   *Example declare_target.2b_functions.cpp* (**omp_5.1**)

```
S-1   #include "classes.hpp"
S-2   int XOR1::foo() { return a^0x01; }
```

9   *Example declare_target.2b_main.cpp* (**omp_5.1**)

```
S-1   #include <iostream>
S-2   using namespace std;
S-3
S-4   #include "classes.hpp"
S-5
S-6   int main (){
S-7
S-8       XOR1 my_XOR1(3);
S-9       int res1;
S-10
S-11      #pragma omp target map(from: res1)
S-12      res1=my_XOR1.foo();
S-13
S-14      cout << res1 << endl;   // OUT1: 2
S-15  }
```

10 The following example shows how the **begin declare target** and **end declare target**
11 directives are used to enclose the declaration of a variable *varY* with a class type **typeY**.

12 This example shows pre-OpenMP 5.0 behavior for the *varY.foo()* function call (an error). The

member function **typeY::foo()** cannot be accessed on a target device because its declaration does not appear between **begin declare target** and **end declare target** directives. As of OpenMP 5.0, the function is implicitly declared with a declare target directive and will successfully execute the function on the device. See previous examples.

Example declare_target.2c.cpp (**omp_5.1**)

```
S-1     struct typeX
S-2     {
S-3        int a;
S-4     };
S-5     class typeY
S-6     {
S-7        int a;
S-8      public:
S-9        int foo() { return a^0x01; }
S-10    };
S-11
S-12    #pragma omp begin declare target
S-13       struct typeX varX;   // ok
S-14       class typeY varY; // ok if varY.foo() not called on target device
S-15    #pragma omp end declare target
S-16
S-17    void foo()
S-18    {
S-19       #pragma omp target
S-20       {
S-21          varX.a = 100;  // ok
S-22          varY.foo(); // error foo() is not available on a target device
S-23       }
S-24    }
```

C++

6.13.3 Declare Target Directive for Variables

The following examples show how the declare target directive is used to indicate that global variables are mapped to the implicit device data environment of each target device.

In the following example, the declarations of the variables *p*, *v1*, and *v2* appear between **begin declare target** and **end declare target** directives indicating that the variables are mapped to the implicit device data environment of each target device. The **target update** directive is then used to manage the consistency of the variables *p*, *v1*, and *v2* between the data environment of the encountering host device task and the implicit device data environment of the default target device.

1   *Example declare_target.3.c* (`omp_5.1`)

```
S-1    #define N 1000
S-2
S-3    #pragma omp begin declare target
S-4    float p[N], v1[N], v2[N];
S-5    #pragma omp end declare target
S-6
S-7    extern void init(float *, float *, int);
S-8    extern void output(float *, int);
S-9
S-10   void vec_mult()
S-11   {
S-12      int i;
S-13      init(v1, v2, N);
S-14      #pragma omp target update to(v1, v2)
S-15      #pragma omp target
S-16      #pragma omp parallel for
S-17      for (i=0; i<N; i++)
S-18        p[i] = v1[i] * v2[i];
S-19      #pragma omp target update from(p)
S-20      output(p, N);
S-21   }
```

2   The Fortran version of the above C code uses a different syntax. Fortran modules use a list syntax
3   on the **declare target** directive to declare mapped variables.

4   *Example declare_target.3.f90* (`omp_4.0`)

```
S-1    module my_arrays
S-2    !$omp declare target (N, p, v1, v2)
S-3    integer, parameter :: N=1000
S-4    real               :: p(N), v1(N), v2(N)
S-5    end module
S-6    subroutine vec_mult()
S-7    use my_arrays
S-8       integer :: i
S-9       call init(v1, v2, N);
S-10      !$omp target update to(v1, v2)
S-11      !$omp target
S-12      !$omp parallel do
S-13      do i = 1,N
S-14        p(i) = v1(i) * v2(i)
S-15      end do
```

```
S-16         !$omp end target
S-17         !$omp target update from (p)
S-18         call output(p, N)
S-19     end subroutine
```

──────────────────────────── Fortran ────────────────────────────

1 The following example also indicates that the function *Pfun( )* is available on the target device, as
2 well as the variable *Q*, which is mapped to the implicit device data environment of each target
3 device. The **target update** directive is then used to manage the consistency of the variable *Q*
4 between the data environment of the encountering host device task and the implicit device data
5 environment of the default target device.

6 In the following example, the function and variable declarations appear between the
7 **begin declare target** and **end declare target** directives.

──────────────────────────── C / C++ ────────────────────────────

8 *Example declare_target.4.c* (**omp_5.1**)

```
S-1      #define N 10000
S-2
S-3      #pragma omp begin declare target
S-4        float Q[N][N];
S-5        float Pfun(const int i, const int k) { return Q[i][k] * Q[k][i]; }
S-6      #pragma omp end declare target
S-7
S-8      float accum(int k)
S-9      {
S-10         float tmp = 0.0;
S-11         #pragma omp target update to(Q)
S-12         #pragma omp target map(tofrom: tmp)
S-13         #pragma omp parallel for reduction(+:tmp)
S-14         for(int i=0; i < N; i++)
S-15             tmp += Pfun(i,k);
S-16         return tmp;
S-17      }
S-18
S-19      /* Note:   The variable tmp is now mapped with tofrom, for correct
S-20                 execution with 4.5 (and pre-4.5) compliant compilers.
S-21                 See Devices Intro.
S-22      */
```

──────────────────────────── C / C++ ────────────────────────────

9   The Fortran version of the above C code uses a different syntax. In Fortran modules a list syntax on
10 the **declare target** directive is used to declare mapped variables and procedures. The *N* and *Q*
11 variables are declared as a comma separated list. When the **declare target** directive is used to
12 declare just the procedure, the procedure name need not be listed – it is implicitly assumed, as
13 illustrated in the *Pfun( )* function.

1   *Example declare_target.4.f90* (**omp_4.0**)

```fortran
S-1     module my_global_array
S-2     !$omp declare target (N,Q)
S-3     integer, parameter :: N=10
S-4     real              :: Q(N,N)
S-5     contains
S-6     function Pfun(i,k)
S-7     !$omp declare target
S-8     real              :: Pfun
S-9     integer,intent(in) :: i,k
S-10       Pfun=(Q(i,k) * Q(k,i))
S-11    end function
S-12    end module
S-13
S-14    function accum(k) result(tmp)
S-15    use my_global_array
S-16    real    :: tmp
S-17    integer :: i, k
S-18       tmp = 0.0e0
S-19       !$omp target map(tofrom: tmp)
S-20       !$omp parallel do reduction(+:tmp)
S-21       do i=1,N
S-22          tmp = tmp + Pfun(k,i)
S-23       end do
S-24       !$omp end target
S-25    end function
S-26
S-27    ! Note:  The variable tmp is now mapped with tofrom, for correct
S-28    ! execution with 4.5 (and pre-4.5) compliant compilers. See Devices Intro.
```

2   ## 6.13.4 Declare Target Directive with `declare simd`

3   The following example shows how the **begin declare target** and **end declare target**
4   directives are used to indicate that a function is available on a target device. The **declare simd**
5   directive indicates that there is a SIMD version of the function *P()* that is available on the target
6   device as well as one that is available on the host device.

1   *Example declare_target.5.c* (**omp_5.1**)

```
S-1    #define N 10000
S-2    #define M 1024
S-3
S-4    #pragma omp begin declare target
S-5    float Q[N][N];
S-6
S-7    #pragma omp declare simd uniform(i) linear(k) notinbranch
S-8    float P(const int i, const int k)
S-9    {
S-10     return Q[i][k] * Q[k][i];
S-11   }
S-12   #pragma omp end declare target
S-13
S-14   float accum(void)
S-15   {
S-16     float tmp = 0.0;
S-17     int i, k;
S-18   #pragma omp target map(tofrom: tmp)
S-19   #pragma omp parallel for reduction(+:tmp)
S-20     for (i=0; i < N; i++) {
S-21       float tmp1 = 0.0;
S-22   #pragma omp simd reduction(+:tmp1)
S-23       for (k=0; k < M; k++) {
S-24         tmp1 += P(i,k);
S-25       }
S-26       tmp += tmp1;
S-27     }
S-28     return tmp;
S-29   }
S-30
S-31   /* Note:   The variable tmp is now mapped with tofrom, for correct
S-32             execution with 4.5 (and pre-4.5) compliant compilers.
S-33             See Devices Intro.
S-34   */
```

2   The Fortran version of the above C code uses a different syntax. Fortran modules use a list syntax
3   of the **declare target** declaration for the mapping. Here the *N* and *Q* variables are declared in
4   the list form as a comma separated list. The function declaration does not use a list and implicitly
5   assumes the function name. In this Fortran example row and column indices are reversed relative to
6   the C/C++ example, as is usual for codes optimized for memory access.

1   *Example declare_target.5.f90* (**omp_4.0**)

```fortran
S-1    module my_global_array
S-2    !$omp declare target (N,Q)
S-3    integer, parameter :: N=10000, M=1024
S-4    real              :: Q(N,N)
S-5    contains
S-6    function P(k,i)
S-7    !$omp declare simd uniform(i) linear(k) notinbranch
S-8    !$omp declare target
S-9    real             :: P
S-10   integer,intent(in) :: k,i
S-11      P=(Q(k,i) * Q(i,k))
S-12   end function
S-13   end module
S-14
S-15   function accum() result(tmp)
S-16   use my_global_array
S-17   real    :: tmp, tmp1
S-18   integer :: i
S-19      tmp = 0.0e0
S-20      !$omp target map(tofrom: tmp)
S-21      !$omp parallel do private(tmp1) reduction(+:tmp)
S-22      do i=1,N
S-23         tmp1 = 0.0e0
S-24         !$omp simd reduction(+:tmp1)
S-25         do k = 1,M
S-26            tmp1 = tmp1 + P(k,i)
S-27         end do
S-28         tmp = tmp + tmp1
S-29      end do
S-30      !$omp end target
S-31   end function
S-32
S-33   ! Note:  The variable tmp is now mapped with tofrom, for correct
S-34   ! execution with 4.5 (and pre-4.5) compliant compilers. See Devices Intro.
```

6.13.5 Declare Target Directive with `link` Clause

In the OpenMP 4.5 standard the declare target directive was extended to allow static data to be mapped, *when needed*, through a `link` clause.

Data storage for items listed in the `link` clause becomes available on the device when it is mapped implicitly or explicitly in a **map** clause, and it persists for the scope of the mapping (as specified by a **target** construct, a **target data** construct, or **target enter/exit data** constructs).

Tip: When all the global data items will not fit on a device and are not needed simultaneously, use the `link` clause and map the data only when it is needed.

The following C and Fortran examples show two sets of data (single precision and double precision) that are global on the host for the entire execution on the host; but are only used globally on the device for part of the program execution. The single precision data are allocated and persist only for the first **target** region. Similarly, the double precision data are in scope on the device only for the second **target** region.

------------------------------ C / C++ ------------------------------

Example declare_target.6.c (`omp_5.1`)

```
S-1    #define N 100000000
S-2
S-3    float   sp[N], sv1[N], sv2[N];
S-4    double dp[N], dv1[N], dv2[N];
S-5    #pragma omp declare target link(sp,sv1,sv2) \
S-6                               link(dp,dv1,dv2)
S-7
S-8    void s_init(float *, float *, int);
S-9    void d_init(double *, double *, int);
S-10   void s_output(float *, int);
S-11   void d_output(double *, int);
S-12
S-13   #pragma omp begin declare target
S-14
S-15   void s_vec_mult_accum()
S-16   {
S-17      int i;
S-18
S-19      #pragma omp parallel for
S-20      for (i=0; i<N; i++)
S-21        sp[i] = sv1[i] * sv2[i];
S-22   }
S-23
S-24   void d_vec_mult_accum()
S-25   {
S-26      int i;
S-27
```

```
S-28        #pragma omp parallel for
S-29        for (i=0; i<N; i++)
S-30          dp[i] = dv1[i] * dv2[i];
S-31     }
S-32     #pragma omp end declare target
S-33
S-34     int main()
S-35     {
S-36        s_init(sv1, sv2, N);
S-37        #pragma omp target map(to:sv1,sv2) map(from:sp)
S-38          s_vec_mult_accum();
S-39        s_output(sp, N);
S-40
S-41        d_init(dv1, dv2, N);
S-42        #pragma omp target map(to:dv1,dv2) map(from:dp)
S-43          d_vec_mult_accum();
S-44        d_output(dp, N);
S-45
S-46      return 0;
S-47     }
```

───────────────────── C / C++ ─────────────────────
───────────────────── Fortran ─────────────────────

1   *Example declare_target.6.f90* (omp_4.5)

```
S-1      module m_dat
S-2         integer, parameter :: N=100000000
S-3         !$omp declare target link(sp,sv1,sv2)
S-4         real :: sp(N), sv1(N), sv2(N)
S-5
S-6         !$omp declare target link(dp,dv1,dv2)
S-7         double precision :: dp(N), dv1(N), dv2(N)
S-8
S-9      contains
S-10        subroutine s_vec_mult_accum()
S-11        !$omp declare target
S-12           integer :: i
S-13
S-14           !$omp parallel do
S-15           do i = 1,N
S-16             sp(i) = sv1(i) * sv2(i)
S-17           end do
S-18
S-19        end subroutine s_vec_mult_accum
S-20
S-21        subroutine d_vec_mult_accum()
S-22        !$omp declare target
```

```
S-23          integer :: i
S-24
S-25          !$omp parallel do
S-26          do i = 1,N
S-27            dp(i) = dv1(i) * dv2(i)
S-28          end do
S-29
S-30       end subroutine
S-31    end module m_dat
S-32
S-33    program prec_vec_mult
S-34       use m_dat
S-35
S-36       call s_init(sv1, sv2, N)
S-37       !$omp target map(to:sv1,sv2) map(from:sp)
S-38         call s_vec_mult_accum()
S-39       !$omp end target
S-40       call s_output(sp, N)
S-41
S-42       call d_init(dv1, dv2, N)
S-43       !$omp target map(to:dv1,dv2) map(from:dp)
S-44         call d_vec_mult_accum()
S-45       !$omp end target
S-46       call d_output(dp, N)
S-47
S-48    end program
```

———————————————————— Fortran ————————————————————

6.14 Lambda Expressions

--------------------------------- C++ ----------------------------------

The following example illustrates the usage of lambda expressions and their corresponding closure objects within a **target** region.

In CASE 1, a lambda expression is defined inside a **target** construct that implicitly maps the structure *s*. Inside the construct, the lambda captures (by reference) the corresponding *s*, and the resulting closure object is assigned to *lambda1*. When the call operator is invoked on *lambda1*, the captured reference to *s* is used in the call. The modified *s* is then copied back to the host device on exit from the **target** construct.

In CASE 2, a lambda expression is instead defined before the **target** construct and captures (by copy) the pointer *sp*. A **target data** construct is used to first map the structure, and then the **target** construct implicitly maps the closure object referenced by *lambda2*, a zero-length array section based on the structure pointer *sp*, and a zero-length array section based on the captured pointer in the closure object. The implicit maps result in attached pointers to the corresponding structure. The call for *lambda2* inside the **target** construct will access *sp->a* and *sp->b* from the corresponding structure.

CASE 3 is similar to CASE 2, except *s* is instead captured by reference by the lambda expression. As for CASE 2, the structure is first mapped by an enclosing **target data** construct, and then the **target** construct implicitly maps *s* and the closure object referenced by *lambda3*. The effect of the map is to make the the call for *lambda3* refer to the corresponding *s* inside the **target** construct rather than the original *s*.

In CASE 4, the program defines a static variable *ss* of the same structure type as *s*. While the body of the lambda expression refers to *ss*, it is not captured. In order for *lambda4* to be callable in the **target** region, the reference to *ss* should be to a device copy of *ss* that also has static storage. This is achieved with the use of the **declare target** directive. Inside the **target** construct, all references to *ss*, including in the *lambda4()* call, will refer to the corresponding *ss* that results from the **declare target** directive. The **always** modifier is used on the **map** clause to transfer the updated values for the structure back to the host device.

Example lambda_expressions.1.cpp (**omp_5.0**)

```
S-1     #include <iostream>
S-2     using namespace std;
S-3
S-4     struct S { int a; int b; };
S-5
S-6     int main()
S-7     {
S-8
S-9     // CASE 1 Lambda defined in target region
S-10
S-11        S s = S {0,1};
```

```
S-12
S-13        #pragma omp target
S-14        {
S-15           auto lambda1 = [&s]() { s.a = s.b * 2; };
S-16           s.b += 2;
S-17           lambda1(); // s.a = 3 * 2
S-18        }
S-19        cout << s.a << " " << s.b << endl; //OUT 6 3
S-20
S-21    // CASE 2 Host defined lambda, Capture pointer to s
S-22
S-23        s = {0,1};
S-24        S *sp = &s;
S-25        auto lambda2 = [sp]() {sp->a = sp->b * 2; };
S-26
S-27        // closure object's sp attaches to corresponding s on target
S-28        // construct
S-29        #pragma omp target data map(sp[0])
S-30        #pragma omp target
S-31        {
S-32           sp->b += 2;
S-33           lambda2();
S-34        }
S-35        cout << s.a << " " << s.b << endl; //OUT 6 3
S-36
S-37    // CASE 3 Host defined lambda, Capture s by reference
S-38
S-39        s = {0,1};
S-40        auto lambda3 = [&s]() {s.a = s.b * 2; };
S-41
S-42        // closure object's s refers to corresponding s in target
S-43        // construct
S-44        #pragma omp target data map(s)
S-45        #pragma omp target
S-46        {
S-47           s.b += 2;
S-48           lambda3();
S-49        }
S-50        cout << s.a << " " << s.b << endl; //OUT 6 3
S-51
S-52    // CASE 4 Host defined lambda, references static variable
S-53
S-54        static S ss = {0,1};
S-55        #pragma omp declare target enter(ss)
S-56        auto lambda4 = [&]() {ss.a = ss.b * 2; };
S-57
S-58        #pragma omp target map(always,from:ss)
```

```
S-59          {
S-60              ss.b += 2;
S-61              lambda4();
S-62          }
S-63          cout << ss.a << " " << ss.b << endl; //OUT 6 3
S-64
S-65          return 0;
S-66      }
```

———————————————————————— C++ ————————————————————————

6.15 `teams` Construct and Related Combined Constructs

6.15.1 `target` and `teams` Constructs with `omp_get_num_teams` and `omp_get_team_num` Routines

The following example shows how the **target** and **teams** constructs are used to create a league of thread teams that execute a region. The **teams** construct creates a league of at most two teams where the primary thread of each team executes the **teams** region.

The **omp_get_num_teams** routine returns the number of teams executing in a **teams** region. The **omp_get_team_num** routine returns the team number, which is an integer between 0 and one less than the value returned by **omp_get_num_teams**. The following example manually distributes a loop across two teams.

--------- C / C++ ---------

Example teams.1.c (`omp_4.0`)

```
S-1    #include <stdlib.h>
S-2    #include <omp.h>
S-3    float dotprod(float B[], float C[], int N)
S-4    {
S-5       float sum0 = 0.0;
S-6       float sum1 = 0.0;
S-7       #pragma omp target map(to: B[:N], C[:N]) map(tofrom: sum0, sum1)
S-8       #pragma omp teams num_teams(2)
S-9       {
S-10         int i;
S-11         if (omp_get_num_teams() != 2)
S-12            abort();
S-13         if (omp_get_team_num() == 0)
S-14         {
S-15            #pragma omp parallel for reduction(+:sum0)
S-16            for (i=0; i<N/2; i++)
S-17               sum0 += B[i] * C[i];
S-18         }
S-19         else if (omp_get_team_num() == 1)
S-20         {
S-21            #pragma omp parallel for reduction(+:sum1)
S-22            for (i=N/2; i<N; i++)
S-23               sum1 += B[i] * C[i];
S-24         }
S-25      }
S-26      return sum0 + sum1;
S-27   }
S-28
```

```
S-29       /* Note:   The variables sum0,sum1 are now mapped with tofrom, for
S-30                  correct execution with 4.5 (and pre-4.5) compliant compilers.
S-31                  See Devices Intro.
S-32       */
```

───────────────────────────── C / C++ ─────────────────────────────
───────────────────────────── Fortran ─────────────────────────────

1   *Example teams.1.f90* (**omp_4.0**)

```
S-1        function dotprod(B,C,N) result(sum)
S-2        use omp_lib, ONLY : omp_get_num_teams, omp_get_team_num
S-3            real     :: B(N), C(N), sum,sum0, sum1
S-4            integer :: N, i
S-5            sum0 = 0.0e0
S-6            sum1 = 0.0e0
S-7            !$omp target map(to: B, C) map(tofrom: sum0, sum1)
S-8            !$omp teams num_teams(2)
S-9              if (omp_get_num_teams() /= 2) stop "2 teams required"
S-10             if (omp_get_team_num() == 0) then
S-11                !$omp parallel do reduction(+:sum0)
S-12                do i=1,N/2
S-13                   sum0 = sum0 + B(i) * C(i)
S-14                end do
S-15             else if (omp_get_team_num() == 1) then
S-16                !$omp parallel do reduction(+:sum1)
S-17                do i=N/2+1,N
S-18                   sum1 = sum1 + B(i) * C(i)
S-19                end do
S-20             end if
S-21           !$omp end teams
S-22           !$omp end target
S-23           sum = sum0 + sum1
S-24       end function
S-25
S-26       ! Note:   The variables sum0,sum1 are now mapped with tofrom, for correct
S-27       ! execution with 4.5 (and pre-4.5) compliant compilers. See Devices Intro.
```
───────────────────────────── Fortran ─────────────────────────────

6.15.2 `target`, `teams`, and `distribute` Constructs

The following example shows how the **target**, **teams**, and **distribute** constructs are used to execute a loop nest in a **target** region. The **teams** construct creates a league and the primary thread of each team executes the **teams** region. The **distribute** construct schedules the subsequent loop iterations across the primary threads of each team.

The number of teams in the league is less than or equal to the variable *num_blocks*. Each team in the league has a number of threads less than or equal to the variable *block_threads*. The iterations in the outer loop are distributed among the primary threads of each team.

When a team's primary thread encounters the parallel loop construct before the inner loop, the other threads in its team are activated. The team executes the **parallel** region and then workshares the execution of the loop.

Each primary thread executing the **teams** region has a private copy of the variable *sum* that is created by the **reduction** clause on the **teams** construct. The primary thread and all threads in its team have a private copy of the variable *sum* that is created by the **reduction** clause on the parallel loop construct. The second private *sum* is reduced into the primary thread's private copy of *sum* created by the **teams** construct. At the end of the **teams** region, each primary thread's private copy of *sum* is reduced into the final *sum* that is implicitly mapped into the **target** region.

─────────────────────────── C / C++ ───────────────────────────

Example teams.2.c (`omp_4.0`)

```
#define min(x, y) (((x) < (y)) ? (x) : (y))

float dotprod(float B[], float C[], int N, int block_size,
  int num_teams, int block_threads)
{
    float sum = 0.0;
    int i, i0;
    #pragma omp target map(to: B[0:N], C[0:N]) map(tofrom: sum)
    #pragma omp teams num_teams(num_teams) thread_limit(block_threads) \
        reduction(+:sum)
    #pragma omp distribute
    for (i0=0; i0<N; i0 += block_size)
        #pragma omp parallel for reduction(+:sum)
        for (i=i0; i< min(i0+block_size,N); i++)
            sum += B[i] * C[i];
    return sum;
}
/* Note:  The variable sum is now mapped with tofrom, for correct
   execution with 4.5 (and pre-4.5) compliant compilers. See
   Devices Intro.
 */
```

─────────────────────────── C / C++ ───────────────────────────

1   *Example teams.2.f90* (**omp_4.0**)

```
S-1    function dotprod(B,C,N, block_size, num_teams, block_threads) result(sum)
S-2    implicit none
S-3        real    :: B(N), C(N), sum
S-4        integer :: N, block_size, num_teams, block_threads, i, i0
S-5        sum = 0.0e0
S-6    !$omp target map(to: B, C) map(tofrom: sum)
S-7    !$omp teams num_teams(num_teams) thread_limit(block_threads) &
S-8    !$omp&   reduction(+:sum)
S-9    !$omp distribute
S-10       do i0=1,N, block_size
S-11          !$omp parallel do reduction(+:sum)
S-12          do i = i0, min(i0+block_size,N)
S-13             sum = sum + B(i) * C(i)
S-14          end do
S-15       end do
S-16    !$omp end teams
S-17    !$omp end target
S-18    end function
S-19
S-20    ! Note:   The variable sum is now mapped with tofrom, for correct
S-21    ! execution with 4.5 (and pre-4.5) compliant compilers. See Devices Intro.
```

6.15.3 `target teams`, and Distribute Parallel Loop Constructs

The following example shows how the **target teams** and distribute parallel loop constructs are used to execute a **target** region. The **target teams** construct creates a league of teams where the primary thread of each team executes the **teams** region.

The distribute parallel loop construct schedules the loop iterations across the primary threads of each team and then across the threads of each team.

1   *Example teams.3.c* (`omp_4.5`)

```
S-1    float dotprod(float B[], float C[], int N)
S-2    {
S-3       float sum = 0;
S-4       int i;
S-5       #pragma omp target teams map(to: B[0:N], C[0:N]) \
S-6                              defaultmap(tofrom:scalar) reduction(+:sum)
S-7       #pragma omp distribute parallel for reduction(+:sum)
S-8       for (i=0; i<N; i++)
S-9          sum += B[i] * C[i];
S-10      return sum;
S-11   }
S-12
S-13   /* Note:   The variable sum is now mapped with tofrom from the defaultmap
S-14             clause on the combined target teams construct, for correct
S-15             execution with 4.5 (and pre-4.5) compliant compilers.
S-16             See Devices Intro.
S-17    */
```

2   *Example teams.3.f90* (`omp_4.5`)

```
S-1    function dotprod(B,C,N) result(sum)
S-2       real    :: B(N), C(N), sum
S-3       integer :: N, i
S-4       sum = 0.0e0
S-5       !$omp target teams map(to: B, C)   &
S-6       !$omp&                 defaultmap(tofrom:scalar) reduction(+:sum)
S-7       !$omp distribute parallel do reduction(+:sum)
S-8          do i = 1,N
S-9             sum = sum + B(i) * C(i)
S-10         end do
S-11      !$omp end target teams
S-12   end function
S-13
S-14   ! Note:   The variable sum is now mapped with tofrom from the defaultmap
S-15   !   clause on the combined target teams construct, for correct
S-16   !   execution with 4.5 (and pre-4.5) compliant compilers. See Devices Intro.
```

6.15.4 `target teams` and Distribute Parallel Loop Constructs with Scheduling Clauses

The following example shows how the **target teams** and distribute parallel loop constructs are used to execute a **target** region. The **teams** construct creates a league of at most eight teams where the primary thread of each team executes the **teams** region. The number of threads in each team is less than or equal to 16.

The **distribute** parallel loop construct schedules the subsequent loop iterations across the primary threads of each team and then across the threads of each team.

The **dist_schedule** clause on the distribute parallel loop construct indicates that loop iterations are distributed to the primary thread of each team in chunks of 1024 iterations.

The **schedule** clause indicates that the 1024 iterations distributed to a primary thread are then assigned to the threads in its associated team in chunks of 64 iterations.

---------- C / C++ ----------

Example teams.4.c (**omp_4.0**)

```
#define N 1024*1024
float dotprod(float B[], float C[])
{
    float sum = 0.0;
    int i;
    #pragma omp target map(to: B[0:N], C[0:N]) map(tofrom: sum)
    #pragma omp teams num_teams(8) thread_limit(16) reduction(+:sum)
    #pragma omp distribute parallel for reduction(+:sum) \
                dist_schedule(static, 1024) schedule(static, 64)
    for (i=0; i<N; i++)
        sum += B[i] * C[i];
    return sum;
}

/* Note:   The variable sum is now mapped with tofrom, for correct
           execution with 4.5 (and pre-4.5) compliant compilers.
           See Devices Intro.
*/
```

---------- C / C++ ----------

1   *Example teams.4.f90* (**omp_4.0**)

```fortran
S-1     module arrays
S-2     integer,parameter :: N=1024*1024
S-3     real :: B(N), C(N)
S-4     end module
S-5     function dotprod() result(sum)
S-6     use arrays
S-7        real     :: sum
S-8        integer :: i
S-9        sum = 0.0e0
S-10       !$omp target map(to: B, C) map(tofrom: sum)
S-11       !$omp teams num_teams(8) thread_limit(16) reduction(+:sum)
S-12       !$omp distribute parallel do reduction(+:sum) &
S-13       !$omp&  dist_schedule(static, 1024) schedule(static, 64)
S-14          do i = 1,N
S-15             sum = sum + B(i) * C(i)
S-16          end do
S-17       !$omp end teams
S-18       !$omp end target
S-19    end function
S-20
S-21    ! Note:  The variable sum is now mapped with tofrom, for correct
S-22    ! execution with 4.5 (and pre-4.5) compliant compilers. See Devices Intro.
```

6.15.5 `target teams` and `distribute simd` Constructs

The following example shows how the **target teams** and **distribute simd** constructs are used to execute a loop in a **target** region. The **target teams** construct creates a league of teams where the primary thread of each team executes the **teams** region.

The **distribute simd** construct schedules the loop iterations across the primary thread of each team and then uses SIMD parallelism to execute the iterations.

C / C++

Example teams.5.c (omp_**4.0**)

```
S-1   extern void init(float *, float *, int);
S-2   extern void output(float *, int);
S-3   void vec_mult(float *p, float *v1, float *v2, int N)
S-4   {
S-5      int i;
S-6      init(v1, v2, N);
S-7      #pragma omp target teams map(to: v1[0:N], v2[:N]) map(from: p[0:N])
S-8      #pragma omp distribute simd
S-9      for (i=0; i<N; i++)
S-10        p[i] = v1[i] * v2[i];
S-11     output(p, N);
S-12  }
```

C / C++

Fortran

Example teams.5.f90 (omp_**4.0**)

```
S-1   subroutine vec_mult(p, v1, v2, N)
S-2      real     ::  p(N), v1(N), v2(N)
S-3      integer ::  i
S-4      call init(v1, v2, N)
S-5      !$omp target teams map(to: v1, v2) map(from: p)
S-6         !$omp distribute simd
S-7            do i=1,N
S-8               p(i) = v1(i) * v2(i)
S-9            end do
S-10     !$omp end target teams
S-11     call output(p, N)
S-12  end subroutine
```

Fortran

6.15.6 `target teams` and Distribute Parallel Loop SIMD Constructs

The following example shows how the **target teams** and the distribute parallel loop SIMD constructs are used to execute a loop in a **target teams** region. The **target teams** construct creates a league of teams where the primary thread of each team executes the **teams** region.

The distribute parallel loop SIMD construct schedules the loop iterations across the primary thread of each team and then across the threads of each team where each thread uses SIMD parallelism.

─────────────────── C / C++ ───────────────────

Example teams.6.c (`omp_4.0`)

```
S-1    extern void init(float *, float *, int);
S-2    extern void output(float *, int);
S-3    void vec_mult(float *p, float *v1, float *v2, int N)
S-4    {
S-5       int i;
S-6       init(v1, v2, N);
S-7       #pragma omp target teams map(to: v1[0:N], v2[:N]) map(from: p[0:N])
S-8       #pragma omp distribute parallel for simd
S-9       for (i=0; i<N; i++)
S-10        p[i] = v1[i] * v2[i];
S-11      output(p, N);
S-12   }
```

─────────────────── C / C++ ───────────────────
─────────────────── Fortran ───────────────────

Example teams.6.f90 (`omp_4.0`)

```
S-1    subroutine vec_mult(p, v1, v2, N)
S-2       real    ::  p(N), v1(N), v2(N)
S-3       integer ::  i
S-4       call init(v1, v2, N)
S-5       !$omp target teams map(to: v1, v2) map(from: p)
S-6         !$omp distribute parallel do simd
S-7           do i=1,N
S-8              p(i) = v1(i) * v2(i)
S-9           end do
S-10      !$omp end target teams
S-11      call output(p, N)
S-12   end subroutine
```

─────────────────── Fortran ───────────────────

1

2

6.16 Asynchronous `target` Execution and Dependences

3 Asynchronous execution of a **target** region can be accomplished by creating an explicit task
4 around the **target** region. Examples with explicit tasks are shown at the beginning of this section.

5 As of OpenMP 4.5 and beyond the **nowait** clause can be used on the **target** directive for
6 asynchronous execution. Examples with **nowait** clauses follow the explicit **task** examples.

7 This section also shows the use of **depend** clauses to order executions through dependences.

6.16.1 Asynchronous `target` with Tasks

9   The following example shows how the **task** and **target** constructs are used to execute multiple
10 **target** regions asynchronously. The task that encounters the **task** construct generates an
11 explicit task that contains a **target** region. The thread executing the explicit task encounters a
12 task scheduling point while waiting for the execution of the **target** region to complete, allowing
13 the thread to switch back to the execution of the encountering task or one of the previously
14 generated explicit tasks.

--------------------------------------- C / C++ ---------------------------------------

15 *Example async_target.1.c* (**omp_5.1**)

```
S-1    #pragma omp begin declare target
S-2    float F(float);
S-3    #pragma omp end declare target
S-4
S-5    #define N 1000000000
S-6    #define CHUNKSZ 1000000
S-7    void init(float *, int);
S-8    float Z[N];
S-9    void pipedF(){
S-10      int C, i;
S-11      init(Z, N);
S-12      for (C=0; C<N; C+=CHUNKSZ){
S-13         #pragma omp task shared(Z)
S-14         #pragma omp target map(Z[C:CHUNKSZ])
S-15         #pragma omp parallel for
S-16         for (i=0; i<CHUNKSZ; i++) Z[i] = F(Z[i]);
S-17      }
S-18      #pragma omp taskwait
S-19   }
```

--------------------------------------- C / C++ ---------------------------------------

The Fortran version has an interface block that contains the **declare target**. An identical statement exists in the function declaration (not shown here).

───────────────────────────── Fortran ─────────────────────────────

Example async_target.1.f90 (**omp_4.0**)

```
S-1     module parameters
S-2     integer, parameter :: N=1000000000, CHUNKSZ=1000000
S-3     end module
S-4     subroutine pipedF()
S-5     use parameters, ONLY: N, CHUNKSZ
S-6     integer          :: C, i
S-7     real             :: z(N)
S-8
S-9     interface
S-10       function F(z)
S-11       !$omp declare target
S-12         real, intent(IN) ::z
S-13         real             ::F
S-14       end function F
S-15    end interface
S-16
S-17       call init(z,N)
S-18
S-19       do C=1,N,CHUNKSZ
S-20
S-21          !$omp task shared(z)
S-22          !$omp target map(z(C:C+CHUNKSZ-1))
S-23          !$omp parallel do
S-24             do i=C,C+CHUNKSZ-1
S-25                z(i) = F(z(i))
S-26             end do
S-27          !$omp end target
S-28          !$omp end task
S-29
S-30       end do
S-31       !$omp taskwait
S-32       print*, z
S-33
S-34    end subroutine pipedF
```

───────────────────────────── Fortran ─────────────────────────────

The following example shows how the **task** and **target** constructs are used to execute multiple **target** regions asynchronously. The task dependence ensures that the storage is allocated and initialized on the device before it is accessed.

1   *Example async_target.2.c* (`omp_5.1`)

```
S-1     #include <stdlib.h>
S-2     #include <omp.h>
S-3
S-4     #pragma omp begin declare target
S-5     extern void init(float *, float *, int);
S-6     #pragma omp end declare target
S-7
S-8     extern void foo();
S-9     extern void output(float *, int);
S-10    void vec_mult(float *p, int N, int dev)
S-11    {
S-12        float *v1, *v2;
S-13        int i;
S-14        #pragma omp task shared(v1, v2) depend(out: v1, v2)
S-15        #pragma omp target device(dev) map(v1, v2)
S-16        {
S-17            // check whether on device dev
S-18            if (omp_is_initial_device())
S-19                abort();
S-20            v1 = (float *)malloc(N*sizeof(float));
S-21            v2 = (float *)malloc(N*sizeof(float));
S-22            init(v1, v2, N);
S-23        }
S-24        foo(); // execute other work asychronously
S-25        #pragma omp task shared(v1, v2, p) depend(in: v1, v2)
S-26        #pragma omp target device(dev) map(to: v1, v2) map(from: p[0:N])
S-27        {
S-28            // check whether on device dev
S-29            if (omp_is_initial_device())
S-30                abort();
S-31            #pragma omp parallel for
S-32            for (i=0; i<N; i++)
S-33                p[i] = v1[i] * v2[i];
S-34            free(v1);
S-35            free(v2);
S-36        }
S-37        #pragma omp taskwait
S-38        output(p, N);
S-39    }
```

2   The Fortran example below is similar to the C version above. Instead of pointers, though, it uses the
3   convenience of Fortran allocatable arrays on the device. In order to preserve the arrays allocated on
4   the device across multiple **target** regions, a **target data** region is used in this case.

If there is no shape specified for an allocatable array in a **map** clause, only the array descriptor (also called a dope vector) is mapped. That is, device space is created for the descriptor, and it is initially populated with host values. In this case, the *v1* and *v2* arrays will be in a non-associated state on the device. When space for *v1* and *v2* is allocated on the device in the first **target** region the addresses to the space will be included in their descriptors.

At the end of the first **target** region, the arrays *v1* and *v2* are preserved on the device for access in the second **target** region. At the end of the second **target** region, the data in array *p* is copied back, the arrays *v1* and *v2* are not.

A **depend** clause is used in the **task** directive to provide a wait at the beginning of the second **target** region, to insure that there is no race condition with *v1* and *v2* in the two tasks. It would be noncompliant to use *v1* and/or *v2* in lieu of *N* in the **depend** clauses, because the use of non-allocated allocatable arrays as list items in a **depend** clause would lead to unspecified behavior.

Note – This example is not strictly compliant with the OpenMP 4.5 specification since the allocation status of allocatable arrays *v1* and *v2* is changed inside the **target** region, which is not allowed. (See the restrictions for the **map** clause in the *Data-mapping Attribute Rules and Clauses* section of the specification.) However, the intention is to relax the restrictions on mapping of allocatable variables in the next release of the specification so that the example will be compliant.

———————————————————————— Fortran ————————————————————————

Example async_target.2.f90 (**omp_4.0**)

```
subroutine mult(p,   N, idev)
  use omp_lib, ONLY: omp_is_initial_device
  real          :: p(N)
  real,allocatable :: v1(:), v2(:)
  integer ::  i, idev
  !$omp declare target (init)

  !$omp target data map(v1,v2)

  !$omp task shared(v1,v2) depend(out: N)
    !$omp target device(idev)
      if( omp_is_initial_device() ) &
         stop "not executing on target device"
      allocate(v1(N),  v2(N))
      call init(v1,v2,N)
    !$omp end target
  !$omp end task

  call foo()   ! execute other work asychronously

  !$omp task shared(v1,v2,p) depend(in: N)
    !$omp target device(idev) map(from: p)
```

```
S-23              if( omp_is_initial_device() ) &
S-24                  stop "not executing on target device"
S-25              !$omp parallel do
S-26                do i = 1,N
S-27                    p(i) = v1(i) * v2(i)
S-28                end do
S-29              deallocate(v1,v2)
S-30
S-31          !$omp end target
S-32      !$omp end task
S-33
S-34      !$omp taskwait
S-35
S-36      !$omp end target data
S-37
S-38      call output(p, N)
S-39
S-40  end subroutine
```

──────────────── Fortran ────────────────

6.16.2 `nowait` Clause on `target` Construct

The following example shows how to execute code asynchronously on a device without an explicit task. The **nowait** clause on a **target** construct allows the thread of the *target task* to perform other work while waiting for the **target** region execution to complete. Hence, the **target** region can execute asynchronously on the device (without requiring a host thread to idle while waiting for the *target task* execution to complete).

In this example the product of two vectors (arrays), *v1* and *v2*, is formed. One half of the operations is performed on the device, and the last half on the host, concurrently.

After a team of threads is formed the primary thread generates the *target task* while the other threads can continue on, without a barrier, to the execution of the host portion of the vector product. The completion of the *target task* (asynchronous target execution) is guaranteed by the synchronization in the implicit barrier at the end of the host vector-product worksharing loop region. See the **barrier** glossary entry in the OpenMP specification for details.

The host loop scheduling is **dynamic**, to balance the host thread executions, since one thread is being used for offload generation. In the situation where little time is spent by the *target task* in setting up and tearing down the target execution, **static** scheduling may be desired.

1   *Example async_target.3.c* (**omp_5.1**)

```c
S-1    #include <stdio.h>
S-2
S-3    #define N 1000000      //N must be even
S-4    void init(int n, float *v1, float *v2);
S-5
S-6    int main(){
S-7       int   i, n=N;
S-8       int   chunk=1000;
S-9       float v1[N],v2[N],vxv[N];
S-10
S-11      init(n,  v1,v2);
S-12
S-13      #pragma omp parallel
S-14      {
S-15
S-16         #pragma omp masked
S-17         #pragma omp target teams distribute parallel for nowait \
S-18                                  map(to:  v1[0:n/2]) \
S-19                                  map(to:  v2[0:n/2]) \
S-20                                  map(from: vxv[0:n/2])
S-21         for(i=0; i<n/2; i++){ vxv[i] = v1[i]*v2[i]; }
S-22
S-23         #pragma omp for schedule(dynamic,chunk)
S-24         for(i=n/2; i<n; i++){ vxv[i] = v1[i]*v2[i]; }
S-25
S-26      }
S-27      printf(" vxv[0] vxv[n-1] %f %f\n", vxv[0], vxv[n-1]);
S-28      return 0;
S-29   }
```

2   *Example async_target.3.f90* (**omp_5.1**)

```fortran
S-1    program concurrent_async
S-2       use omp_lib
S-3       integer,parameter :: n=1000000   !!n must be even
S-4       integer           :: i, chunk=1000
S-5       real              :: v1(n),v2(n),vxv(n)
S-6
S-7       call init(n, v1,v2)
S-8
S-9       !$omp parallel
S-10
```

```
S-11          !$omp masked
S-12          !$omp target teams distribute parallel do nowait &
S-13          !$omp&                map(to: v1(1:n/2))    &
S-14          !$omp&                map(to: v2(1:n/2))    &
S-15          !$omp&                map(from: vxv(1:n/2))
S-16          do i = 1,n/2;    vxv(i) = v1(i)*v2(i); end do
S-17          !$omp end masked
S-18
S-19          !$omp do schedule(dynamic,chunk)
S-20          do i = n/2+1,n;  vxv(i) = v1(i)*v2(i); end do
S-21
S-22        !$omp end parallel
S-23
S-24        print*, " vxv(1) vxv(n) :", vxv(1), vxv(n)
S-25
S-26    end program
```

———————————————————— Fortran ————————————————————

6.16.3 Asynchronous `target` with `nowait` and `depend` Clauses

More details on dependences can be found in Section 5.3 on page 105, Task Dependences. In this example, there are three flow dependences. In the first two dependences the target task does not execute until the preceding explicit tasks have finished. These dependences are produced by arrays *v1* and *v2* with the **out** dependence type in the first two tasks, and the **in** dependence type in the target task.

The last dependence is produced by array *p* with the **out** dependence type in the target task, and the **in** dependence type in the last task. The last task does not execute until the target task finishes.

The **nowait** clause on the **target** construct creates a deferrable *target task*, allowing the encountering task to continue execution without waiting for the completion of the *target task*.

———————————————————— C / C++ ————————————————————

Example async_target.4.c (**omp_4.5**)

```
S-1
S-2     extern void init(  float*, int);
S-3     extern void output(float*, int);
S-4
S-5     void vec_mult(int N)
S-6     {
S-7        int i;
S-8        float p[N], v1[N], v2[N];
S-9
```

```
S-10        #pragma omp parallel num_threads(2)
S-11        {
S-12          #pragma omp single
S-13          {
S-14            #pragma omp task depend(out:v1)
S-15            init(v1, N);
S-16
S-17            #pragma omp task depend(out:v2)
S-18            init(v2, N);
S-19
S-20            #pragma omp target nowait depend(in:v1,v2) depend(out:p) \
S-21                                  map(to:v1,v2) map( from: p)
S-22            #pragma omp parallel for private(i)
S-23            for (i=0; i<N; i++)
S-24              p[i] = v1[i] * v2[i];
S-25
S-26            #pragma omp task depend(in:p)
S-27            output(p, N);
S-28          }
S-29        }
S-30        }
```

—————————————————— C / C++ ——————————————————
—————————————————— Fortran ——————————————————

1   *Example async_target.4.f90* (**omp_4.5**)

```
S-1
S-2    subroutine vec_mult(N)
S-3       implicit none
S-4       integer          :: i, N
S-5       real, allocatable :: p(:), v1(:), v2(:)
S-6       allocate( p(N), v1(N), v2(N) )
S-7
S-8       !$omp parallel num_threads(2)
S-9
S-10        !$omp single
S-11
S-12          !$omp task depend(out:v1)
S-13          call init(v1, N)
S-14          !$omp end task
S-15
S-16          !$omp task depend(out:v2)
S-17          call init(v2, N)
S-18          !$omp end task
S-19
S-20          !$omp target nowait depend(in:v1,v2) depend(out:p) &
S-21          !$omp&                    map(to:v1,v2)  map(from: p)
```

```
S-22              !$omp parallel do
S-23              do i=1,N
S-24                  p(i) = v1(i) * v2(i)
S-25              end do
S-26              !$omp end target
S-27
S-28
S-29              !$omp task depend(in:p)
S-30              call output(p, N)
S-31              !$omp end task
S-32
S-33          !$omp end single
S-34       !$omp end parallel
S-35
S-36       deallocate( p, v1, v2 )
S-37
S-38   end subroutine
```

Fortran

6.17 Device Routines

2

6.17.1 `omp_is_initial_device` Routine

The following example shows how the **omp_is_initial_device** runtime library routine can
be used to query if a code is executing on the initial host device or on a target device. The example
then sets the number of threads in the **parallel** region based on where the code is executing.

——————————— C / C++ ———————————

Example device.1.c (`omp_5.1`)

```
S-1    #include <stdio.h>
S-2    #include <omp.h>
S-3
S-4    #pragma omp begin declare target
S-5        void vec_mult(float *p, float *v1, float *v2, int N);
S-6        extern float *p, *v1, *v2;
S-7        extern int N;
S-8    #pragma omp end declare target
S-9
S-10   extern void init_vars(float *, float *, int);
S-11   extern void output(float *, int);
S-12
S-13   void foo()
S-14   {
S-15       init_vars(v1, v2, N);
S-16       #pragma omp target device(42) map(p[:N], v1[:N], v2[:N])
S-17       {
S-18           vec_mult(p, v1, v2, N);
S-19       }
S-20       output(p, N);
S-21   }
S-22
S-23   void vec_mult(float *p, float *v1, float *v2, int N)
S-24   {
S-25       int i;
S-26       int nthreads;
S-27       if (!omp_is_initial_device())
S-28       {
S-29           printf("1024 threads on target device\n");
S-30           nthreads = 1024;
S-31       }
S-32       else
S-33       {
S-34           printf("8 threads on initial device\n");
S-35           nthreads = 8;
S-36       }
```

```
S-37        #pragma omp parallel for private(i) num_threads(nthreads)
S-38        for (i=0; i<N; i++)
S-39          p[i] = v1[i] * v2[i];
S-40    }
```

——————————————————————— C / C++ ———————————————————————
——————————————————————— Fortran ———————————————————————

1   *Example device.1.f90* (omp_4.0)

```
S-1     module params
S-2         integer,parameter :: N=1024
S-3     end module params
S-4     module vmult
S-5     contains
S-6         subroutine vec_mult(p, v1, v2, N)
S-7         use omp_lib, ONLY : omp_is_initial_device
S-8         !$omp declare target
S-9         real     :: p(N), v1(N), v2(N)
S-10        integer :: i, nthreads, N
S-11          if (.not. omp_is_initial_device()) then
S-12              print*, "1024 threads on target device"
S-13              nthreads = 1024
S-14          else
S-15              print*, "8 threads on initial device"
S-16              nthreads = 8
S-17          endif
S-18          !$omp parallel do private(i) num_threads(nthreads)
S-19          do i = 1,N
S-20            p(i) = v1(i) * v2(i)
S-21          end do
S-22        end subroutine vec_mult
S-23    end module vmult
S-24    program prog_vec_mult
S-25    use params
S-26    use vmult
S-27    real :: p(N), v1(N), v2(N)
S-28        call init(v1,v2,N)
S-29        !$omp target device(42) map(p, v1, v2)
S-30          call vec_mult(p, v1, v2, N)
S-31        !$omp end target
S-32        call output(p, N)
S-33    end program
```

——————————————————————— Fortran ———————————————————————

6.17.2 `omp_get_num_devices` Routine

The following example shows how the **`omp_get_num_devices`** runtime library routine can be used to determine the number of devices.

─────────────────────── C / C++ ───────────────────────

Example device.2.c (**omp_4.0**)

```
S-1    #include <omp.h>
S-2    extern void init(float *, float *, int);
S-3    extern void output(float *, int);
S-4    void vec_mult(float *p, float *v1, float *v2, int N)
S-5    {
S-6       int i;
S-7       init(v1, v2, N);
S-8       int ndev = omp_get_num_devices();
S-9       int do_offload = (ndev>0 && N>1000000);
S-10      #pragma omp target if(do_offload) \
S-11                         map(to: v1[0:N], v2[:N]) \
S-12                         map(from: p[0:N])
S-13      #pragma omp parallel for if(N>1000) private(i)
S-14      for (i=0; i<N; i++)
S-15        p[i] = v1[i] * v2[i];
S-16      output(p, N);
S-17   }
```

─────────────────────── C / C++ ───────────────────────
─────────────────────── Fortran ───────────────────────

Example device.2.f90 (**omp_4.0**)

```
S-1    subroutine vec_mult(p, v1, v2, N)
S-2    use omp_lib, ONLY : omp_get_num_devices
S-3    real      :: p(N), v1(N), v2(N)
S-4    integer :: N, i, ndev
S-5    logical :: do_offload
S-6       call init(v1, v2, N)
S-7       ndev = omp_get_num_devices()
S-8       do_offload = (ndev>0) .and. (N>1000000)
S-9       !$omp target if(do_offload) map(to: v1, v2) map(from: p)
S-10      !$omp parallel do if(N>1000)
S-11         do i=1,N
S-12            p(i) = v1(i) * v2(i)
S-13         end do
S-14      !$omp end target
S-15      call output(p, N)
S-16   end subroutine
```

─────────────────────── Fortran ───────────────────────

6.17.3 `omp_set_default_device` and `omp_get_default_device` Routines

The following example shows how the **omp_set_default_device** and
omp_get_default_device runtime library routines can be used to set the default device and
determine the default device respectively.

───────────────────── C / C++ ─────────────────────

Example device.3.c (**omp_4.0**)

```
S-1    #include <omp.h>
S-2    #include <stdio.h>
S-3    void foo(void)
S-4    {
S-5       int default_device = omp_get_default_device();
S-6       printf("Default device = %d\n", default_device);
S-7       omp_set_default_device(default_device+1);
S-8       if (omp_get_default_device() != default_device+1)
S-9          printf("Default device is still = %d\n", default_device);
S-10   }
```

───────────────────── C / C++ ─────────────────────
───────────────────── Fortran ─────────────────────

Example device.3.f90 (**omp_4.0**)

```
S-1    program foo
S-2    use omp_lib, ONLY : omp_get_default_device, omp_set_default_device
S-3    integer :: old_default_device, new_default_device
S-4       old_default_device = omp_get_default_device()
S-5       print*, "Default device = ", old_default_device
S-6       new_default_device = old_default_device + 1
S-7       call omp_set_default_device(new_default_device)
S-8       if (omp_get_default_device() == old_default_device) &
S-9          print*,"Default device is STILL = ", old_default_device
S-10   end program
```

───────────────────── Fortran ─────────────────────

6.17.4 Device and Host Memory Association

The association of device memory with host memory can be established by calling the `omp_target_associate_ptr` API routine as part of the mapping. The following example shows the use of this routine to associate device memory of size *CS*, allocated by the `omp_target_alloc` routine and pointed to by the device pointer *dev_ptr*, with a chunk of the host array *arr* starting at index *ioff*. In Fortran, the intrinsic function **c_loc** is called to obtain the corresponding C pointer (*h_ptr*) of *arr(ioff)* for use in the call to the API routine.

Since the reference count of the resulting mapping is infinite, it is necessary to use the **target update** directive (or the **always** modifier in a **map** clause) to accomplish a data transfer between host and device. The explicit mapping of the array section *arr[ioff:CS]* (or *arr(ioff:ioff+CS-1)* in Fortran) on the **target** construct ensures that the allocated and associated device memory is used when referencing the array *arr* in the **target** region. The device pointer *dev_ptr* cannot be accessed directly after a call to the `omp_target_associate_ptr` routine.

After the **target** region, the device pointer is disassociated from the current chunk of the host memory by calling the `omp_target_disassociate_ptr` routine before working on the next chunk. The device memory is freed by calling the `omp_target_free` routine at the end.

───────────────────────────── C / C++ ─────────────────────────────

Example target_associate_ptr.1.c (**omp_4.5**)

```
#include <stdio.h>
#include <omp.h>

#define CS 50
#define N   (CS*2)

int main() {
  int arr[N];
  int *dev_ptr;
  int dev;

  for (int i = 0; i < N; i++)
    arr[i] = i;

  dev = omp_get_default_device();

  // Allocate device memory
  dev_ptr = (int *)omp_target_alloc(sizeof(int) * CS, dev);

  // Loop over chunks
  for (int ioff = 0; ioff < N; ioff += CS) {

    // Associate device memory with one chunk of host memory
    omp_target_associate_ptr(&arr[ioff], dev_ptr,
```

```
S-25                                    sizeof(int) * CS, 0, dev);
S-26
S-27        printf("before: arr[%d]=%d\n", ioff, arr[ioff]);
S-28
S-29        // Update the device data
S-30        #pragma omp target update to(arr[ioff:CS]) device(dev)
S-31
S-32        // Explicit mapping of arr to make sure that we use the allocated
S-33        // and associated memory.  No host-device data update here.
S-34        #pragma omp target map(tofrom : arr[ioff:CS]) device(dev)
S-35          for (int i = 0; i < CS; i++) {
S-36            arr[i+ioff]++;
S-37          }
S-38
S-39        // Update the host data
S-40        #pragma omp target update from(arr[ioff:CS]) device(dev)
S-41
S-42        printf("after: arr[%d]=%d\n", ioff, arr[ioff]);
S-43
S-44        // Disassociate device pointer from the current chunk of host memory
S-45        // before next use
S-46        omp_target_disassociate_ptr(&arr[ioff], dev);
S-47      }
S-48
S-49      // Free device memory
S-50      omp_target_free(dev_ptr, dev);
S-51
S-52      return 0;
S-53    }
S-54    /* Outputs:
S-55      before: arr[0]=0
S-56      after: arr[0]=1
S-57      before: arr[50]=50
S-58      after: arr[50]=51
S-59    */
```

———————————————————————————— C / C++ ————————————————————————————
———————————————————————————— Fortran ————————————————————————————

1   *Example target_associate_ptr.1.f90* (**omp_5.1**)

```
S-1     program target_associate
S-2       use omp_lib
S-3       use, intrinsic :: iso_c_binding
S-4       implicit none
S-5
S-6       integer, parameter :: CS = 50
S-7       integer, parameter :: N  = CS*2
```

```
S-8        integer, target :: arr(N)
S-9        type(c_ptr) :: h_ptr, dev_ptr
S-10       integer(c_size_t) :: csize, dev_off
S-11       integer(c_int) :: dev
S-12       integer :: i, ioff, s
S-13
S-14       do i = 1, N
S-15         arr(i) = i
S-16       end do
S-17
S-18       dev = omp_get_default_device()
S-19       csize = c_sizeof(arr(1)) * CS
S-20
S-21       ! Allocate device memory
S-22       dev_ptr = omp_target_alloc(csize, dev)
S-23       dev_off = 0
S-24
S-25       ! Loop over chunks
S-26       do ioff = 1, N, CS
S-27
S-28         ! Associate device memory with one chunk of host memory
S-29         h_ptr = c_loc(arr(ioff))
S-30         s = omp_target_associate_ptr(h_ptr, dev_ptr, csize, dev_off, dev)
S-31
S-32         print *, "before: arr(", ioff, ")=", arr(ioff)
S-33
S-34         ! Update the device data
S-35         !$omp target update to(arr(ioff:ioff+CS-1)) device(dev)
S-36
S-37         ! Explicit mapping of arr to make sure that we use the allocated
S-38         ! and associated memory.  No host-device data update here.
S-39         !$omp target map(tofrom: arr(ioff:ioff+CS-1)) device(dev)
S-40           do i = 0, CS-1
S-41             arr(i+ioff) = arr(i+ioff) + 1
S-42           end do
S-43         !$omp end target
S-44
S-45         ! Update the host data
S-46         !$omp target update from(arr(ioff:ioff+CS-1)) device(dev)
S-47
S-48         print *, "after: arr(", ioff, ")=", arr(ioff)
S-49
S-50         ! Disassociate device pointer from the current chunk of host memory
S-51         ! before next use
S-52         s = omp_target_disassociate_ptr(h_ptr, dev)
S-53       end do
S-54
```

```
S-55      ! Free device memory
S-56        call omp_target_free(dev_ptr, dev)
S-57
S-58    end
S-59    ! Outputs:
S-60    !   before: arr( 1 )= 1
S-61    !   after: arr( 1 )= 2
S-62    !   before: arr( 51 )= 51
S-63    !   after: arr( 51 )= 52
```

———————————————————————— Fortran ————————————————————————

6.17.5 Target Memory and Device Pointers Routines

The following example shows how to create space on a device, transfer data to and from that space, and free the space, using API calls. The API calls directly execute allocation, copy and free operations on the device, without invoking any mapping through a **target** directive. The **omp_target_alloc** routine allocates space and returns a device pointer for referencing the space in the **omp_target_memcpy** API routine on the host. The **omp_target_free** routine frees the space on the device.

The example also illustrates how to access that space in a **target** region by exposing the device pointer in an **is_device_ptr** clause.

The example creates an array of cosine values on the default device, to be used on the host device. The function fails if a default device is not available.

▼——————————————————————— C / C++ ———————————————————————▼

Example device.4.c (**omp_4.5**)

```
S-1     #include <stdio.h>
S-2     #include <math.h>
S-3     #include <stdlib.h>
S-4     #include <omp.h>
S-5
S-6     void get_dev_cos(double *mem, size_t s)
S-7     {
S-8         int h, t, i;
S-9         double * mem_dev_cpy;
S-10        h = omp_get_initial_device();
S-11        t = omp_get_default_device();
S-12
S-13        if (omp_get_num_devices() < 1 || t < 0){
S-14            printf(" ERROR: No device found.\n");
S-15            exit(1);
S-16        }
S-17
```

```
S-18        mem_dev_cpy = (double *)omp_target_alloc( sizeof(double) * s, t);
S-19        if(mem_dev_cpy == NULL){
S-20           printf(" ERROR: No space left on device.\n");
S-21           exit(1);
S-22        }
S-23
S-24                          /* dst   src */
S-25        omp_target_memcpy(mem_dev_cpy, mem, sizeof(double)*s,
S-26                              0,    0,
S-27                              t,    h);
S-28
S-29        #pragma omp target is_device_ptr(mem_dev_cpy) device(t)
S-30        #pragma omp teams distribute parallel for
S-31          for(i=0;i<s;i++){ mem_dev_cpy[i] = cos((double)i); } /* init data */
S-32
S-33                     /* dst   src */
S-34        omp_target_memcpy(mem, mem_dev_cpy, sizeof(double)*s,
S-35                           0,           0,
S-36                           h,           t);
S-37
S-38        omp_target_free(mem_dev_cpy, t);
S-39     }
```

———————————————————————— C / C++ ————————————————————————

1   The following Fortran example illustrates how to use the **omp_target_alloc** and
2   **omp_target_memcpy** functions to directly allocate device storage and transfer data to and from
3   a device. It also shows how to check for the presence of device data with the
4   **omp_target_is_present** function and to associate host and device storage with the
5   **omp_target_associate_ptr** function.

6   In Section 1 of the code, 40 bytes of storage are allocated on the default device with the
7   **omp_target_alloc** function, which returns a value (of type C_PTR) that contains the device
8   address of the storage. In the subsequent **target** construct, cp is specified on the
9   **is_device_ptr** clause to instruct the compiler that cp is a device pointer. The device pointer
10 (cp) is then associated with the Fortran pointer (fp) via the c_f_pointer routine inside the
11 **target** construct. As a result, fp points to the storage on the device that is allocated by the
12 **omp_target_alloc** routine. In the **target** region, the value 4 is assigned to the storage on
13 the device, using the Fortran pointer. A trivial test checks that all values were correctly assigned.
14 The Fortran pointer (fp) is nullified before the end of the **target** region. After the **target**
15 construct, the space on the device is freed with the **omp_target_free** function, using the
16 device cp pointer which is set to null after the call.

17 In Section 2, the content of the storage allocated on the host is directly copied to the OpenMP
18 allocated storage on the device. First, storage is allocated for the device and host using
19 **omp_target_alloc**. Next, on the host the device pointer, returned from the allocation
20 **omp_target_alloc** function, is associated with a Fortran pointer, and values are assigned to

the storage. Similarly, values are assigned on the device to the device storage, after associating a
Fortran pointer (`fp_dst`) with the device's storage pointer (`cp_dst`).

Next the **omp_target_memcpy** function directly copies the host data to the device storage,
specified by the respective host and device pointers. This copy will overwrite -1 values in the
device storage, and is checked in the next **target** construct. Keyword arguments are used here for
clarity. (A positional argument list is used in the next Section.)

In Section 3, space is allocated (with a Fortran ALLOCATE statement) and initialized using a host
Fortran pointer (`h_fp`), and the address of the storage is directly assigned to a host C pointer
(`h_cp`). The following **omp_target_is_present** function returns 0 (false, of integer(C_INT)
type) to indicate that `h_cp` does not have any corresponding storage on the default device.

Next, the same amount of space is allocated on the default device with the **omp_target_alloc**
function, which returns a device pointer (`d_cp`). The device pointer `d_cp` and host pointer `h_cp`
are then associated using the **omp_target_associate_ptr** function. The device storage to
which `d_cp` points becomes the corresponding storage of the host storage to which `h_cp` points.
The following **omp_target_is_present** call confirms this, by returning a non-zero value of
integer(C_INT) type for true.

After the association, the content of the host storage is copied to the device using the
omp_target_memcpy function. In the final **target** construct an array section of `h_fp` is
mapped to the device, and evaluated for correctness. The mapping establishes a connection of
`h_fp` with the corresponding device data in the **target** construct, but does not produce an update
on the device because the previous **omp_target_associate_ptr** routine sets the reference
count of the mapped object to infinity, meaning a mapping without the **always** modifier will not
update the device object.

——————————————— Fortran ———————————————

Example device.4.f90 (**omp_5.0**)

```
program device_mem
  use omp_lib
  use, intrinsic              :: iso_c_binding

  integer(kind=4),parameter :: N = 10
  type(c_ptr)               :: cp
  integer(c_int), pointer   :: fp(:)
  integer(c_int)            :: rc, host_dev, targ_dev
  integer(c_size_t)         :: int_bytes

  integer, pointer :: fp_src(:), fp_dst(:)    ! Section 2 vars
  type(c_ptr)      :: cp_src,    cp_dst       ! Section 2 vars

  integer, pointer :: h_fp(:)                 ! Section 3 vars
  type(c_ptr)      :: h_cp,    d_cp           ! Section 3 vars
```

```
S-17        integer :: i
S-18
S-19      host_dev  = omp_get_initial_device()
S-20      targ_dev  = omp_get_default_device()
S-21      int_bytes = C_SIZEOF(rc)
S-22
S-23    !--------------------------------------------------Section 1 vv-----------
S-24      cp = omp_target_alloc(N*int_bytes, targ_dev)
S-25
S-26      !$omp target is_device_ptr(cp) device(targ_dev) !fp implicit map
S-27         call c_f_pointer(cp, fp, [ N ])                  !fp becomes associated
S-28         fp(:) = 4
S-29         if( all(fp == 4) ) print*,"PASSED 1 of 5"
S-30         nullify(fp)                      !fp must be returned as disassociated
S-31      !$omp end target
S-32
S-33      call omp_target_free(cp, targ_dev)
S-34      cp = c_null_ptr
S-35
S-36    !--------------------------------------------------Section 2 vv-----------
S-37
S-38      cp_src = omp_target_alloc((N+1)*int_bytes, host_dev)
S-39      cp_dst = omp_target_alloc(  N  *int_bytes, targ_dev)
S-40
S-41    !          Initialize host array (src)
S-42      call c_f_pointer(cp_src, fp_src, [N+1])
S-43      fp_src = [(i,i=1,N+1)]
S-44
S-45      !$omp target device(targ_dev) is_device_ptr(cp_dst)
S-46         call c_f_pointer(cp_dst, fp_dst, [N])   ! fp_dst becomes associated
S-47         fp_dst(:) = -1                          ! Initial device storage
S-48         nullify(fp_dst)                         ! return as disassociated
S-49      !$omp end target
S-50
S-51    !  Copy subset of host (src) array to device (dst) array
S-52      rc = omp_target_memcpy(                                              &
S-53              dst=cp_dst,              src=cp_src,     length=N*int_bytes, &
S-54              dst_offset=0_c_size_t,   src_offset=int_bytes,               &
S-55              dst_device_num=targ_dev,src_device_num=host_dev)
S-56
S-57    !  Check dst array on device
S-58
S-59      !$omp target device(targ_dev) is_device_ptr(cp_dst)
S-60         call c_f_pointer(cp_dst, fp_dst, [N])
S-61         if ( all(fp_dst == [(i,i=1,N)]) ) print*,"PASSED 2 of 5"
S-62         nullify(fp_dst)
S-63      !$omp end target
```

```
S-64
S-65     !-------------------------------------------------Section 3 vv-----------
S-66
S-67         !allocate host memory and initialize.
S-68         allocate(h_fp(N), source=[(i,i=1,N)])
S-69
S-70         h_cp = c_loc(h_fp)
S-71                  ! Device is not aware of allocation on host
S-72         if(omp_target_is_present(h_cp, targ_dev) == 0) &
S-73             print*, "PASSED 3 of 5"
S-74
S-75                  ! Allocate device memory
S-76         d_cp = omp_target_alloc(c_sizeof(h_fp(1))*size(h_fp), targ_dev)
S-77
S-78                  ! now associate host and device storage
S-79         rc=omp_target_associate_ptr(h_cp,d_cp,c_sizeof(h_fp(1))*size(h_fp), &
S-80                                  0_c_size_t,targ_dev)
S-81
S-82                  ! check presence of device data, associated w. host pointer
S-83         if(omp_target_is_present(h_cp, targ_dev) /= 0) &
S-84             print*,"PASSED 4 of 5"
S-85
S-86                  ! copy from host to device via C pointers
S-87         rc=omp_target_memcpy(d_cp,        h_cp,c_sizeof(h_fp(1))*size(h_fp), &
S-88                          0_c_size_t, 0_c_size_t,                          &
S-89                          targ_dev,    host_dev)
S-90
S-91                  ! validate the device data in the target region
S-92                  ! no data copy here since the reference count is infinity
S-93         !$omp target device(targ_dev) map(h_fp)
S-94             if ( all(h_fp == [(i,i=1,N)]) ) print*, "PASSED 5 of 5"
S-95         !$omp end target
S-96
S-97         call omp_target_free(d_cp,targ_dev)
S-98         deallocate(h_fp)
S-99     end program
```

——————————————— Fortran ———————————————

7 SIMD

Single instruction, multiple data (SIMD) is a form of parallel execution in which the same operation is performed on multiple data elements independently in hardware vector processing units (VPU), also called SIMD units. The addition of two vectors to form a third vector is a SIMD operation. Many processors have SIMD (vector) units that can perform simultaneously 2, 4, 8 or more executions of the same operation (by a single SIMD unit).

Loops without loop-carried backward dependency (or with dependency preserved using ordered simd) are candidates for vectorization by the compiler for execution with SIMD units. In addition, with state-of-the-art vectorization technology and **declare simd** directive extensions for function vectorization in the OpenMP 4.5 specification, loops with function calls can be vectorized as well. The basic idea is that a scalar function call in a loop can be replaced by a vector version of the function, and the loop can be vectorized simultaneously by combining a loop vectorization (**simd** directive on the loop) and a function vectorization (**declare simd** directive on the function).

A **simd** construct states that SIMD operations be performed on the data within the loop. A number of clauses are available to provide data-sharing attributes (**private**, **linear**, **reduction** and **lastprivate**). Other clauses provide vector length preference/restrictions (**simdlen** / **safelen**), loop fusion (**collapse**), and data alignment (**aligned**).

The **declare simd** directive designates that a vector version of the function should also be constructed for execution within loops that contain the function and have a **simd** directive. Clauses provide argument specifications (**linear**, **uniform**, and **aligned**), a requested vector length (**simdlen**), and designate whether the function is always/never called conditionally in a loop (**notinbranch**/**inbranch**). The latter is for optimizing performance.

Also, the **simd** construct has been combined with the worksharing loop constructs (**for simd** and **do simd**) to enable simultaneous thread execution in different SIMD units.

7.1 `simd` and `declare simd` Directives

The following example illustrates the basic use of the **simd** construct to assure the compiler that the loop can be vectorized.

C / C++

Example SIMD.1.c (omp_4.0)

```
S-1   void star( double *a, double *b, double *c, int n, int *ioff )
S-2   {
S-3      int i;
S-4      #pragma omp simd
S-5      for ( i = 0; i < n; i++ )
S-6         a[i] *= b[i] * c[i+ *ioff];
S-7   }
```

C / C++

Fortran

Example SIMD.1.f90 (omp_4.0)

```
S-1   subroutine star(a,b,c,n,ioff_ptr)
S-2      implicit none
S-3      double precision :: a(*),b(*),c(*)
S-4      integer          :: n, i
S-5      integer, pointer :: ioff_ptr
S-6
S-7      !$omp simd
S-8      do i = 1,n
S-9         a(i) = a(i) * b(i) * c(i+ioff_ptr)
S-10     end do
S-11
S-12  end subroutine
```

Fortran

When a function can be inlined within a loop the compiler has an opportunity to vectorize the loop. By guaranteeing SIMD behavior of a function's operations, characterizing the arguments of the function and privatizing temporary variables of the loop, the compiler can often create faster, vector code for the loop. In the examples below the **declare simd** directive is used on the *add1* and *add2* functions to enable creation of their corresponding SIMD function versions for execution within the associated SIMD loop. The functions characterize two different approaches of accessing data within the function: by a single variable and as an element in a data array, respectively. The *add3* C function uses dereferencing.

The **declare simd** directives also illustrate the use of **uniform** and **linear** clauses. The **uniform(fact)** clause indicates that the variable *fact* is invariant across the SIMD lanes. In the *add2* function *a* and *b* are included in the **uniform** list because the C pointer and the Fortran array references are constant. The *i* index used in the *add2* function is included in a **linear** clause with a constant-linear-step of 1, to guarantee a unity increment of the associated loop. In the **declare simd** directive for the *add3* C function the **linear(a,b:1)** clause instructs the compiler to generate unit-stride loads across the SIMD lanes; otherwise, costly *gather* instructions would be generated for the unknown sequence of access of the pointer dereferences.

In the **simd** constructs for the loops the **private(tmp)** clause is necessary to assure that the each vector operation has its own *tmp* variable.

———————————————————————— C / C++ ————————————————————————

Example SIMD.2.c (**omp_4.0**)

```
#include <stdio.h>

#pragma omp declare simd uniform(fact)
double add1(double a, double b, double fact)
{
   double c;
   c = a + b + fact;
   return c;
}

#pragma omp declare simd uniform(a,b,fact) linear(i:1)
double add2(double *a, double *b, int i, double fact)
{
   double c;
   c = a[i] + b[i] + fact;
   return c;
}

#pragma omp declare simd uniform(fact) linear(a,b:1)
double add3(double *a, double *b, double fact)
{
   double c;
   c = *a + *b + fact;
   return c;
}

void work( double *a, double *b, int n )
{
   int i;
   double tmp;
   #pragma omp simd private(tmp)
   for ( i = 0; i < n; i++ ) {
      tmp  = add1( a[i],   b[i], 1.0);
      a[i] = add2( a,      b, i, 1.0) + tmp;
      a[i] = add3(&a[i], &b[i], 1.0);
   }
}

int main(){
   int i;
   const int N=32;
```

```
S-42        double a[N], b[N];
S-43
S-44        for ( i=0; i<N; i++ ) {
S-45            a[i] = i; b[i] = N-i;
S-46        }
S-47
S-48        work(a, b, N );
S-49
S-50        for ( i=0; i<N; i++ ) {
S-51            printf("%d %f\n", i, a[i]);
S-52        }
S-53
S-54        return 0;
S-55    }
```

───────────────────────── C / C++ ─────────────────────────
───────────────────────── Fortran ─────────────────────────

1   *Example SIMD.2.f90* (omp_4.0)

```
S-1     program main
S-2         implicit none
S-3         integer, parameter :: N=32
S-4         integer :: i
S-5         double precision    :: a(N), b(N)
S-6         do i = 1,N
S-7             a(i) = i-1
S-8             b(i) = N-(i-1)
S-9         end do
S-10        call work(a, b, N )
S-11        do i = 1,N
S-12            print*, i,a(i)
S-13        end do
S-14    end program
S-15
S-16    function add1(a,b,fact) result(c)
S-17        implicit none
S-18    !$omp declare simd(add1) uniform(fact)
S-19        double precision :: a,b,fact, c
S-20        c = a + b + fact
S-21    end function
S-22
S-23    function add2(a,b,i, fact) result(c)
S-24        implicit none
S-25    !$omp declare simd(add2) uniform(a,b,fact) linear(i:1)
S-26        integer        :: i
S-27        double precision :: a(*),b(*),fact, c
S-28        c = a(i) + b(i) + fact
```

```
S-29    end function
S-30
S-31    subroutine work(a, b, n )
S-32       implicit none
S-33       double precision              :: a(n),b(n), tmp
S-34       integer                       :: n, i
S-35       double precision, external :: add1, add2
S-36
S-37       !$omp simd private(tmp)
S-38       do i = 1,n
S-39          tmp  = add1(a(i), b(i), 1.0d0)
S-40          a(i) = add2(a,     b, i, 1.0d0) + tmp
S-41          a(i) = a(i) + b(i) + 1.0d0
S-42       end do
S-43    end subroutine
```

────────────────────────── Fortran ──────────────────────────

A thread that encounters a SIMD construct executes a vectorized code of the iterations. Similar to
the concerns of a worksharing loop a loop vectorized with a SIMD construct must assure that
temporary and reduction variables are privatized and declared as reductions with clauses. The
example below illustrates the use of **private** and **reduction** clauses in a SIMD construct.

────────────────────────── C / C++ ──────────────────────────

Example SIMD.3.c (**omp_4.0**)

```
S-1     double work( double *a, double *b, int n )
S-2     {
S-3        int i;
S-4        double tmp, sum;
S-5        sum = 0.0;
S-6        #pragma omp simd private(tmp) reduction(+:sum)
S-7        for (i = 0; i < n; i++) {
S-8           tmp = a[i] + b[i];
S-9           sum += tmp;
S-10       }
S-11       return sum;
S-12    }
```

────────────────────────── C / C++ ──────────────────────────

1   *Example SIMD.3.f90* (`omp_4.0`)

```fortran
S-1    subroutine work( a, b, n, sum )
S-2       implicit none
S-3       integer :: i, n
S-4       double precision :: a(n), b(n), sum, tmp
S-5
S-6       sum = 0.0d0
S-7       !$omp simd private(tmp) reduction(+:sum)
S-8       do i = 1,n
S-9          tmp = a(i) + b(i)
S-10          sum = sum + tmp
S-11       end do
S-12
S-13    end subroutine work
```

2   A **safelen(N)** clause in a **simd** construct assures the compiler that there are no loop-carried
3   dependencies for vectors of size *N* or below. If the **safelen** clause is not specified, then the
4   default safelen value is the number of loop iterations.

5   The **safelen(16)** clause in the example below guarantees that the vector code is safe for vectors
6   up to and including size 16. In the loop, *m* can be 16 or greater, for correct code execution. If the
7   value of *m* is less than 16, the behavior is undefined.

8   *Example SIMD.4.c* (`omp_4.0`)

```c
S-1    void work( float *b, int n, int m )
S-2    {
S-3       int i;
S-4       #pragma omp simd safelen(16)
S-5       for (i = m; i < n; i++)
S-6          b[i] = b[i-m] - 1.0f;
S-7    }
```

1   *Example SIMD.4.f90* (`omp_4.0`)

```
S-1    subroutine work( b, n, m )
S-2       implicit none
S-3       real        :: b(n)
S-4       integer     :: i,n,m
S-5
S-6       !$omp simd safelen(16)
S-7       do i = m+1, n
S-8          b(i) = b(i-m) - 1.0
S-9       end do
S-10   end subroutine work
```

2   The following SIMD construct instructs the compiler to collapse the *i* and *j* loops into a single
3   SIMD loop in which SIMD chunks are executed by threads of the team. Within the workshared
4   loop chunks of a thread, the SIMD chunks are executed in the lanes of the vector units.

5   *Example SIMD.5.c* (`omp_4.0`)

```
S-1    void work( double **a, double **b, double **c, int n )
S-2    {
S-3       int i, j;
S-4       double tmp;
S-5       #pragma omp for simd collapse(2) private(tmp)
S-6       for (i = 0; i < n; i++) {
S-7          for (j = 0; j < n; j++) {
S-8             tmp = a[i][j] + b[i][j];
S-9             c[i][j] = tmp;
S-10         }
S-11      }
S-12   }
```

1 *Example SIMD.5.f90* (**omp_4.0**)

```fortran
S-1    subroutine work( a, b, c,  n )
S-2       implicit none
S-3       integer :: i,j,n
S-4       double precision :: a(n,n), b(n,n), c(n,n), tmp
S-5
S-6       !$omp do simd collapse(2) private(tmp)
S-7       do j = 1,n
S-8          do i = 1,n
S-9             tmp = a(i,j) + b(i,j)
S-10            c(i,j) = tmp
S-11         end do
S-12      end do
S-13
S-14   end subroutine work
```

7.2 `inbranch` and `notinbranch` Clauses

2

3 The following examples illustrate the use of the **declare simd** directive with the **inbranch**
4 and **notinbranch** clauses. The **notinbranch** clause informs the compiler that the function
5 *foo* is never called conditionally in the SIMD loop of the function *myaddint*. On the other hand, the
6 **inbranch** clause for the function goo indicates that the function is always called conditionally in
7 the SIMD loop inside the function *myaddfloat*.

8 *Example SIMD.6.c* (**omp_4.0**)

```c
S-1    #pragma omp declare simd linear(p:1) notinbranch
S-2    int foo(int *p){
S-3      *p = *p + 10;
S-4      return *p;
S-5    }
S-6
S-7    int myaddint(int *a, int *b, int n)
S-8    {
S-9    #pragma omp simd
S-10     for (int i=0; i<n; i++){
S-11        a[i]  = foo(&b[i]);   /* foo is not called under a condition */
S-12     }
S-13     return a[n-1];
S-14   }
```

```
S-15
S-16    #pragma omp declare simd linear(p:1) inbranch
S-17    float goo(float *p){
S-18      *p = *p + 18.5f;
S-19      return *p;
S-20    }
S-21
S-22    int myaddfloat(float *x, float *y, int n)
S-23    {
S-24    #pragma omp simd
S-25      for (int i=0; i<n; i++){
S-26        x[i] = (x[i] > y[i]) ? goo(&y[i]) : y[i];
S-27          /* goo is called under the condition (or within a branch) */
S-28      }
S-29      return x[n-1];
S-30    }
```

———————————————————— C / C++ ————————————————————
———————————————————— Fortran ————————————————————

1   *Example SIMD.6.f90* (omp_4.0)

```
S-1     function foo(p) result(r)
S-2       implicit none
S-3     !$omp declare simd(foo) notinbranch
S-4       integer :: p, r
S-5       p = p + 10
S-6       r = p
S-7     end function foo
S-8
S-9     function myaddint(a, b,  n) result(r)
S-10      implicit none
S-11      integer :: a(*), b(*), n, r
S-12      integer :: i
S-13      integer, external :: foo
S-14
S-15      !$omp simd
S-16      do i=1, n
S-17          a(i) = foo(b(i))   ! foo is not called under a condition
S-18      end do
S-19      r = a(n)
S-20
S-21    end function myaddint
S-22
S-23    function goo(p) result(r)
S-24      implicit none
S-25    !$omp declare simd(goo) inbranch
S-26      real :: p, r
```

```
S-27        p = p + 18.5
S-28        r = p
S-29     end function goo
S-30
S-31     function myaddfloat(x, y, n) result(r)
S-32        implicit none
S-33        real :: x(*), y(*), r
S-34        integer :: n
S-35        integer :: i
S-36        real, external :: goo
S-37
S-38        !$omp simd
S-39        do i=1, n
S-40           if (x(i) > y(i)) then
S-41              x(i) = goo(y(i))
S-42              ! goo is called under the condition (or within a branch)
S-43           else
S-44              x(i) = y(i)
S-45           endif
S-46        end do
S-47
S-48        r = x(n)
S-49     end function myaddfloat
```

———————————————————————— Fortran ————————————————————————

In the code below, the function *fib()* is called in the main program and also recursively called in the function *fib()* within an **if** condition. The compiler creates a masked vector version and a non-masked vector version for the function *fib()* while retaining the original scalar version of the *fib()* function.

———————————————————————— C / C++ ————————————————————————

Example SIMD.7.c (`omp_4.0`)

```
S-1      #include <stdio.h>
S-2      #include <stdlib.h>
S-3
S-4      #define N 45
S-5      int a[N], b[N], c[N];
S-6
S-7      #pragma omp declare simd inbranch
S-8      int fib( int n )
S-9      {
S-10        if (n <= 1)
S-11           return n;
S-12        else {
S-13           return fib(n-1) + fib(n-2);
S-14        }
```

```
S-15      }
S-16
S-17      int main(void)
S-18      {
S-19          int i;
S-20
S-21          #pragma omp simd
S-22          for (i=0; i < N; i++) b[i] = i;
S-23
S-24          #pragma omp simd
S-25          for (i=0; i < N; i++) {
S-26              a[i] = fib(b[i]);
S-27          }
S-28          printf("Done a[%d] = %d\n", N-1, a[N-1]);
S-29          return 0;
S-30      }
```

—————————————————————————————— C / C++ ——————————————————————————————
—————————————————————————————— Fortran ——————————————————————————————

1   *Example SIMD.7.f90* (`omp_4.0`)

```
S-1       program fibonacci
S-2          implicit none
S-3          integer,parameter :: N=45
S-4          integer           :: a(0:N-1), b(0:N-1)
S-5          integer           :: i
S-6          integer, external :: fib
S-7
S-8          !$omp simd
S-9          do i = 0,N-1
S-10            b(i) = i
S-11         end do
S-12
S-13         !$omp simd
S-14         do i=0,N-1
S-15            a(i) = fib(b(i))
S-16         end do
S-17
S-18         write(*,*) "Done a(", N-1, ") = ", a(N-1)
S-19                              ! 44   701408733
S-20      end program
S-21
S-22      recursive function fib(n) result(r)
S-23         implicit none
S-24      !$omp declare simd(fib) inbranch
S-25         integer :: n, r
S-26
```

```
S-27        if (n <= 1) then
S-28            r = n
S-29        else
S-30            r = fib(n-1) + fib(n-2)
S-31        endif
S-32
S-33    end function fib
```

———————————————————————— Fortran ————————————————————————

7.3 Loop-Carried Lexical Forward Dependence

The following example tests the restriction on an SIMD loop with the loop-carried lexical forward-dependence. This dependence must be preserved for the correct execution of SIMD loops.

A loop can be vectorized even though the iterations are not completely independent when it has loop-carried dependences that are forward lexical dependences, indicated in the code below by the read of $A[j+1]$ and the write to $A[j]$ in C/C++ code (or $A(j+1)$ and $A(j)$ in Fortran). That is, the read of $A[j+1]$ (or $A(j+1)$ in Fortran) before the write to $A[j]$ (or $A(j)$ in Fortran) ordering must be preserved for each iteration in j for valid SIMD code generation.

This test assures that the compiler preserves the loop carried lexical forward-dependence for generating a correct SIMD code.

―――――――――――――――――――――― C / C++ ――――――――――――――――――――――

Example SIMD.8.c (`omp_4.0`)

```
S-1    #include <stdio.h>
S-2    #include <math.h>
S-3
S-4    int    P[1000];
S-5    float A[1000];
S-6
S-7    float do_work(float *arr)
S-8    {
S-9      float pri;
S-10     int i;
S-11   #pragma omp simd lastprivate(pri)
S-12     for (i = 0; i < 999; ++i) {
S-13       int j = P[i];
S-14
S-15       pri = 0.5f;
S-16       if (j % 2 == 0) {
S-17         pri = A[j+1] + arr[i];
S-18       }
S-19       A[j] = pri * 1.5f;
S-20       pri = pri + A[j];
S-21     }
S-22     return pri;
S-23   }
S-24
S-25   int main(void)
S-26   {
S-27     float pri, arr[1000];
S-28     int i;
S-29
S-30     for (i = 0; i < 1000; ++i) {
```

```
S-31        P[i]   = i;
S-32        A[i]   = i * 1.5f;
S-33        arr[i] = i * 1.8f;
S-34     }
S-35     pri = do_work(&arr[0]);
S-36     if (pri == 8237.25) {
S-37       printf("passed: result pri = %7.2f (8237.25) \n", pri);
S-38     }
S-39     else {
S-40       printf("failed: result pri = %7.2f (8237.25) \n", pri);
S-41     }
S-42     return 0;
S-43  }
```

———————————————————————— C / C++ ————————————————————————
———————————————————————— Fortran ————————————————————————

1   *Example SIMD.8.f90* (`omp_4.0`)

```
S-1    module work
S-2
S-3    integer :: P(1000)
S-4    real    :: A(1000)
S-5
S-6    contains
S-7    function do_work(arr) result(pri)
S-8      implicit none
S-9      real, dimension(*) :: arr
S-10
S-11     real :: pri
S-12     integer :: i, j
S-13
S-14     !$omp simd private(j) lastprivate(pri)
S-15     do i = 1, 999
S-16       j = P(i)
S-17
S-18       pri = 0.5
S-19       if (mod(j-1, 2) == 0) then
S-20         pri = A(j+1) + arr(i)
S-21       endif
S-22       A(j) = pri * 1.5
S-23       pri = pri + A(j)
S-24     end do
S-25
S-26   end function do_work
S-27
S-28   end module work
S-29
```

```
S-30      program simd_8f
S-31        use work
S-32        implicit none
S-33        real :: pri, arr(1000)
S-34        integer :: i
S-35
S-36        do i = 1, 1000
S-37          P(i)   = i
S-38          A(i)   = (i-1) * 1.5
S-39          arr(i) = (i-1) * 1.8
S-40        end do
S-41        pri = do_work(arr)
S-42        if (pri == 8237.25) then
S-43          print 2, "passed", pri
S-44        else
S-45          print 2, "failed", pri
S-46        endif
S-47      2 format(a, ": result pri = ", f7.2, " (8237.25)")
S-48
S-49      end program
```

——————————————————————— Fortran ———————————————————————

7.4 `ref`, `val`, `uval` Modifiers for `linear` Clause

When generating vector functions from **declare simd** directives, it is important for a compiler to know the proper types of function arguments in order to generate efficient codes. This is especially true for C++ reference types and Fortran arguments.

In the following example, the function *add_one2* has a C++ reference parameter (or Fortran argument) p. Variable p gets incremented by 1 in the function. The caller loop i in the main program passes a variable k as a reference to the function *add_one2* call. The **ref** modifier for the **linear** clause on the **declare simd** directive specifies that the reference-type parameter p is to match the property of the variable k in the loop. This use of reference type is equivalent to the second call to *add_one2* with a direct passing of the array element *a[i]*. In the example, the preferred vector length 8 is specified for both the caller loop and the callee function.

When **linear(p: ref)** is applied to an argument passed by reference, it tells the compiler that the addresses in its vector argument are consecutive, and so the compiler can generate a single vector load or store instead of a gather or scatter. This allows more efficient SIMD code to be generated with less source changes.

1   *Example linear_modifier.1.cpp* (**omp_5.2**)

```cpp
#include <stdio.h>

#define NN 1023
int a[NN];

#pragma omp declare simd linear(p: ref) simdlen(8)
void add_one2(int& p)
{
    p += 1;
}

int main(void)
{
    int i;
    int* p = a;

    for (i = 0; i < NN; i++) {
        a[i] = i;
    }

#pragma omp simd linear(p) simdlen(8)
    for (i = 0; i < NN; i++) {
        int& k = *p;
        add_one2(k);
        add_one2(a[i]);
        p++;
    }

    for (i = 0; i < NN; i++) {
        if (a[i] != i+2) {
            printf("failed\n");
            return 1;
        }
    }
    printf("passed\n");
    return 0;
}
```

1   *Example linear_modifier.1.f90* (**omp_5.2**)

```fortran
S-1    module m
S-2       integer, parameter :: NN = 1023
S-3       integer :: a(NN)
S-4
S-5     contains
S-6       subroutine add_one2(p)
S-7       !$omp declare simd(add_one2) linear(p: ref) simdlen(8)
S-8       implicit none
S-9       integer :: p
S-10
S-11      p = p + 1
S-12      end subroutine
S-13   end module
S-14
S-15   program main
S-16      use m
S-17      implicit none
S-18      integer :: i, p
S-19
S-20      do i = 1, NN
S-21         a(i) = i
S-22      end do
S-23
S-24      p = 1
S-25      !$omp simd linear(p) simdlen(8)
S-26      do i = 1, NN
S-27         associate(k => a(p))
S-28            call add_one2(k)
S-29         end associate
S-30         call add_one2(a(i))
S-31         p = p + 1
S-32      end do
S-33
S-34      do i = 1, NN
S-35         if (a(i) /= i+2) then
S-36            print *, "failed"
S-37            stop
S-38         endif
S-39      end do
S-40      print *, "passed"
S-41   end program
S-42
```

The following example is a variant of the above example. The function *add_one2* in the C++ code includes an additional C++ reference parameter *i*. The loop index *i* of the caller loop *i* in the main program is passed as a reference to the function *add_one2* call. The loop index *i* has a uniform address with linear value of step 1 across SIMD lanes. Thus, the **uval** modifier is used for the **linear** clause to specify that the C++ reference-type parameter *i* is to match the property of loop index *i*.

In the corresponding Fortran code the arguments *p* and *i* in the routine *add_on2* are passed by references. Similar modifiers are used for these variables in the **linear** clauses to match with the property at the caller loop in the main program.

When **linear(i: uval)** is applied to an argument passed by reference, it tells the compiler that its addresses in the vector argument are uniform so that the compiler can generate a scalar load or scalar store and create linear values. This allows more efficient SIMD code to be generated with less source changes.

C++

Example linear_modifier.2.cpp (**omp_5.2**)

```
S-1    #include <stdio.h>
S-2
S-3    #define NN 1023
S-4    int a[NN];
S-5
S-6    #pragma omp declare simd linear(p: ref) linear(i: uval)
S-7    void add_one2(int& p, const int& i)
S-8    {
S-9        p += i;
S-10   }
S-11
S-12   int main(void)
S-13   {
S-14       int i;
S-15       int* p = a;
S-16
S-17       for (i = 0; i < NN; i++) {
S-18           a[i] = i;
S-19       }
S-20
S-21       #pragma omp simd linear(p)
S-22       for (i = 0; i < NN; i++) {
S-23           int& k = *p;
S-24           add_one2(k, i);
S-25           p++;
S-26       }
S-27
S-28       for (i = 0; i < NN; i++) {
```

```
S-29            if (a[i] != i*2) {
S-30                printf("failed\n");
S-31                return 1;
S-32            }
S-33        }
S-34        printf("passed\n");
S-35        return 0;
S-36    }
```

─────────────────────── C++ ───────────────────────

─────────────────────── Fortran ───────────────────────

Example linear_modifier.2.f90 (**omp_5.2**)

```
S-1     module m
S-2        integer, parameter :: NN = 1023
S-3        integer :: a(NN)
S-4
S-5      contains
S-6        subroutine add_one2(p, i)
S-7        !$omp declare simd(add_one2) linear(p: ref) linear(i: uval)
S-8        implicit none
S-9        integer :: p
S-10       integer, intent(in) :: i
S-11
S-12       p = p + i
S-13       end subroutine
S-14    end module
S-15
S-16    program main
S-17       use m
S-18       implicit none
S-19       integer :: i, p
S-20
S-21       do i = 1, NN
S-22          a(i) = i
S-23       end do
S-24
S-25       p = 1
S-26       !$omp simd linear(p)
S-27       do i = 1, NN
S-28          call add_one2(a(p), i)
S-29          p = p + 1
S-30       end do
S-31
S-32       do i = 1, NN
S-33          if (a(i) /= i*2) then
```

```
S-34              print *, "failed"
S-35                stop
S-36            endif
S-37          end do
S-38          print *, "passed"
S-39      end program
```

─────────────────────── Fortran ───────────────────────

In the following example, the function *func* takes arrays *x* and *y* as arguments, and accesses the array elements referenced by the index *i*. The caller loop *i* in the main program passes a linear copy of the variable *k* to the function *func*. The **val** modifier is used for the **linear** clause in the **declare simd** directive for the function *func* to specify that the argument *i* is to match the property of the actual argument *k* passed in the SIMD loop. Arrays *x* and *y* have uniform addresses across SIMD lanes.

When **linear(i: val,step(1))** is applied to an argument, it tells the compiler that its addresses in the vector argument may not be consecutive, however, their values are linear (with stride 1 here). When the value of *i* is used in subscript of array references (e.g., *x[i]*), the compiler can generate a vector load or store instead of a gather or scatter. This allows more efficient SIMD code to be generated with less source changes.

─────────────────────── C / C++ ───────────────────────

Example linear_modifier.3.c (**omp_5.2**)

```
S-1     #include <stdio.h>
S-2
S-3     #define N 128
S-4
S-5     #pragma omp declare simd simdlen(4) uniform(x, y) linear(i:val,step(1))
S-6     double func(double x[], double y[], int i)
S-7     {
S-8         return (x[i] + y[i]);
S-9     }
S-10
S-11    int main(void)
S-12    {
S-13        double x[N], y[N], z1[N], z2;
S-14        int i, k;
S-15
S-16        for (i = 0; i < N; i++) {
S-17            x[i] = (double)i;
S-18            y[i] = (double)i*2;
S-19        }
S-20
S-21        k = 0;
S-22    #pragma omp simd linear(k)
S-23        for (i = 0; i < N; i++) {
```

```
S-24            z1[i] = func(x, y, k);
S-25            k++;
S-26        }
S-27
S-28        for (i = 0; i < N; i++) {
S-29            z2 = (double)(i + i*2);
S-30            if (z1[i] != z2) {
S-31                printf("failed\n");
S-32                return 1;
S-33            }
S-34        }
S-35        printf("passed\n");
S-36        return 0;
S-37    }
```

———————————————————— C / C++ ————————————————————
———————————————————— Fortran ————————————————————

1   *Example linear_modifier.3.f90* (**omp_5.2**)

```
S-1     module func_mod
S-2     contains
S-3        real(8) function func(x, y, i)
S-4     !$omp declare simd(func) simdlen(4) uniform(x, y) linear(i:val,step(1))
S-5            implicit none
S-6            real(8), intent(in) :: x(*), y(*)
S-7            integer, intent(in) :: i
S-8
S-9            func = x(i) + y(i)
S-10
S-11       end function func
S-12    end module func_mod
S-13
S-14    program main
S-15       use func_mod
S-16       implicit none
S-17       integer, parameter :: n = 128
S-18       real(8) :: x(n), y(n), z1(n), z2
S-19       integer :: i, k
S-20
S-21       do i=1, n
S-22          x(i) = real(i, kind=8)
S-23          y(i) = real(i*2, kind=8)
S-24       enddo
S-25
S-26       k = 1
S-27    !$omp simd linear(k)
S-28       do i=1, n
```

```
S-29            z1(i) = func(x, y, k)
S-30            k = k + 1
S-31        enddo
S-32
S-33        do i=1, n
S-34            z2 = real(i+i*2, kind=8)
S-35            if (z1(i) /= z2) then
S-36                print *, 'failed'
S-37                stop
S-38            endif
S-39        enddo
S-40        print *, 'passed'
S-41    end program main
```

———————————————————————— Fortran ————————————————————————

8 Loop Transformations

To obtain better performance on a platform, code may need to be restructured relative to the way it is written (which is often for best readability). User-directed loop transformations accomplish this goal by providing a means to separate code semantics and its optimization.

A loop transformation construct states that a transformation operation is to be performed on set of nested loops. This directive approach can target specific loops for transformation, rather than applying more time-consuming general compiler heuristics methods with compiler options that may not be able to discover optimal transformations.

Loop transformations can be augmented by preprocessor support or OpenMP **metadirective** directives, to select optimal dimension and size parameters for specific platforms, facilitating a single code base for multiple platforms. Moreover, directive-based transformations make experimenting easier: whereby specific hot spots can be affected by transformation directives.

8.1 `tile` Construct

In the following example a **tile** construct transforms two nested loops within the func1 function into four nested loops. The tile sizes in the **sizes** clause are applied from outermost to innermost loops (left-to-right). The effective tiling operation is illustrated in the func2 function. (For easier illustration, tile sizes for all examples in this section evenly divide the iteration counts so that there are no remainders.)

In the following C/C++ code the inner loop traverses columns and the outer loop traverses the rows of a 100x128 (row x column) matrix. The **sizes(5,16)** clause of the **tile** construct specifies a 5x16 blocking, applied to the outer (row) and inner (column) loops. The worksharing-loop construct before the **tile** construct is applied after the transform.

────────────────────────── C / C++ ──────────────────────────

Example tile.1.c (**omp_5.1**)

```
void func1(int A[100][128])
{
    #pragma omp parallel for
    #pragma omp tile sizes(5,16)
    for (int i = 0; i < 100; ++i)
        for (int j = 0; j < 128; ++j)
            A[i][j] = i*1000 + j;
}
```

```
S-10    void func2(int A[100][128])
S-11    {
S-12        #pragma omp parallel for
S-13        for (int i1 = 0; i1 < 100; i1+=5)
S-14            for (int j1 = 0; j1 < 128; j1+=16)
S-15                for (int i2 = i1; i2 < i1+5; ++i2)
S-16                    for (int j2 = j1; j2 < j1+16; ++j2)
S-17                        A[i2][j2] = i2*1000 + j2;
S-18    }
```

──────────────────────── C / C++ ────────────────────────

In the following Fortran code the inner loop traverses rows and the outer loop traverses the columns
of a 128x100 (row x column) matrix. The **sizes(5,16)** clause of the **tile** construct specifies a
5x16 blocking, applied to the outer (column) and inner (row) loops. The worksharing-loop
construct before the **tile** construct is applied after the transform.

──────────────────────── Fortran ────────────────────────

Example tile.1.f90 (**omp_5.1**)

```
S-1
S-2     subroutine func1(A)
S-3         integer :: A(128,100)
S-4         integer :: i, j
S-5         !$omp parallel do
S-6         !$omp tile sizes(5,16)
S-7         do i = 1, 100
S-8         do j = 1, 128
S-9             A(j,i) = j*1000 + i
S-10        end do; end do
S-11    end subroutine
S-12
S-13    subroutine func2(A)
S-14        integer :: A(128,100)
S-15        integer :: i1, j1, i2, j2
S-16        !$omp parallel do
S-17        do i1 = 1, 100,5
S-18        do j1 = 1, 128,16
S-19            do i2 = i1, i1+( 5-1)
S-20            do j2 = j1, j1+(16-1)
S-21                A(j2,i2) = j2*1000 + i2
S-22            end do; end do
S-23        end do; end do
S-24    end subroutine
```

──────────────────────── Fortran ────────────────────────

This example illustrates transformation nesting. Here, a 4x4 "outer" **tile** construct is applied to the "inner" tile transform shown in the example above. The effect of the inner loop is shown in `func2` (cf. `func2` in tile.1.c). The outer **tile** construct's **sizes(4,4)** clause applies a 4x4 tile upon the resulting blocks of the inner transform. The effective looping is shown in `func3`.

─────────────────────────── C / C++ ───────────────────────────

Example tile.2.c (**omp_5.1**)

```
void func1(int A[100][128])
{
   #pragma omp tile sizes(4, 4)
   #pragma omp tile sizes(5,16)
   for (int i = 0; i < 100; ++i)
       for (int j = 0; j < 128; ++j)
           A[i][j] = i*1000 + j;
}

void func2(int A[100][128])
{
   #pragma omp tile sizes(4,4)
   for (int i1 = 0; i1 < 100; i1+=5)
       for (int j1 = 0; j1 < 128; j1+=16)
           for (int i2 = i1; i2 < i1+5; ++i2)
               for (int j2 = j1; j2 < j1+16; ++j2)
                   A[i2][j2] = i2*1000 + j2;
}

void func3(int A[100][128])
{
   for (int i11 = 0; i11 < 100; i11+= 5*4)
   for (int j11 = 0; j11 < 128; j11+=16*4)

       for (int i12 = i11; i12 < i11+( 5*4); i12+= 5)
       for (int j12 = j11; j12 < j11+(16*4); j12+=16)

           for (int i2 = i12; i2 < i12+ 5; ++i2)
           for (int j2 = j12; j2 < j12+16; ++j2)
               A[i2][j2] = i2*1000 + j2;
}
```

─────────────────────────── C / C++ ───────────────────────────

1   *Example tile.2.f90* (`omp_5.1`)

```
S-1
S-2      subroutine func1(A)
S-3          integer :: A(128,100)
S-4          integer :: i, j
S-5          !$omp tile sizes(4, 4)
S-6          !$omp tile sizes(5,16)
S-7          do i = 1, 100
S-8          do j = 1, 128
S-9              A(j,i) = j*1000 + i
S-10         end do; end do
S-11     end subroutine
S-12
S-13     subroutine func2(A)
S-14         integer :: A(128,100)
S-15         integer :: i1, j1, i2, j2
S-16         !$omp tile sizes(4,4)
S-17         do i1 = 1, 100,5
S-18         do j1 = 1, 128,16
S-19             do i2 = i1, i1+( 5-1)
S-20             do j2 = j1, j1+(16-1)
S-21                 A(j2,i2) = j2*1000 + i2
S-22             end do; end do
S-23         end do; end do
S-24
S-25     end subroutine
S-26
S-27     subroutine func3(A)
S-28         integer :: A(128,100)
S-29         integer :: i11, j11, i12, j12, i2, j2
S-30         do i11 = 1, 100,   5*4
S-31         do j11 = 1, 128,  16*4
S-32             do i12 = i11, i11+( 5*4-1),   5
S-33             do j12 = j11, j11+(16*4-1),  16
S-34                 do i2 = i12, i12+ 5-1
S-35                 do j2 = j12, j12+16-1
S-36                     A(j2,i2) = j2*1000 + i2
S-37                 enddo; enddo;
S-38             enddo; enddo;
S-39         enddo; enddo
S-40
S-41     end subroutine
```

8.2 `unroll` Construct

The **unroll** construct is a loop transformation that increases the number of loop blocks in a loop, while reducing the number of iterations. The **full** clause specifies that the loop is to be completely unrolled. That is, a loop block for each iteration is created, and the loop is removed. A **partial** clause with a *unroll-factor* specifies that the number of iterations will be reduced multiplicatively by the factor while the number of blocks will be increased by the same factor. Operationally, the loop is tiled by the factor, and the tiled loop is fully expanded, resulting in a single loop with multiple blocks.

Unrolling can reduce control-flow overhead and provide additional optimization opportunities for the compiler and the processor pipeline. Nevertheless, unrolling can increase the code size, and saturate the instruction cache. Hence, the trade-off may need to be assessed. Unrolling a loop does not change the code's semantics. Also, compilers may unroll loops without explicit directives, at various optimization levels.

In the example below, the **unroll** construct is used without any clause, and then with a **full** clause, in the first two functions, respectively. When no clause is used, it is up to the implementation (compiler) to decide if and how the loop is to be unrolled. The iteration count can have a run time value. In the second function, the **unroll** construct uses a **full** clause to completely unroll the loop. A compile-time constant is required for the iteration count. The statements in the third function (*unroll_full_equivalent*) illustrates equivalent code for the full unrolling in the second function.

--------------------------------- C / C++ ---------------------------------

Example unroll.1.c (**omp_5.1**)

```
void unroll(double A[], int n)
{
   #pragma omp unroll
   for (int i = 0; i < n; ++i)
     A[i] = 0;
}

void unroll_full(double A[])
{
   #pragma omp unroll full
   for (int i = 0; i < 4; ++i)
     A[i] = 0;
}

void unroll_full_equivalent(double A[])
{
   A[0] = 0;
   A[1] = 0;
   A[2] = 0;
   A[3] = 0;
```

```
S-21      }
S-22
```

───────────────────────────── C / C++ ─────────────────────────────
───────────────────────────── Fortran ─────────────────────────────

1   *Example unroll.1.f90* (`omp_5.1`)

```
S-1     subroutine unroll(A, n)
S-2        implicit none
S-3        integer          :: i,n
S-4        double precision :: A(n)
S-5
S-6        !$omp unroll
S-7        do i = 1,n
S-8           A(i) = 0.0d0
S-9        end do
S-10    end subroutine
S-11
S-12    subroutine unroll_full(A)
S-13       implicit none
S-14       integer :: i
S-15       double precision :: A(*)
S-16
S-17       !$omp unroll full
S-18       do i = 1,4
S-19          A(i) = 0.0d0
S-20       end do
S-21    end subroutine
S-22
S-23    subroutine unroll_full_equivalent(A)
S-24       implicit none
S-25       double precision :: A(*)
S-26
S-27       A(1) = 0.0d0
S-28       A(2) = 0.0d0
S-29       A(3) = 0.0d0
S-30       A(4) = 0.0d0
S-31    end subroutine
```

───────────────────────────── Fortran ─────────────────────────────

2   The next example shows cases when it is incorrect to use full unrolling.

1

———————————————— C / C++ ————————————————

Example unroll.2.c (omp_5.1)

```
S-1    void illegal_2a(double A[])
S-2    {
S-3        #pragma omp for
S-4        #pragma omp unroll full  // ERROR: No loop left after full unrolling.
S-5        for (int i = 0; i < 12; ++i)
S-6            A[i] = 0;
S-7    }
S-8
S-9    void illegal_2b(double A[])
S-10   {
S-11       // Loop might be fully unrolled (or a partially unrolled loop
S-12       // replacement). Hence, no canonical for-loop, resulting in
S-13       // non-compliant code. Implementations may suggest adding a
S-14       // "partial" clause.
S-15
S-16       #pragma omp for              //          Requires a canonical loop
S-17       #pragma omp unroll           // ERROR: may result in non-compliant code
S-18       for (int i = 0; i < 12; ++i)
S-19           A[i] = 0;
S-20   }
S-21
S-22   void illegal_2c(int n, double A[])
S-23   {
S-24       #pragma omp unroll full  // ERROR: Constant iteration count required.
S-25       for (int i = 0; i < n; ++i)
S-26           A[i] = 0;
S-27   }
```

———————————————— C / C++ ————————————————
———————————————— Fortran ————————————————

Example unroll.2.f90 (omp_5.1)

```
S-1    subroutine illegal_2a(A)
S-2        implicit none
S-3        double precision :: A(*)
S-4        integer :: i
S-5
S-6        !$omp do
S-7        !$omp unroll full  !! ERROR: No loop left after full unrolling
S-8        do i = 1,12
S-9            A(i) = 0.0d0
S-10       end do
S-11   end subroutine
S-12
```

```
S-13    subroutine illegal_2b(A)
S-14       implicit none
S-15       double precision :: A(*)
S-16       integer :: i
S-17
S-18       !! Loop might be fully unrolled (or a partially unrolled loop
S-19       !! replacement).  Hence, no canonical do-loop will exist,
S-20       !! resulting in non-compliant code.
S-21       !! Implementations may suggest to adding a "partial" clause.
S-22
S-23       !$omp do            !!         Requires a canonical loop
S-24       !$omp unroll        !! ERROR: may result in non-compliant code
S-25       do i = 1,12
S-26          A(i) = 0.0d0
S-27       end do
S-28    end subroutine
S-29
S-30    subroutine illegal_2c(n, A)
S-31       implicit none
S-32       integer          :: i,n
S-33       double precision :: A(*)
S-34
S-35       !$omp unroll full  !! Full unroll requires constant iteration count
S-36       do i = 1,n
S-37          A(i) = 0.0d0
S-38       end do
S-39    end subroutine
```

————————————————————— Fortran —————————————————————

In many cases, when the iteration count is large and/or dynamic, it is reasonable to partially unroll a
loop by including a **partial** clause. In the *unroll3_partial* function below, the *unroll-factor*
value of 4 is used to create a tile size of 4 that is unrolled to create 4 unrolled statements. The
equivalent "hand unrolled" loop code is presented in the *unroll3_partial_equivalent* function. If the
unroll-factor is omitted, as in the *unroll3_partial_nofactor* function, the implementation may
optimally select a factor from 1 (no unrolling) to the iteration count (full unrolling). In the latter
case the construct generates a loop with a single iteration.

————————————————————— C / C++ —————————————————————

Example unroll.3.c (**omp_5.1**)

```
S-1    void unroll3_partial(double A[])
S-2    {
S-3       #pragma omp unroll partial(4)
S-4       for (int i = 0; i < 128; ++i)
S-5          A[i] = 0;
S-6    }
S-7
```

```
S-8     void unroll3_partial_equivalent(double A[])
S-9     {
S-10        for (int i_iv = 0; i_iv < 32; ++i_iv) {
S-11            A[i_iv * 4 + 0] = 0;
S-12            A[i_iv * 4 + 1] = 0;
S-13            A[i_iv * 4 + 2] = 0;
S-14            A[i_iv * 4 + 3] = 0;
S-15        }
S-16     }
S-17
S-18     void unroll3_partial_nofactor(double A[])
S-19     {
S-20        #pragma omp unroll partial
S-21        for (int i = 0; i < 128; ++i)
S-22            A[i] = 0;
S-23     }
```

──────────────────────── C / C++ ────────────────────────
──────────────────────── Fortran ────────────────────────

1   *Example unroll.3.f90* (**omp_5.1**)

```
S-1     subroutine unroll3_partial(A)
S-2        implicit none
S-3        double precision :: A(*)
S-4        integer :: i
S-5
S-6        !$omp unroll partial(4)
S-7        do i = 1,128
S-8            A(i) = 0
S-9        end do
S-10    end subroutine
S-11
S-12    subroutine unroll3_partial_equivalent(A)
S-13        implicit none
S-14        double precision :: A(*)
S-15        integer :: i_iv
S-16
S-17        do i_iv = 0, 31
S-18            A(i_iv * 4 + 1) = 0
S-19            A(i_iv * 4 + 2) = 0
S-20            A(i_iv * 4 + 3) = 0
S-21            A(i_iv * 4 + 4) = 0
S-22        end do
S-23    end subroutine
S-24
S-25    subroutine unroll3_partial_nofactor(A)
S-26        implicit none
```

```
S-27        double precision :: A(*)
S-28        integer :: i
S-29
S-30        !$omp unroll partial
S-31        do i = 1, 128
S-32          A(i) = 0
S-33        end do
S-34    end subroutine
```

───────────────────────────── Fortran ─────────────────────────────

When the iteration count is not a multiple of the *unroll-factor*, iterations that should not produce executions must be conditionally protected from execution. In this example, the first function unrolls a loop that has a variable iteration count. Since the **unroll** construct uses a **partial(** *4* **)** clause, the compiler will need to create code that can account for cases when the iteration count is not a multiple of 4. A brute-force, simple-to-understand approach for implementing the conditionals is shown in the *unroll_partial_remainder_option1* function.

The remaining two functions show more optimal algorithms the compiler may select to implement the transformation. Optimal approaches may reduce the number of conditionals as shown in *unroll_partial_remainder_option2*, and may eliminate conditionals completely by peeling off a "remainder" into a separate loop as in *unroll_partial_remainder_option3*.

Regardless of the optimization, implementations must ensure that the semantics remain the same, especially when additional directives are applied to the unrolled loop. For the case in the *unroll_partial_remainder_option3* function, the fission of the worksharing-loop construct may result in a different distribution of threads to the iterations. Since no reproducible scheduling is specified on the work-sharing construct, the worksharing-loop and unrolling are compliant.

───────────────────────────── C / C++ ─────────────────────────────

Example unroll.4.c (**omp_5.1**)

```
S-1     void unroll_partial_remainder(int n, int A[])
S-2     {
S-3         #pragma omp parallel for
S-4         #pragma omp unroll partial(4)
S-5         for (int i = 0; i < n; ++i)
S-6             A[i] = i;
S-7     }
S-8
S-9     void unroll_partial_remainder_option1(int n, int A[])
S-10    {
S-11        #pragma omp parallel for
S-12        for (int i_iv = 0; i_iv < (n+3)/4; ++i_iv) {
S-13                                 A[i_iv * 4 + 0] = i_iv * 4 + 0;
S-14            if (i_iv * 4 + 1 < n) A[i_iv * 4 + 1] = i_iv * 4 + 1;
S-15            if (i_iv * 4 + 2 < n) A[i_iv * 4 + 2] = i_iv * 4 + 2;
S-16            if (i_iv * 4 + 3 < n) A[i_iv * 4 + 3] = i_iv * 4 + 3;
```

```
S-17            }
S-18        }
S-19
S-20    void unroll_partial_remainder_option2(int n, int A[])
S-21    {
S-22        #pragma omp parallel for
S-23        for (int i_iv = 0; i_iv < (n+3)/4; ++i_iv) {
S-24            if (i_iv < n/4) {
S-25                A[i_iv * 4 + 0] = i_iv * 4 + 0;
S-26                A[i_iv * 4 + 1] = i_iv * 4 + 1;
S-27                A[i_iv * 4 + 2] = i_iv * 4 + 2;
S-28                A[i_iv * 4 + 3] = i_iv * 4 + 3;
S-29            } else {
S-30                // remainder loop
S-31                for (int i_rem = i_iv*4; i_rem < n; ++i_rem)
S-32                    A[i_rem] = i_rem;
S-33            }
S-34        }
S-35    }
S-36
S-37    void unroll_partial_remainder_option3(int n, int A[])
S-38    {
S-39        // main loop
S-40        #pragma omp parallel for
S-41        for (int i_iv = 0; i_iv < n/4; ++i_iv) {
S-42            A[i_iv * 4 + 0] = i_iv * 4 + 0;
S-43            A[i_iv * 4 + 1] = i_iv * 4 + 1;
S-44            A[i_iv * 4 + 2] = i_iv * 4 + 2;
S-45            A[i_iv * 4 + 3] = i_iv * 4 + 3;
S-46        }
S-47
S-48        // remainder loop
S-49        #pragma omp parallel for
S-50        for (int i_rem = (n/4)*4; i_rem < n; ++i_rem)
S-51            A[i_rem] = i_rem;
S-52    }
S-53
S-54    #include <stdio.h>
S-55    #define NT 12
S-56
S-57    int main(){
S-58    int error=0, A[NT],C[NT];
S-59    for(int i = 0; i<NT; i++){ A[i]=0; C[i]=i; }
S-60
S-61        for(int i = 0; i<NT; i++) A[i]=0.0;
S-62        unroll_partial_remainder(NT,A);
S-63        for(int i = 0; i<NT; i++) if(A[i] != C[i]) error=1;
```

```
S-64
S-65         for(int i = 0; i<NT; i++) A[i]=0.0;
S-66         unroll_partial_remainder_option1(NT,A);
S-67         for(int i = 0; i<NT; i++) if(A[i] != C[i]) error=1;
S-68
S-69         for(int i = 0; i<NT; i++) A[i]=0.0;
S-70         unroll_partial_remainder_option2(NT,A);
S-71         for(int i = 0; i<NT; i++) if(A[i] != C[i]) error=1;
S-72
S-73         for(int i = 0; i<NT; i++) A[i]=0.0;
S-74         unroll_partial_remainder_option3(NT,A);
S-75         for(int i = 0; i<NT; i++) if(A[i] != C[i]) error=1;
S-76
S-77      if(!error) printf("OUT: Passed\n");
S-78      if( error) printf("OUT: Failed\n");
S-79    }
```

C / C++
Fortran
---

1   *Example unroll.4.f90* (`omp_5.1`)

```
S-1     subroutine unroll_partial_remainder(n, A)
S-2        implicit none
S-3        integer :: n, i
S-4        integer :: A(*)
S-5
S-6         !$omp parallel do
S-7         !$omp unroll partial(4)
S-8         do i = 1, n
S-9            A(i) = i
S-10        end do
S-11
S-12    end subroutine
S-13
S-14    subroutine unroll_partial_remainder_option1(n, A)
S-15       implicit none
S-16       integer :: n, i_iv
S-17       integer :: A(*)
S-18
S-19        !$omp parallel do
S-20        do i_iv = 0,(n+3)/4 -1
S-21                                  A(i_iv * 4 + 1) = i_iv * 4 + 1
S-22            if (i_iv * 4 + 2 <= n) A(i_iv * 4 + 2) = i_iv * 4 + 2
S-23            if (i_iv * 4 + 3 <= n) A(i_iv * 4 + 3) = i_iv * 4 + 3
S-24            if (i_iv * 4 + 4 <= n) A(i_iv * 4 + 4) = i_iv * 4 + 4
S-25        end do
S-26
```

```
S-27     end subroutine
S-28
S-29     subroutine unroll_partial_remainder_option2(n, A)
S-30        implicit none
S-31        integer :: n, i_iv, i_rem
S-32        integer :: A(*)
S-33
S-34        !$omp parallel do
S-35        do i_iv = 0, (n+3)/4 -1
S-36            if (i_iv < n/4) then
S-37                A(i_iv * 4 + 1) = i_iv * 4 + 1
S-38                A(i_iv * 4 + 2) = i_iv * 4 + 2
S-39                A(i_iv * 4 + 3) = i_iv * 4 + 3
S-40                A(i_iv * 4 + 4) = i_iv * 4 + 4
S-41            else
S-42                !! remainder loop
S-43                do i_rem = i_iv*4 +1, n
S-44                    A(i_rem) = i_rem
S-45                end do
S-46            end if
S-47        end do
S-48
S-49     end subroutine
S-50
S-51     subroutine unroll_partial_remainder_option3(n, A)
S-52        implicit none
S-53        integer :: n, i_iv, i_rem
S-54        integer :: A(*)
S-55
S-56        !$omp parallel do
S-57        do i_iv = 0, (n/4) -1
S-58
S-59            A(i_iv * 4 + 1) = i_iv * 4 + 1
S-60            A(i_iv * 4 + 2) = i_iv * 4 + 2
S-61            A(i_iv * 4 + 3) = i_iv * 4 + 3
S-62            A(i_iv * 4 + 4) = i_iv * 4 + 4
S-63        end do
S-64
S-65        !! remainder loop
S-66        !$omp parallel do
S-67        do i_rem = (n/4)*4 +1, n
S-68            A(i_rem) = i_rem
S-69        end do
S-70
S-71     end subroutine
S-72
S-73     program main
```

```
S-74      implicit none
S-75      integer, parameter :: NT=12
S-76
S-77      integer :: i
S-78      logical :: error=.false.
S-79      integer    :: A(NT), C(NT)=[ (i, i=1,NT) ]
S-80
S-81         A(1:NT)=0
S-82         call unroll_partial_remainder(NT, A)
S-83         if( .not. all(A(1:NT) == C(1:NT)) ) error = .true.
S-84
S-85         A(1:NT)=0
S-86         call unroll_partial_remainder_option1(NT, A)
S-87         if( .not. all(A(1:NT) == C(1:NT)) ) error = .true.
S-88
S-89         A(1:NT)=0
S-90         call unroll_partial_remainder_option2(NT, A)
S-91         if( .not. all(A(1:NT) == C(1:NT)) ) error = .true.
S-92
S-93         A(1:NT)=0
S-94         call unroll_partial_remainder_option3(NT, A)
S-95         if( .not. all(A(1:NT) == C(1:NT)) ) error = .true.
S-96
S-97         if(.not. error) print*, "OUT: Passed."
S-98         if(      error) print*, "OUT: Failed"
S-99      end program
```

———————————————————— Fortran ————————————————————

8.3 Incomplete Tiles

Optimal performance for tiled loops is achieved when the loop iteration count is a multiple of the tile size. When this condition does not exist, the implementation is free to execute the partial loops in a manner that optimizes performance, while preserving the specified order of iterations in the complete-tile loops.

Figure 8.1a shows an example of a 2-by-2 tiling for a 5-by-5 iteration space. There are nine resulting tiles. Four are *complete* 2-by-2 tiles, and the remaining five tiles are *partial* tiles.

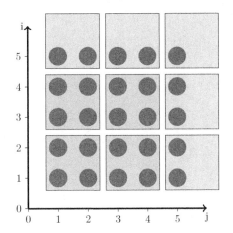

(A) 2-dimensional tiling with partial tiles

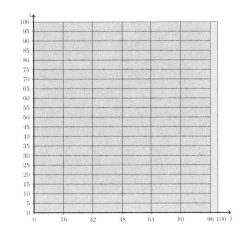

(B) Partial tiles of Example *partial_tile.1*

FIGURE 8.1: Tiling illustrations

In the following example, function *func1* uses the **tile** construct with a **sizes(4,16)** tiling clause. Because the second tile dimension of 16 does not evenly divide into the iteration count of the j-loop, the iterations corresponding to the remainder for the j-loop correspond to partial tiles as shown in Figure 8.1b. Each remaining function illustrates a code implementation that a compiler may generate to implement the **tile** construct in *func1*.

The order of tile execution relative to other tiles can be changed, but execution order of iterations within the same tile must be preserved. Implementations must ensure that dependencies that are valid with any tile size need to be preserved (including tile size of 1 and tiles as large as the iteration space).

Functions *func2* through *func6* are valid implementations of *func1*. In *func2* the unrolling is illustrated as a pair of nested loops with a simple adjustment in the size of the final iteration block in the *j2* iteration space for the partial tile.

Performance of the implementation depends on the hardware architecture, the instruction set and compiler optimization goals. Functions *func3*, *func4*, and *func5* have the advantage that the

1 innermost loop for the complete tile is a constant size and can be replaced with SIMD instructions.
2 If the target platform has masked SIMD instructions with no overhead, then avoiding the
3 construction of a remainder loop, as in *func5*, might be the best option. Another option is to use a
4 remainder loop without tiling, as shown in *func6*, to reduce control-flow overhead.

──────────────────────────── C / C++ ────────────────────────────

5 *Example partial_tile.1.c* (omp_5.1)

```
S-1    int min(int a, int b){ return (a < b)? a : b; }
S-2
S-3    void func1(double A[100][100])
S-4    {
S-5        #pragma omp tile sizes(4,16)
S-6        for (int i = 0; i < 100; ++i)
S-7            for (int j = 0; j < 100; ++j)
S-8                A[i][j] = A[i][j] + 1;
S-9    }
S-10
S-11   void func2(double A[100][100])
S-12   {
S-13       for (int i1 = 0; i1 < 100; i1+=4)
S-14           for (int j1 = 0; j1 < 100; j1+=16)
S-15               for (int i2 = i1; i2 < i1+4; ++i2)
S-16                   for (int j2 = j1; j2 < min(j1+16,100); ++j2)
S-17                       A[i2][j2] = A[i2][j2] + 1;
S-18   }
S-19
S-20   void func3(double A[100][100])
S-21   {
S-22       // complete tiles
S-23       for (int i1 = 0; i1 < 100; i1+=4)
S-24           for (int j1 = 0; j1 < 96; j1+=16)
S-25               for (int i2 = i1; i2 < i1+4; ++i2)
S-26                   for (int j2 = j1; j2 < j1+16; ++j2)
S-27                       A[i2][j2] = A[i2][j2] + 1;
S-28       // partial tiles / remainder
S-29       for (int i1 = 0; i1 < 100; i1+=4)
S-30           for (int i2 = i1; i2 < i1+4; ++i2)
S-31               for (int j = 96; j < 100; j+=1)
S-32                   A[i2][j] = A[i2][j] + 1;
S-33   }
S-34
S-35   void func4(double A[100][100])
S-36   {
S-37       for (int i1 = 0; i1 < 100; i1+=4) {
S-38           // complete tiles
S-39           for (int j1 = 0; j1 < 96; j1+=16)
```

```
S-40              for (int i2 = i1;  i2 < i1+4;  ++i2)
S-41                  for (int j2 = j1;  j2 < j1+16;  ++j2)
S-42                      A[i2][j2] = A[i2][j2] + 1;
S-43          // partial tiles
S-44          for (int i2 = i1;  i2 < i1+4;  ++i2)
S-45              for (int j = 96;  j < 100;  j+=1)
S-46                  A[i2][j] = A[i2][j] + 1;
S-47      }
S-48  }
S-49
S-50  void func5(double A[100][100])
S-51  {
S-52      for (int i1 = 0;  i1 < 100;  i1+=4)
S-53          for (int j1 = 0;  j1 < 100;  j1+=16)
S-54              for (int i2 = i1;  i2 < i1+4;  ++i2)
S-55                  for (int j2 = j1;  j2 <j1+16;  ++j2)
S-56                      if (j2 < 100)
S-57                          A[i2][j2] = A[i2][j2] + 1;
S-58  }
S-59
S-60  void func6(double A[100][100])
S-61  {
S-62      // complete tiles
S-63      for (int i1 = 0;  i1 < 100;  i1+=4)
S-64          for (int j1 = 0;  j1 < 96;  j1+=16)
S-65              for (int i2 = i1;  i2 < i1+4;  ++i2)
S-66                  for (int j2 = j1;  j2 < j1+16;  ++j2)
S-67                      A[i2][j2] = A[i2][j2] + 1;
S-68      // partial tiles / remainder (not tiled)
S-69      for (int i = 0;  i < 100;  ++i)
S-70          for (int j = 96;  j < 100;  ++j)
S-71                  A[i][j] = A[i][j] + 1;
S-72  }
```

———————————————— C / C++ ————————————————
———————————————— Fortran ————————————————

1   *Example partial_tile.1.f90* (**omp_5.1**)

```
S-1
S-2   subroutine func1(A)
S-3      implicit none
S-4      double precision   :: A(100,100)
S-5      integer            :: i,j
S-6
S-7      !$omp tile sizes(4,16)
S-8      do i = 1, 100
S-9      do j = 1, 100
```

```
S-10            A(j,i)  = A(j,i) + 1
S-11        end do; end do
S-12
S-13    end subroutine
S-14
S-15
S-16    subroutine func2(A)
S-17        implicit none
S-18        double precision    :: A(100,100)
S-19        integer             :: i1,i2,j1,j2
S-20
S-21        do i1 =  1, 100,  4
S-22        do j1 =  1, 100, 16
S-23        do i2 = i1,  i1 + 3
S-24        do j2 = j1, min(j1+15,100)
S-25           A(j2,i2) = A(j2,i2) + 1
S-26        end do; end do; end do; end do
S-27
S-28    end subroutine
S-29
S-30
S-31    subroutine func3(A)
S-32        implicit none
S-33        double precision    :: A(100,100)
S-34        integer             :: i1,i2,j1,j2, j
S-35
S-36        !! complete tiles
S-37        do i1 =  1, 100,  4
S-38        do j1 =  1,  96, 16
S-39        do i2 = i1,  i1 + 3
S-40        do j2 = j1,   j1 +15
S-41           A(j2,i2) = A(j2,i2) + 1
S-42        end do; end do; end do; end do
S-43
S-44        !! partial tiles / remainder
S-45        do i1 =  1, 100,  4
S-46        do i2 = i1,  i1 +3
S-47        do  j = 97, 100
S-48           A(j,i2) = A(j,i2) + 1
S-49        end do; end do; end do
S-50
S-51    end subroutine
S-52
S-53
S-54    subroutine func4(A)
S-55        implicit none
S-56        double precision    :: A(100,100)
```

```
S-57        integer              :: i1,i2,j1,j2, j
S-58
S-59        do i1 =  1, 100,  4
S-60
S-61           !! complete tiles
S-62           do j1 =  1,   96, 16
S-63           do i2 = i1,   i1 + 3
S-64           do j2 = j1,   j1 +15
S-65              A(j2,i2) = A(j2,i2) + 1
S-66           end do; end do; end do
S-67
S-68           !! partial tiles
S-69           do i2 = i1,   i1 +3
S-70           do   j = 97, 100
S-71              A(j,i2) = A(j,i2) + 1
S-72           end do; end do
S-73
S-74        end do
S-75
S-76     end subroutine
S-77
S-78
S-79     subroutine func5(A)
S-80        implicit none
S-81        double precision   :: A(100,100)
S-82        integer              :: i1,i2,j1,j2
S-83
S-84        do i1 =  1, 100,  4
S-85        do j1 =  1, 100, 16
S-86        do i2 = i1,   i1 + 3
S-87        do j2 = j1,   j1 +15
S-88           if (j2 < 101) A(j2,i2) = A(j2,i2) + 1
S-89        end do; end do; end do; end do
S-90
S-91     end subroutine
S-92
S-93
S-94     subroutine func6(A)
S-95        implicit none
S-96        double precision   :: A(100,100)
S-97        integer              :: i1,i2,j1,j2, i,j
S-98
S-99        !! complete tiles
S-100       do i1 =  1, 100,  4
S-101       do j1 =  1,   96, 16
S-102       do i2 = i1,   i1 + 3
S-103       do j2 = j1,   j1 +15
```

```
S-104                A(j2,i2) = A(j2,i2) + 1
S-105            end do; end do; end do; end do
S-106
S-107            !! partial tiles / remainder (not tiled)
S-108            do i =  1, 100
S-109            do j = 97, 100
S-110                A(j,i) = A(j,i) + 1
S-111            end do; end do
S-112
S-113        end subroutine
```

———————————————————— Fortran ————————————————————

In the following example, function *func7* tiles nested loops with a size of (4,16), resulting in partial
tiles that cover the last 4 iterations of the j-loop, as in the previous example. However, the outer
loop is parallelized with a **parallel** worksharing-loop construct.

Functions *func8* and *func9* illustrate two implementations of the tiling with **parallel** and
worksharing-loop directives. Function *func8* uses a single outer loop, with a *min* function to
accommodate the partial tiles. Function *func9* uses two sets of nested loops, the first iterates over
the complete tiles and the second covers iterations from the partial tiles. When fissioning loops that
are in a **parallel** worksharing-loop region, each iteration of each worksharing loop must be
executed on the same thread as in an un-fissioned loop. The **schedule(static)** clause in
func7 forces the implementation to use static scheduling and allows the fission in function *func8*.
When dynamic scheduling is prescribed, fissioning is not allowed. When no scheduling is
specified, the compiler implementation will select a scheduling *kind* and adhere to its restrictions.

———————————————————— C / C++ ————————————————————

Example *partial_tile.2.c* (**omp_5.1**)

```
S-1     int min(int a, int b){ return (a < b)? a : b; }
S-2
S-3     void func7(double A[100][100])
S-4     {
S-5         #pragma omp parallel for schedule(static)
S-6         #pragma omp tile sizes(4,16)
S-7         for (int i = 0; i < 100; ++i)
S-8             for (int j = 0; j < 100; ++j)
S-9                 A[i][j] = A[i][j] + 1;
S-10    }
S-11
S-12    void func8(double A[100][100])
S-13    {
S-14        #pragma omp parallel for schedule(static)
S-15        for (int i1 = 0; i1 < 100; i1+=4)
S-16            for (int j1 = 0; j1 < 100; j1+=16)
S-17                for (int i2 = i1; i2 < i1+4; ++i2)
S-18                    for (int j2 = j1; j2 < min(j1+16,100); ++j2)
```

```
S-19                              A[i2][j2] = A[i2][j2] + 1;
S-20      }
S-21
S-22    void func9(double A[100][100])
S-23    {
S-24        #pragma omp parallel
S-25        {
S-26            #pragma omp for schedule(static) nowait
S-27            for (int i1 = 0; i1 < 100; i1+=4)
S-28                for (int j1 = 0; j1 < 96; j1+=16)
S-29                    for (int i2 = i1; i2 < i1+4; ++i2)
S-30                        for (int j2 = j1; j2 < j1+16; ++j2)
S-31                            A[i2][j2] = A[i2][j2] + 1;
S-32            #pragma omp for schedule(static)
S-33            for (int i1 = 0; i1 < 100; i1+=4)
S-34                for (int i2 = i1; i2 < i1+4; ++i2)
S-35                    for (int j = 96; j < 100; j+=1)
S-36                        A[i2][j] = A[i2][j] + 1;
S-37        }
S-38    }
```

———————————————————————————— C / C++ ————————————————————————————
———————————————————————————— Fortran ————————————————————————————

1   *Example partial_tile.2.f90* (omp_5.1)

```
S-1
S-2     subroutine func7(A)
S-3        implicit none
S-4        double precision   :: A(100,100)
S-5        integer            :: i,j
S-6
S-7        !$omp parallel do schedule(static)
S-8        !$omp tile sizes(4,16)
S-9        do i=1,100
S-10       do j = 1, 100
S-11          A(j,i)  = A(j,i) + 1
S-12       end do; end do
S-13
S-14    end subroutine
S-15
S-16    subroutine func8(A)
S-17       implicit none
S-18       double precision   :: A(100,100)
S-19       integer            :: i1,i2,j1,j2
S-20
S-21       do i1 =  1, 100,  4
S-22       do j1 =  1, 100, 16
```

```
S-23          do i2 = i1,   i1 + 3
S-24          do j2 = j1, min(j1+15,100)
S-25             A(j2,i2) = A(j2,i2) + 1
S-26          end do; end do; end do; end do
S-27

S-28       end subroutine
S-29

S-30       subroutine func9(A)
S-31          implicit none
S-32          double precision     :: A(100,100)
S-33          integer              :: i1,i2,j1,j2,j
S-34

S-35          !$omp parallel
S-36

S-37             !$omp do schedule(static)
S-38             do i1 =   1, 100,   4
S-39             do j1 =   1,  96, 16
S-40             do i2 = i1,   i1 + 3
S-41             do j2 = j1,   j1 +15
S-42                A(j2,i2) = A(j2,i2) + 1
S-43             end do; end do; end do; end do
S-44             !$omp end do nowait
S-45

S-46             !$omp do schedule(static)
S-47             do i1 =   1, 100, 4
S-48             do i2 = i1,   i1 +3
S-49             do  j = 97, 100
S-50                A(j,i2) = A(j,i2) + 1
S-51             end do; end do; end do;
S-52

S-53          !$omp end parallel
S-54

S-55       end subroutine
```
─────────────────────── Fortran ───────────────────────

9 Synchronization

The **barrier** construct is a stand-alone directive that requires all threads of a team (within a contention group) to execute the barrier and complete execution of all tasks within the region, before continuing past the barrier.

The **critical** construct is a directive that contains a structured block. The construct allows only a single thread at a time to execute the structured block (region). Multiple critical regions may exist in a parallel region, and may act cooperatively (only one thread at a time in all **critical** regions), or separately (only one thread at a time in each **critical** regions when a unique name is supplied on each **critical** construct). An optional (lock) **hint** clause may be specified on a named **critical** construct to provide the OpenMP runtime guidance in selection a locking mechanism.

On a finer scale the **atomic** construct allows only a single thread at a time to have atomic access to a storage location involving a single read, write, update or capture statement, and a limited number of combinations when specifying the **capture** *atomic-clause* clause. The *atomic-clause* clause is required for some expression statements, but is not required for **update** statements. The *memory-order* clause can be used to specify the degree of memory ordering enforced by an **atomic** construct. From weakest to strongest, they are **relaxed** (the default), acquire and/or release clauses (specified with **acquire**, **release**, or **acq_rel**), and **seq_cst**. Please see the details in the *atomic Construct* subsection of the *Directives* chapter in the OpenMP Specifications document.

The **ordered** construct either specifies a structured block in a loop, simd, or loop SIMD region that will be executed in the order of the loop iterations. The ordered construct sequentializes and orders the execution of ordered regions while allowing code outside the region to run in parallel.

Since OpenMP 4.5 the **ordered** construct can also be a stand-alone directive that specifies cross-iteration dependences in a doacross loop nest. The **depend** clause uses a **sink** *dependence-type*, along with an iteration vector argument (vec) to indicate the iteration that satisfies the dependence. The **depend** clause with a **source** *dependence-type* specifies dependence satisfaction.

The **flush** directive is a stand-alone construct for enforcing consistency between a thread's view of memory and the view of memory for other threads (see the Memory Model chapter of this document for more details). When the construct is used with an explicit variable list, a *strong flush* that forces a thread's temporary view of memory to be consistent with the actual memory is applied to all listed variables. When the construct is used without an explicit variable list and without a *memory-order* clause, a strong flush is applied to all locally thread-visible data as defined by the base language, and additionally the construct provides both acquire and release memory ordering semantics. When an explicit variable list is not present and a *memory-order* clause is present, the construct provides acquire and/or release memory ordering semantics according to the *memory-order* clause, but no strong flush is performed. A resulting strong flush that applies to a set of variables effectively ensures that no memory (load or store) operation for the affected variables may be reordered across the **flush** directive.

General-purpose routines provide mutual exclusion semantics through locks, represented by lock variables. The semantics allows a task to *set*, and hence *own* a lock, until it is *unset* by the task that set it. A *nestable* lock can be set multiple times by a task, and is used when in code requires nested control of locks. A *simple lock* can only be set once by the owning task. There are specific calls for the two types of locks, and the variable of a specific lock type cannot be used by the other lock type.

Any explicit task will observe the synchronization prescribed in a **barrier** construct and an implied barrier. Also, additional synchronizations are available for tasks. All children of a task will wait at a **taskwait** (for their siblings to complete). A **taskgroup** construct creates a region in which the current task is suspended at the end of the region until all sibling tasks, and their descendants, have completed. Scheduling constraints on task execution can be prescribed by the **depend** clause to enforce dependence on previously generated tasks. More details on controlling task executions can be found in the *Tasking* Chapter in the OpenMP Specifications document.

9.1 `critical` Construct

The following example includes several **critical** constructs. The example illustrates a queuing model in which a task is dequeued and worked on. To guard against multiple threads dequeuing the same task, the dequeuing operation must be in a **critical** region. Because the two queues in this example are independent, they are protected by **critical** constructs with different names, *xaxis* and *yaxis*.

──────────────────── C / C++ ────────────────────

Example critical.1.c

```
S-1   int dequeue(float *a);
S-2   void work(int i, float *a);
S-3
S-4   void critical_example(float *x, float *y)
S-5   {
S-6     int ix_next, iy_next;
S-7
S-8     #pragma omp parallel shared(x, y) private(ix_next, iy_next)
S-9     {
S-10      #pragma omp critical (xaxis)
S-11        ix_next = dequeue(x);
S-12      work(ix_next, x);
S-13
S-14      #pragma omp critical (yaxis)
S-15        iy_next = dequeue(y);
S-16      work(iy_next, y);
S-17    }
S-18
S-19  }
```

──────────────────── C / C++ ────────────────────

──────────────────── Fortran ────────────────────

Example critical.1.f

```
S-1         SUBROUTINE CRITICAL_EXAMPLE(X, Y)
S-2
S-3           REAL X(*), Y(*)
S-4           INTEGER IX_NEXT, IY_NEXT
S-5
S-6   !$OMP PARALLEL SHARED(X, Y) PRIVATE(IX_NEXT, IY_NEXT)
S-7
S-8   !$OMP CRITICAL(XAXIS)
S-9           CALL DEQUEUE(IX_NEXT, X)
S-10  !$OMP END CRITICAL(XAXIS)
S-11          CALL WORK(IX_NEXT, X)
S-12
```

```
S-13    !$OMP CRITICAL(YAXIS)
S-14           CALL DEQUEUE(IY_NEXT,Y)
S-15    !$OMP END CRITICAL(YAXIS)
S-16           CALL WORK(IY_NEXT, Y)
S-17
S-18    !$OMP END PARALLEL
S-19
S-20           END SUBROUTINE CRITICAL_EXAMPLE
```

―――――――――――――――――――――――― Fortran ――――――――――――――――――――――――

The following example extends the previous example by adding the **hint** clause to the **critical** constructs.

―――――――――――――――――――――――― C / C++ ――――――――――――――――――――――――

Example critical.2.c (**omp_5.0**)

```
S-1    #include <omp.h>
S-2
S-3    int dequeue(float *a);
S-4    void work(int i, float *a);
S-5
S-6    void critical_example(float *x, float *y)
S-7    {
S-8      int ix_next, iy_next;
S-9
S-10     #pragma omp parallel shared(x, y) private(ix_next, iy_next)
S-11     {
S-12       #pragma omp critical (xaxis) hint(omp_sync_hint_contended)
S-13         ix_next = dequeue(x);
S-14       work(ix_next, x);
S-15
S-16       #pragma omp critical (yaxis) hint(omp_sync_hint_contended)
S-17         iy_next = dequeue(y);
S-18       work(iy_next, y);
S-19     }
S-20
S-21   }
```

―――――――――――――――――――――――― C / C++ ――――――――――――――――――――――――

1   *Example critical.2.f* (**omp_5.0**)

```
S-1          SUBROUTINE CRITICAL_EXAMPLE(X, Y)
S-2            USE OMP_LIB           ! or INCLUDE "omp_lib.h"
S-3
S-4            REAL X(*), Y(*)
S-5            INTEGER IX_NEXT, IY_NEXT
S-6
S-7    !$OMP PARALLEL SHARED(X, Y) PRIVATE(IX_NEXT, IY_NEXT)
S-8
S-9    !$OMP CRITICAL(XAXIS) HINT(OMP_SYNC_HINT_CONTENDED)
S-10           CALL DEQUEUE(IX_NEXT, X)
S-11   !$OMP END CRITICAL(XAXIS)
S-12           CALL WORK(IX_NEXT, X)
S-13
S-14   !$OMP CRITICAL(YAXIS) HINT(OMP_SYNC_HINT_CONTENDED)
S-15           CALL DEQUEUE(IY_NEXT,Y)
S-16   !$OMP END CRITICAL(YAXIS)
S-17           CALL WORK(IY_NEXT, Y)
S-18
S-19   !$OMP END PARALLEL
S-20
S-21           END SUBROUTINE CRITICAL_EXAMPLE
```

9.2 Worksharing Constructs Inside a `critical` Construct

The following example demonstrates using a worksharing construct inside a **critical** construct. This example is conforming because the worksharing **single** region is not closely nested inside the **critical** region. A single thread executes the one and only section in the **sections** region, and executes the **critical** region. The same thread encounters the nested **parallel** region, creates a new team of threads, and becomes the primary thread of the new team. One of the threads in the new team enters the **single** region and increments **i** by **1**. At the end of this example **i** is equal to **2**.

--- C / C++ ---

Example worksharing_critical.1.c

```
void critical_work()
{
  int i = 1;
  #pragma omp parallel sections
  {
    #pragma omp section
    {
      #pragma omp critical (name)
      {
        #pragma omp parallel
        {
          #pragma omp single
          {
            i++;
          }
        }
      }
    }
  }
}
```

--- C / C++ ---

1   *Example worksharing_critical.1.f*

```
S-1          SUBROUTINE CRITICAL_WORK()
S-2
S-3           INTEGER I
S-4           I = 1
S-5
S-6  !$OMP    PARALLEL SECTIONS
S-7  !$OMP      SECTION
S-8  !$OMP        CRITICAL (NAME)
S-9  !$OMP          PARALLEL
S-10 !$OMP            SINGLE
S-11                    I = I + 1
S-12 !$OMP            END SINGLE
S-13 !$OMP          END PARALLEL
S-14 !$OMP        END CRITICAL (NAME)
S-15 !$OMP    END PARALLEL SECTIONS
S-16         END SUBROUTINE CRITICAL_WORK
```

9.3 Binding of `barrier` Regions

The binding rules call for a **barrier** region to bind to the closest enclosing **parallel** region.

In the following example, the call from the main program to *sub2* is conforming because the **barrier** region (in *sub3*) binds to the **parallel** region in *sub2*. The call from the main program to *sub1* is conforming because the **barrier** region binds to the **parallel** region in subroutine *sub2*.

The call from the main program to *sub3* is conforming because the **barrier** region binds to the implicit inactive **parallel** region enclosing the sequential part. Also note that the **barrier** region in *sub3* when called from *sub2* only synchronizes the team of threads in the enclosing **parallel** region and not all the threads created in *sub1*.

C / C++

Example barrier_regions.1.c

```
void work(int n) {}

void sub3(int n)
{
  work(n);
  #pragma omp barrier
  work(n);
}

void sub2(int k)
{
  #pragma omp parallel shared(k)
    sub3(k);
}

void sub1(int n)
{
  int i;
  #pragma omp parallel private(i) shared(n)
  {
    #pragma omp for
    for (i=0; i<n; i++)
      sub2(i);
  }
}

int main()
{
  sub1(2);
  sub2(2);
```

```
S-31        sub3(2);
S-32        return 0;
S-33    }
```

———————————————— C / C++ ————————————————
———————————————— Fortran ————————————————

1   *Example barrier_regions.1.f*

```
S-1             SUBROUTINE WORK(N)
S-2               INTEGER N
S-3             END SUBROUTINE WORK
S-4
S-5             SUBROUTINE SUB3(N)
S-6             INTEGER N
S-7               CALL WORK(N)
S-8     !$OMP    BARRIER
S-9               CALL WORK(N)
S-10            END SUBROUTINE SUB3
S-11
S-12            SUBROUTINE SUB2(K)
S-13            INTEGER K
S-14    !$OMP    PARALLEL SHARED(K)
S-15               CALL SUB3(K)
S-16    !$OMP    END PARALLEL
S-17            END SUBROUTINE SUB2
S-18
S-19
S-20            SUBROUTINE SUB1(N)
S-21            INTEGER N
S-22              INTEGER I
S-23    !$OMP    PARALLEL PRIVATE(I) SHARED(N)
S-24    !$OMP      DO
S-25              DO I = 1, N
S-26                CALL SUB2(I)
S-27              END DO
S-28    !$OMP    END PARALLEL
S-29            END SUBROUTINE SUB1
S-30
S-31            PROGRAM EXAMPLE
S-32              CALL SUB1(2)
S-33              CALL SUB2(2)
S-34              CALL SUB3(2)
S-35            END PROGRAM EXAMPLE
```

———————————————— Fortran ————————————————

9.4 `atomic` Construct

The following example avoids race conditions (simultaneous updates of an element of *x* by multiple threads) by using the **atomic** construct .

The advantage of using the **atomic** construct in this example is that it allows updates of two different elements of *x* to occur in parallel. If a **critical** construct were used instead, then all updates to elements of *x* would be executed serially (though not in any guaranteed order).

Note that the **atomic** directive applies only to the statement immediately following it. As a result, elements of *y* are not updated atomically in this example.

―――――――――――――――― C / C++ ――――――――――――――――

Example atomic.1.c (`omp_3.1`)

```
float work1(int i)
{
  return 1.0 * i;
}


float work2(int i)
{
   return 2.0 * i;
}

void atomic_example(float *x, float *y, int *index, int n)
{
  int i;

  #pragma omp parallel for shared(x, y, index, n)
    for (i=0; i<n; i++) {
      #pragma omp atomic update
      x[index[i]] += work1(i);
      y[i] += work2(i);
    }
}

int main()
{
  float x[1000];
  float y[10000];
  int index[10000];
  int i;

  for (i = 0; i < 10000; i++) {
    index[i] = i % 1000;
    y[i]=0.0;
  }
```

```
S-34        for (i = 0; i < 1000; i++)
S-35          x[i] = 0.0;
S-36        atomic_example(x, y, index, 10000);
S-37        return 0;
S-38      }
```

—————————————— C / C++ ——————————————
—————————————— Fortran ——————————————

1   *Example atomic.1.f* (omp_3.1)

```
S-1              REAL FUNCTION WORK1(I)
S-2                INTEGER I
S-3                WORK1 = 1.0 * I
S-4                RETURN
S-5              END FUNCTION WORK1
S-6
S-7              REAL FUNCTION WORK2(I)
S-8                INTEGER I
S-9                WORK2 = 2.0 * I
S-10               RETURN
S-11             END FUNCTION WORK2
S-12
S-13             SUBROUTINE SUB(X, Y, INDEX, N)
S-14               REAL X(*), Y(*)
S-15               INTEGER INDEX(*), N
S-16
S-17               INTEGER I
S-18
S-19     !$OMP    PARALLEL DO SHARED(X, Y, INDEX, N)
S-20               DO I=1,N
S-21     !$OMP        ATOMIC UPDATE
S-22                   X(INDEX(I)) = X(INDEX(I)) + WORK1(I)
S-23                 Y(I) = Y(I) + WORK2(I)
S-24               ENDDO
S-25
S-26             END SUBROUTINE SUB
S-27
S-28             PROGRAM ATOMIC_EXAMPLE
S-29               REAL X(1000), Y(10000)
S-30               INTEGER INDEX(10000)
S-31               INTEGER I
S-32
S-33               DO I=1,10000
S-34                 INDEX(I) = MOD(I, 1000) + 1
S-35                 Y(I) = 0.0
S-36               ENDDO
S-37
```

```
S-38          DO I = 1,1000
S-39            X(I) = 0.0
S-40          ENDDO
S-41
S-42          CALL SUB(X, Y, INDEX, 10000)
S-43
S-44          END PROGRAM ATOMIC_EXAMPLE
```

───────────────── *Fortran* ─────────────────

1   The following example illustrates the **read** and **write** clauses for the **atomic** directive. These
2   clauses ensure that the given variable is read or written, respectively, as a whole. Otherwise, some
3   other thread might read or write part of the variable while the current thread was reading or writing
4   another part of the variable. Note that most hardware provides atomic reads and writes for some set
5   of properly aligned variables of specific sizes, but not necessarily for all the variable types
6   supported by the OpenMP API.

───────────────── C / C++ ─────────────────

7   *Example atomic.2.c* (**omp_3.1**)

```
S-1    int atomic_read(const int *p)
S-2    {
S-3        int value;
S-4    /* Guarantee that the entire value of *p is read atomically. No part of
S-5     * *p can change during the read operation.
S-6     */
S-7    #pragma omp atomic read
S-8        value = *p;
S-9        return value;
S-10   }
S-11
S-12   void atomic_write(int *p, int value)
S-13   {
S-14   /* Guarantee that value is stored atomically into *p. No part of *p can
S-15   change
S-16    * until after the entire write operation is completed.
S-17    */
S-18   #pragma omp atomic write
S-19       *p = value;
S-20   }
```

───────────────── C / C++ ─────────────────

1 *Example atomic.2.f* (**omp_3.1**)

```
S-1            function atomic_read(p)
S-2            integer :: atomic_read
S-3            integer, intent(in) :: p
S-4    ! Guarantee that the entire value of p is read atomically. No part of
S-5    ! p can change during the read operation.
S-6
S-7    !$omp atomic read
S-8            atomic_read = p
S-9            return
S-10           end function atomic_read
S-11
S-12           subroutine atomic_write(p, value)
S-13           integer, intent(out) :: p
S-14           integer, intent(in) :: value
S-15   ! Guarantee that value is stored atomically into p. No part of p can change
S-16   ! until after the entire write operation is completed.
S-17   !$omp atomic write
S-18           p = value
S-19           end subroutine atomic_write
```

2 The following example illustrates the **capture** clause for the **atomic** directive. In this case the
3 value of a variable is captured, and then the variable is incremented. These operations occur
4 atomically. This example could be implemented using the fetch-and-add instruction available on
5 many kinds of hardware. The example also shows a way to implement a spin lock using the
6 **capture** and **read** clauses.

7 *Example atomic.3.c* (**omp_3.1**)

```
S-1    int fetch_and_add(int *p)
S-2    {
S-3        /* Atomically read the value of *p and then increment it. The
S-4           previous value is returned. This can be used to implement a
S-5           simple lock as shown below.
S-6        */
S-7        int old;
S-8    #pragma omp atomic capture
S-9        { old = *p; (*p)++; }
S-10       return old;
S-11   }
S-12
S-13   /*
```

```
S-14        * Use fetch_and_add to implement a lock
S-15        */
S-16     struct locktype {
S-17        int ticketnumber;
S-18        int turn;
S-19     };
S-20     void do_locked_work(struct locktype *lock)
S-21     {
S-22        int atomic_read(const int *p);
S-23        void work();
S-24
S-25        // Obtain the lock
S-26        int myturn = fetch_and_add(&lock->ticketnumber);
S-27        while (atomic_read(&lock->turn) != myturn)
S-28           ;
S-29        // Do some work. The flush is needed to ensure visibility of
S-30        // variables not involved in atomic directives
S-31
S-32        #pragma omp flush
S-33        work();
S-34        #pragma omp flush
S-35        // Release the lock
S-36        fetch_and_add(&lock->turn);
S-37     }
```

———————————————————— C / C++ ————————————————————
———————————————————————— Fortran ————————————————————

1   *Example atomic.3.f* (omp_3.1)

```
S-1              function fetch_and_add(p)
S-2              integer:: fetch_and_add
S-3              integer, intent(inout) :: p
S-4
S-5      ! Atomically read the value of p and then increment it. The previous value
S-6      ! is returned. This can be used to implement a simple lock as shown below.
S-7      !$omp atomic capture
S-8              fetch_and_add = p
S-9              p = p + 1
S-10     !$omp end atomic
S-11             end function fetch_and_add
S-12             module m
S-13             interface
S-14               function fetch_and_add(p)
S-15                 integer :: fetch_and_add
S-16                 integer, intent(inout) :: p
S-17               end function
S-18               function atomic_read(p)
```

```
S-19            integer :: atomic_read
S-20            integer, intent(in) :: p
S-21          end function
S-22        end interface
S-23        type locktype
S-24          integer ticketnumber
S-25          integer turn
S-26        end type
S-27        contains
S-28        subroutine do_locked_work(lock)
S-29        type(locktype), intent(inout) :: lock
S-30        integer myturn
S-31        integer junk
S-32  ! obtain the lock
S-33          myturn = fetch_and_add(lock%ticketnumber)
S-34          do while (atomic_read(lock%turn) .ne. myturn)
S-35            continue
S-36          enddo
S-37  ! Do some work. The flush is needed to ensure visibility of variables
S-38  ! not involved in atomic directives
S-39  !$omp flush
S-40          call work
S-41  !$omp flush
S-42  ! Release the lock
S-43          junk = fetch_and_add(lock%turn)
S-44        end subroutine
S-45        end module
```

———————————————————— Fortran ————————————————————

9.5 Restrictions on the `atomic` Construct

The following non-conforming examples illustrate the restrictions on the **atomic** construct.

---------------------------- C / C++ ----------------------------

Example atomic_restrict.1.c (**omp_3.1**)

```
S-1    void atomic_wrong ()
S-2    {
S-3     union {int n; float x;} u;
S-4
S-5    #pragma omp parallel
S-6       {
S-7    #pragma omp atomic update
S-8        u.n++;
S-9
S-10   #pragma omp atomic update
S-11       u.x += 1.0;
S-12
S-13   /* Incorrect because the atomic constructs reference the same location
S-14      through incompatible types */
S-15      }
S-16   }
```

---------------------------- C / C++ ----------------------------

---------------------------- Fortran ----------------------------

Example atomic_restrict.1.f (**omp_3.1**)

```
S-1            SUBROUTINE ATOMIC_WRONG()
S-2              INTEGER:: I
S-3              REAL:: R
S-4              EQUIVALENCE(I,R)
S-5
S-6    !$OMP     PARALLEL
S-7    !$OMP      ATOMIC UPDATE
S-8                I = I + 1
S-9    !$OMP      ATOMIC UPDATE
S-10               R = R + 1.0
S-11   ! incorrect because I and R reference the same location
S-12   ! but have different types
S-13   !$OMP     END PARALLEL
S-14           END SUBROUTINE ATOMIC_WRONG
```

---------------------------- Fortran ----------------------------

1   *Example atomic_restrict.2.c* (**omp_3.1**)

```
S-1    void atomic_wrong2 ()
S-2    {
S-3     int   x;
S-4     int *i;
S-5     float    *r;
S-6
S-7     i = &x;
S-8     r = (float *)&x;
S-9
S-10   #pragma omp parallel
S-11     {
S-12   #pragma omp atomic update
S-13       *i += 1;
S-14
S-15   #pragma omp atomic update
S-16       *r += 1.0;
S-17
S-18   /* Incorrect because the atomic constructs reference the same location
S-19      through incompatible types */
S-20
S-21     }
S-22   }
```

2
3   The following example is non-conforming because **I** and **R** reference the same location but have different types.

4   *Example atomic_restrict.2.f* (**omp_3.1**)

```
S-1            SUBROUTINE SUB()
S-2              COMMON /BLK/ R
S-3              REAL R
S-4
S-5    !$OMP    ATOMIC UPDATE
S-6                R = R + 1.0
S-7            END SUBROUTINE SUB
S-8
S-9            SUBROUTINE ATOMIC_WRONG2()
S-10             COMMON /BLK/ I
S-11             INTEGER I
S-12
S-13   !$OMP    PARALLEL
S-14
```

```
S-15     !$OMP     ATOMIC UPDATE
S-16               I = I + 1
S-17               CALL SUB()
S-18     !$OMP   END PARALLEL
S-19           END SUBROUTINE ATOMIC_WRONG2
```

Although the following example might work on some implementations, this is also non-conforming:

Example atomic_restrict.3.f (`omp_3.1`)

```
S-1           SUBROUTINE ATOMIC_WRONG3
S-2             INTEGER:: I
S-3             REAL:: R
S-4             EQUIVALENCE(I,R)
S-5
S-6     !$OMP   PARALLEL
S-7     !$OMP     ATOMIC UPDATE
S-8               I = I + 1
S-9     ! incorrect because I and R reference the same location
S-10    ! but have different types
S-11    !$OMP   END PARALLEL
S-12
S-13    !$OMP   PARALLEL
S-14    !$OMP     ATOMIC UPDATE
S-15              R = R + 1.0
S-16    ! incorrect because I and R reference the same location
S-17    ! but have different types
S-18    !$OMP   END PARALLEL
S-19
S-20          END SUBROUTINE ATOMIC_WRONG3
```

─────────────────────────── Fortran ───────────────────────────

9.6 `flush` Construct without a List

The following example distinguishes the shared variables affected by a **flush** construct with no list from the shared objects that are not affected:

———————————————————— C / C++ ————————————————————

Example flush_nolist.1.c

```
int x, *p = &x;

void f1(int *q)
{
  *q = 1;
  #pragma omp flush
  /* x, p, and *q are flushed */
  /* because they are shared and accessible */
  /* q is not flushed because it is not shared. */
}

void f2(int *q)
{
  #pragma omp barrier
  *q = 2;
  #pragma omp barrier

  /* a barrier implies a flush */
  /* x, p, and *q are flushed */
  /* because they are shared and accessible */
  /* q is not flushed because it is not shared. */
}

int g(int n)
{
  int i = 1, j, sum = 0;
  *p = 1;
  #pragma omp parallel reduction(+: sum) num_threads(10)
  {
    f1(&j);

    /* i, n and sum were not flushed */
    /* because they were not accessible in f1 */
    /* j was flushed because it was accessible */
    sum += j;

    f2(&j);

    /* i, n, and sum were not flushed */
```

S-1
S-2
S-3
S-4
S-5
S-6
S-7
S-8
S-9
S-10
S-11
S-12
S-13
S-14
S-15
S-16
S-17
S-18
S-19
S-20
S-21
S-22
S-23
S-24
S-25
S-26
S-27
S-28
S-29
S-30
S-31
S-32
S-33
S-34
S-35
S-36
S-37
S-38
S-39

1
2
3
4

```
S-40        /* because they were not accessible in f2 */
S-41        /* j was flushed because it was accessible */
S-42          sum += i + j + *p + n;
S-43      }
S-44    return sum;
S-45  }
S-46
S-47  int main()
S-48  {
S-49    int result = g(7);
S-50    return result;
S-51  }
```

———————————————————————— C / C++ ————————————————————————
———————————————————————— Fortran ————————————————————————

1   *Example flush_nolist.1.f*

```
S-1              SUBROUTINE F1(Q)
S-2                COMMON /DATA/ X, P
S-3                INTEGER, TARGET  :: X
S-4                INTEGER, POINTER :: P
S-5                INTEGER Q
S-6
S-7                Q = 1
S-8   !$OMP    FLUSH
S-9                ! X, P and Q are flushed
S-10               ! because they are shared and accessible
S-11             END SUBROUTINE F1
S-12
S-13             SUBROUTINE F2(Q)
S-14               COMMON /DATA/ X, P
S-15               INTEGER, TARGET  :: X
S-16               INTEGER, POINTER :: P
S-17               INTEGER Q
S-18
S-19  !$OMP    BARRIER
S-20               Q = 2
S-21  !$OMP    BARRIER
S-22               ! a barrier implies a flush
S-23               ! X, P and Q are flushed
S-24               ! because they are shared and accessible
S-25             END SUBROUTINE F2
S-26
S-27             INTEGER FUNCTION G(N)
S-28               COMMON /DATA/ X, P
S-29               INTEGER, TARGET  :: X
S-30               INTEGER, POINTER :: P
```

```
S-31          INTEGER N
S-32          INTEGER I, J, SUM
S-33
S-34          I = 1
S-35          SUM = 0
S-36          P = 1
S-37  !$OMP   PARALLEL REDUCTION(+: SUM) NUM_THREADS(10)
S-38            CALL F1(J)
S-39              ! I, N and SUM were not flushed
S-40              !   because they were not accessible in F1
S-41              ! J was flushed because it was accessible
S-42            SUM = SUM + J
S-43
S-44            CALL F2(J)
S-45              ! I, N, and SUM were not flushed
S-46              !   because they were not accessible in f2
S-47              ! J was flushed because it was accessible
S-48            SUM = SUM + I + J + P + N
S-49  !$OMP   END PARALLEL
S-50
S-51          G = SUM
S-52        END FUNCTION G
S-53
S-54        PROGRAM FLUSH_NOLIST
S-55          COMMON /DATA/ X, P
S-56          INTEGER, TARGET  :: X
S-57          INTEGER, POINTER :: P
S-58          INTEGER RESULT, G
S-59
S-60          P => X
S-61          RESULT = G(7)
S-62          PRINT *, RESULT
S-63        END PROGRAM FLUSH_NOLIST
```

———————————————— Fortran ————————————————

9.7 Synchronization Based on Acquire/Release Semantics

As explained in the Memory Model chapter of this document, a flush operation may be an *acquire flush* and/or a *release flush*, and OpenMP 5.0 defines acquire/release semantics in terms of these fundamental flush operations. For any synchronization between two threads that is specified by OpenMP, a release flush logically occurs at the source of the synchronization and an acquire flush logically occurs at the sink of the synchronization. OpenMP 5.0 added memory ordering clauses – **acquire**, **release**, and **acq_rel** – to the **flush** and **atomic** constructs for explicitly requesting acquire/release semantics. Furthermore, implicit flushes for all OpenMP constructs and runtime routines that synchronize OpenMP threads in some manner were redefined in terms of synchronizing release and acquire flushes to avoid the requirement of strong memory fences (see the *Flush Synchronization and Happens Before* and *Implicit Flushes* sections of the OpenMP Specifications document).

The examples that follow in this section illustrate how acquire and release flushes may be employed, implicitly or explicitly, for synchronizing threads. A **flush** directive without a list and without any memory ordering clause can also function as both an acquire and release flush for facilitating thread synchronization. Flushes implied on entry to, or exit from, an atomic operation (specified by an **atomic** construct) may function as an acquire flush or a release flush if a memory ordering clause appears on the construct. On entry to and exit from a **critical** construct there is now an implicit acquire flush and release flush, respectively.

The first example illustrates how the release and acquire flushes implied by a **critical** region guarantee a value written by the first thread is visible to a read of the value on the second thread. Thread 0 writes to *x* and then executes a **critical** region in which it writes to *y*; the write to *x* happens before the execution of the **critical** region, consistent with the program order of the thread. Meanwhile, thread 1 executes a **critical** region in a loop until it reads a non-zero value from *y* in the **critical** region, after which it prints the value of *x*; again, the execution of the **critical** regions happen before the read from *x* based on the program order of the thread. The **critical** regions executed by the two threads execute in a serial manner, with a pairwise synchronization from the exit of one **critical** region to the entry to the next **critical** region. These pairwise synchronizations result from the implicit release flushes that occur on exit from **critical** regions and the implicit acquire flushes that occur on entry to **critical** regions; hence, the execution of each **critical** region in the sequence happens before the execution of the next **critical** region. A "happens before" order is therefore established between the assignment to *x* by thread 0 and the read from *x* by thread 1, and so thread 1 must see that *x* equals 10.

————————————— C / C++ —————————————

1   *Example acquire_release.1.c* (**omp_5.0**)

```
S-1
S-2    #include <stdio.h>
S-3    #include <omp.h>
S-4
S-5    int main()
S-6    {
S-7       int x = 0, y = 0;
S-8       #pragma omp parallel num_threads(2)
S-9       {
S-10         int thrd = omp_get_thread_num();
S-11         if (thrd == 0) {
S-12            x = 10;
S-13            #pragma omp critical
S-14            { y = 1; }
S-15         } else {
S-16            int tmp = 0;
S-17            while (tmp == 0) {
S-18               #pragma omp critical
S-19               { tmp = y; }
S-20            }
S-21            printf("x = %d\n", x); // always "x = 10"
S-22         }
S-23      }
S-24      return 0;
S-25   }
```

————————————— C / C++ —————————————
————————————— Fortran —————————————

2   *Example acquire_release.1.f90* (**omp_5.0**)

```
S-1
S-2    program rel_acq_ex1
S-3       use omp_lib
S-4       integer :: x, y, thrd, tmp
S-5       x = 0
S-6       y = 0
S-7       !$omp parallel num_threads(2) private(thrd, tmp)
S-8          thrd = omp_get_thread_num()
S-9          if (thrd == 0) then
S-10            x = 10
S-11            !$omp critical
S-12            y = 1
S-13            !$omp end critical
S-14         else
```

```
S-15                tmp = 0
S-16                do while (tmp == 0)
S-17                   !$omp critical
S-18                   tmp = y
S-19                   !$omp end critical
S-20                end do
S-21                print *, "x = ", x  !! always "x = 10"
S-22             end if
S-23          !$omp end parallel
S-24    end program
```

—————————————————————— *Fortran* ——————————————————————

In the second example, the **critical** constructs are exchanged with **atomic** constructs that have *explicit* memory ordering specified. When the atomic read operation on thread 1 reads a non-zero value from *y*, this results in a release/acquire synchronization that in turn implies that the assignment to *x* on thread 0 happens before the read of *x* on thread 1. Therefore, thread 1 will print "x = 10".

—————————————————————— C / C++ ——————————————————————

Example acquire_release.2.c (**omp_5.0**)

```
S-1
S-2     #include <stdio.h>
S-3     #include <omp.h>
S-4
S-5     int main()
S-6     {
S-7        int x = 0, y = 0;
S-8        #pragma omp parallel num_threads(2)
S-9        {
S-10          int thrd = omp_get_thread_num();
S-11          if (thrd == 0) {
S-12             x = 10;
S-13             #pragma omp atomic write release // or seq_cst
S-14             y = 1;
S-15          } else {
S-16             int tmp = 0;
S-17             while (tmp == 0) {
S-18                #pragma omp atomic read acquire // or seq_cst
S-19                tmp = y;
S-20             }
S-21             printf("x = %d\n", x); // always "x = 10"
S-22          }
S-23       }
S-24       return 0;
S-25    }
```

—————————————————————— C / C++ ——————————————————————

1   *Example acquire_release.2.f90* (**omp_5.0**)

```
S-1
S-2    program rel_acq_ex2
S-3       use omp_lib
S-4       integer :: x, y, thrd, tmp
S-5       x = 0
S-6       y = 0
S-7       !$omp parallel num_threads(2) private(thrd, tmp)
S-8          thrd = omp_get_thread_num()
S-9          if (thrd == 0) then
S-10            x = 10
S-11            !$omp atomic write release ! or seq_cst
S-12             y = 1
S-13            !$omp end atomic
S-14         else
S-15            tmp = 0
S-16            do while (tmp == 0)
S-17               !$omp atomic read acquire ! or seq_cst
S-18               tmp = y
S-19               !$omp end atomic
S-20            end do
S-21            print *, "x = ", x  !! always "x = 10"
S-22         end if
S-23      !$omp end parallel
S-24   end program
```

In the third example, **atomic** constructs that specify relaxed atomic operations are used with explicit **flush** directives to enforce memory ordering between the two threads. The explicit **flush** directive on thread 0 must specify a release flush and the explicit **flush** directive on thread 1 must specify an acquire flush to establish a release/acquire synchronization between the two threads. The **flush** and **atomic** constructs encountered by thread 0 can be replaced by the **atomic** construct used in Example 2 for thread 0, and similarly the **flush** and **atomic** constructs encountered by thread 1 can be replaced by the **atomic** construct used in Example 2 for thread 1.

——————————————————— C / C++ ———————————————————

Example acquire_release.3.c (**omp_5.0**)

```
#include <stdio.h>
#include <omp.h>

int main()
{
    int x = 0, y = 0;
    #pragma omp parallel num_threads(2)
    {
        int thrd = omp_get_thread_num();
        if (thrd == 0) {
            x = 10;
            #pragma omp flush // or with acq_rel or release clause
            #pragma omp atomic write // or with relaxed clause
            y = 1;
        } else {
            int tmp = 0;
            while (tmp == 0) {
                #pragma omp atomic read // or with relaxed clause
                tmp = y;
            }
            #pragma omp flush // or with acq_rel or acquire clause
            printf("x = %d\n", x);  // always "x = 10"
        }
    }
    return 0;
}
```

——————————————————— C / C++ ———————————————————

1   *Example acquire_release.3.f90* (**omp_5.0**)

```
S-1
S-2    program rel_acq_ex3
S-3       use omp_lib
S-4       integer :: x, y, thrd, tmp
S-5       x = 0
S-6       y = 0
S-7       !$omp parallel num_threads(2) private(thrd, tmp)
S-8          thrd = omp_get_thread_num()
S-9          if (thrd == 0) then
S-10            x = 10
S-11            !$omp flush ! or with acq_rel or release clause
S-12            !$omp atomic write
S-13            y = 1
S-14            !$omp end atomic
S-15         else
S-16            tmp = 0
S-17            do while (tmp == 0)
S-18               !$omp atomic read
S-19               tmp = y
S-20               !$omp end atomic
S-21            end do
S-22            !$omp flush ! or with acq_rel or acquire clause
S-23            print *, "x = ", x  !! always "x = 10"
S-24         end if
S-25      !$omp end parallel
S-26   end program
```

2   Example 4 will fail to order the write to *x* on thread 0 before the read from *x* on thread 1.
3   Importantly, the implicit release flush on exit from the **critical** region will not synchronize with
4   the acquire flush that occurs on the atomic read operation performed by thread 1. This is because
5   implicit release flushes that occur on a given construct may only synchronize with implicit acquire
6   flushes on a compatible construct (and vice-versa) that internally makes use of the same
7   synchronization variable. For a **critical** construct, this might correspond to a *lock* object that is
8   used by a given implementation (for the synchronization semantics of other constructs due to
9   implicit release and acquire flushes, refer to the *Implicit Flushes* section of the OpenMP
10   Specifications document). Either an explicit **flush** directive that provides a release flush (i.e., a
11   flush without a list that does not have the **acquire** clause) must be specified between the
12   **critical** construct and the atomic write, or an atomic operation that modifies *y* and provides
13   release semantics must be specified.

1   *Example acquire_release_broke.4.c* (**omp_5.0**)

```
S-1
S-2     #include <stdio.h>
S-3     #include <omp.h>
S-4
S-5     int main()
S-6     {
S-7
S-8     // !!! THIS CODE WILL FAIL TO PRODUCE CONSISTENT RESULTS !!!!!!!
S-9     // !!! DO NOT PROGRAM SYNCHRONIZATION THIS WAY !!!!!!!
S-10
S-11        int x = 0, y;
S-12        #pragma omp parallel num_threads(2)
S-13        {
S-14           int thrd = omp_get_thread_num();
S-15           if (thrd == 0) {
S-16              #pragma omp critical
S-17              { x = 10; }
S-18              // an explicit flush directive that provides
S-19              // release semantics is needed here
S-20              // to complete the synchronization.
S-21              #pragma omp atomic write
S-22              y = 1;
S-23           } else {
S-24              int tmp = 0;
S-25              while (tmp == 0) {
S-26                 #pragma omp atomic read acquire // or seq_cst
S-27                 tmp = y;
S-28              }
S-29              #pragma omp critical
S-30              { printf("x = %d\n", x); }  // !! NOT ALWAYS 10
S-31           }
S-32        }
S-33        return 0;
S-34     }
```

1   *Example acquire_release_broke.4.f90* (**omp_5.0**)

```fortran
program rel_acq_ex4
   use omp_lib
   integer :: x, y, thrd
   integer :: tmp
   x = 0

!! !!! THIS CODE WILL FAIL TO PRODUCE CONSISTENT RESULTS !!!!!!!
!! !!! DO NOT PROGRAM SYNCHRONIZATION THIS WAY !!!!!!!

   !$omp parallel num_threads(2) private(thrd) private(tmp)
      thrd = omp_get_thread_num()
      if (thrd == 0) then
         !$omp critical
         x = 10
         !$omp end critical
         ! an explicit flush directive that provides
         ! release semantics is needed here to
         ! complete the synchronization.
         !$omp atomic write
         y = 1
         !$omp end atomic
      else
         tmp = 0
         do while(tmp == 0)
            !$omp atomic read acquire ! or seq_cst
            tmp = x
            !$omp end atomic
         end do
         !$omp critical
         print *, "x = ", x  !! !! NOT ALWAYS 10
         !$omp end critical
      end if
   !$omp end parallel
end program
```

9.8 ordered Clause and ordered Construct

2
3

Ordered constructs are useful for sequentially ordering the output from work that is done in parallel. The following program prints out the indices in sequential order:

───────────────────────────── C / C++ ─────────────────────────────

4   *Example ordered.1.c*

```
S-1    #include <stdio.h>
S-2
S-3    void work(int k)
S-4    {
S-5      #pragma omp ordered
S-6        printf(" %d\n", k);
S-7    }
S-8
S-9    void ordered_example(int lb, int ub, int stride)
S-10   {
S-11     int i;
S-12
S-13     #pragma omp parallel for ordered schedule(dynamic)
S-14     for (i=lb; i<ub; i+=stride)
S-15       work(i);
S-16   }
S-17
S-18   int main()
S-19   {
S-20     ordered_example(0, 100, 5);
S-21     return 0;
S-22   }
```

───────────────────────────── C / C++ ─────────────────────────────
───────────────────────────── Fortran ─────────────────────────────

5   *Example ordered.1.f*

```
S-1            SUBROUTINE WORK(K)
S-2               INTEGER k
S-3
S-4    !$OMP ORDERED
S-5               WRITE(*,*) K
S-6    !$OMP END ORDERED
S-7
S-8            END SUBROUTINE WORK
S-9
S-10           SUBROUTINE SUB(LB, UB, STRIDE)
S-11              INTEGER LB, UB, STRIDE
S-12              INTEGER I
```

```
S-13
S-14    !$OMP PARALLEL DO ORDERED SCHEDULE(DYNAMIC)
S-15          DO I=LB,UB,STRIDE
S-16            CALL WORK(I)
S-17          END DO
S-18    !$OMP END PARALLEL DO
S-19
S-20          END SUBROUTINE SUB
S-21
S-22          PROGRAM ORDERED_EXAMPLE
S-23            CALL SUB(1,100,5)
S-24          END PROGRAM ORDERED_EXAMPLE
```

———————————————————————— Fortran ————————————————————————

It is possible to have multiple **ordered** constructs within a loop region with the **ordered** clause specified. The first example is non-conforming because all iterations execute two **ordered** regions. An iteration of a loop must not execute more than one **ordered** region:

———————————————————————— C / C++ ————————————————————————

Example ordered.2.c

```
S-1     void work(int i) {}
S-2
S-3     void ordered_wrong(int n)
S-4     {
S-5       int i;
S-6       #pragma omp for ordered
S-7       for (i=0; i<n; i++) {
S-8     /* incorrect because an iteration may not execute more than one
S-9        ordered region */
S-10        #pragma omp ordered
S-11          work(i);
S-12        #pragma omp ordered
S-13          work(i+1);
S-14      }
S-15    }
```

———————————————————————— C / C++ ————————————————————————

Example ordered.2.f

```
S-1          SUBROUTINE WORK(I)
S-2          INTEGER I
S-3          END SUBROUTINE WORK
S-4
S-5          SUBROUTINE ORDERED_WRONG(N)
S-6          INTEGER N
S-7
S-8           INTEGER I
S-9   !$OMP    DO ORDERED
S-10          DO I = 1, N
S-11  ! incorrect because an iteration may not execute more than one
S-12  ! ordered region
S-13  !$OMP      ORDERED
S-14              CALL WORK(I)
S-15  !$OMP      END ORDERED
S-16
S-17  !$OMP      ORDERED
S-18              CALL WORK(I+1)
S-19  !$OMP      END ORDERED
S-20           END DO
S-21          END SUBROUTINE ORDERED_WRONG
```

The following is a conforming example with more than one **ordered** construct. Each iteration
will execute only one **ordered** region:

Example ordered.3.c

```
S-1   void work(int i) {}
S-2   void ordered_good(int n)
S-3   {
S-4     int i;
S-5   #pragma omp for ordered
S-6     for (i=0; i<n; i++) {
S-7       if (i <= 10) {
S-8         #pragma omp ordered
S-9            work(i);
S-10      }
S-11      if (i > 10) {
S-12        #pragma omp ordered
S-13           work(i+1);
S-14      }
```

```
S-15        }
S-16    }
```

─────────────── C / C++ ───────────────
─────────────── Fortran ───────────────

1   *Example ordered.3.f*

```
S-1         SUBROUTINE ORDERED_GOOD(N)
S-2         INTEGER N
S-3
S-4   !$OMP    DO ORDERED
S-5         DO I = 1,N
S-6            IF (I <= 10) THEN
S-7   !$OMP       ORDERED
S-8               CALL WORK(I)
S-9   !$OMP       END ORDERED
S-10           ENDIF
S-11
S-12           IF (I > 10) THEN
S-13  !$OMP       ORDERED
S-14              CALL WORK(I+1)
S-15  !$OMP       END ORDERED
S-16           ENDIF
S-17        ENDDO
S-18      END SUBROUTINE ORDERED_GOOD
```

─────────────── Fortran ───────────────

9.9 `depobj` Construct

The stand-alone **depobj** construct provides a mechanism to create a *depend object* that expresses a dependence to be used subsequently in the **depend** clause of another construct. The dependence is created from a dependence type and a storage location, within a **depend** clause of an **depobj** construct; and it is stored in the depend object. The depend object is represented by a variable of type **omp_depend_t** in C/C++ (by a scalar variable of integer kind **omp_depend_kind** in Fortran).

In the example below the stand-alone **depobj** construct uses the **depend**, **update** and **destroy** clauses to *initialize*, *update* and *uninitialize* a depend object (**obj**).

The first **depobj** construct initializes the **obj** depend object with an **inout** dependence type with a storage location defined by variable **a**. This dependence is passed into the *driver* routine via the **obj** depend object.

In the first *driver* routine call, *Task 1* uses the dependence of the object (**inout**), while *Task 2* uses an **in** dependence specified directly in a **depend** clause. For these task dependences *Task 1* must execute and complete before *Task 2* begins.

Before the second call to *driver*, **obj** is updated using the **depobj** construct to represent an **in** dependence. Hence, in the second call to *driver*, *Task 1* will have an **in** dependence; and *Task 1* and *Task 2* can execute simultaneously. Note: in an **update** clause, only the dependence type can be (is) updated.

The third **depobj** construct uses the **destroy** clause. It frees resources as it puts the depend object in an uninitialized state– effectively destroying the depend object. After an object has been uninitialized it can be initialized again with a new dependence type *and* a new variable.

C / C++

Example depobj.1.c (**omp_5.2**)

```
#include <stdio.h>
#include <omp.h>

#define N 100
#define TRUE  1
#define FALSE 0

void driver(int update, float a[], float b[], int n, omp_depend_t *obj);

void update_copy(int update, float a[], float b[], int n);
void checkpoint(float a[],int n);
void init(float a[], int n);


int main(){
```

```
S-17
S-18        float a[N],b[N];
S-19        omp_depend_t obj;
S-20
S-21        init(a, N);
S-22
S-23        #pragma omp depobj(obj) depend(inout: a)
S-24
S-25        driver(TRUE,  a,b,N, &obj);  // updating a occurs
S-26
S-27        #pragma omp depobj(obj) update(in)
S-28
S-29        driver(FALSE, a,b,N, &obj);  // no updating of a
S-30
S-31        #pragma omp depobj(obj) destroy(obj)  // obj is set to uninitialized
S-32                                              // state, resources are freed
S-33        return 0;
S-34
S-35    }
S-36
S-37    void driver(int update, float a[], float b[], int n, omp_depend_t *obj)
S-38    {
S-39        #pragma omp parallel num_threads(2)
S-40        #pragma omp single
S-41        {
S-42
S-43          #pragma omp task depend(depobj: *obj) // Task 1, uses depend object
S-44             update_copy(update, a,b,n); // may update a, always copy a to b
S-45
S-46          #pragma omp task depend(in: a[:n])    // Task 2, only read a
S-47             checkpoint(a,n);
S-48        }
S-49    }
S-50
S-51    void update_copy(int update, float a[], float b[], int n)
S-52    {
S-53        if(update) for(int i=0;i<n;i++) a[i]+=1.0f;
S-54
S-55        for(int i=0;i<n;i++) b[i]=a[i];
S-56    }
S-57
S-58    void checkpoint(float a[], int n)
S-59    {
S-60        for(int i=0;i<n;i++) printf(" %f ",a[i]);
S-61        printf("\n");
S-62    }
S-63
```

```
S-64    void init(float a[], int n)
S-65    {
S-66        for(int i=0;i<n;i++) a[i]=i;
S-67    }
S-68
```

———————————————————————————————— C / C++ ————————————————————————————————
———————————————————————————————— Fortran ————————————————————————————————

1   *Example depobj.1.f90* (`omp_5.2`)

```
S-1
S-2     program main
S-3         use omp_lib
S-4         implicit none
S-5
S-6         integer,parameter       :: N=100
S-7         real                    :: a(N),b(N)
S-8         integer(omp_depend_kind) :: obj
S-9
S-10        call init(a, N)
S-11
S-12        !$omp depobj(obj) depend(inout: a)
S-13
S-14        call driver(.true.,  a,b,N, obj)   !! updating occurs
S-15
S-16        !$omp depobj(obj) update(in)
S-17
S-18        call driver(.false., a,b,N, obj)   !! no updating
S-19
S-20        !$omp depobj(obj) destroy(obj)     !! obj is set to uninitialized
S-21                                           !! state, resources are freed
S-22
S-23    end program
S-24
S-25    subroutine driver(update, a, b, n, obj)
S-26        use omp_lib
S-27        implicit none
S-28        logical :: update
S-29        real    :: a(n), b(n)
S-30        integer :: n
S-31        integer(omp_depend_kind) :: obj
S-32
S-33        !$omp parallel num_threads(2)
S-34
S-35          !$omp single
S-36
S-37            !$omp task depend(depobj: obj)        !! Task 1, uses depend object
```

```
S-38            call update_copy(update, a,b,n)
S-39                  !! update a or not, always copy a to b
S-40          !$omp end task
S-41
S-42          !$omp task depend(in: a)              !! Task 2, only read a
S-43            call checkpoint(a,n)
S-44          !$omp end task
S-45
S-46       !$omp end single
S-47
S-48      !$omp end parallel
S-49
S-50   end subroutine
S-51
S-52   subroutine update_copy(update, a, b, n)
S-53      implicit none
S-54      logical :: update
S-55      real     :: a(n), b(n)
S-56      integer :: n
S-57
S-58      if (update) a = a + 1.0
S-59
S-60      b = a
S-61
S-62   end subroutine
S-63
S-64   subroutine checkpoint( a, n)
S-65      implicit none
S-66      integer :: n
S-67      real     :: a(n)
S-68      integer :: i
S-69
S-70      write(*,'( *(f5.0) )') (a(i), i=1,n)
S-71   end subroutine
S-72
S-73   subroutine init(a,n)
S-74      implicit none
S-75      integer :: n
S-76      real     :: a(n)
S-77      integer :: i
S-78
S-79      a=[ (i, i=1,n) ]
S-80   end subroutine
```

Fortran

9.10 Doacross Loop Nest

An **ordered** clause can be used on a loop construct with an integer parameter argument to define the number of associated loops within a *doacross loop nest* where cross-iteration dependences exist. A **doacross** clause on an **ordered** construct within an ordered loop describes the dependences of the *doacross* loops.

In the code below, the **doacross(sink:i-1)** clause defines an *i-1* to *i* cross-iteration dependence that specifies a wait point for the completion of computation from iteration *i-1* before proceeding to the subsequent statements. The **doacross(source:omp_cur_iteration)** or **doacross(source:)** clause indicates the completion of computation from the current iteration (*i*) to satisfy the cross-iteration dependence that arises from the iteration. The **omp_cur_iteration** keyword is optional for the **source** dependence type. For this example the same sequential ordering could have been achieved with an **ordered** clause without a parameter, on the loop directive, and a single **ordered** directive without the **doacross** clause specified for the statement executing the *bar* function.

---------------------------------- C / C++ ----------------------------------

Example doacross.1.c (**omp_5.2**)

```
float foo(int i);
float bar(float a, float b);
float baz(float b);

void work( int N, float *A, float *B, float *C )
{
  int i;

  #pragma omp for ordered(1)
  for (i=1; i<N; i++)
  {
    A[i] = foo(i);

  #pragma omp ordered doacross(sink: i-1)
    B[i] = bar(A[i], B[i-1]);
  #pragma omp ordered doacross(source: omp_cur_iteration)

    C[i] = baz(B[i]);
  }
}
```

---------------------------------- C / C++ ----------------------------------

Example doacross.1.f90 (`omp_5.2`)

```
S-1
S-2    subroutine work( N, A, B, C )
S-3      integer :: N, i
S-4      real, dimension(N) :: A, B, C
S-5      real, external :: foo, bar, baz
S-6
S-7      !$omp do ordered(1)
S-8      do i=2, N
S-9        A(i) = foo(i)
S-10
S-11     !$omp ordered doacross(sink: i-1)
S-12       B(i) = bar(A(i), B(i-1))
S-13     !$omp ordered doacross(source: omp_cur_iteration)
S-14
S-15       C(i) = baz(B(i))
S-16     end do
S-17   end subroutine
```

The following code is similar to the previous example but with *doacross loop nest* extended to two nested loops, *i* and *j*, as specified by the **ordered(2)** clause on the loop directive. In the C/C++ code, the *i* and *j* loops are the first and second associated loops, respectively, whereas in the Fortran code, the *j* and *i* loops are the first and second associated loops, respectively. The **doacross(sink:i-1,j)** and **doacross(sink:i,j-1)** clauses in the C/C++ code define cross-iteration dependences in two dimensions from iterations $(i\text{-}1, j)$ and $(i, j\text{-}1)$ to iteration (i, j). Likewise, the **doacross(sink:j-1,i)** and **doacross(sink:j,i-1)** clauses in the Fortran code define cross-iteration dependences from iterations $(j\text{-}1, i)$ and $(j, i\text{-}1)$ to iteration (j, i).

Example doacross.2.c (`omp_5.2`)

```
S-1
S-2    float foo(int i, int j);
S-3    float bar(float a, float b, float c);
S-4    float baz(float b);
S-5
S-6    void work( int N, int M, float **A, float **B, float **C )
S-7    {
S-8      int i, j;
S-9
S-10     #pragma omp for ordered(2)
S-11     for (i=1; i<N; i++)
S-12     {
```

```
S-13          for (j=1; j<M; j++)
S-14          {
S-15            A[i][j] = foo(i, j);
S-16
S-17      #pragma omp ordered doacross(sink: i-1,j) doacross(sink: i,j-1)
S-18            B[i][j] = bar(A[i][j], B[i-1][j], B[i][j-1]);
S-19      #pragma omp ordered doacross(source:)
S-20
S-21            C[i][j] = baz(B[i][j]);
S-22          }
S-23        }
S-24   }
```

———————————————— C / C++ ————————————————
———————————————— Fortran ————————————————

1   *Example doacross.2.f90* (**omp_5.2**)

```
S-1
S-2    subroutine work( N, M, A, B, C )
S-3      integer :: N, M, i, j
S-4      real, dimension(M,N) :: A, B, C
S-5      real, external :: foo, bar, baz
S-6
S-7      !$omp do ordered(2)
S-8      do j=2, N
S-9        do i=2, M
S-10         A(i,j) = foo(i, j)
S-11
S-12       !$omp ordered doacross(sink: j-1,i) doacross(sink: j,i-1)
S-13         B(i,j) = bar(A(i,j), B(i-1,j), B(i,j-1))
S-14       !$omp ordered doacross(source:)
S-15
S-16         C(i,j) = baz(B(i,j))
S-17       end do
S-18     end do
S-19   end subroutine
```

———————————————— Fortran ————————————————

2   The following example shows the incorrect use of the **ordered** directive with a **doacross**
3   clause. There are two issues with the code. The first issue is a missing
4   **ordered doacross(source:)** directive, which could cause a deadlock. The second issue is
5   the **doacross(sink:i+1,j)** and **doacross(sink:i, j+1)** clauses define dependences
6   on lexicographically later source iterations $(i+1, j)$ and $(i, j+1)$, which could cause a deadlock as
7   well since they may not start to execute until the current iteration completes.

1   *Example doacross.3.c* (**omp_5.2**)

```
S-1
S-2    #define N 100
S-3
S-4    void work_wrong(double p[][N][N])
S-5    {
S-6      int i, j, k;
S-7
S-8      #pragma omp parallel for ordered(2) private(i,j,k)
S-9      for (i=1; i<N-1; i++)
S-10     {
S-11       for (j=1; j<N-1; j++)
S-12       {
S-13     #pragma omp ordered doacross(sink: i-1,j) doacross(sink: i+1,j) \
S-14                     doacross(sink: i,j-1) doacross(sink: i,j+1)
S-15       for (k=1; k<N-1; k++)
S-16       {
S-17         double tmp1 = p[i-1][j][k] + p[i+1][j][k];
S-18         double tmp2 = p[i][j-1][k] + p[i][j+1][k];
S-19         double tmp3 = p[i][j][k-1] + p[i][j][k+1];
S-20         p[i][j][k] = (tmp1 + tmp2 + tmp3) / 6.0;
S-21       }
S-22   /* missing #pragma omp ordered doacross(source:) */
S-23       }
S-24     }
S-25   }
```

2   *Example doacross.3.f90* (**omp_5.2**)

```
S-1
S-2    subroutine work_wrong(N, p)
S-3      integer :: N
S-4      real(8), dimension(N,N,N) :: p
S-5      integer :: i, j, k
S-6      real(8) :: tmp1, tmp2, tmp3
S-7
S-8    !$omp parallel do ordered(2) private(i,j,k,tmp1,tmp2,tmp3)
S-9      do i=2, N-1
S-10       do j=2, N-1
S-11       !$omp ordered doacross(sink: i-1,j) doacross(sink: i+1,j) &
S-12       !$omp&          doacross(sink: i,j-1) doacross(sink: i,j+1)
S-13        do k=2, N-1
S-14          tmp1 = p(k-1,j,i) + p(k+1,j,i)
```

```
S-15              tmp2 = p(k,j-1,i) + p(k,j+1,i)
S-16              tmp3 = p(k,j,i-1) + p(k,j,i+1)
S-17              p(k,j,i) = (tmp1 + tmp2 + tmp3) / 6.0
S-18           end do
S-19   ! missing !$omp ordered doacross(source:)
S-20         end do
S-21      end do
S-22   end subroutine
```

—————————————————————————— Fortran ——————————————————————————

The following example illustrates the use of the **collapse** clause for a *doacross loop nest*. The *i* and *j* loops are the associated loops for the collapsed loop as well as for the *doacross loop nest*. The example also shows a compliant usage of the dependence source directive placed before the corresponding sink directive. Checking the completion of computation from previous iterations at the sink point can occur after the source statement.

—————————————————————————— C / C++ ——————————————————————————

Example doacross.4.c (**omp_5.2**)

```
S-1
S-2    double foo(int i, int j);
S-3
S-4    void work( int N, int M, double **A, double **B, double **C )
S-5    {
S-6      int i, j;
S-7      double alpha = 1.2;
S-8
S-9      #pragma omp for collapse(2) ordered(2)
S-10     for (i = 1; i < N-1; i++)
S-11     {
S-12       for (j = 1; j < M-1; j++)
S-13       {
S-14         A[i][j] = foo(i, j);
S-15     #pragma omp ordered doacross(source:)
S-16
S-17         B[i][j] = alpha * A[i][j];
S-18
S-19     #pragma omp ordered doacross(sink: i-1,j) doacross(sink: i,j-1)
S-20         C[i][j] = 0.2 * (A[i-1][j] + A[i+1][j] +
S-21                     A[i][j-1] + A[i][j+1] + A[i][j]);
S-22       }
S-23     }
S-24   }
```

—————————————————————————— C / C++ ——————————————————————————

1   *Example doacross.4.f90* (**omp_5.2**)

```
S-1
S-2     subroutine work( N, M, A, B, C )
S-3       integer :: N, M
S-4       real(8), dimension(M, N) :: A, B, C
S-5       real(8), external :: foo
S-6       integer :: i, j
S-7       real(8) :: alpha = 1.2
S-8
S-9       !$omp do collapse(2) ordered(2)
S-10      do j=2, N-1
S-11        do i=2, M-1
S-12          A(i,j) = foo(i, j)
S-13          !$omp ordered doacross(source:)
S-14
S-15          B(i,j) = alpha * A(i,j)
S-16
S-17          !$omp ordered doacross(sink: j,i-1) doacross(sink: j-1,i)
S-18          C(i,j) = 0.2 * (A(i-1,j) + A(i+1,j) +  &
S-19                    A(i,j-1) + A(i,j+1) + A(i,j))
S-20        end do
S-21      end do
S-22    end subroutine
```

9.11 Lock Routines

This section is about the use of lock routines for synchronization.

9.11.1 `omp_init_lock` Routine

The following example demonstrates how to initialize an array of locks in a **parallel** region by using `omp_init_lock`.

——————————————————— C++ ———————————————————

Example init_lock.1.cpp

```cpp
S-1    #include <omp.h>
S-2
S-3    omp_lock_t *new_locks() {
S-4      int i;
S-5      omp_lock_t *lock = new omp_lock_t[1000];
S-6
S-7      #pragma omp parallel for private(i)
S-8        for (i=0; i<1000; i++)
S-9        { omp_init_lock(&lock[i]); }
S-10
S-11     return lock;
S-12   }
```

——————————————————— C++ ———————————————————

——————————————————— Fortran ———————————————————

Example init_lock.1.f

```fortran
S-1            FUNCTION NEW_LOCKS()
S-2              USE OMP_LIB          ! or INCLUDE "omp_lib.h"
S-3              INTEGER(OMP_LOCK_KIND), DIMENSION(1000) :: NEW_LOCKS
S-4              INTEGER I
S-5
S-6    !$OMP    PARALLEL DO PRIVATE(I)
S-7              DO I=1,1000
S-8                CALL OMP_INIT_LOCK(NEW_LOCKS(I))
S-9              END DO
S-10   !$OMP    END PARALLEL DO
S-11
S-12            END FUNCTION NEW_LOCKS
```

——————————————————— Fortran ———————————————————

9.11.2 `omp_init_lock_with_hint` Routine

The following example demonstrates how to initialize an array of locks in a **parallel** region by using **`omp_init_lock_with_hint`**. Note, hints are combined with an | or + operator in C/C++ and a + operator in Fortran.

――――――――――――― C++ ―――――――――――――

Example init_lock_with_hint.1.cpp (**omp_5.0**)

```
#include <omp.h>

omp_lock_t *new_locks()
{
  int i;
  omp_lock_t *lock = new omp_lock_t[1000];

  #pragma omp parallel for private(i)
    for (i=0; i<1000; i++)
      {
        omp_init_lock_with_hint(&lock[i],
          static_cast<omp_lock_hint_t>(omp_sync_hint_contended |
                                       omp_sync_hint_speculative));
      }
    return lock;
}
```

――――――――――――― C++ ―――――――――――――

――――――――――――― Fortran ―――――――――――――

Example init_lock_with_hint.1.f (**omp_5.0**)

```
          FUNCTION NEW_LOCKS()
            USE OMP_LIB          ! or INCLUDE "omp_lib.h"
            INTEGER(OMP_LOCK_KIND), DIMENSION(1000) :: NEW_LOCKS

            INTEGER I

!$OMP   PARALLEL DO PRIVATE(I)
            DO I=1,1000
              CALL OMP_INIT_LOCK_WITH_HINT(NEW_LOCKS(I),
     &              OMP_SYNC_HINT_CONTENDED + OMP_SYNC_HINT_SPECULATIVE)
            END DO
!$OMP   END PARALLEL DO

          END FUNCTION NEW_LOCKS
```

――――――――――――― Fortran ―――――――――――――

9.11.3 Ownership of Locks

Ownership of locks has changed since OpenMP 2.5. In OpenMP 2.5, locks are owned by threads; so a lock released by the **omp_unset_lock** routine must be owned by the same thread executing the routine. Beginning with OpenMP 3.0, locks are owned by task regions; so a lock released by the **omp_unset_lock** routine in a task region must be owned by the same task region.

This change in ownership requires extra care when using locks. The following program is conforming in OpenMP 2.5 because the thread that releases the lock **lck** in the parallel region is the same thread that acquired the lock in the sequential part of the program (primary thread of parallel region and the initial thread are the same). However, it is not conforming beginning with OpenMP 3.0, because the task region that releases the lock **lck** is different from the task region that acquires the lock.

─────────────────────────── C / C++ ───────────────────────────

Example lock_owner.1.c (**omp_5.1**)

```
#include <stdlib.h>
#include <stdio.h>
#include <omp.h>

int main()
{
  int x;
  omp_lock_t lck;

  omp_init_lock (&lck);
  omp_set_lock (&lck);
  x = 0;

#pragma omp parallel shared (x)
  {
    #pragma omp masked
      {
        x = x + 1;
        omp_unset_lock (&lck);
      }

    /* Some more stuff. */
  }
  omp_destroy_lock (&lck);
  return 0;
}
```

─────────────────────────── C / C++ ───────────────────────────

1   *Example lock_owner.1.f* (**omp_5.1**)

```
S-1              program lock
S-2              use omp_lib
S-3              integer :: x
S-4              integer (kind=omp_lock_kind) :: lck
S-5
S-6              call omp_init_lock (lck)
S-7              call omp_set_lock(lck)
S-8              x = 0
S-9
S-10   !$omp parallel shared (x)
S-11   !$omp masked
S-12             x = x + 1
S-13             call omp_unset_lock(lck)
S-14   !$omp end masked
S-15
S-16   !        Some more stuff.
S-17   !$omp end parallel
S-18
S-19             call omp_destroy_lock(lck)
S-20
S-21             end
```

9.11.4 Simple Lock Routines

In the following example, the lock routines cause the threads to be idle while waiting for entry to the first critical section, but to do other work while waiting for entry to the second. The **omp_set_lock** function blocks, but the **omp_test_lock** function does not, allowing the work in **skip** to be done.

Note that the argument to the lock routines should have type **omp_lock_t** (or **omp_lock_kind** in Fortran), and that there is no need to flush the lock variable (*lck*).

1   *Example simple_lock.1.c*

```c
S-1     #include <stdio.h>
S-2     #include <omp.h>
S-3     void skip(int i) {}
S-4     void work(int i) {}
S-5     int main()
S-6     {
S-7       omp_lock_t lck;
S-8       int id;
S-9       omp_init_lock(&lck);
S-10
S-11      #pragma omp parallel shared(lck) private(id)
S-12      {
S-13        id = omp_get_thread_num();
S-14
S-15        omp_set_lock(&lck);
S-16        /*  only one thread at a time can execute this printf */
S-17        printf("My thread id is %d.\n", id);
S-18        omp_unset_lock(&lck);
S-19
S-20        while (! omp_test_lock(&lck)) {
S-21          skip(id);    /* we do not yet have the lock,
S-22                          so we must do something else */
S-23        }
S-24
S-25        work(id);      /* we now have the lock
S-26                          and can do the work */
S-27
S-28        omp_unset_lock(&lck);
S-29      }
S-30      omp_destroy_lock(&lck);
S-31
S-32      return 0;
S-33    }
```

1   *Example simple_lock.1.f*

```
S-1          SUBROUTINE SKIP(ID)
S-2          END SUBROUTINE SKIP
S-3
S-4          SUBROUTINE WORK(ID)
S-5          END SUBROUTINE WORK
S-6
S-7          PROGRAM SIMPLELOCK
S-8
S-9             INCLUDE "omp_lib.h"        ! or USE OMP_LIB
S-10
S-11            INTEGER(OMP_LOCK_KIND) LCK
S-12            INTEGER ID
S-13
S-14            CALL OMP_INIT_LOCK(LCK)
S-15
S-16   !$OMP    PARALLEL SHARED(LCK) PRIVATE(ID)
S-17               ID = OMP_GET_THREAD_NUM()
S-18               CALL OMP_SET_LOCK(LCK)
S-19               PRINT *, 'My thread id is ', ID
S-20               CALL OMP_UNSET_LOCK(LCK)
S-21
S-22               DO WHILE (.NOT. OMP_TEST_LOCK(LCK))
S-23                 CALL SKIP(ID)     ! We do not yet have the lock
S-24                                   ! so we must do something else
S-25               END DO
S-26
S-27               CALL WORK(ID)       ! We now have the lock
S-28                                   ! and can do the work
S-29
S-30               CALL OMP_UNSET_LOCK( LCK )
S-31
S-32   !$OMP    END PARALLEL
S-33
S-34            CALL OMP_DESTROY_LOCK( LCK )
S-35
S-36         END PROGRAM SIMPLELOCK
```

9.11.5 Nestable Lock Routines

The following example demonstrates how a nestable lock can be used to synchronize updates both to a whole structure and to one of its members.

─────────────── C / C++ ───────────────

Example nestable_lock.1.c

```
#include <omp.h>

typedef struct {
    int a,b;
    omp_nest_lock_t lck;
} pair;

int work1();
int work2();
int work3();

void incr_a(pair *p, int a)
{

  /* Called only from incr_pair, no need to lock. */
  p->a += a;

}

void incr_b(pair *p, int b)
{

  /* Called both from incr_pair and elsewhere, */
  /* so need a nestable lock. */

  omp_set_nest_lock(&p->lck);
  p->b += b;
  omp_unset_nest_lock(&p->lck);

}

void incr_pair(pair *p, int a, int b)
{

  omp_set_nest_lock(&p->lck);
  incr_a(p, a);
  incr_b(p, b);
  omp_unset_nest_lock(&p->lck);

```

```
S-41        }
S-42
S-43     void nestlock(pair *p)
S-44     {
S-45
S-46        #pragma omp parallel sections
S-47        {
S-48           #pragma omp section
S-49             incr_pair(p, work1(), work2());
S-50           #pragma omp section
S-51             incr_b(p, work3());
S-52        }
S-53
S-54     }
```

——————————————— C / C++ ———————————————
——————————————— Fortran ———————————————

1   *Example nestable_lock.1.f*

```
S-1            MODULE DATA
S-2              USE OMP_LIB, ONLY: OMP_NEST_LOCK_KIND
S-3              TYPE LOCKED_PAIR
S-4                INTEGER A
S-5                INTEGER B
S-6                INTEGER (OMP_NEST_LOCK_KIND) LCK
S-7             END TYPE
S-8            END MODULE DATA
S-9
S-10           SUBROUTINE INCR_A(P, A)
S-11             ! called only from INCR_PAIR, no need to lock
S-12             USE DATA
S-13             TYPE(LOCKED_PAIR) :: P
S-14             INTEGER A
S-15             P%A = P%A + A
S-16           END SUBROUTINE INCR_A
S-17
S-18           SUBROUTINE INCR_B(P, B)
S-19             ! called from both INCR_PAIR and elsewhere,
S-20             ! so we need a nestable lock
S-21             USE OMP_LIB        ! or INCLUDE "omp_lib.h"
S-22             USE DATA
S-23             TYPE(LOCKED_PAIR) :: P
S-24             INTEGER B
S-25             CALL OMP_SET_NEST_LOCK(P%LCK)
S-26             P%B = P%B + B
S-27             CALL OMP_UNSET_NEST_LOCK(P%LCK)
S-28           END SUBROUTINE INCR_B
```

```
S-29
S-30          SUBROUTINE INCR_PAIR(P, A, B)
S-31            USE OMP_LIB        ! or INCLUDE "omp_lib.h"
S-32            USE DATA
S-33            TYPE(LOCKED_PAIR) :: P
S-34            INTEGER A
S-35            INTEGER B
S-36
S-37            CALL OMP_SET_NEST_LOCK(P%LCK)
S-38            CALL INCR_A(P, A)
S-39            CALL INCR_B(P, B)
S-40            CALL OMP_UNSET_NEST_LOCK(P%LCK)
S-41          END SUBROUTINE INCR_PAIR
S-42
S-43          SUBROUTINE NESTLOCK(P)
S-44            USE OMP_LIB        ! or INCLUDE "omp_lib.h"
S-45            USE DATA
S-46            TYPE(LOCKED_PAIR) :: P
S-47            INTEGER WORK1, WORK2, WORK3
S-48            EXTERNAL WORK1, WORK2, WORK3
S-49
S-50  !$OMP    PARALLEL SECTIONS
S-51
S-52  !$OMP    SECTION
S-53              CALL INCR_PAIR(P, WORK1(), WORK2())
S-54  !$OMP    SECTION
S-55              CALL INCR_B(P, WORK3())
S-56  !$OMP    END PARALLEL SECTIONS
S-57
S-58          END SUBROUTINE NESTLOCK
```
———————————————————————— Fortran ————————————————————————

10 Data Environment

The OpenMP *data environment* contains data attributes of variables and objects. Many constructs (such as **parallel**, **simd**, **task**) accept clauses to control *data-sharing* attributes of referenced variables in the construct, where *data-sharing* applies to whether the attribute of the variable is *shared*, is *private* storage, or has special operational characteristics (as found in the **firstprivate**, **lastprivate**, **linear**, or **reduction** clause).

The data environment for a device (distinguished as a *device data environment*) is controlled on the host by *data-mapping* attributes, which determine the relationship of the data on the host, the *original* data, and the data on the device, the *corresponding* data.

DATA-SHARING ATTRIBUTES

Data-sharing attributes of variables can be classified as being *predetermined*, *explicitly determined* or *implicitly determined*.

Certain variables and objects have predetermined attributes. A commonly found case is the loop iteration variable in associated loops of a **for** or **do** construct. It has a private data-sharing attribute. Variables with predetermined data-sharing attributes cannot be listed in a data-sharing clause; but there are some exceptions (mainly concerning loop iteration variables).

Variables with explicitly determined data-sharing attributes are those that are referenced in a given construct and are listed in a data-sharing attribute clause on the construct. Some of the common data-sharing clauses are: **shared**, **private**, **firstprivate**, **lastprivate**, **linear**, and **reduction**.

Variables with implicitly determined data-sharing attributes are those that are referenced in a given construct, do not have predetermined data-sharing attributes, and are not listed in a data-sharing attribute clause of an enclosing construct. For a complete list of variables and objects with predetermined and implicitly determined attributes, please refer to the *Data-sharing Attribute Rules for Variables Referenced in a Construct* subsection of the OpenMP Specifications document.

DATA-MAPPING ATTRIBUTES

The **map** clause on a device construct explicitly specifies how the list items in the clause are mapped from the encountering task's data environment (on the host) to the corresponding item in the device data environment (on the device). The common *list items* are arrays, array sections, scalars, pointers, and structure elements (members).

Procedures and global variables have predetermined data mapping if they appear within the list or block of a **declare target** directive. Also, a C/C++ pointer is mapped as a zero-length array section, as is a C++ variable that is a reference to a pointer.

Without explicit mapping, non-scalar and non-pointer variables within the scope of the **target** construct are implicitly mapped with a *map-type* of **tofrom**. Without explicit mapping, scalar variables within the scope of the **target** construct are not mapped, but have an implicit firstprivate data-sharing attribute. (That is, the value of the original variable is given to a private variable of the same name on the device.) This behavior can be changed with the **defaultmap** clause.

The **map** clause can appear on **target**, **target data** and **target enter/exit data** constructs. The operations of creation and removal of device storage as well as assignment of the original list item values to the corresponding list items may be complicated when the list item appears on multiple constructs or when the host and device storage is shared. In these cases the item's reference count, the number of times it has been referenced (+1 on entry and -1 on exited) in nested (structured) map regions and/or accumulative (unstructured) mappings, determines the operation. Details of the **map** clause and reference count operation are specified in the *map Clause* subsection of the OpenMP Specifications document.

10.1 `threadprivate` Directive

The following examples demonstrate how to use the **threadprivate** directive to give each thread a separate counter.

---- C / C++ ----

Example threadprivate.1.c

```
S-1   int counter = 0;
S-2   #pragma omp threadprivate(counter)
S-3
S-4   int increment_counter()
S-5   {
S-6     counter++;
S-7     return(counter);
S-8   }
```

---- C / C++ ----
---- Fortran ----

Example threadprivate.1.f

```
S-1          INTEGER FUNCTION INCREMENT_COUNTER()
S-2            COMMON/INC_COMMON/COUNTER
S-3   !$OMP    THREADPRIVATE(/INC_COMMON/)
S-4
S-5            COUNTER = COUNTER +1
S-6            INCREMENT_COUNTER = COUNTER
S-7            RETURN
S-8          END FUNCTION INCREMENT_COUNTER
```

---- Fortran ----
---- C / C++ ----

The following example uses **threadprivate** on a static variable:

Example threadprivate.2.c

```
S-1   int increment_counter_2()
S-2   {
S-3     static int counter = 0;
S-4     #pragma omp threadprivate(counter)
S-5     counter++;
S-6     return(counter);
S-7   }
```

The following example demonstrates unspecified behavior for the initialization of a **threadprivate** variable. A **threadprivate** variable is initialized once at an unspecified point before its first reference. Because **a** is constructed using the value of **x** (which is modified by the statement **x++**), the value of **a.val** at the start of the **parallel** region could be either 1 or 2. This problem is avoided for **b**, which uses an auxiliary **const** variable and a copy-constructor.

Example threadprivate.3.cpp

```
class T {
  public:
    int val;
    T (int);
    T (const T&);
};

T :: T (int v){
    val = v;
}

T :: T (const T& t) {
    val = t.val;
}

void g(T a, T b){
    a.val += b.val;
}

int x = 1;
T a(x);
const T b_aux(x); /* Capture value of x = 1 */
T b(b_aux);
#pragma omp threadprivate(a, b)

void f(int n) {
    x++;
    #pragma omp parallel for
    /* In each thread:
     * a is constructed from x (with value 1 or 2?)
     * b is copy-constructed from b_aux
     */

    for (int i=0; i<n; i++) {
        g(a, b); /* Value of a is unspecified. */
    }
}
```

―――――――――――――――― C / C++ ――――――――――――――――

The following examples show non-conforming uses and correct uses of the **threadprivate** directive.

──────────────── Fortran ────────────────

The following example is non-conforming because the common block is not declared local to the subroutine that refers to it:

Example threadprivate.2.f

```
S-1          MODULE INC_MODULE
S-2             COMMON /T/ A
S-3          END MODULE INC_MODULE
S-4
S-5          SUBROUTINE INC_MODULE_WRONG()
S-6             USE INC_MODULE
S-7   !$OMP    THREADPRIVATE(/T/)
S-8             !non-conforming because /T/ not declared in INC_MODULE_WRONG
S-9          END SUBROUTINE INC_MODULE_WRONG
```

The following example is also non-conforming because the common block is not declared local to the subroutine that refers to it:

Example threadprivate.3.f

```
S-1          SUBROUTINE INC_WRONG()
S-2             COMMON /T/ A
S-3   !$OMP    THREADPRIVATE(/T/)
S-4
S-5             CONTAINS
S-6                SUBROUTINE INC_WRONG_SUB()
S-7   !$OMP          PARALLEL COPYIN(/T/)
S-8             !non-conforming because /T/ not declared in INC_WRONG_SUB
S-9   !$OMP          END PARALLEL
S-10               END SUBROUTINE INC_WRONG_SUB
S-11         END SUBROUTINE INC_WRONG
```

The following example is a correct rewrite of the previous example:

Example threadprivate.4.f

```
S-1          SUBROUTINE INC_GOOD()
S-2             COMMON /T/ A
S-3   !$OMP    THREADPRIVATE(/T/)
S-4
S-5             CONTAINS
S-6                SUBROUTINE INC_GOOD_SUB()
S-7                   COMMON /T/ A
S-8   !$OMP          THREADPRIVATE(/T/)
S-9
S-10  !$OMP          PARALLEL COPYIN(/T/)
```

```
S-11    !$OMP          END PARALLEL
S-12                 END SUBROUTINE INC_GOOD_SUB
S-13                END SUBROUTINE INC_GOOD
```

1   The following is an example of the use of **threadprivate** for local variables:

2   *Example threadprivate.5.f*

```
S-1                PROGRAM INC_GOOD2
S-2                  INTEGER, ALLOCATABLE, SAVE :: A(:)
S-3                  INTEGER, POINTER, SAVE :: PTR
S-4                  INTEGER, SAVE :: I
S-5                  INTEGER, TARGET :: TARG
S-6                  LOGICAL :: FIRSTIN = .TRUE.
S-7     !$OMP        THREADPRIVATE(A, I, PTR)
S-8
S-9                  ALLOCATE (A(3))
S-10                 A = (/1,2,3/)
S-11                 PTR => TARG
S-12                 I = 5
S-13
S-14    !$OMP        PARALLEL COPYIN(I, PTR)
S-15    !$OMP          CRITICAL
S-16                     IF (FIRSTIN) THEN
S-17                       TARG = 4                ! Update target of ptr
S-18                       I = I + 10
S-19                       IF (ALLOCATED(A)) A = A + 10
S-20                       FIRSTIN = .FALSE.
S-21                     END IF
S-22
S-23                     IF (ALLOCATED(A)) THEN
S-24                       PRINT *, 'a = ', A
S-25                     ELSE
S-26                       PRINT *, 'A is not allocated'
S-27                     END IF
S-28
S-29                     PRINT *, 'ptr = ', PTR
S-30                     PRINT *, 'i = ', I
S-31                     PRINT *
S-32
S-33    !$OMP          END CRITICAL
S-34    !$OMP        END PARALLEL
S-35                END PROGRAM INC_GOOD2
```

3   The above program, if executed by two threads, will print one of the following two sets of output:

```
1            a = 11 12 13
2            ptr = 4
3            i = 15

4            A is not allocated
5            ptr = 4
6            i = 5

7            or

8            A is not allocated
9            ptr = 4
10           i = 15

11           a = 1 2 3
12           ptr = 4
13           i = 5
```

14 The following is an example of the use of **threadprivate** for module variables:

15 *Example threadprivate.6.f*

```
S-1          MODULE INC_MODULE_GOOD3
S-2            REAL, POINTER :: WORK(:)
S-3            SAVE WORK
S-4   !$OMP    THREADPRIVATE(WORK)
S-5          END MODULE INC_MODULE_GOOD3
S-6
S-7          SUBROUTINE SUB1(N)
S-8          USE INC_MODULE_GOOD3
S-9   !$OMP    PARALLEL PRIVATE(THE_SUM)
S-10           ALLOCATE(WORK(N))
S-11           CALL SUB2(THE_SUM)
S-12          WRITE(*,*)THE_SUM
S-13  !$OMP    END PARALLEL
S-14         END SUBROUTINE SUB1
S-15
S-16         SUBROUTINE SUB2(THE_SUM)
S-17           USE INC_MODULE_GOOD3
S-18           WORK(:) = 10
S-19           THE_SUM=SUM(WORK)
S-20         END SUBROUTINE SUB2
S-21
S-22         PROGRAM INC_GOOD3
S-23           N = 10
S-24           CALL SUB1(N)
```

—————————————————————————— Fortran ——————————————————————————

—————————————————————————— C++ ——————————————————————————

1   The following example illustrates initialization of **threadprivate** variables for class-type **T**. **t1**
2   is default constructed, **t2** is constructed taking a constructor accepting one argument of integer
3   type, **t3** is copy constructed with argument **f()**:

4   *Example threadprivate.4.cpp*

```
S-1    struct T { T (); T (int); ~T (); int t; };
S-2    int f();
S-3    static T t1;
S-4    #pragma omp threadprivate(t1)
S-5    static T t2( 23 );
S-6    #pragma omp threadprivate(t2)
S-7    static T t3 = f();
S-8    #pragma omp threadprivate(t3)
```

5   The following example illustrates the use of **threadprivate** for static class members. The
6   **threadprivate** directive for a static class member must be placed inside the class definition.

7   *Example threadprivate.5.cpp*

```
S-1    class T {
S-2     public:
S-3       static int i;
S-4    #pragma omp threadprivate(i)
S-5    };
```

—————————————————————————— C++ ——————————————————————————

10.2 `default(none)` Clause

The following example distinguishes the variables that are affected by the **default(none)** clause from those that are not.

———————————————————— C / C++ ————————————————————

Beginning with OpenMP 4.0, variables with **const**-qualified type and no mutable member are no longer predetermined shared. Thus, these variables (variable *c* in the example) need to be explicitly listed in data-sharing attribute clauses when the **default(none)** clause is specified.

Example default_none.1.c

```
S-1    #include <omp.h>
S-2    int x, y, z[1000];
S-3    #pragma omp threadprivate(x)
S-4
S-5    void default_none(int a) {
S-6      const int c = 1;
S-7      int i = 0;
S-8
S-9      #pragma omp parallel default(none) private(a) shared(z, c)
S-10     {
S-11         int j = omp_get_num_threads();
S-12             /* O.K.  - j is declared within parallel region */
S-13         a = z[j];    /* O.K.  - a is listed in private clause */
S-14                      /*       - z is listed in shared clause */
S-15         x = c;       /* O.K.  - x is threadprivate */
S-16                      /*       - c has const-qualified type and
S-17                                  is listed in shared clause */
S-18         z[i] = y;    /* Error - cannot reference i or y here */
S-19
S-20     #pragma omp for firstprivate(y)
S-21             /* Error - Cannot reference y in the firstprivate clause */
S-22         for (i=0; i<10 ; i++) {
S-23             z[i] = i; /* O.K. - i is the loop iteration variable */
S-24         }
S-25
S-26         z[i] = y;    /* Error - cannot reference i or y here */
S-27     }
S-28   }
```

———————————————————— C / C++ ————————————————————

1   *Example default_none.1.f*

```
S-1          SUBROUTINE DEFAULT_NONE(A)
S-2          INCLUDE "omp_lib.h"        ! or USE OMP_LIB
S-3
S-4          INTEGER A
S-5
S-6          INTEGER X, Y, Z(1000)
S-7          COMMON/BLOCKX/X
S-8          COMMON/BLOCKY/Y
S-9          COMMON/BLOCKZ/Z
S-10   !$OMP THREADPRIVATE(/BLOCKX/)
S-11
S-12          INTEGER I, J
S-13          i = 1
S-14
S-15   !$OMP    PARALLEL DEFAULT(NONE) PRIVATE(A) SHARED(Z) PRIVATE(J)
S-16          J = OMP_GET_NUM_THREADS();
S-17                    ! O.K.  - J is listed in PRIVATE clause
S-18          A = Z(J) ! O.K.  - A is listed in PRIVATE clause
S-19                 !        - Z is listed in SHARED clause
S-20          X = 1    ! O.K.  - X is THREADPRIVATE
S-21          Z(I) = Y ! Error - cannot reference I or Y here
S-22
S-23   !$OMP DO firstprivate(y)
S-24       ! Error - Cannot reference y in the firstprivate clause
S-25          DO I = 1,10
S-26            Z(I) = I ! O.K. - I is the loop iteration variable
S-27          END DO
S-28
S-29
S-30          Z(I) = Y    ! Error - cannot reference I or Y here
S-31   !$OMP    END PARALLEL
S-32        END SUBROUTINE DEFAULT_NONE
```

10.3 `private` Clause

In the following example, the values of original list items *i* and *j* are retained on exit from the **parallel** region, while the private list items *i* and *j* are modified within the **parallel** construct.

——————————————————— C / C++ ———————————————————

Example private.1.c

```
S-1    #include <stdio.h>
S-2    #include <assert.h>
S-3
S-4    int main()
S-5    {
S-6      int i, j;
S-7      int *ptr_i, *ptr_j;
S-8
S-9      i = 1;
S-10     j = 2;
S-11
S-12     ptr_i = &i;
S-13     ptr_j = &j;
S-14
S-15     #pragma omp parallel private(i) firstprivate(j)
S-16     {
S-17       i = 3;
S-18       j = j + 2;
S-19       assert (*ptr_i == 1 && *ptr_j == 2);
S-20     }
S-21
S-22     assert(i == 1 && j == 2);
S-23
S-24     return 0;
S-25   }
```

——————————————————— C / C++ ———————————————————

1 *Example private.1.f*

```fortran
S-1            PROGRAM PRIV_EXAMPLE
S-2              INTEGER I, J
S-3
S-4              I = 1
S-5              J = 2
S-6
S-7   !$OMP    PARALLEL PRIVATE(I) FIRSTPRIVATE(J)
S-8                I = 3
S-9                J = J + 2
S-10  !$OMP    END PARALLEL
S-11
S-12             PRINT *, I, J  ! I .eq. 1 .and. J .eq. 2
S-13             END PROGRAM PRIV_EXAMPLE
```

2 In the following example, all uses of the variable *a* within the loop construct in the routine *f* refer to
3 a private list item *a*, while it is unspecified whether references to *a* in the routine *g* are to a private
4 list item or the original list item.

5 *Example private.2.c*

```c
S-1   int a;
S-2
S-3   void g(int k) {
S-4     a = k; /* Accessed in the region but outside of the construct;
S-5               * therefore unspecified whether original or private list
S-6               * item is modified. */
S-7   }
S-8
S-9
S-10  void f(int n) {
S-11    int a = 0;
S-12
S-13    #pragma omp parallel for private(a)
S-14    for (int i=1; i<n; i++) {
S-15        a = i;
S-16        g(a*2);       /* Private copy of "a" */
S-17      }
S-18  }
```

1   *Example private.2.f*

```
S-1            MODULE PRIV_EXAMPLE2
S-2              REAL A
S-3
S-4            CONTAINS
S-5
S-6              SUBROUTINE G(K)
S-7                REAL K
S-8                A = K   ! Accessed in the region but outside of the
S-9                        ! construct; therefore unspecified whether
S-10                       ! original or private list item is modified.
S-11             END SUBROUTINE G
S-12
S-13             SUBROUTINE F(N)
S-14             INTEGER N
S-15             REAL A
S-16
S-17               INTEGER I
S-18   !$OMP         PARALLEL DO PRIVATE(A)
S-19                 DO I = 1,N
S-20                   A = I
S-21                     CALL G(A*2)
S-22                 ENDDO
S-23   !$OMP         END PARALLEL DO
S-24             END SUBROUTINE F
S-25
S-26          END MODULE PRIV_EXAMPLE2
```

2   The following example demonstrates that a list item that appears in a **private** clause in a
3   **parallel** construct may also appear in a **private** clause in an enclosed worksharing construct,
4   which results in an additional private copy.

5   *Example private.3.c*

```
S-1    #include <assert.h>
S-2    void priv_example3()
S-3    {
S-4      int i, a;
S-5
S-6      #pragma omp parallel private(a)
S-7      {
S-8        a = 1;
S-9        #pragma omp parallel for private(a)
```

```
S-10          for (i=0; i<10; i++)
S-11        {
S-12          a = 2;
S-13        }
S-14      assert (a == 1);
S-15    }
S-16  }
```

————————————————— C / C++ —————————————————

————————————————— Fortran —————————————————

1   *Example private.3.f*

```
S-1           SUBROUTINE PRIV_EXAMPLE3()
S-2             INTEGER I, A
S-3
S-4   !$OMP     PARALLEL PRIVATE(A)
S-5             A = 1
S-6   !$OMP       PARALLEL DO PRIVATE(A)
S-7             DO I = 1, 10
S-8               A = 2
S-9             END DO
S-10  !$OMP       END PARALLEL DO
S-11            PRINT *, A ! Outer A still has value 1
S-12  !$OMP     END PARALLEL
S-13          END SUBROUTINE PRIV_EXAMPLE3
```

————————————————— Fortran —————————————————

10.4 Fortran Private Loop Iteration Variables

Fortran

In general loop iteration variables will be private, when used in the *do-loop* of a **do** and **parallel do** construct or in sequential loops in a **parallel** construct (see Section 2.7.1 and Section 2.14.1 of the OpenMP 4.0 specification). In the following example of a sequential loop in a **parallel** construct the loop iteration variable *I* will be private.

Example fort_loopvar.1.f90

```
S-1     SUBROUTINE PLOOP_1(A,N)
S-2     INCLUDE "omp_lib.h"        ! or USE OMP_LIB
S-3
S-4     REAL A(*)
S-5     INTEGER I, MYOFFSET, N
S-6
S-7     !$OMP PARALLEL PRIVATE(MYOFFSET)
S-8           MYOFFSET = OMP_GET_THREAD_NUM()*N
S-9           DO I = 1, N
S-10            A(MYOFFSET+I) = FLOAT(I)
S-11          ENDDO
S-12    !$OMP END PARALLEL
S-13
S-14    END SUBROUTINE PLOOP_1
```

In exceptional cases, loop iteration variables can be made shared, as in the following example:

Example fort_loopvar.2.f90

```
S-1     SUBROUTINE PLOOP_2(A,B,N,I1,I2)
S-2     REAL A(*), B(*)
S-3     INTEGER I1, I2, N
S-4
S-5     !$OMP PARALLEL SHARED(A,B,I1,I2)
S-6     !$OMP SECTIONS
S-7     !$OMP SECTION
S-8           DO I1 = I1, N
S-9             IF (A(I1).NE.0.0) EXIT
S-10          ENDDO
S-11    !$OMP SECTION
S-12          DO I2 = I2, N
S-13            IF (B(I2).NE.0.0) EXIT
S-14          ENDDO
S-15    !$OMP END SECTIONS
S-16    !$OMP SINGLE
S-17        IF (I1.LE.N) PRINT *, 'ITEMS IN A UP TO ', I1, 'ARE ALL ZERO.'
S-18        IF (I2.LE.N) PRINT *, 'ITEMS IN B UP TO ', I2, 'ARE ALL ZERO.'
S-19    !$OMP END SINGLE
```

```
S-20    !$OMP END PARALLEL
S-21
S-22    END SUBROUTINE PLOOP_2
```

1   Note however that the use of shared loop iteration variables can easily lead to race conditions.

━━━━━━━━━━━━━━━━━━━━ Fortran ━━━━━━━━━━━━━━━━━━━━

10.5 Fortran Restrictions on `shared` and `private` Clauses with Common Blocks

──────────────────────── Fortran ────────────────────────

When a named common block is specified in a **private**, **firstprivate**, or **lastprivate** clause of a construct, none of its members may be declared in another data-sharing attribute clause on that construct. The following examples illustrate this point.

The following example is conforming:

Example fort_sp_common.1.f

```
S-1           SUBROUTINE COMMON_GOOD()
S-2             COMMON /C/ X,Y
S-3             REAL X, Y
S-4
S-5   !$OMP     PARALLEL PRIVATE (/C/)
S-6                ! do work here
S-7   !$OMP     END PARALLEL
S-8   !$OMP     PARALLEL SHARED (X,Y)
S-9                ! do work here
S-10  !$OMP     END PARALLEL
S-11          END SUBROUTINE COMMON_GOOD
```

The following example is also conforming:

Example fort_sp_common.2.f

```
S-1           SUBROUTINE COMMON_GOOD2()
S-2             COMMON /C/ X,Y
S-3             REAL X, Y
S-4             INTEGER I
S-5   !$OMP     PARALLEL
S-6   !$OMP       DO PRIVATE(/C/)
S-7               DO I=1,1000
S-8                  ! do work here
S-9               ENDDO
S-10  !$OMP       END DO
S-11  !$OMP       DO PRIVATE(X)
S-12              DO I=1,1000
S-13                 ! do work here
S-14              ENDDO
S-15  !$OMP       END DO
S-16  !$OMP     END PARALLEL
S-17          END SUBROUTINE COMMON_GOOD2
```

The following example is conforming:

Example fort_sp_common.3.f

```
S-1          SUBROUTINE COMMON_GOOD3()
S-2            COMMON /C/ X,Y
S-3   !$OMP    PARALLEL PRIVATE (/C/)
S-4              ! do work here
S-5   !$OMP    END PARALLEL
S-6   !$OMP    PARALLEL SHARED (/C/)
S-7              ! do work here
S-8   !$OMP    END PARALLEL
S-9          END SUBROUTINE COMMON_GOOD3
```

The following example is non-conforming because **x** is a constituent element of **c**:

Example fort_sp_common.4.f

```
S-1          SUBROUTINE COMMON_WRONG()
S-2            COMMON /C/ X,Y
S-3   ! Incorrect because X is a constituent element of C
S-4   !$OMP    PARALLEL PRIVATE(/C/), SHARED(X)
S-5              ! do work here
S-6   !$OMP    END PARALLEL
S-7          END SUBROUTINE COMMON_WRONG
```

The following example is non-conforming because a common block may not be declared both shared and private:

Example fort_sp_common.5.f

```
S-1          SUBROUTINE COMMON_WRONG2()
S-2            COMMON /C/ X,Y
S-3   ! Incorrect: common block C cannot be declared both
S-4   ! shared and private
S-5   !$OMP    PARALLEL PRIVATE (/C/), SHARED(/C/)
S-6              ! do work here
S-7   !$OMP    END PARALLEL
S-8
S-9          END SUBROUTINE COMMON_WRONG2
```

—————————————————— Fortran ——————————————————

10.6 Fortran Restrictions on Storage Association with the `private` Clause

---
Fortran

The following non-conforming examples illustrate the implications of the **private** clause rules with regard to storage association.

Example fort_sa_private.1.f

```
S-1              SUBROUTINE SUB()
S-2              COMMON /BLOCK/ X
S-3              PRINT *,X              ! X is undefined
S-4              END SUBROUTINE SUB
S-5
S-6              PROGRAM PRIV_RESTRICT
S-7                COMMON /BLOCK/ X
S-8                X = 1.0
S-9      !$OMP     PARALLEL PRIVATE (X)
S-10               X = 2.0
S-11               CALL SUB()
S-12     !$OMP     END PARALLEL
S-13             END PROGRAM PRIV_RESTRICT
```

Example fort_sa_private.2.f

```
S-1              PROGRAM PRIV_RESTRICT2
S-2                COMMON /BLOCK2/ X
S-3                X = 1.0
S-4
S-5      !$OMP     PARALLEL PRIVATE (X)
S-6                X = 2.0
S-7                CALL SUB()
S-8      !$OMP     END PARALLEL
S-9
S-10             CONTAINS
S-11
S-12               SUBROUTINE SUB()
S-13               COMMON /BLOCK2/ Y
S-14
S-15               PRINT *,X              ! X is undefined
S-16               PRINT *,Y              ! Y is undefined
S-17               END SUBROUTINE SUB
S-18
S-19             END PROGRAM PRIV_RESTRICT2
```

1   *Example fort_sa_private.3.f*

```
S-1          PROGRAM PRIV_RESTRICT3
S-2            EQUIVALENCE (X,Y)
S-3            X = 1.0
S-4
S-5   !$OMP    PARALLEL PRIVATE(X)
S-6            PRINT *,Y                    ! Y is undefined
S-7            Y = 10
S-8            PRINT *,X                    ! X is undefined
S-9   !$OMP    END PARALLEL
S-10           END PROGRAM PRIV_RESTRICT3
```

2   *Example fort_sa_private.4.f*

```
S-1          PROGRAM PRIV_RESTRICT4
S-2            INTEGER I, J
S-3            INTEGER A(100), B(100)
S-4            EQUIVALENCE (A(51), B(1))
S-5
S-6   !$OMP PARALLEL DO DEFAULT(PRIVATE) PRIVATE(I,J) LASTPRIVATE(A)
S-7            DO I=1,100
S-8              DO J=1,100
S-9                B(J) = J - 1
S-10             ENDDO
S-11
S-12             DO J=1,100
S-13               A(J) = J   ! B becomes undefined at this point
S-14             ENDDO
S-15
S-16             DO J=1,50
S-17               B(J) = B(J) + 1  ! B is undefined
S-18                              ! A becomes undefined at this point
S-19             ENDDO
S-20           ENDDO
S-21  !$OMP END PARALLEL DO        ! The LASTPRIVATE write for A has
S-22                              ! undefined results
S-23
S-24           PRINT *, B    ! B is undefined since the LASTPRIVATE
S-25                              ! write of A was not defined
S-26           END PROGRAM PRIV_RESTRICT4
```

3   *Example fort_sa_private.5.f* (`omp_5.1`)

```
S-1          SUBROUTINE SUB1(X)
S-2            DIMENSION X(10)
```

```
S-3
S-4                ! This use of X does not conform to the
S-5                ! specification. It would be legal Fortran 90,
S-6                ! but the OpenMP private directive allows the
S-7                ! compiler to break the sequence association that
S-8                ! A had with the rest of the common block.
S-9
S-10               FORALL (I = 1:10) X(I) = I
S-11          END SUBROUTINE SUB1
S-12
S-13          PROGRAM PRIV_RESTRICT5
S-14            COMMON /BLOCK5/ A
S-15
S-16            DIMENSION B(10)
S-17            EQUIVALENCE (A,B(1))
S-18
S-19            ! the common block has to be at least 10 words
S-20            A = 0
S-21
S-22    !$OMP     PARALLEL PRIVATE(/BLOCK5/)
S-23
S-24               ! Without the private clause,
S-25               ! we would be passing a member of a sequence
S-26               ! that is at least ten elements long.
S-27               ! With the private clause, A may no longer be
S-28               ! sequence-associated.
S-29
S-30               CALL SUB1(A)
S-31    !$OMP     MASKED
S-32                 PRINT *, A
S-33    !$OMP     END MASKED
S-34
S-35    !$OMP     END PARALLEL
```
———————————————— Fortran ————————————————

10.7 C/C++ Arrays in a `firstprivate` Clause

--------------------------------- C / C++ ---------------------------------

The following example illustrates the size and value of list items of array or pointer type in a **firstprivate** clause . The size of new list items is based on the type of the corresponding original list item, as determined by the base language.

In this example:

- The type of **A** is array of two arrays of two ints.
- The type of **B** is adjusted to pointer to array of **n** ints, because it is a function parameter.
- The type of **C** is adjusted to pointer to int, because it is a function parameter.
- The type of **D** is array of two arrays of two ints.
- The type of **E** is array of **n** arrays of **n** ints.

Note that **B** and **E** involve variable length array types.

The new items of array type are initialized as if each integer element of the original array is assigned to the corresponding element of the new array. Those of pointer type are initialized as if by assignment from the original item to the new item.

Example carrays_fpriv.1.c

```
S-1     #include <assert.h>
S-2
S-3     int A[2][2] = {1, 2, 3, 4};
S-4
S-5     void f(int n, int B[n][n], int C[])
S-6     {
S-7       int D[2][2] = {1, 2, 3, 4};
S-8       int E[n][n];
S-9
S-10      assert(n >= 2);
S-11      E[1][1] = 4;
S-12
S-13      #pragma omp parallel firstprivate(B, C, D, E)
S-14      {
S-15        assert(sizeof(B) == sizeof(int (*)[n]));
S-16        assert(sizeof(C) == sizeof(int*));
S-17        assert(sizeof(D) == 4 * sizeof(int));
S-18        assert(sizeof(E) == n * n * sizeof(int));
S-19
S-20        /* Private B and C have values of original B and C. */
S-21        assert(&B[1][1] == &A[1][1]);
S-22        assert(&C[3] == &A[1][1]);
S-23        assert(D[1][1] == 4);
```

```
S-24          assert(E[1][1] == 4);
S-25       }
S-26    }
S-27
S-28    int main() {
S-29      f(2, A, A[0]);
S-30      return 0;
S-31    }
```

————————————— C / C++ —————————————

10.8 `lastprivate` Clause

Correct execution sometimes depends on the value that the last iteration of a loop assigns to a variable. Such programs must list all such variables in a **lastprivate** clause so that the values of the variables are the same as when the loop is executed sequentially.

───────────────────────────── C / C++ ─────────────────────────────

Example lastprivate.1.c

```
S-1    void lastpriv (int n, float *a, float *b)
S-2    {
S-3      int i;
S-4
S-5      #pragma omp parallel
S-6      {
S-7        #pragma omp for lastprivate(i)
S-8        for (i=0; i<n-1; i++)
S-9          a[i] = b[i] + b[i+1];
S-10     }
S-11
S-12     a[i]=b[i];        /* i == n-1 here */
S-13   }
```

───────────────────────────── C / C++ ─────────────────────────────
───────────────────────────── Fortran ─────────────────────────────

Example lastprivate.1.f

```
S-1           SUBROUTINE LASTPRIV(N, A, B)
S-2
S-3             INTEGER N
S-4             REAL A(*), B(*)
S-5             INTEGER I
S-6    !$OMP PARALLEL
S-7    !$OMP DO LASTPRIVATE(I)
S-8
S-9             DO I=1,N-1
S-10              A(I) = B(I) + B(I+1)
S-11            ENDDO
S-12
S-13   !$OMP END PARALLEL
S-14            A(I) = B(I)       ! I has the value of N here
S-15
S-16            END SUBROUTINE LASTPRIV
```

───────────────────────────── Fortran ─────────────────────────────

The next example illustrates the use of the **conditional** modifier in a **lastprivate** clause to return the last value when it may not come from the last iteration of a loop. That is, users can preserve the serial equivalence semantics of the loop. The conditional lastprivate ensures the final value of the variable after the loop is as if the loop iterations were executed in a sequential order.

———————————————————— C / C++ ————————————————————

Example lastprivate.2.c (**omp_5.0**)

```
#include <math.h>

float condlastprivate(float *a, int n)
{
    float x = 0.0f;

    #pragma omp parallel for simd lastprivate(conditional: x)
    for (int k = 0; k < n; k++) {
        if (a[k] < 108.5 || a[k] > 208.5) {
            x = sinf(a[k]);
        }
    }

    return x;
}
```

———————————————————— C / C++ ————————————————————
———————————————————— Fortran ————————————————————

Example lastprivate.2.f90 (**omp_5.0**)

```
function condlastprivate(a, n) result(x)
    implicit none
    real a(*), x
    integer n, k

    x = 0.0

    !$omp parallel do simd lastprivate(conditional: x)
    do k = 1, n
        if (a(k) < 108.5 .or. a(k) > 208.5) then
            x = sin(a(k))
        endif
    end do

end function condlastprivate
```

———————————————————— Fortran ————————————————————

10.9 Reduction

This section covers ways to perform reductions in parallel, task, taskloop, and SIMD regions.

10.9.1 `reduction` Clause

The following example demonstrates the **`reduction`** clause; note that some reductions can be expressed in the loop in several ways, as shown for the **max** and **min** reductions below:

───────────────── C / C++ ─────────────────

Example reduction.1.c (**omp_3.1**)

```
S-1    #include <math.h>
S-2    void reduction1(float *x, int *y, int n)
S-3    {
S-4      int i, b, c;
S-5      float a, d;
S-6      a = 0.0;
S-7      b = 0;
S-8      c = y[0];
S-9      d = x[0];
S-10     #pragma omp parallel for private(i) shared(x, y, n) \
S-11                             reduction(+:a) reduction(^:b) \
S-12                             reduction(min:c) reduction(max:d)
S-13       for (i=0; i<n; i++) {
S-14         a += x[i];
S-15         b ^= y[i];
S-16         if (c > y[i]) c = y[i];
S-17         d = fmaxf(d,x[i]);
S-18       }
S-19   }
```

───────────────── C / C++ ─────────────────

1

Example reduction.1.f90

```fortran
S-1    SUBROUTINE REDUCTION1(A, B, C, D, X, Y, N)
S-2       REAL :: X(*), A, D
S-3       INTEGER :: Y(*), N, B, C
S-4       INTEGER :: I
S-5       A = 0
S-6       B = 0
S-7       C = Y(1)
S-8       D = X(1)
S-9       !$OMP PARALLEL DO PRIVATE(I) SHARED(X, Y, N) REDUCTION(+:A) &
S-10      !$OMP& REDUCTION(IEOR:B) REDUCTION(MIN:C)  REDUCTION(MAX:D)
S-11        DO I=1,N
S-12          A = A + X(I)
S-13          B = IEOR(B, Y(I))
S-14          C = MIN(C, Y(I))
S-15          IF (D < X(I)) D = X(I)
S-16        END DO
S-17
S-18    END SUBROUTINE REDUCTION1
```

2
3

A common implementation of the preceding example is to treat it as if it had been written as follows:

4

Example reduction.2.c

```c
S-1    #include <limits.h>
S-2    #include <math.h>
S-3    void reduction2(float *x, int *y, int n)
S-4    {
S-5      int i, b, b_p, c, c_p;
S-6      float a, a_p, d, d_p;
S-7      a = 0.0f;
S-8      b = 0;
S-9      c = y[0];
S-10     d = x[0];
S-11     #pragma omp parallel shared(a, b, c, d, x, y, n) \
S-12                           private(a_p, b_p, c_p, d_p)
S-13     {
S-14       a_p = 0.0f;
S-15       b_p = 0;
S-16       c_p = INT_MAX;
S-17       d_p = -HUGE_VALF;
S-18       #pragma omp for private(i)
```

```
S-19        for (i=0; i<n; i++) {
S-20          a_p += x[i];
S-21          b_p ^= y[i];
S-22          if (c_p > y[i]) c_p = y[i];
S-23          d_p = fmaxf(d_p,x[i]);
S-24        }
S-25        #pragma omp critical
S-26        {
S-27          a += a_p;
S-28          b ^= b_p;
S-29          if( c > c_p ) c = c_p;
S-30          d = fmaxf(d,d_p);
S-31        }
S-32      }
S-33    }
```

──────────────────────────── C / C++ ────────────────────────────
──────────────────────────── Fortran ────────────────────────────

1   *Example reduction.2.f90*

```
S-1     SUBROUTINE REDUCTION2(A, B, C, D, X, Y, N)
S-2       REAL :: X(*), A, D
S-3       INTEGER :: Y(*), N, B, C
S-4       REAL :: A_P, D_P
S-5       INTEGER :: I, B_P, C_P
S-6       A = 0
S-7       B = 0
S-8       C = Y(1)
S-9       D = X(1)
S-10      !$OMP PARALLEL SHARED(X, Y, A, B, C, D, N) &
S-11      !$OMP&          PRIVATE(A_P, B_P, C_P, D_P)
S-12        A_P = 0.0
S-13        B_P = 0
S-14        C_P = HUGE(C_P)
S-15        D_P = -HUGE(D_P)
S-16        !$OMP DO PRIVATE(I)
S-17        DO I=1,N
S-18          A_P = A_P + X(I)
S-19          B_P = IEOR(B_P, Y(I))
S-20          C_P = MIN(C_P, Y(I))
S-21          IF (D_P < X(I)) D_P = X(I)
S-22        END DO
S-23        !$OMP CRITICAL
S-24          A = A + A_P
S-25          B = IEOR(B, B_P)
S-26          C = MIN(C, C_P)
S-27          D = MAX(D, D_P)
```

```
S-28              !$OMP END CRITICAL
S-29            !$OMP END PARALLEL
S-30          END SUBROUTINE REDUCTION2
```

1　　The following program is non-conforming because the reduction is on the *intrinsic procedure name*
2　　**MAX** but that name has been redefined to be the variable named **MAX**.

3　　*Example reduction.3.f90*

```
S-1     PROGRAM REDUCTION_WRONG
S-2     MAX = HUGE(0)
S-3     M = 0
S-4
S-5     !$OMP PARALLEL DO REDUCTION(MAX: M)
S-6     ! MAX is no longer the intrinsic so this is non-conforming
S-7     DO I = 1, 100
S-8        CALL SUB(M,I)
S-9     END DO
S-10
S-11    END PROGRAM REDUCTION_WRONG
S-12
S-13    SUBROUTINE SUB(M,I)
S-14       M = MAX(M,I)
S-15    END SUBROUTINE SUB
```

4　　The following conforming program performs the reduction using the *intrinsic procedure name* **MAX**
5　　even though the intrinsic **MAX** has been renamed to **REN**.

6　　*Example reduction.4.f90*

```
S-1     MODULE M
S-2        INTRINSIC MAX
S-3     END MODULE M
S-4
S-5     PROGRAM REDUCTION3
S-6        USE M, REN => MAX
S-7        N = 0
S-8     !$OMP PARALLEL DO REDUCTION(REN: N)        ! still does MAX
S-9        DO I = 1, 100
S-10          N = MAX(N,I)
S-11       END DO
S-12    END PROGRAM REDUCTION3
```

7　　The following conforming program performs the reduction using *intrinsic procedure name* **MAX**
8　　even though the intrinsic **MAX** has been renamed to **MIN**.

9　　*Example reduction.5.f90*

```
S-1     MODULE MOD
S-2        INTRINSIC MAX, MIN
S-3     END MODULE MOD
S-4
S-5     PROGRAM REDUCTION4
S-6        USE MOD, MIN=>MAX, MAX=>MIN
S-7        REAL :: R
S-8        R = -HUGE(0.0)
S-9
S-10    !$OMP PARALLEL DO REDUCTION(MIN: R)        ! still does MAX
S-11       DO I = 1, 1000
S-12          R = MIN(R, SIN(REAL(I)))
S-13       END DO
S-14       PRINT *, R
S-15    END PROGRAM REDUCTION4
```

───────────────────────────── Fortran ─────────────────────────────

The following example is non-conforming because the initialization (a = 0) of the original list
item **a** is not synchronized with the update of **a** as a result of the reduction computation in the **for**
loop. Therefore, the example may print an incorrect value for **a**.

To avoid this problem, the initialization of the original list item **a** should complete before any
update of **a** as a result of the **reduction** clause. This can be achieved by adding an explicit
barrier after the assignment **a = 0**, or by enclosing the assignment **a = 0** in a **single** directive
(which has an implied barrier), or by initializing **a** before the start of the **parallel** region.

───────────────────────────── C / C++ ─────────────────────────────

Example reduction.6.c (**omp_5.1**)

```
S-1     #include <stdio.h>
S-2
S-3     int main (void)
S-4     {
S-5       int a, i;
S-6
S-7       #pragma omp parallel shared(a) private(i)
S-8       {
S-9         #pragma omp masked
S-10        a = 0;
S-11
S-12        // To avoid race conditions, add a barrier here.
S-13
S-14        #pragma omp for reduction(+:a)
S-15        for (i = 0; i < 10; i++) {
S-16            a += i;
S-17        }
S-18
```

```
S-19        #pragma omp single
S-20        printf ("Sum is %d\n", a);
S-21      }
S-22    return 0;
S-23  }
```

———————————————— C / C++ ————————————————
———————————————— Fortran ————————————————

1   *Example reduction.6.f* (**omp_5.1**)

```
S-1          INTEGER A, I
S-2
S-3    !$OMP PARALLEL SHARED(A) PRIVATE(I)
S-4
S-5    !$OMP MASKED
S-6          A = 0
S-7    !$OMP END MASKED
S-8
S-9          ! To avoid race conditions, add a barrier here.
S-10
S-11   !$OMP DO REDUCTION(+:A)
S-12         DO I= 0, 9
S-13            A = A + I
S-14         END DO
S-15
S-16   !$OMP SINGLE
S-17         PRINT *, "Sum is ", A
S-18   !$OMP END SINGLE
S-19
S-20   !$OMP END PARALLEL
S-21
S-22         END
```

———————————————— Fortran ————————————————

2   The following example demonstrates the reduction of array *a*. In C/C++ this is illustrated by the
3   explicit use of an array section *a[0:N]* in the **reduction** clause. The corresponding Fortran
4   example uses array syntax supported in the base language. As of the OpenMP 4.5 specification the
5   explicit use of array section in the **reduction** clause in Fortran is not permitted. But this
6   oversight has been fixed in the OpenMP 5.0 specification.

1   *Example reduction.7.c* (omp_4.5)

```c
S-1    #include <stdio.h>
S-2
S-3    #define N 100
S-4    void init(int n, float (*b)[N]);
S-5
S-6    int main(){
S-7
S-8      int i,j;
S-9      float a[N], b[N][N];
S-10
S-11     init(N,b);
S-12
S-13     for(i=0; i<N; i++) a[i]=0.0e0;
S-14
S-15     #pragma omp parallel for reduction(+:a[0:N]) private(j)
S-16     for(i=0; i<N; i++){
S-17       for(j=0; j<N; j++){
S-18         a[j] +=  b[i][j];
S-19       }
S-20     }
S-21     printf(" a[0] a[N-1]: %f %f\n", a[0], a[N-1]);
S-22
S-23     return 0;
S-24   }
```

2   *Example reduction.7.f90*

```fortran
S-1    program array_red
S-2
S-3      integer,parameter :: n=100
S-4      integer           :: j
S-5      real              :: a(n), b(n,n)
S-6
S-7      call init(n,b)
S-8
S-9      a(:) = 0.0e0
S-10
S-11     !$omp parallel do reduction(+:a)
S-12     do j = 1, n
S-13        a(:) = a(:) + b(:,j)
S-14     end do
S-15
```

```
S-16         print*, " a(1) a(n): ", a(1), a(n)
S-17
S-18     end program
```
──────────────────────────── Fortran ────────────────────────────

10.9.2 Task Reduction

In OpenMP 5.0 the **task_reduction** clause was created for the **taskgroup** construct, to allow reductions among explicit tasks that have an **in_reduction** clause.

In the *task_reduction.1* example below a reduction is performed as the algorithm traverses a linked list. The reduction statement is assigned to be an explicit task using a **task** construct and is specified to be a reduction participant with the **in_reduction** clause. A **taskgroup** construct encloses the tasks participating in the reduction, and specifies, with the **task_reduction** clause, that the taskgroup has tasks participating in a reduction. After the **taskgroup** region the original variable will contain the final value of the reduction.

Note: The *res* variable is private in the *linked_list_sum* routine and is not required to be shared (as in the case of a **parallel** construct reduction).

──────────────────────────── C / C++ ────────────────────────────

Example task_reduction.1.c (**omp_5.0**)

```
S-1      #include<stdlib.h>
S-2      #include<stdio.h>
S-3      #define N 10
S-4
S-5      typedef struct node_tag {
S-6          int val;
S-7          struct node_tag *next;
S-8      } node_t;
S-9
S-10     int linked_list_sum(node_t *p)
S-11     {
S-12         int res = 0;
S-13
S-14         #pragma omp taskgroup task_reduction(+: res)
S-15         {
S-16             node_t* aux = p;
S-17             while(aux != 0)
S-18             {
S-19                 #pragma omp task in_reduction(+: res)
S-20                 res += aux->val;
S-21
S-22                 aux = aux->next;
```

```
S-23                }
S-24            }
S-25        return res;
S-26    }
S-27
S-28
S-29    int main(int argc, char *argv[]) {
S-30        int i;
S-31    //                          Create the root node.
S-32        node_t* root = (node_t*) malloc(sizeof(node_t));
S-33        root->val = 1;
S-34
S-35        node_t* aux = root;
S-36
S-37    //                          Create N-1 more nodes.
S-38        for(i=2;i<=N;++i){
S-39            aux->next = (node_t*) malloc(sizeof(node_t));
S-40            aux = aux->next;
S-41            aux->val = i;
S-42        }
S-43
S-44        aux->next = 0;
S-45
S-46        #pragma omp parallel
S-47        #pragma omp single
S-48        {
S-49            int result = linked_list_sum(root);
S-50            printf( "Calculated: %d  Analytic:%d\n", result, (N*(N+1)/2) );
S-51        }
S-52
S-53        return 0;
S-54    }
S-55
```

———————————————————————————— C / C++ ————————————————————————————
———————————————————————————— Fortran ————————————————————————————

1   *Example task_reduction.1.f90* (**omp_5.0**)

```
S-1    module m
S-2        type node_t
S-3            integer :: val
S-4            type(node_t), pointer :: next
S-5        end type
S-6    end module m
S-7
S-8    function linked_list_sum(p) result(res)
S-9        use m
```

```
S-10        implicit none
S-11        type(node_t), pointer :: p
S-12        type(node_t), pointer :: aux
S-13        integer :: res
S-14
S-15        res = 0
S-16
S-17        !$omp taskgroup task_reduction(+: res)
S-18            aux => p
S-19            do while (associated(aux))
S-20                !$omp task in_reduction(+: res)
S-21                    res = res + aux%val
S-22                !$omp end task
S-23                aux => aux%next
S-24            end do
S-25        !$omp end taskgroup
S-26    end function linked_list_sum
S-27
S-28
S-29    program main
S-30        use m
S-31        implicit none
S-32        type(node_t), pointer :: root, aux
S-33        integer :: res, i
S-34        integer, parameter :: N=10
S-35
S-36        interface
S-37            function linked_list_sum(p) result(res)
S-38                use m
S-39                implicit none
S-40                type(node_t), pointer :: p
S-41                integer :: res
S-42            end function
S-43        end interface
S-44    !                       Create the root node.
S-45        allocate(root)
S-46        root%val = 1
S-47        aux => root
S-48
S-49    !                       Create N-1 more nodes.
S-50        do i = 2,N
S-51            allocate(aux%next)
S-52            aux => aux%next
S-53            aux%val = i
S-54        end do
S-55
S-56        aux%next => null()
```

```
S-57
S-58        !$omp parallel
S-59        !$omp single
S-60            res = linked_list_sum(root)
S-61            print *, "Calculated:", res, " Analytic:", (N*(N+1))/2
S-62        !$omp end single
S-63        !$omp end parallel
S-64
S-65     end program main
S-66
```

──────────────────────── Fortran ────────────────────────

1   In OpenMP 5.0 the **task** *reduction-modifier* for the **reduction** clause was introduced to
2   provide a means of performing reductions among implicit and explicit tasks.

3   The **reduction** clause of a **parallel** or worksharing construct may specify the **task**
4   *reduction-modifier* to include explicit task reductions within their region, provided the reduction
5   operators (*reduction-identifiers*) and variables (*list items*) of the participating tasks match those of
6   the implicit tasks.

7   There are 2 reduction use cases (identified by USE CASE #) in the *task_reduction.2* example below.

8   In USE CASE 1 a **task** modifier in the **reduction** clause of the **parallel** construct is used to
9   include the reductions of any participating tasks, those with an **in_reduction** clause and
10   matching *reduction-identifiers* (**+**) and list items (**x**).

11   Note, a **taskgroup** construct (with a **task_reduction** clause) in not necessary to scope the
12   explicit task reduction (as seen in the example above). Hence, even without the implicit task
13   reduction statement (without the C **x++** and Fortran **x=x+1** statements), the **task**
14   *reduction-modifier* in a **reduction** clause of the **parallel** construct can be used to avoid
15   having to create a **taskgroup** construct (and its **task_reduction** clause) around the task
16   generating structure.

17   In USE CASE 2 tasks participating in the reduction are within a worksharing region (a parallel
18   worksharing-loop construct). Here, too, no **taskgroup** is required, and the *reduction-identifier*
19   (**+**) and list item (variable **x**) match as required.

──────────────────────── C / C++ ────────────────────────

20   *Example task_reduction.2.c* (**omp_5.0**)

```
S-1     #include <stdio.h>
S-2     int main(void) {
S-3         int N=100, M=10;
S-4         int i, x;
S-5
S-6     // USE CASE 1   explicit-task reduction + parallel reduction clause
S-7         x=0;
S-8         #pragma omp parallel num_threads(M) reduction(task,+:x)
```

```
S-9          {
S-10
S-11            x++;                        // implicit task reduction statement
S-12
S-13          #pragma omp single
S-14          for(i=0;i<N;i++)
S-15            #pragma omp task in_reduction(+:x)
S-16            x++;
S-17
S-18          }
S-19        printf("x=%d  =M+N\n",x);   // x= 110  =M+N
S-20
S-21
S-22  // USE CASE 2  task reduction +  worksharing reduction clause
S-23        x=0;
S-24        #pragma omp parallel for num_threads(M) reduction(task,+:x)
S-25        for(i=0; i< N; i++){
S-26
S-27          x++;
S-28
S-29          if( i%2 == 0){
S-30            #pragma omp task in_reduction(+:x)
S-31            x--;
S-32          }
S-33        }
S-34        printf("x=%d  =N-N/2\n",x);   // x= 50  =N-N/2
S-35
S-36        return 0;
S-37  }
```

———————————————— C / C++ ————————————————
———————————————— Fortran ————————————————

1 *Example task_reduction.2.f90* (omp_5.0)

```
S-1
S-2   program task_modifier
S-3
S-4       integer :: N=100, M=10
S-5       integer :: i, x
S-6
S-7   ! USE CASE 1  explicit-task reduction + parallel reduction clause
S-8       x=0
S-9       !$omp parallel num_threads(M) reduction(task,+:x)
S-10
S-11        x=x+1                        !! implicit task reduction statement
S-12
S-13        !$omp single
```

```
S-14              do i = 1,N
S-15                !$omp task in_reduction(+:x)
S-16                  x=x+1
S-17                !$omp end task
S-18              end do
S-19            !$omp end single
S-20
S-21         !$omp end parallel
S-22         write(*,'("x=",I0," =M+N")') x    ! x= 110 =M+N
S-23
S-24
S-25      ! USE CASE 2  task reduction +  worksharing reduction clause
S-26         x=0
S-27         !$omp parallel do num_threads(M) reduction(task,+:x)
S-28          do i = 1,N
S-29
S-30              x=x+1
S-31
S-32              if( mod(i,2) == 0) then
S-33                  !$omp task in_reduction(+:x)
S-34                    x=x-1
S-35                  !$omp end task
S-36              endif
S-37
S-38          end do
S-39         write(*,'("x=",I0,"  =N-N/2")') x    ! x= 50 =N-N/2
S-40
S-41      end program
```

—————————————— Fortran ——————————————

10.9.3 Reduction on Combined Target Constructs

When a **reduction** clause appears on a combined construct that combines a **target** construct with another construct, there is an implicit map of the list items with a **tofrom** map type for the **target** construct. Otherwise, the list items (if they are scalar variables) would be treated as firstprivate by default in the **target** construct, which is unlikely to provide the intended behavior since the result of the reduction that is in the firstprivate variable would be discarded at the end of the **target** region.

In the following example, the use of the **reduction** clause on **sum1** or **sum2** should, by default, result in an implicit **tofrom** map for that variable. So long as neither **sum1** nor **sum2** were already present on the device, the mapping behavior ensures the value for **sum1** computed in the first **target** construct is used in the second **target** construct.

1   *Example target_reduction.1.c* (**omp_5.0**)

```
S-1    #include <stdio.h>
S-2    int f(int);
S-3    int g(int);
S-4    int main()
S-5    {
S-6       int sum1=0, sum2=0;
S-7       int i;
S-8       const int n = 100;
S-9
S-10      #pragma omp target teams distribute reduction(+:sum1)
S-11      for (int i = 0; i < n; i++) {
S-12         sum1 += f(i);
S-13      }
S-14
S-15      #pragma omp target teams distribute reduction(+:sum2)
S-16      for (int i = 0; i < n; i++) {
S-17         sum2 += g(i) * sum1;
S-18      }
S-19
S-20      printf( "sum1 = %d, sum2 = %d\n", sum1, sum2);
S-21      //OUTPUT: sum1 = 9900, sum2 = 147015000
S-22      return 0;
S-23   }
S-24
S-25   int f(int res){ return res*2; }
S-26   int g(int res){ return res*3; }
```

2   *Example target_reduction.1.f90* (**omp_5.0**)

```
S-1    program target_reduction_ex1
S-2       interface
S-3          function f(res)
S-4                integer :: f, res
S-5             end function
S-6          function g(res)
S-7                integer :: g, res
S-8             end function
S-9       end interface
S-10      integer :: sum1, sum2, i
S-11      integer, parameter :: n = 100
S-12      sum1 = 0
S-13      sum2 = 0
```

```
S-14        !$omp target teams distribute reduction(+:sum1)
S-15            do i=1,n
S-16                sum1 = sum1 + f(i)
S-17            end do
S-18        !$omp target teams distribute reduction(+:sum2)
S-19            do i=1,n
S-20                sum2 = sum2 + g(i)*sum1
S-21            end do
S-22        print *, "sum1 = ", sum1, ", sum2 = ", sum2
S-23        !!OUTPUT: sum1 =       10100 , sum2 = 153015000
S-24    end program
S-25
S-26
S-27    integer function f(res)
S-28        integer :: res
S-29        f = res*2
S-30    end function
S-31    integer function g(res)
S-32        integer :: res
S-33        g = res*3
S-34    end function
```

▲────────────────────────── Fortran ──────────────────────────▲

1   In next example, the variables **sum1** and **sum2** remain on the device for the duration of the
2   **target data** region so that it is their device copies that are updated by the reductions. Note the
3   significance of mapping **sum1** on the second **target** construct; otherwise, it would be treated by
4   default as firstprivate and the result computed for **sum1** in the prior **target** region may not be
5   used. Alternatively, a **target update** construct could be used between the two **target**
6   constructs to update the host version of **sum1** with the value that is in the corresponding device
7   version after the completion of the first construct.

▼────────────────────────── C / C++ ──────────────────────────▼

8   *Example target_reduction.2.c* (**omp_5.0**)

```
S-1     #include <stdio.h>
S-2     int f(int);
S-3     int g(int);
S-4     int main()
S-5     {
S-6         int sum1=0, sum2=0;
S-7         int i;
S-8         const int n = 100;
S-9
S-10        #pragma omp target data map(sum1,sum2)
S-11        {
S-12            #pragma omp target teams distribute reduction(+:sum1)
S-13            for (int i = 0; i < n; i++) {
```

```
S-14              sum1 += f(i);
S-15          }
S-16
S-17          #pragma omp target teams distribute map(sum1) reduction(+:sum2)
S-18          for (int i = 0; i < n; i++) {
S-19              sum2 += g(i) * sum1;
S-20          }
S-21      }
S-22      printf(  "sum1 = %d, sum2 = %d\n", sum1, sum2);
S-23      //OUTPUT: sum1 = 9900, sum2 = 147015000
S-24      return 0;
S-25  }
S-26
S-27  int f(int res){ return res*2; }
S-28  int g(int res){ return res*3; }
```

———————————————— C / C++ ————————————————
———————————————— Fortran ————————————————

Example target_reduction.2.f90 (**omp_5.0**)

```
S-1
S-2   program target_reduction_ex2
S-3      interface
S-4         function f(res)
S-5              integer :: f, res
S-6            end function
S-7         function g(res)
S-8              integer :: g, res
S-9            end function
S-10     end interface
S-11     integer :: sum1, sum2, i
S-12     integer, parameter :: n = 100
S-13     sum1 = 0
S-14     sum2 = 0
S-15     !$omp target data map(sum1, sum2)
S-16        !$omp target teams distribute reduction(+:sum1)
S-17           do i=1,n
S-18              sum1 = sum1 + f(i)
S-19           end do
S-20        !$omp target teams distribute map(sum1) reduction(+:sum2)
S-21           do i=1,n
S-22              sum2 = sum2 + g(i)*sum1
S-23           end do
S-24     !$omp end target data
S-25     print *, "sum1 = ", sum1, ", sum2 = ", sum2
S-26     !!OUTPUT: sum1 =      10100 , sum2 = 153015000
S-27  end program
```

```
S-28
S-29
S-30    integer function f(res)
S-31       integer :: res
S-32       f = res*2
S-33    end function
S-34    integer function g(res)
S-35       integer :: res
S-36       g = res*3
S-37    end function
```

———————————————————— Fortran ————————————————————

10.9.4 Task Reduction with Target Constructs

The following examples illustrate how task reductions can apply to target tasks that result from a
target construct with the **in_reduction** clause. Here, the **in_reduction** clause specifies
that the target task participates in the task reduction defined in the scope of the enclosing
taskgroup construct. Partial results from all tasks participating in the task reduction will be
combined (in some order) into the original variable listed in the **task_reduction** clause before
exiting the **taskgroup** region.

▼———————————————————— C / C++ ————————————————————▼

Example target_task_reduction.1.c (**omp_5.2**)

```
S-1
S-2     #include <stdio.h>
S-3     #pragma omp declare target enter(device_compute)
S-4     void device_compute(int *);
S-5     void host_compute(int *);
S-6     int main()
S-7     {
S-8        int sum = 0;
S-9
S-10       #pragma omp parallel masked
S-11       #pragma omp taskgroup task_reduction(+:sum)
S-12       {
S-13          #pragma omp target in_reduction(+:sum) nowait
S-14             device_compute(&sum);
S-15
S-16          #pragma omp task in_reduction(+:sum)
S-17             host_compute(&sum);
S-18       }
S-19       printf(  "sum = %d\n", sum);
S-20       //OUTPUT: sum = 2
S-21       return 0;
```

```
S-22    }
S-23
S-24    void device_compute(int *sum){ *sum = 1; }
S-25    void   host_compute(int *sum){ *sum = 1; }
```

――――――――――――――――――――――――――― C / C++ ―――――――――――――――――――――――――――

――――――――――――――――――――――――――― Fortran ―――――――――――――――――――――――――――

1   *Example target_task_reduction.1.f90* (`omp_5.2`)

```
S-1
S-2     program target_task_reduction_ex1
S-3        interface
S-4           subroutine device_compute(res)
S-5           !$omp declare target enter(device_compute)
S-6              integer :: res
S-7           end subroutine device_compute
S-8           subroutine host_compute(res)
S-9              integer :: res
S-10          end subroutine host_compute
S-11       end interface
S-12       integer :: sum
S-13       sum = 0
S-14       !$omp parallel masked
S-15          !$omp taskgroup task_reduction(+:sum)
S-16             !$omp target in_reduction(+:sum) nowait
S-17                call device_compute(sum)
S-18             !$omp end target
S-19             !$omp task in_reduction(+:sum)
S-20                call host_compute(sum)
S-21             !$omp end task
S-22          !$omp end taskgroup
S-23       !$omp end parallel masked
S-24       print *, "sum = ", sum
S-25       !!OUTPUT: sum = 2
S-26    end program
S-27
S-28    subroutine device_compute(sum)
S-29       integer :: sum
S-30       sum = 1
S-31    end subroutine
S-32    subroutine host_compute(sum)
S-33       integer :: sum
S-34       sum = 1
S-35    end subroutine
```

――――――――――――――――――――――――――― Fortran ―――――――――――――――――――――――――――

In the next pair of examples, the task reduction is defined by a **reduction** clause with the **task** modifier, rather than a **task_reduction** clause on a **taskgroup** construct. Again, the partial results from the participating tasks will be combined in some order into the original reduction variable, **sum**.

C / C++

Example target_task_reduction.2a.c (**omp_5.2**)

```
S-1    #include <stdio.h>
S-2    #pragma omp declare target enter(device_compute)
S-3    extern void device_compute(int *);
S-4    extern void host_compute(int *);
S-5    int main()
S-6    {
S-7       int sum = 0;
S-8
S-9       #pragma omp parallel sections reduction(task, +:sum)
S-10      {
S-11         #pragma omp section
S-12            {
S-13                #pragma omp target in_reduction(+:sum)
S-14                device_compute(&sum);
S-15            }
S-16         #pragma omp section
S-17            {
S-18                host_compute(&sum);
S-19            }
S-20      }
S-21      printf(  "sum = %d\n", sum);
S-22      //OUTPUT: sum = 2
S-23      return 0;
S-24   }
S-25
S-26   void device_compute(int *sum){ *sum = 1; }
S-27   void   host_compute(int *sum){ *sum = 1; }
```

C / C++

---

1   *Example target_task_reduction.2a.f90* (**omp_5.2**)

```
S-1
S-2    program target_task_reduction_ex2
S-3       interface
S-4          subroutine device_compute(res)
S-5          !$omp declare target enter(device_compute)
S-6             integer :: res
S-7          end subroutine device_compute
S-8          subroutine host_compute(res)
S-9             integer :: res
S-10         end subroutine host_compute
S-11      end interface
S-12      integer :: sum
S-13      sum = 0
S-14      !$omp parallel sections reduction(task,+:sum)
S-15         !$omp section
S-16            !$omp target in_reduction(+:sum) nowait
S-17               call device_compute(sum)
S-18            !$omp end target
S-19         !$omp section
S-20            call host_compute(sum)
S-21      !$omp end parallel sections
S-22      print *, "sum = ", sum
S-23      !!OUTPUT: sum = 2
S-24   end program
S-25
S-26   subroutine device_compute(sum)
S-27      integer :: sum
S-28      sum = 1
S-29   end subroutine
S-30   subroutine host_compute(sum)
S-31      integer :: sum
S-32      sum = 1
S-33   end subroutine
```

2   Next, the **task** modifier is again used to define a task reduction over participating tasks. This time,
3   the participating tasks are a target task resulting from a **target** construct with the
4   **in_reduction** clause, and the implicit task (executing on the primary thread) that calls
5   **host_compute**. As before, the partial results from these participating tasks are combined in
6   some order into the original reduction variable.

1   *Example target_task_reduction.2b.c* (**omp_5.2**)

```
S-1    #include <stdio.h>
S-2    #pragma omp declare target enter(device_compute)
S-3    extern void device_compute(int *);
S-4    extern void host_compute(int *);
S-5    int main()
S-6    {
S-7       int sum = 0;
S-8
S-9       #pragma omp parallel masked reduction(task, +:sum)
S-10      {
S-11          #pragma omp target in_reduction(+:sum) nowait
S-12          device_compute(&sum);
S-13
S-14          host_compute(&sum);
S-15      }
S-16      printf(  "sum = %d\n", sum);
S-17      //OUTPUT: sum = 2
S-18      return 0;
S-19   }
S-20
S-21   void device_compute(int *sum){ *sum = 1; }
S-22   void   host_compute(int *sum){ *sum = 1; }
```

2   *Example target_task_reduction.2b.f90* (**omp_5.2**)

```
S-1
S-2    program target_task_reduction_ex2b
S-3       interface
S-4          subroutine device_compute(res)
S-5          !$omp declare target enter(device_compute)
S-6             integer :: res
S-7          end subroutine device_compute
S-8          subroutine host_compute(res)
S-9             integer :: res
S-10         end subroutine host_compute
S-11      end interface
S-12      integer :: sum
S-13      sum = 0
S-14      !$omp parallel masked reduction(task,+:sum)
S-15            !$omp target in_reduction(+:sum) nowait
S-16              call device_compute(sum)
S-17            !$omp end target
```

```
S-18              call host_compute(sum)
S-19        !$omp end parallel masked
S-20        print *, "sum = ", sum
S-21        !!OUTPUT: sum = 2
S-22     end program
S-23
S-24
S-25     subroutine device_compute(sum)
S-26        integer :: sum
S-27        sum = 1
S-28     end subroutine
S-29     subroutine host_compute(sum)
S-30        integer :: sum
S-31        sum = 1
S-32     end subroutine
S-33
```

——————————————————————— Fortran ———————————————————————

10.9.5 Taskloop Reduction

In the OpenMP 5.0 Specification the **taskloop** construct was extended to include the reductions.

The following two examples show how to implement a reduction over an array using taskloop reduction in two different ways. In the first example we apply the **reduction** clause to the **taskloop** construct. As it was explained above in the task reduction examples, a reduction over tasks is divided in two components: the scope of the reduction, which is defined by a **taskgroup** region, and the tasks that participate in the reduction. In this example, the **reduction** clause defines both semantics. First, it specifies that the implicit **taskgroup** region associated with the **taskloop** construct is the scope of the reduction, and second, it defines all tasks created by the **taskloop** construct as participants of the reduction. About the first property, it is important to note that if we add the **nogroup** clause to the **taskloop** construct the code will be nonconforming, basically because we have a set of tasks that participate in a reduction that has not been defined.

————————————————————————— C / C++ —————————————————————————

Example taskloop_reduction.1.c (**omp_5.0**)

```
S-1     #include <stdio.h>
S-2
S-3     int array_sum(int n, int *v) {
S-4         int i;
S-5         int res = 0;
S-6
S-7         #pragma omp taskloop reduction(+: res)
S-8         for(i = 0; i < n; ++i)
```

```
S-9              res += v[i];
S-10
S-11          return res;
S-12      }
S-13
S-14      int main(int argc, char *argv[]) {
S-15          int n = 10;
S-16          int v[10] = {1,2,3,4,5,6,7,8,9,10};
S-17
S-18          #pragma omp parallel
S-19          #pragma omp single
S-20          {
S-21              int res = array_sum(n, v);
S-22              printf("The result is %d\n", res);
S-23          }
S-24          return 0;
S-25      }
```

——————————————————————— C / C++ ———————————————————————
——————————————————————— Fortran ———————————————————————

1   *Example taskloop_reduction.1.f90* (**omp_5.0**)

```
S-1      function array_sum(n, v) result(res)
S-2          implicit none
S-3          integer :: n, v(n), res
S-4          integer :: i
S-5
S-6          res = 0
S-7          !$omp taskloop reduction(+: res)
S-8          do i=1, n
S-9              res = res + v(i)
S-10          end do
S-11          !$omp end taskloop
S-12
S-13      end function array_sum
S-14
S-15      program main
S-16          implicit none
S-17          integer :: n, v(10), res
S-18          integer :: i
S-19
S-20          integer, external :: array_sum
S-21
S-22          n = 10
S-23          do i=1, n
S-24              v(i) = i
S-25          end do
```

```
S-26
S-27          !$omp parallel
S-28          !$omp single
S-29          res = array_sum(n, v)
S-30          print *, "The result is", res
S-31          !$omp end single
S-32          !$omp end parallel
S-33      end program main
```

———————————————————— Fortran ————————————————————

The second example computes exactly the same value as in the preceding *taskloop_reduction.1*
code section, but in a very different way. First, in the *array_sum* function a **taskgroup** region is
created that defines the scope of a new reduction using the **task_reduction** clause. After that,
a task and also the tasks generated by a taskloop participate in that reduction by using the
in_reduction clause on the **task** and **taskloop** constructs, respectively. Note that the
nogroup clause was added to the **taskloop** construct. This is allowed because what is
expressed with the **in_reduction** clause is different from what is expressed with the
reduction clause. In one case the generated tasks are specified to participate in a previously
declared reduction (**in_reduction** clause) whereas in the other case creation of a new reduction
is specified and also all tasks generated by the taskloop will participate on it.

———————————————————— C / C++ ————————————————————

Example taskloop_reduction.2.c (**omp_5.0**)

```
S-1   #include <stdio.h>
S-2
S-3   int array_sum(int n, int *v) {
S-4       int i;
S-5       int res = 0;
S-6
S-7       #pragma omp taskgroup task_reduction(+: res)
S-8       {
S-9           if (n > 0) {
S-10              #pragma omp task in_reduction(+: res)
S-11              res = res + v[0];
S-12
S-13              #pragma omp taskloop in_reduction(+: res) nogroup
S-14              for(i = 1; i < n; ++i)
S-15                  res += v[i];
S-16          }
S-17      }
S-18
S-19      return res;
S-20  }
S-21
S-22  int main(int argc, char *argv[]) {
```

```
S-23        int n = 10;
S-24        int v[10] = {1,2,3,4,5,6,7,8,9,10};
S-25
S-26        #pragma omp parallel
S-27        #pragma omp single
S-28        {
S-29            int res = array_sum(n, v);
S-30            printf("The result is %d\n", res);
S-31        }
S-32        return 0;
S-33    }
```

———————————————————— C / C++ ————————————————————
———————————————————— Fortran ————————————————————

1   *Example taskloop_reduction.2.f90* (**omp_5.0**)

```
S-1     function array_sum(n, v) result(res)
S-2         implicit none
S-3         integer :: n, v(n), res
S-4         integer :: i
S-5
S-6         res = 0
S-7         !$omp taskgroup task_reduction(+: res)
S-8         if (n > 0) then
S-9             !$omp task in_reduction(+: res)
S-10            res = res + v(1)
S-11            !$omp end task
S-12
S-13            !$omp taskloop in_reduction(+: res) nogroup
S-14            do i=2, n
S-15                res = res + v(i)
S-16            end do
S-17            !$omp end taskloop
S-18        endif
S-19        !$omp end taskgroup
S-20
S-21    end function array_sum
S-22
S-23    program main
S-24        implicit none
S-25        integer :: n, v(10), res
S-26        integer :: i
S-27
S-28        integer, external :: array_sum
S-29
S-30        n = 10
S-31        do i=1, n
```

```
S-32            v(i) = i
S-33        end do
S-34
S-35        !$omp parallel
S-36        !$omp single
S-37        res = array_sum(n, v)
S-38        print *, "The result is", res
S-39        !$omp end single
S-40        !$omp end parallel
S-41    end program main
```

———————————————— Fortran ————————————————

In the OpenMP 5.0 Specification, **reduction** clauses for the **taskloop simd** construct were also added.

The examples below compare reductions for the **taskloop** and the **taskloop simd** constructs. These examples illustrate the use of **reduction** clauses within "stand-alone" **taskloop** constructs, and the use of **in_reduction** clauses for tasks of taskloops to participate with other reductions within the scope of a parallel region.

taskloop reductions:

In the *taskloop reductions* section of the example below, *taskloop 1* uses the **reduction** clause in a **taskloop** construct for a sum reduction, accumulated in *asum*. The behavior is as though a **taskgroup** construct encloses the taskloop region with a **task_reduction** clause, and each taskloop task has an **in_reduction** clause with the specifications of the **reduction** clause. At the end of the taskloop region *asum* contains the result of the reduction.

The next taskloop, *taskloop 2*, illustrates the use of the **in_reduction** clause to participate in a previously defined reduction scope of a **parallel** construct.

The task reductions of *task 2* and *taskloop 2* are combined across the **taskloop** construct and the single **task** construct, as specified in the **reduction(task, +:asum)** clause of the **parallel** construct. At the end of the parallel region *asum* contains the combined result of all reductions.

taskloop simd reductions:

Reductions for the **taskloop simd** construct are shown in the second half of the code. Since each component construct, **taskloop** and **simd**, can accept a reduction-type clause, the **taskloop simd** construct is a composite construct, and the specific application of the reduction clause is defined within the **taskloop simd** construct section of the OpenMP 5.0 Specification. The code below illustrates use cases for these reductions.

In the *taskloop simd reduction* section of the example below, *taskloop simd 3* uses the **reduction** clause in a **taskloop simd** construct for a sum reduction within a loop. For this case a **reduction** clause is used, as one would use for a **simd** construct. The SIMD reductions of each task are combined, and the results of these tasks are further combined just as in the **taskloop**

construct with the **reduction** clause for *taskloop 1*. At the end of the taskloop region *asum*
contains the combined result of all reductions.

If a **taskloop simd** construct is to participate in a previously defined reduction scope, the
reduction participation should be specified with a **in_reduction** clause, as shown in the
parallel region enclosing *task 4* and *taskloop simd 4* code sections.

Here the **taskloop simd** construct's **in_reduction** clause specifies participation of the
construct's tasks as a task reduction within the scope of the parallel region. That is, the results of
each task of the **taskloop** construct component contribute to the reduction in a broader level, just
as in *parallel reduction a* code section above. Also, each **simd**-component construct occurs as if it
has a **reduction** clause, and the SIMD results of each task are combined as though to form a
single result for each task (that participates in the **in_reduction** clause). At the end of the
parallel region *asum* contains the combined result of all reductions.

─────────────────────────── C / C++ ───────────────────────────

Example taskloop_simd_reduction.1.c (**omp_5.1**)

```
S-1    #include <stdio.h>
S-2    #define N 100
S-3
S-4    int main(){
S-5       int i, a[N], asum=0;
S-6
S-7       for(i=0;i<N;i++) a[i]=i;
S-8
S-9       // taskloop reductions
S-10
S-11      #pragma omp parallel masked
S-12      #pragma omp taskloop reduction(+:asum) // taskloop 1
S-13         for(i=0;i<N;i++){ asum += a[i]; }
S-14
S-15
S-16      #pragma omp parallel reduction(task, +:asum) // parallel reduction a
S-17      {
S-18         #pragma omp masked
S-19         #pragma omp task               in_reduction(+:asum) // task 2
S-20            for(i=0;i<N;i++){ asum += a[i]; }
S-21
S-22         #pragma omp masked taskloop in_reduction(+:asum) // taskloop 2
S-23            for(i=0;i<N;i++){ asum += a[i]; }
S-24      }
S-25
S-26      // taskloop simd reductions
S-27
S-28      #pragma omp parallel masked
S-29      #pragma omp taskloop simd reduction(+:asum) // taskloop simd 3
```

```
S-30            for(i=0;i<N;i++){ asum += a[i]; }
S-31
S-32
S-33         #pragma omp parallel reduction(task, +:asum) // parallel reduction b
S-34         {
S-35            #pragma omp masked
S-36            #pragma omp task                     in_reduction(+:asum) // task 4
S-37               for(i=0;i<N;i++){ asum += a[i]; }
S-38
S-39            #pragma omp masked taskloop simd in_reduction(+:asum) // taskloop
S-40               for(i=0;i<N;i++){ asum += a[i]; }                   // simd 4
S-41
S-42         }
S-43
S-44         printf("asum=%d \n",asum); // output: asum=29700
S-45      }
```

———————————————————— C / C++ ————————————————————
———————————————————— Fortran ————————————————————

Example taskloop_simd_reduction.1.f90 (**omp_5.1**)

```
S-1     program main
S-2
S-3       use omp_lib
S-4       integer, parameter ::  N=100
S-5       integer            ::  i, a(N), asum=0
S-6
S-7       a = [( i, i=1,N )]     !! initialize
S-8
S-9     !! taskloop reductions
S-10
S-11      !$omp parallel masked
S-12      !$omp taskloop reduction(+:asum)                  !! taskloop 1
S-13        do i=1,N;  asum = asum + a(i);   enddo
S-14      !$omp end taskloop
S-15      !$omp end parallel masked
S-16
S-17
S-18      !$omp parallel reduction(task, +:asum)            !! parallel reduction a
S-19
S-20         !$omp masked
S-21         !$omp task              in_reduction(+:asum)   !! task 2
S-22           do i=1,N;  asum = asum + a(i);   enddo
S-23         !$omp end task
S-24         !$omp end masked
S-25
S-26         !$omp masked taskloop in_reduction(+:asum)     !! taskloop 2
```

```
S-27              do i=1,N;   asum = asum + a(i);   enddo
S-28          !$omp end masked taskloop
S-29
S-30      !$omp end parallel
S-31
S-32    !! taskloop simd reductions
S-33
S-34      !$omp parallel masked
S-35      !$omp taskloop simd reduction(+:asum)                    !! taskloop simd 3
S-36        do i=1,N;   asum = asum + a(i);   enddo
S-37      !$omp end taskloop simd
S-38      !$omp end parallel masked
S-39
S-40
S-41      !$omp parallel reduction(task, +:asum)                   !! parallel reduction b
S-42
S-43        !$omp masked
S-44        !$omp task                      in_reduction(+:asum)  !! task 4
S-45          do i=1,N;   asum = asum + a(i);   enddo
S-46        !$omp end task
S-47        !$omp end masked
S-48
S-49        !$omp masked taskloop simd in_reduction(+:asum) !! taskloop simd 4
S-50          do i=1,N;   asum = asum + a(i);   enddo
S-51        !$omp end masked taskloop simd
S-52
S-53      !$omp end parallel
S-54
S-55      print*,"asum=",asum    !! output: asum=30300
S-56
S-57    end program
```

———————————————————— Fortran ————————————————————

10.9.6 Reduction with the scope Construct

The following example illustrates the use of the **scope** construct to perform a reduction in a **parallel** region. The case is useful for producing a reduction and accessing reduction variables inside a **parallel** region without using a worksharing-loop construct.

C++
---

1   *Example scope_reduction.1.cpp* (**omp_5.1**)

```
S-1    #include <stdio.h>
S-2    void do_work(int n, float a[], float &s)
S-3    {
S-4       float loc_s = 0.0f;           // local sum
S-5       static int nthrs;
S-6       #pragma omp for
S-7          for (int i = 0; i < n; i++)
S-8             loc_s += a[i];
S-9       #pragma omp single
S-10      {
S-11         s = 0.0f;                  // total sum
S-12         nthrs = 0;
S-13      }
S-14      #pragma omp scope reduction(+:s,nthrs)
S-15      {
S-16         s += loc_s;
S-17         nthrs++;
S-18      }
S-19      #pragma omp masked
S-20         printf("total sum = %f, nthrs = %d\n", s, nthrs);
S-21   }
S-22
S-23   float work(int n, float a[])
S-24   {
S-25      float s;
S-26      #pragma omp parallel
S-27      {
S-28         do_work(n, a, s);
S-29      }
S-30      return s;
S-31   }
```

C++
---

1   *Example scope_reduction.1.f90* (**omp_5.1**)

```fortran
S-1    subroutine do_work(n, a, s)
S-2       implicit none
S-3       integer n, i
S-4       real a(*), s, loc_s
S-5       integer, save :: nthrs
S-6
S-7       loc_s = 0.0                   ! local sum
S-8    !$omp do
S-9       do i = 1, n
S-10         loc_s = loc_s + a(i)
S-11      end do
S-12   !$omp single
S-13      s = 0.0                       ! total sum
S-14      nthrs = 0
S-15   !$omp end single
S-16   !$omp scope reduction(+:s,nthrs)
S-17      s = s + loc_s
S-18      nthrs = nthrs + 1
S-19   !$omp end scope
S-20   !$omp masked
S-21      print *, "total sum = ", s, ", nthrs = ", nthrs
S-22   !$omp end masked
S-23   end subroutine
S-24
S-25   function work(n, a) result(s)
S-26      implicit none
S-27      integer n
S-28      real a(*), s
S-29
S-30   !$omp parallel
S-31      call do_work(n, a, s)
S-32   !$omp end parallel
S-33   end function
```

10.9.7 User-Defined Reduction

The **declare reduction** directive can be used to specify user-defined reductions (UDR) for user data types.

In the following example, **declare reduction** directives are used to define *min* and *max* operations for the *point* data structure for computing the rectangle that encloses a set of 2-D points.

Each **declare reduction** directive defines new reduction identifiers, *min* and *max*, to be used in a **reduction** clause. The next item in the declaration list is the data type (*struct point*) used in the reduction, followed by the combiner, here the functions *minproc* and *maxproc* perform the min and max operations, respectively, on the user data (of type *struct point*). In the function argument list are two special OpenMP variable identifiers, **omp_in** and **omp_out**, that denote the two values to be combined in the "real" function; the **omp_out** identifier indicates which one is to hold the result.

The initializer of the **declare reduction** directive specifies the initial value for the private variable of each implicit task. The **omp_priv** identifier is used to denote the private variable.

───────────────────────── C / C++ ─────────────────────────

Example udr.1.c (**omp_4.0**)

```
#include <stdio.h>
#include <limits.h>

struct point {
  int x;
  int y;
};

void minproc ( struct point *out, struct point *in )
{
  if ( in->x < out->x ) out->x = in->x;
  if ( in->y < out->y ) out->y = in->y;
}

void maxproc ( struct point *out, struct point *in )
{
  if ( in->x > out->x ) out->x = in->x;
  if ( in->y > out->y ) out->y = in->y;
}

#pragma omp declare reduction(min : struct point : \
        minproc(&omp_out, &omp_in)) \
        initializer( omp_priv = { INT_MAX, INT_MAX } )

#pragma omp declare reduction(max : struct point : \
        maxproc(&omp_out, &omp_in)) \
        initializer( omp_priv = { 0, 0 } )

void find_enclosing_rectangle ( int n, struct point points[] )
{
  struct point minp = { INT_MAX, INT_MAX }, maxp = {0,0};
  int i;
```

```
S-34    #pragma omp parallel for reduction(min:minp) reduction(max:maxp)
S-35      for ( i = 0; i < n; i++ ) {
S-36        minproc(&minp, &points[i]);
S-37        maxproc(&maxp, &points[i]);
S-38      }
S-39      printf("min = (%d, %d)\n", minp.x, minp.y);
S-40      printf("max = (%d, %d)\n", maxp.x, maxp.y);
S-41    }
```

──────────────────────── C / C++ ────────────────────────

1   The following example shows the corresponding code in Fortran. The **declare reduction**
2   directives are specified as part of the declaration in subroutine *find_enclosing_rectangle* and the
3   procedures that perform the min and max operations are specified as subprograms.

──────────────────────── Fortran ────────────────────────

4   *Example udr.1.f90* (**omp_4.0**)

```
S-1     module data_type
S-2
S-3       type :: point
S-4         integer :: x
S-5         integer :: y
S-6       end type
S-7
S-8     end module data_type
S-9
S-10    subroutine find_enclosing_rectangle ( n, points )
S-11      use data_type
S-12      implicit none
S-13      integer :: n
S-14      type(point) :: points(*)
S-15
S-16      !$omp declare reduction(min : point : minproc(omp_out, omp_in)) &
S-17      !$omp&  initializer( omp_priv = point( HUGE(0), HUGE(0) ) )
S-18
S-19      !$omp declare reduction(max : point : maxproc(omp_out, omp_in)) &
S-20      !$omp&  initializer( omp_priv = point( 0, 0 ) )
S-21
S-22      type(point) :: minp = point( HUGE(0), HUGE(0) ), maxp = point( 0, 0 )
S-23      integer :: i
S-24
S-25      !$omp parallel do reduction(min:minp) reduction(max:maxp)
S-26      do i = 1, n
S-27         call minproc(minp, points(i))
S-28         call maxproc(maxp, points(i))
S-29      end do
S-30      print *, "min = (", minp%x, minp%y, ")"
```

```
S-31        print *, "max = (", maxp%x, maxp%y, ")"
S-32
S-33    contains
S-34      subroutine minproc ( out, in )
S-35        implicit none
S-36        type(point), intent(inout) :: out
S-37        type(point), intent(in) :: in
S-38
S-39        out%x = min( out%x, in%x )
S-40        out%y = min( out%y, in%y )
S-41      end subroutine minproc
S-42
S-43      subroutine maxproc ( out, in )
S-44        implicit none
S-45        type(point), intent(inout) :: out
S-46        type(point), intent(in) :: in
S-47
S-48        out%x = max( out%x, in%x )
S-49        out%y = max( out%y, in%y )
S-50      end subroutine maxproc
S-51
S-52    end subroutine
```

———————————————————————— Fortran ————————————————————————

1   The following example shows the same computation as *udr.1* but it illustrates that you can craft
2   complex expressions in the user-defined reduction declaration. In this case, instead of calling the
3   *minproc* and *maxproc* functions we inline the code in a single expression.

———————————————————————— C / C++ ————————————————————————

4   *Example udr.2.c* (`omp_4.0`)

```
S-1    #include <stdio.h>
S-2    #include <limits.h>
S-3
S-4    struct point {
S-5      int x;
S-6      int y;
S-7    };
S-8
S-9    #pragma omp declare reduction(min : struct point : \
S-10           omp_out.x = omp_in.x > omp_out.x ? omp_out.x : omp_in.x, \
S-11           omp_out.y = omp_in.y > omp_out.y ? omp_out.y : omp_in.y ) \
S-12           initializer( omp_priv = { INT_MAX, INT_MAX } )
S-13
S-14   #pragma omp declare reduction(max : struct point : \
S-15           omp_out.x = omp_in.x < omp_out.x ? omp_out.x : omp_in.x, \
S-16           omp_out.y = omp_in.y < omp_out.y ? omp_out.y : omp_in.y ) \
```

```
S-17                 initializer( omp_priv = { 0, 0 } )
S-18
S-19     void find_enclosing_rectangle ( int n, struct point points[] )
S-20     {
S-21       struct point minp = { INT_MAX, INT_MAX }, maxp = {0,0};
S-22       int i;
S-23
S-24     #pragma omp parallel for reduction(min:minp) reduction(max:maxp)
S-25       for ( i = 0; i < n; i++ ) {
S-26         if ( points[i].x < minp.x ) minp.x = points[i].x;
S-27         if ( points[i].y < minp.y ) minp.y = points[i].y;
S-28         if ( points[i].x > maxp.x ) maxp.x = points[i].x;
S-29         if ( points[i].y > maxp.y ) maxp.y = points[i].y;
S-30       }
S-31       printf("min = (%d, %d)\n", minp.x, minp.y);
S-32       printf("max = (%d, %d)\n", maxp.x, maxp.y);
S-33     }
```

———————————————————————— C / C++ ————————————————————————

1 The corresponding code of the same example in Fortran is very similar except that the assignment
2 expression in the **declare reduction** directive can only be used for a single variable, in this
3 case through a type structure constructor *point(...)*.

———————————————————————— Fortran ————————————————————————

4 *Example udr.2.f90* (**omp_4.0**)

```
S-1      module data_type
S-2
S-3        type :: point
S-4          integer :: x
S-5          integer :: y
S-6        end type
S-7
S-8      end module data_type
S-9
S-10     subroutine find_enclosing_rectangle ( n, points )
S-11       use data_type
S-12       implicit none
S-13       integer :: n
S-14       type(point) :: points(*)
S-15
S-16       !$omp declare reduction( min : point :   &
S-17       !$omp&    omp_out = point(min( omp_out%x, omp_in%x ), &
S-18       !$omp&                    min( omp_out%y, omp_in%y )) ) &
S-19       !$omp&    initializer( omp_priv = point( HUGE(0), HUGE(0) ) )
S-20
S-21       !$omp declare reduction( max : point :   &
```

```
S-22        !$omp&    omp_out = point(max( omp_out%x, omp_in%x ), &
S-23        !$omp&                     max( omp_out%y, omp_in%y )) ) &
S-24        !$omp&    initializer( omp_priv = point( 0, 0 ) )
S-25
S-26        type(point) :: minp = point( HUGE(0), HUGE(0) ), maxp = point( 0, 0 )
S-27        integer :: i
S-28
S-29        !$omp parallel do reduction(min: minp) reduction(max: maxp)
S-30        do i = 1, n
S-31          minp%x = min(minp%x, points(i)%x)
S-32          minp%y = min(minp%y, points(i)%y)
S-33          maxp%x = max(maxp%x, points(i)%x)
S-34          maxp%y = max(maxp%y, points(i)%y)
S-35        end do
S-36        print *, "min = (", minp%x, minp%y, ")"
S-37        print *, "max = (", maxp%x, maxp%y, ")"
S-38
S-39    end subroutine
```

———————————————————————— Fortran ————————————————————————

The following example shows the use of special variables in arguments for combiner (**omp_in** and
omp_out) and initializer (**omp_priv** and **omp_orig**) routines. This example returns the
maximum value of an array and the corresponding index value. The **declare reduction**
directive specifies a user-defined reduction operation *maxloc* for data type *struct mx_s*. The
function *mx_combine* is the combiner and the function *mx_init* is the initializer.

———————————————————————— C / C++ ————————————————————————

Example udr.3.c (**omp_4.0**)

```
S-1
S-2     #include <stdio.h>
S-3     #define N 100
S-4
S-5     struct mx_s {
S-6        float value;
S-7        int index;
S-8     };
S-9
S-10    /* prototype functions for combiner and initializer in
S-11       the declare reduction */
S-12    void mx_combine(struct mx_s *out, struct mx_s *in);
S-13    void mx_init(struct mx_s *priv, struct mx_s *orig);
S-14
S-15    #pragma omp declare reduction(maxloc: struct mx_s: \
S-16            mx_combine(&omp_out, &omp_in)) \
S-17            initializer(mx_init(&omp_priv, &omp_orig))
S-18
```

```
S-19    void mx_combine(struct mx_s *out, struct mx_s *in)
S-20    {
S-21       if ( out->value < in->value ) {
S-22          out->value = in->value;
S-23          out->index = in->index;
S-24       }
S-25    }
S-26
S-27    void mx_init(struct mx_s *priv, struct mx_s *orig)
S-28    {
S-29       priv->value = orig->value;
S-30       priv->index = orig->index;
S-31    }
S-32
S-33    int main(void)
S-34    {
S-35       struct mx_s mx;
S-36       float val[N], d;
S-37       int i, count = N;
S-38
S-39       for (i = 0; i < count; i++) {
S-40          d = (N*0.8f - i);
S-41          val[i] = N * N - d * d;
S-42       }
S-43
S-44       mx.value = val[0];
S-45       mx.index = 0;
S-46       #pragma omp parallel for reduction(maxloc: mx)
S-47       for (i = 1; i < count; i++) {
S-48          if (mx.value < val[i])
S-49          {
S-50             mx.value = val[i];
S-51             mx.index = i;
S-52          }
S-53       }
S-54
S-55       printf("max value = %g, index = %d\n", mx.value, mx.index);
S-56       /* prints 10000, 80 */
S-57
S-58       return 0;
S-59    }
```

-- C / C++ --

Below is the corresponding Fortran version of the above example. The **declare reduction**
directive specifies the user-defined operation *maxloc* for user-derived type *mx_s*. The combiner
mx_combine and the initializer *mx_init* are specified as subprograms.

1   *Example udr.3.f90* (`omp_4.0`)

```
S-1    program max_loc
S-2      implicit none
S-3
S-4      type :: mx_s
S-5        real value
S-6        integer index
S-7      end type
S-8
S-9      !$omp declare reduction(maxloc: mx_s: &
S-10     !$omp&          mx_combine(omp_out, omp_in)) &
S-11     !$omp&          initializer(mx_init(omp_priv, omp_orig))
S-12
S-13     integer, parameter :: N = 100
S-14     type(mx_s) :: mx
S-15     real :: val(N), d
S-16     integer :: i, count
S-17
S-18     count = N
S-19     do i = 1, count
S-20        d = N*0.8 - i + 1
S-21        val(i) = N * N - d * d
S-22     enddo
S-23
S-24     mx%value = val(1)
S-25     mx%index = 1
S-26     !$omp parallel do reduction(maxloc: mx)
S-27     do i = 2, count
S-28        if (mx%value < val(i)) then
S-29           mx%value = val(i)
S-30           mx%index = i
S-31        endif
S-32     enddo
S-33
S-34     print *, 'max value = ', mx%value, ' index = ', mx%index
S-35     ! prints 10000, 81
S-36
S-37   contains
S-38
S-39   subroutine mx_combine(out, in)
S-40     implicit none
S-41     type(mx_s), intent(inout) :: out
S-42     type(mx_s), intent(in) :: in
S-43
S-44     if ( out%value < in%value ) then
```

```
S-45        out%value = in%value
S-46        out%index = in%index
S-47      endif
S-48    end subroutine mx_combine
S-49
S-50    subroutine mx_init(priv, orig)
S-51      implicit none
S-52      type(mx_s), intent(out) :: priv
S-53      type(mx_s), intent(in) :: orig
S-54
S-55      priv%value = orig%value
S-56      priv%index = orig%index
S-57    end subroutine mx_init
S-58
S-59  end program
```

───────────────────────── Fortran ─────────────────────────

The following example explains a few details of the user-defined reduction in Fortran through
modules. The **declare reduction** directive is declared in a module (*data_red*). The
reduction-identifier *.add.* is a user-defined operator that is to allow accessibility in the scope that
performs the reduction operation. The user-defined operator *.add.* and the subroutine *dt_init*
specified in the **initializer** clause are defined in the same subprogram.

The reduction operation (that is, the **reduction** clause) is in the main program. The reduction
identifier *.add.* is accessible by use association. Since *.add.* is a user-defined operator, the explicit
interface should also be accessible by use association in the current program unit. Since the
declare reduction associated to this **reduction** clause has the **initializer** clause,
the subroutine specified on the clause must be accessible in the current scoping unit. In this case, the
subroutine *dt_init* is accessible by use association.

───────────────────────── Fortran ─────────────────────────

Example udr.4.f90 (**omp_4.0**)

```
S-1   module data_red
S-2   ! Declare data type.
S-3     type dt
S-4       real :: r1
S-5       real :: r2
S-6     end type
S-7
S-8   ! Declare the user-defined operator .add.
S-9     interface operator(.add.)
S-10      module procedure addc
S-11    end interface
S-12
S-13  ! Declare the user-defined reduction operator .add.
S-14  !$omp declare reduction(.add.:dt:omp_out=omp_out.add.omp_in) &
```

```
S-15      !$omp& initializer(dt_init(omp_priv))
S-16
S-17       contains
S-18      ! Declare the initialization routine.
S-19        subroutine dt_init(u)
S-20          type(dt) :: u
S-21          u%r1 = 0.0
S-22          u%r2 = 0.0
S-23        end subroutine
S-24
S-25      ! Declare the specific procedure for the .add. operator.
S-26        function addc(x1, x2) result(xresult)
S-27          type(dt), intent(in) :: x1, x2
S-28          type(dt) :: xresult
S-29          xresult%r1 = x1%r1 + x2%r2
S-30          xresult%r2 = x1%r2 + x2%r1
S-31        end function
S-32
S-33      end module data_red
S-34
S-35      program main
S-36        use data_red, only : dt, dt_init, operator(.add.)
S-37
S-38        type(dt) :: xdt1, xdt2
S-39        integer :: i
S-40
S-41        xdt1 = dt(1.0,2.0)
S-42        xdt2 = dt(2.0,3.0)
S-43
S-44      ! The reduction operation
S-45      !$omp parallel do reduction(.add.: xdt1)
S-46        do i = 1, 10
S-47          xdt1 = xdt1 .add. xdt2
S-48        end do
S-49      !$omp end parallel do
S-50
S-51        print *, xdt1
S-52
S-53      end program
```

———————————————— Fortran ————————————————

1   The following example uses user-defined reductions to declare a plus (+) reduction for a C++ class.
2   As the **declare reduction** directive is inside the context of the *V* class the expressions in the
3   **declare reduction** directive are resolved in the context of the class. Also, note that the
4   **initializer** clause uses a copy constructor to initialize the private variables of the reduction
5   and it uses as parameter to its original variable by using the special variable **omp_orig**.

1   *Example udr.5.cpp* (**omp_4.0**)

```
S-1     class V {
S-2         float *p;
S-3         int n;
S-4
S-5     public:
S-6         V( int _n )      : n(_n)  { p = new float[n]; }
S-7         V( const V& m ) : n(m.n) { p = new float[n]; }
S-8         ~V() { delete[] p; }
S-9
S-10        V& operator+= ( const V& );
S-11
S-12        #pragma omp declare reduction( + : V : omp_out += omp_in ) \
S-13                initializer(omp_priv(omp_orig))
S-14    };
```

2   The following examples shows how user-defined reductions can be defined for some STL
3   containers. The first **declare reduction** defines the plus (+) operation for *std::vector<int>* by
4   making use of the *std::transform* algorithm. The second and third define the merge (or
5   concatenation) operation for *std::vector<int>* and *std::list<int>*. It shows how the user-defined
6   reduction operation can be applied to specific data types of an STL.

7   *Example udr.6.cpp* (**omp_4.0**)

```
S-1     #include <algorithm>
S-2     #include <list>
S-3     #include <vector>
S-4
S-5     #pragma omp declare reduction( + : std::vector<int> : \
S-6         std::transform (omp_out.begin(), omp_out.end(),  \
S-7                         omp_in.begin(), omp_in.end(),std::plus<int>()))
S-8
S-9     #pragma omp declare reduction( merge : std::vector<int> : \
S-10        omp_out.insert(omp_out.end(), omp_in.begin(), omp_in.end()))
S-11
S-12    #pragma omp declare reduction( merge : std::list<int> : \
S-13        omp_out.merge(omp_in))
```

10.10 scan Directive

The following examples illustrate how to parallelize a loop that saves the *prefix sum* of a reduction. This is accomplished by using the **inscan** modifier in the **reduction** clause for the input variable of the scan, and specifying with a **scan** directive whether the storage statement includes or excludes the scan input of the present iteration (k).

Basically, the **inscan** modifier connects a loop and/or SIMD reduction to the scan operation, and a **scan** construct with an **inclusive** or **exclusive** clause specifies whether the "scan phase" (lexical block before and after the directive, respectively) is to use an *inclusive* or *exclusive* scan value for the list item (x).

The first example uses the *inclusive* scan operation on a composite loop-SIMD construct. The **scan** directive separates the reduction statement on variable x from the use of x (saving to array b). The order of the statements in this example indicates that value $a[k]$ ($a(k)$ in Fortran) is included in the computation of the prefix sum $b[k]$ ($b(k)$ in Fortran) for iteration k.

---------- C / C++ ----------

Example scan.1.c (**omp_5.0**)

```
#include <stdio.h>
#define N 100

int main(void)
{
   int a[N], b[N];
   int x = 0;

   // initialization
   for (int k = 0; k < N; k++)
     a[k] = k + 1;

   // a[k] is included in the computation of producing results in b[k]
   #pragma omp parallel for simd reduction(inscan,+: x)
   for (int k = 0; k < N; k++) {
      x += a[k];
      #pragma omp scan inclusive(x)
      b[k] = x;
   }

   printf("x = %d, b[0:3] = %d %d %d\n", x, b[0], b[1], b[2]);
   //            5050,         1  3  6

   return 0;
}
```

---------- C / C++ ----------

1 *Example scan.1.f90* (**omp_5.0**)

```fortran
S-1    program inclusive_scan
S-2       implicit none
S-3       integer, parameter :: n = 100
S-4       integer a(n), b(n)
S-5       integer x, k
S-6
S-7       ! initialization
S-8       x = 0
S-9       do k = 1, n
S-10         a(k) = k
S-11      end do
S-12
S-13      ! a(k) is included in the computation of producing results in b(k)
S-14      !$omp parallel do simd reduction(inscan,+: x)
S-15      do k = 1, n
S-16         x = x + a(k)
S-17         !$omp scan inclusive(x)
S-18         b(k) = x
S-19      end do
S-20
S-21      print *,'x =', x, ', b(1:3) =', b(1:3)
S-22      !              5050,              1  3  6
S-23
S-24   end program
```

2 The second example uses the *exclusive* scan operation on a composite loop-SIMD construct. The
3 **scan** directive separates the use of x (saving to array b) from the reduction statement on variable
4 x. The order of the statements in this example indicates that value a[k] (a(k) in Fortran) is
5 excluded from the computation of the prefix sum b[k] (b(k) in Fortran) for iteration k.

6 *Example scan.2.c* (**omp_5.0**)

```c
S-1    #include <stdio.h>
S-2    #define N 100
S-3
S-4    int main(void)
S-5    {
S-6       int a[N], b[N];
S-7       int x = 0;
S-8
S-9       // initialization
```

```
S-10         for (int k = 0; k < N; k++)
S-11             a[k] = k + 1;
S-12
S-13         // a[k] is not included in the computation of producing
S-14         // results in b[k]
S-15         #pragma omp parallel for simd reduction(inscan,+: x)
S-16         for (int k = 0; k < N; k++) {
S-17             b[k] = x;
S-18             #pragma omp scan exclusive(x)
S-19             x += a[k];
S-20         }
S-21
S-22         printf("x = %d, b[0:3] = %d %d %d\n", x, b[0], b[1], b[2]);
S-23         //              5050,         0  1  3
S-24
S-25         return 0;
S-26     }
```

─────────────────── C / C++ ───────────────────
─────────────────── Fortran ───────────────────

Example scan.2.f90 (**omp_5.0**)

```
S-1     program exclusive_scan
S-2         implicit none
S-3         integer, parameter :: n = 100
S-4         integer a(n), b(n)
S-5         integer x, k
S-6
S-7         ! initialization
S-8         x = 0
S-9         do k = 1, n
S-10            a(k) = k
S-11        end do
S-12
S-13        ! a(k) is not included in the computation of producing results in b(k)
S-14        !$omp parallel do simd reduction(inscan,+: x)
S-15        do k = 1, n
S-16            b(k) = x
S-17            !$omp scan exclusive(x)
S-18            x = x + a(k)
S-19        end do
S-20
S-21        print *,'x =', x, ', b(1:3) =', b(1:3)
S-22        !              5050,        0  1  3
S-23
S-24    end program
```

─────────────────── Fortran ───────────────────

10.11 `copyin` Clause

The **copyin** clause is used to initialize threadprivate data upon entry to a **parallel** region. The value of the threadprivate variable in the primary thread is copied to the threadprivate variable of each other team member.

───────────────────────────── C / C++ ─────────────────────────────

Example copyin.1.c

```c
#include <stdlib.h>

float* work;
int size;
float tol;

#pragma omp threadprivate(work,size,tol)

void build()
{
  int i;
  work = (float*)malloc( sizeof(float)*size );
  for( i = 0; i < size; ++i ) work[i] = tol;
}

void copyin_example( float t, int n )
{
  tol = t;
  size = n;
  #pragma omp parallel copyin(tol,size)
  {
    build();
  }
}
```

───────────────────────────── C / C++ ─────────────────────────────

1   *Example copyin.1.f*

```
S-1          MODULE M
S-2            REAL, POINTER, SAVE :: WORK(:)
S-3            INTEGER :: SIZE
S-4            REAL :: TOL
S-5   !$OMP    THREADPRIVATE(WORK,SIZE,TOL)
S-6          END MODULE M
S-7
S-8          SUBROUTINE COPYIN_EXAMPLE( T, N )
S-9            USE M
S-10           REAL :: T
S-11           INTEGER :: N
S-12           TOL = T
S-13           SIZE = N
S-14  !$OMP    PARALLEL COPYIN(TOL,SIZE)
S-15           CALL BUILD
S-16  !$OMP    END PARALLEL
S-17         END SUBROUTINE COPYIN_EXAMPLE
S-18
S-19         SUBROUTINE BUILD
S-20           USE M
S-21           ALLOCATE(WORK(SIZE))
S-22           WORK = TOL
S-23         END SUBROUTINE BUILD
```

10.12 `copyprivate` Clause

The `copyprivate` clause can be used to broadcast values acquired by a single thread directly to all instances of the private variables in the other threads. In this example, if the routine is called from the sequential part, its behavior is not affected by the presence of the directives. If it is called from a `parallel` region, then the actual arguments with which **a** and **b** are associated must be private.

The thread that executes the structured block associated with the `single` construct broadcasts the values of the private variables **a**, **b**, **x**, and **y** from its implicit task's data environment to the data environments of the other implicit tasks in the thread team. The broadcast completes before any of the threads have left the barrier at the end of the construct.

───────────────────── C / C++ ─────────────────────

Example copyprivate.1.c

```c
#include <stdio.h>
float x, y;
#pragma omp threadprivate(x, y)

void init(float a,  float b ) {
    #pragma omp single copyprivate(a,b,x,y)
    {
        scanf("%f %f %f %f", &a, &b, &x, &y);
    }
}
```

───────────────────── C / C++ ─────────────────────

───────────────────── Fortran ─────────────────────

Example copyprivate.1.f

```fortran
          SUBROUTINE INIT(A,B)
          REAL A, B
            COMMON /XY/ X,Y
!$OMP     THREADPRIVATE (/XY/)

!$OMP     SINGLE
              READ (11) A,B,X,Y
!$OMP     END SINGLE COPYPRIVATE (A,B,/XY/)

          END SUBROUTINE INIT
```

───────────────────── Fortran ─────────────────────

In this example, assume that the input must be performed by the primary thread. Since the `masked` construct does not support the `copyprivate` clause, it cannot broadcast the input value that is read. However, `copyprivate` is used to broadcast an address where the input value is stored.

1   *Example copyprivate.2.c* (`omp_5.1`)

```c
#include <stdio.h>
#include <stdlib.h>

float read_next( ) {
  float * tmp;
  float return_val;

  #pragma omp single copyprivate(tmp)
  {
    tmp = (float *) malloc(sizeof(float));
  }  /* copies the pointer only */


  #pragma omp masked
  {
    scanf("%f", tmp);
  }

  #pragma omp barrier
  return_val = *tmp;
  #pragma omp barrier

  #pragma omp single nowait
  {
    free(tmp);
  }

  return return_val;
}
```

2   *Example copyprivate.2.f* (`omp_5.1`)

```fortran
      REAL FUNCTION READ_NEXT()
      REAL, POINTER :: TMP

!$OMP    SINGLE
          ALLOCATE (TMP)
!$OMP    END SINGLE COPYPRIVATE (TMP)    ! copies the pointer only

!$OMP    MASKED
          READ (11) TMP
!$OMP    END MASKED
```

```
S-11
S-12    !$OMP    BARRIER
S-13             READ_NEXT = TMP
S-14    !$OMP    BARRIER
S-15
S-16    !$OMP    SINGLE
S-17             DEALLOCATE (TMP)
S-18    !$OMP    END SINGLE NOWAIT
S-19             END FUNCTION READ_NEXT
```

──────────────────────── Fortran ────────────────────────

Suppose that the number of lock variables required within a **parallel** region cannot easily be determined prior to entering it. The **copyprivate** clause can be used to provide access to shared lock variables that are allocated within that **parallel** region.

──────────────────────── C / C++ ────────────────────────

Example copyprivate.3.c

```
S-1     #include <stdio.h>
S-2     #include <stdlib.h>
S-3     #include <omp.h>
S-4
S-5     omp_lock_t *new_lock()
S-6     {
S-7       omp_lock_t *lock_ptr;
S-8
S-9       #pragma omp single copyprivate(lock_ptr)
S-10      {
S-11        lock_ptr = (omp_lock_t *) malloc(sizeof(omp_lock_t));
S-12        omp_init_lock( lock_ptr );
S-13      }
S-14
S-15      return lock_ptr;
S-16    }
```

──────────────────────── C / C++ ────────────────────────

1   *Example copyprivate.3.f*

```
S-1        FUNCTION NEW_LOCK()
S-2        USE OMP_LIB         ! or INCLUDE "omp_lib.h"
S-3          INTEGER(OMP_LOCK_KIND), POINTER :: NEW_LOCK
S-4
S-5   !$OMP   SINGLE
S-6            ALLOCATE(NEW_LOCK)
S-7            CALL OMP_INIT_LOCK(NEW_LOCK)
S-8   !$OMP   END SINGLE COPYPRIVATE(NEW_LOCK)
S-9        END FUNCTION NEW_LOCK
```

2   Note that the effect of the **copyprivate** clause on a variable with the **allocatable** attribute
3   is different than on a variable with the **pointer** attribute. The value of **A** is copied (as if by
4   intrinsic assignment) and the pointer **B** is copied (as if by pointer assignment) to the corresponding
5   list items in the other implicit tasks belonging to the **parallel** region.

6   *Example copyprivate.4.f*

```
S-1        SUBROUTINE S(N)
S-2        INTEGER N
S-3
S-4          REAL, DIMENSION(:), ALLOCATABLE :: A
S-5          REAL, DIMENSION(:), POINTER :: B
S-6
S-7          ALLOCATE (A(N))
S-8   !$OMP   SINGLE
S-9            ALLOCATE (B(N))
S-10           READ (11) A,B
S-11  !$OMP   END SINGLE COPYPRIVATE(A,B)
S-12           ! Variable A is private and is
S-13           ! assigned the same value in each thread
S-14           ! Variable B is shared
S-15
S-16  !$OMP   BARRIER
S-17  !$OMP   SINGLE
S-18           DEALLOCATE (B)
S-19  !$OMP   END SINGLE NOWAIT
S-20       END SUBROUTINE S
```

10.13 C++ Reference in Data-Sharing Clauses

C++

C++ reference types are allowed in data-sharing attribute clauses as of OpenMP 4.5, except for the
threadprivate, **copyin** and **copyprivate** clauses. (See the Data-Sharing Attribute
Clauses Section of the 4.5 OpenMP specification.) When a variable with C++ reference type is
privatized, the object the reference refers to is privatized in addition to the reference itself. The
following example shows the use of reference types in data-sharing clauses in the usual way.
Additionally it shows how the data-sharing of formal arguments with a C++ reference type on an
orphaned task generating construct is determined implicitly. (See the Data-sharing Attribute Rules
for Variables Referenced in a Construct Section of the 4.5 OpenMP specification.)

Example cpp_reference.1.cpp (**omp_4.5**)

```
void task_body (int &);
void gen_task (int &x) { // on orphaned task construct reference argument
  #pragma omp task // x is implicitly determined firstprivate(x)
  task_body (x);
}
void test (int &y, int &z) {
  #pragma omp parallel private(y)
  {
    y = z + 2;
    gen_task (y); // no matter if the argument is determined private
    gen_task (z); // or shared in the enclosing context.

    y++;          // each thread has its own int object y refers to
    gen_task (y);
  }
}
```

C++

10.14 Fortran ASSOCIATE Construct

---------------------------- Fortran ----------------------------

The following is an invalid example of specifying an associate name on a data-sharing attribute clause. The constraint in the Data Sharing Attribute Rules section in the OpenMP 4.0 API Specifications states that an associate name preserves the association with the selector established at the **ASSOCIATE** statement. The associate name *b* is associated with the shared variable *a*. With the predetermined data-sharing attribute rule, the associate name *b* is not allowed to be specified on the **private** clause.

Example associate.1.f (**omp_4.0**)

```
S-1          program example_broken
S-2          real :: a, c
S-3          associate (b => a)
S-4    !$omp parallel private(b, c)          ! invalid to privatize b
S-5          c = 2.0*b
S-6    !$omp end parallel
S-7          end associate
S-8          end program
```

In next example, within the **parallel** construct, the association name *thread_id* is associated with the private copy of *i*. The print statement should output the unique thread number.

Example associate.2.f (**omp_4.0**)

```
S-1          program example
S-2          use omp_lib
S-3          integer  i
S-4    !$omp parallel private(i)
S-5          i = omp_get_thread_num()
S-6          associate(thread_id => i)
S-7            print *, thread_id          ! print private i value
S-8          end associate
S-9    !$omp end parallel
S-10         end program
```

The following example illustrates the effect of specifying a selector name on a data-sharing attribute clause. The associate name *u* is associated with *v* and the variable *v* is specified on the **private** clause of the **parallel** construct. The construct association is established prior to the **parallel** region. The association between *u* and the original *v* is retained (see the Data Sharing Attribute Rules section in the OpenMP 4.0 API Specifications). Inside the **parallel** region, *v* has the value of -1 and *u* has the value of the original *v*.

1   *Example associate.3.f90* (**omp_4.0**)

```
S-1    program example
S-2      integer :: v
S-3      v = 15
S-4    associate(u => v)
S-5    !$omp parallel private(v)
S-6      v = -1
S-7      print *, v                ! private v=-1
S-8      print *, u                ! original v=15
S-9    !$omp end parallel
S-10   end associate
S-11   end program
```

2   The following example illustrates mapping behavior for a Fortran associate name and its selector
3   for a **target** construct.

4   For the first 3 **target** constructs the associate name *a_aray* is associated with the selector *aray*,
5   an array. For the **target** construct of code block TARGET 1 just the selector *aray* is used and is
6   implicitly mapped, likewise for the associate name *a_aray* in the TARGET 2 block. However,
7   mapping an associate name and its selector is not valid for the same **target** construct. Hence the
8   TARGET 3 block is non-conforming.

9   In TARGET 4, the *scalr* selector used in the **target** region has an implicit data-sharing attribute
10   of firstprivate since it is a scalar. Hence, the assigned value is not returned. In TARGET 5, the
11   associate name *a_scalr* is implicitly mapped and the assigned value is returned to the host (default
12   **tofrom** mapping behavior). In TARGET 6, the use of the associate name and its selector in the
13   **target** region is conforming because the scalar firstprivate behavior of the selector and the
14   implicit mapping of the associate name are allowed. At the end of the **target** region only the
15   associate name's value is returned to the host. In TARGET 7, the selector and associate name
16   appear in an explicit mapping for the same **target** construct, hence the code block is
17   non-conforming.

18   *Example associate.4.f90* (**omp_5.1**)

```
S-1    program main
S-2      integer :: scalr, aray(3)
S-3      scalr = -1 ; aray = -1
S-4
S-5      associate(a_scalr=>scalr, a_aray=>aray)
S-6
S-7    !$omp target              !! TARGET 1
S-8        aray = [1,2,3]
S-9    !$omp end target
S-10     print *, a_aray, aray !! 1 2 3   1 2 3
```

```
S-11
S-12        !$omp target              !! TARGET 2
S-13          a_aray = [4,5,6]
S-14        !$omp end target
S-15        print *, a_aray, aray  !! 4 5 6   4 5 6
S-16
S-17    !!!$omp target              !! TARGET 3
S-18    !!                          !! mapping, in this case implicit,
S-19    !!                          !! of aray AND a_aray NOT ALLOWED
S-20    !!     aray = [4,5,6]
S-21    !!   a_aray = [1,2,3]
S-22    !!!$omp end target
S-23
S-24
S-25        !$omp target              !! TARGET 4
S-26          scalr = 1               !! scalr is firstprivate
S-27        !$omp end target
S-28        print *, a_scalr, scalr   !! -1  -1
S-29
S-30        !$omp target              !! TARGET 5
S-31          a_scalr = 2             !! a_scalr implicitly mapped
S-32        !$omp end target
S-33        print *, a_scalr, scalr   !! 2   2
S-34
S-35        !$omp target              !! TARGET 6
S-36          scalr = 3               !!          scalr is firstprivate
S-37          print *, a_scalr, scalr !! 2   3
S-38          a_scalr = 4             !!          a_scalr implicitly mapped
S-39          print *, a_scalr, scalr !! 4   3
S-40        !$omp end target
S-41        print *, a_scalr, scalr   !! 4   4
S-42
S-43    !!!$omp target map(a_scalr,scalr)  !! TARGET 7
S-44                                        !! mapping, in this case explicit,
S-45                                        !! of scalr AND a_sclar NOT ALLOWED
S-46    !!     scalr = 5
S-47    !!   a_scalr = 5
S-48    !!!$omp end target
S-49
S-50      end associate
S-51
S-52    end program
```

Fortran

This page intentionally left blank

11 Memory Model

OpenMP provides a shared-memory model that allows all threads on a given device shared access to *memory*. For a given OpenMP region that may be executed by more than one thread or SIMD lane, variables in memory may be *shared* or *private* with respect to those threads or SIMD lanes. A variable's data-sharing attribute indicates whether it is shared (the *shared* attribute) or private (the *private*, *firstprivate*, *lastprivate*, *linear*, and *reduction* attributes) in the data environment of an OpenMP region. While private variables in an OpenMP region are new copies of the original variable (with same name) that may then be concurrently accessed or modified by their respective threads or SIMD lanes, a shared variable in an OpenMP region is the same as the variable of the same name in the enclosing region. Concurrent accesses or modifications to a shared variable may therefore require synchronization to avoid data races.

OpenMP's memory model also includes a *temporary view* of memory that is associated with each thread. Two different threads may see different values for a given variable in their respective temporary views. Threads may employ flush operations for the purposes of making their temporary view of a variable consistent with the value of the variable in memory. The effect of a given flush operation is characterized by its flush properties – some combination of *strong*, *release*, and *acquire* – and, for *strong* flushes, a *flush-set*.

A *strong* flush will force consistency between the temporary view and the memory for all variables in its *flush-set*. Furthermore, all strong flushes in a program that have intersecting flush-sets will execute in some total order, and within a thread strong flushes may not be reordered with respect to other memory operations on variables in its flush-set. *Release* and *acquire* flushes operate in pairs. A release flush may "synchronize" with an acquire flush, and when it does so the local memory operations that precede the release flush will appear to have been completed before the local memory operations on the same variables that follow the acquire flush.

Flush operations arise from explicit **flush** directives, implicit **flush** directives, and also from the execution of **atomic** constructs. The **flush** directive forces a consistent view of local variables of the thread executing the **flush**. When a list is supplied on the directive, only the items (variables) in the list are guaranteed to be flushed. Implied flushes exist at prescribed locations of certain constructs. For the complete list of these locations and associated constructs, please refer to the *flush Construct* section of the OpenMP Specifications document.

In this chapter, examples illustrate how race conditions may arise for accesses to variables with a *shared* data-sharing attribute when flush operations are not properly employed. A race condition can exist when two or more threads are involved in accessing a variable and at least one of the accesses modifies the variable. In particular, a data race will arise when conflicting accesses do not have a well-defined *completion order*. The existence of data races in OpenMP programs result in undefined behavior, and so they should generally be avoided for programs to be correct. The completion order of accesses to a shared variable is guaranteed in OpenMP through a set of memory consistency rules that are described in the *OpenMP Memory Consistency* section of the OpenMP Specifications document.

11.1 OpenMP Memory Model

The following examples illustrate two major concerns for concurrent thread execution: ordering of thread execution and memory accesses that may or may not lead to race conditions.

In the following example, at Print 1, the value of **xval** could be either 2 or 5, depending on the timing of the threads. The **atomic** directives are necessary for the accesses to **x** by threads 1 and 2 to avoid a data race. If the atomic write completes before the atomic read, thread 1 is guaranteed to see 5 in **xval**. Otherwise, thread 1 is guaranteed to see 2 in **xval**.

The barrier after Print 1 contains implicit flushes on all threads, as well as a thread synchronization, so the programmer is guaranteed that the value 5 will be printed by both Print 2 and Print 3. Since neither Print 2 or Print 3 are modifying **x**, they may concurrently access **x** without requiring **atomic** directives to avoid a data race.

———————————————— C / C++ ————————————————

Example mem_model.1.c (**omp_3.1**)

```
#include <stdio.h>
#include <omp.h>

int main(){
  int x;

  x = 2;
  #pragma omp parallel num_threads(2) shared(x)
  {

    if (omp_get_thread_num() == 0) {
       #pragma omp atomic write
       x = 5;
    } else {
      int xval;
      #pragma omp atomic read
      xval = x;
    /* Print 1: xval can be 2 or 5 */
      printf("1: Thread# %d: x = %d\n", omp_get_thread_num(), xval);
    }

    #pragma omp barrier

    if (omp_get_thread_num() == 0) {
    /* Print 2 */
```

```
S-26          printf("2: Thread# %d: x = %d\n", omp_get_thread_num(), x);
S-27        } else {
S-28        /* Print 3 */
S-29          printf("3: Thread# %d: x = %d\n", omp_get_thread_num(), x);
S-30        }
S-31     }
S-32     return 0;
S-33   }
```

———————————————————— C / C++ ————————————————————
———————————————————— Fortran ————————————————————

1   *Example mem_model.1.f90* (omp_3.1)

```
S-1    PROGRAM MEMMODEL
S-2      INCLUDE "omp_lib.h"        ! or USE OMP_LIB
S-3      INTEGER X, XVAL
S-4
S-5      X = 2
S-6    !$OMP PARALLEL NUM_THREADS(2) SHARED(X)
S-7
S-8        IF (OMP_GET_THREAD_NUM() .EQ. 0) THEN
S-9        !$OMP ATOMIC WRITE
S-10         X = 5
S-11       ELSE
S-12       !$OMP ATOMIC READ
S-13         XVAL = X
S-14       ! PRINT 1: XVAL can be 2 or 5
S-15         PRINT *,"1: THREAD# ", OMP_GET_THREAD_NUM(), "X = ", XVAL
S-16       ENDIF
S-17
S-18     !$OMP BARRIER
S-19
S-20       IF (OMP_GET_THREAD_NUM() .EQ. 0) THEN
S-21       ! PRINT 2
S-22         PRINT *,"2: THREAD# ", OMP_GET_THREAD_NUM(), "X = ", X
S-23       ELSE
S-24       ! PRINT 3
S-25         PRINT *,"3: THREAD# ", OMP_GET_THREAD_NUM(), "X = ", X
S-26       ENDIF
S-27
S-28    !$OMP END PARALLEL
S-29
S-30    END PROGRAM MEMMODEL
```
———————————————————— Fortran ————————————————————

The following example demonstrates why synchronization is difficult to perform correctly through variables. The write to **flag** on thread 0 and the read from **flag** in the loop on thread 1 must be atomic to avoid a data race. When thread 1 breaks out of the loop, **flag** will have the value of 1. However, **data** will still be undefined at the first print statement. Only after the flush of both **flag** and **data** after the first print statement will **data** have the well-defined value of 42.

--------------------------------- C / C++ ---------------------------------

Example mem_model.2.c (`omp_3.1`)

```
#include <omp.h>
#include <stdio.h>
int main()
{
    int data;
    int flag=0;
    #pragma omp parallel num_threads(2)
    {
      if (omp_get_thread_num()==0)
      {
      /* Write to the data buffer that will be
       * read by thread */
         data = 42;
      /* Flush data to thread 1 and strictly order
       * the write to data relative to the write to the flag */
         #pragma omp flush(flag, data)
      /* Set flag to release thread 1 */
         #pragma omp atomic write
         flag = 1;
      }
      else if(omp_get_thread_num()==1)
      {
      /* Loop until we see the update to the flag */
         #pragma omp flush(flag, data)
         int flag_val = 0;
         while (flag_val < 1)
         {
             #pragma omp atomic read
             flag_val = flag;
         }
      /* Value of flag is 1; value of data is undefined */
         printf("flag=%d data=%d\n", flag, data);
         #pragma omp flush(flag, data)
      /* Value of flag is 1; value of data is 42 */
         printf("flag=%d data=%d\n", flag, data);
      }
    }
```

```
S-38        return 0;
S-39    }
```

──────────────────────────── C / C++ ────────────────────────────
──────────────────────────── Fortran ────────────────────────────

Example mem_model.2.f (`omp_3.1`)

```
S-1             PROGRAM EXAMPLE
S-2             INCLUDE "omp_lib.h" ! or USE OMP_LIB
S-3             INTEGER DATA
S-4             INTEGER FLAG, FLAG_VAL
S-5
S-6             FLAG = 0
S-7     !$OMP   PARALLEL NUM_THREADS(2)
S-8               IF(OMP_GET_THREAD_NUM() .EQ. 0) THEN
S-9               ! Write to the data buffer that will be read by thread 1
S-10                DATA = 42
S-11
S-12              ! Flush DATA to thread 1 and strictly order the write to DATA
S-13              ! relative to the write to the FLAG
S-14    !$OMP       FLUSH(FLAG, DATA)
S-15
S-16              ! Set FLAG to release thread 1
S-17    !$OMP       ATOMIC WRITE
S-18                FLAG = 1
S-19
S-20              ELSE IF(OMP_GET_THREAD_NUM() .EQ. 1) THEN
S-21              ! Loop until we see the update to the FLAG
S-22    !$OMP       FLUSH(FLAG, DATA)
S-23                FLAG_VAL = 0
S-24                DO WHILE(FLAG_VAL .LT. 1)
S-25    !$OMP          ATOMIC READ
S-26                    FLAG_VAL = FLAG
S-27                ENDDO
S-28
S-29              ! Value of FLAG is 1; value of DATA is undefined
S-30                PRINT *, 'FLAG=', FLAG, ' DATA=', DATA
S-31
S-32    !$OMP       FLUSH(FLAG, DATA)
S-33              ! Value of FLAG is 1; value of DATA is 42
S-34                PRINT *, 'FLAG=', FLAG, ' DATA=', DATA
S-35
S-36              ENDIF
S-37    !$OMP   END PARALLEL
S-38            END
```

──────────────────────────── Fortran ────────────────────────────

The next example demonstrates why synchronization is difficult to perform correctly through variables. As in the preceding example, the updates to **flag** and the reading of **flag** in the loops on threads 1 and 2 are performed atomically to avoid data races on **flag**. However, the code still contains data race due to the incorrect use of "flush with a list" after the assignment to **data1** on thread 1. By not including **flag** in the flush-set of that **flush** directive, the assignment can be reordered with respect to the subsequent atomic update to **flag**. Consequentially, **data1** is undefined at the print statement on thread 2.

─────────────────────────── C / C++ ───────────────────────────

Example mem_model.3.c (**omp_3.1**)

```
S-1     #include <omp.h>
S-2     #include <stdio.h>
S-3
S-4     int data0 = 0, data1 = 0;
S-5
S-6     int main()
S-7     {
S-8         int flag=0;
S-9
S-10        #pragma omp parallel num_threads(3)
S-11        {
S-12            if(omp_get_thread_num()==0)
S-13            {
S-14                data0 = 17;
S-15                #pragma omp flush
S-16                /* Set flag to release thread 1 */
S-17                #pragma omp atomic update
S-18                flag++;
S-19                /* Flush of flag is implied by the atomic directive */
S-20            }
S-21            else if(omp_get_thread_num()==1)
S-22            {
S-23                int flag_val = 0;
S-24                /* Loop until we see that flag reaches 1*/
S-25                while(flag_val < 0)
S-26                {
S-27                    #pragma omp atomic read
S-28                    flag_val = flag;
S-29                }
S-30                #pragma omp flush(data0)
S-31                /* data0 is 17 here */
S-32                printf("Thread 1 awoken (data0 = %d)\n", data0);
S-33                data1 = 42;
S-34                #pragma omp flush(data1)
S-35                /* Set flag to release thread 2 */
S-36                #pragma omp atomic update
```

```
S-37              flag++;
S-38              /* Flush of flag is implied by the atomic directive */
S-39          }
S-40          else if(omp_get_thread_num()==2)
S-41          {
S-42              int flag_val = 0;
S-43              /* Loop until we see that flag reaches 2 */
S-44              while(flag_val < 2)
S-45              {
S-46                  #pragma omp atomic read
S-47                  flag_val = flag;
S-48              }
S-49              #pragma omp flush(data0,data1)
S-50              /* there is a data race here;
S-51                 data0 is 17 and data1 is undefined */
S-52              printf("Thread 2 awoken (data0 = %d, data1 = %d)\n",
S-53                  data0, data1);
S-54          }
S-55      }
S-56      return 0;
S-57  }
```

──────────────────── C / C++ ────────────────────
──────────────────── Fortran ────────────────────

Example mem_model.3.f (**omp_3.1**)

```
S-1           PROGRAM EXAMPLE
S-2           INCLUDE "omp_lib.h" ! or USE OMP_LIB
S-3           INTEGER FLAG, FLAG_VAL
S-4           INTEGER DATA0, DATA1
S-5
S-6           FLAG = 0
S-7   !$OMP   PARALLEL NUM_THREADS(3)
S-8             IF(OMP_GET_THREAD_NUM() .EQ. 0) THEN
S-9                 DATA0 = 17
S-10  !$OMP         FLUSH
S-11
S-12             ! Set flag to release thread 1
S-13  !$OMP         ATOMIC UPDATE
S-14                 FLAG = FLAG + 1
S-15             ! Flush of FLAG is implied by the atomic directive
S-16
S-17             ELSE IF(OMP_GET_THREAD_NUM() .EQ. 1) THEN
S-18             ! Loop until we see that FLAG reaches 1
S-19  !$OMP         FLUSH(FLAG, DATA)
S-20                 FLAG_VAL = 0
S-21                 DO WHILE(FLAG_VAL .LT. 1)
```

```
S-22   !$OMP          ATOMIC READ
S-23                    FLAG_VAL = FLAG
S-24                  ENDDO
S-25   !$OMP          FLUSH
S-26

S-27           ! DATA0 is 17 here
S-28              PRINT *, 'Thread 1 awoken. DATA0 = ', DATA0
S-29

S-30              DATA1 = 42
S-31   !$OMP      FLUSH(DATA1)
S-32

S-33           ! Set FLAG to release thread 2
S-34   !$OMP      ATOMIC UPDATE
S-35              FLAG = FLAG + 1
S-36           ! Flush of FLAG is implied by the atomic directive
S-37

S-38           ELSE IF(OMP_GET_THREAD_NUM() .EQ. 2) THEN
S-39           ! Loop until we see that FLAG reaches 2
S-40              FLAG_VAL = 0
S-41              DO WHILE(FLAG_VAL .LT. 2)
S-42   !$OMP          ATOMIC READ
S-43                    FLAG_VAL = FLAG
S-44                  ENDDO
S-45   !$OMP          FLUSH(DATA0, DATA1)
S-46

S-47           ! There is a data race here; data0 is 17 and data1 is undefined
S-48              PRINT *, 'Thread 2 awoken. DATA0 = ', DATA0,
S-49        &                ' and DATA1 = ', DATA1
S-50

S-51           ENDIF
S-52   !$OMP   END PARALLEL
S-53           END
```

─────────────────── Fortran ───────────────────

1   The following two examples illustrate the ordering properties of the *flush* operation. The *flush*
2   operations are strong flushes that are applied to the specified flush lists. However, use of a **flush**
3   construct with a list is extremely error prone and users are strongly discouraged from attempting it.
4   In the codes the programmer intends to prevent simultaneous execution of the protected section by
5   the two threads. The atomic directives in the codes ensure that the accesses to shared variables *a*
6   and *b* are atomic write and atomic read operations. Otherwise both examples would contain data
7   races and automatically result in unspecified behavior.

8   In the following incorrect code example, operations on variables *a* and *b* are not ordered with
9   respect to each other. For instance, nothing prevents the compiler from moving the flush of *b* on
10 thread 0 or the flush of *a* on thread 1 to a position completely after the protected section (assuming
11 that the protected section on thread 0 does not reference *b* and the protected section on thread 1
12 does not reference *a*). If either re-ordering happens, both threads can simultaneously execute the

protected section. Any shared data accessed in the protected section is not guaranteed to be current
or consistent during or after the protected section.

———————————————————————— C / C++ ————————————————————————

Example mem_model.4a.c (**omp_3.1**)

```
S-1    #include <omp.h>
S-2
S-3    void flush_incorrect()
S-4    {
S-5      int a, b;
S-6      a = b = 0;
S-7      #pragma omp parallel num_threads(2)
S-8      {
S-9        int myid = omp_get_thread_num();
S-10       int tmp;
S-11
S-12       if ( myid == 0 ) {          // thread 0
S-13         #pragma omp atomic write
S-14           b = 1;
S-15         #pragma omp flush(b)     // flushes are not ordered
S-16         #pragma omp flush(a)     // compiler may move them around
S-17         #pragma omp atomic read
S-18           tmp = a;
S-19       }
S-20       else {                      // thread 1
S-21         #pragma omp atomic write
S-22           a = 1;
S-23         #pragma omp flush(a)     // flushes are not ordered
S-24         #pragma omp flush(b)     // compiler may move them around
S-25         #pragma omp atomic read
S-26           tmp = b;
S-27       }
S-28       if ( tmp == 0 ) {          // exclusive access not guaranteed
S-29         /* protected section */
S-30       }
S-31     }
S-32   }
```

———————————————————————— C / C++ ————————————————————————

1   *Example mem_model.4a.f90* (`omp_3.1`)

```fortran
S-1    subroutine flush_incorrect
S-2      use omp_lib
S-3      implicit none
S-4      integer a, b, tmp
S-5      integer myid
S-6
S-7      a = 0; b = 0
S-8      !$omp parallel private(myid,tmp) num_threads(2)
S-9        myid = omp_get_thread_num()
S-10
S-11       if ( myid == 0 ) then       ! thread 0
S-12         !$omp atomic write
S-13           b = 1
S-14         !$omp flush(b)            ! flushes are not ordered
S-15         !$omp flush(a)            ! compiler may move them around
S-16         !$omp atomic read
S-17           tmp = a
S-18       else                        ! thread 1
S-19         !$omp atomic write
S-20           a = 1
S-21         !$omp flush(a)            ! flushes are not ordered
S-22         !$omp flush(b)            ! compiler may move them around
S-23         !$omp atomic read
S-24           tmp = b
S-25       endif
S-26       if ( tmp == 0 ) then        ! exclusive access not guaranteed
S-27         !! protected section
S-28       endif
S-29     !$omp end parallel
S-30   end subroutine
```

2   The following code example correctly ensures that the protected section is executed by only one
3   thread at a time. Execution of the protected section by neither thread is considered correct in this
4   example. This occurs if both flushes complete prior to either thread executing its **if** statement for
5   the protected section. The compiler is prohibited from moving the flush at all for either thread,
6   ensuring that the respective assignment is complete and the data is flushed before the **if** statement
7   is executed.

1 *Example mem_model.4b.c* (`omp_3.1`)

```
S-1    #include <omp.h>
S-2
S-3    void flush_correct()
S-4    {
S-5      int a, b;
S-6      a = b = 0;
S-7      #pragma omp parallel num_threads(2)
S-8      {
S-9        int myid = omp_get_thread_num();
S-10       int tmp;
S-11
S-12       if ( myid == 0 ) {            // thread 0
S-13         #pragma omp atomic write
S-14           b = 1;
S-15         #pragma omp flush(a,b)      // flushes are ordered
S-16         #pragma omp atomic read
S-17           tmp = a;
S-18       }
S-19       else {                        // thread 1
S-20         #pragma omp atomic write
S-21           a = 1;
S-22         #pragma omp flush(a,b)      // flushes are ordered
S-23         #pragma omp atomic read
S-24           tmp = b;
S-25       }
S-26       if ( tmp == 0 ) {             // access by single thread
S-27         /* protected section */
S-28       }
S-29     }
S-30   }
```

2 *Example mem_model.4b.f90* (`omp_3.1`)

```
S-1    subroutine flush_correct
S-2      use omp_lib
S-3      implicit none
S-4      integer a, b, tmp
S-5      integer myid
S-6
S-7      a = 0; b = 0
S-8      !$omp parallel private(myid,tmp) num_threads(2)
S-9        myid = omp_get_thread_num()
```

```
S-10
S-11          if ( myid == 0 ) then        ! thread 0
S-12            !$omp atomic write
S-13              b = 1
S-14            !$omp flush(a,b)            ! flushes are ordered
S-15            !$omp atomic read
S-16              tmp = a
S-17          else                         ! thread 1
S-18            !$omp atomic write
S-19              a = 1
S-20            !$omp flush(a,b)            ! flushes are ordered
S-21            !$omp atomic read
S-22              tmp = b
S-23          endif
S-24          if ( tmp == 0 ) then         ! access by single thread
S-25            !! protected section
S-26          endif
S-27        !$omp end parallel
S-28    end subroutine
```

——————————————————— Fortran ———————————————————

11.2 Memory Allocators

OpenMP memory allocators can be used to allocate memory with specific allocator traits. In the following example an OpenMP allocator is used to specify an alignment for arrays *x* and *y*. The general approach for attributing traits to variables allocated by OpenMP is to create or specify a pre-defined *memory space*, create an array of *traits*, and then form an *allocator* from the memory space and trait. The allocator is then specified in an OpenMP allocation (using an API *omp_alloc()* function for C/C++ code and an **allocators** directive for Fortran code in the *allocators.1* example).

In the example below the *xy_memspace* variable is declared and assigned the default memory space (*omp_default_mem_space*). Next, an array for *traits* is created. Since only one trait will be used, the array size is *1*. A trait is a structure in C/C++ and a derived type in Fortran, containing 2 components: a key and a corresponding value (key-value pair). The trait key used here is *omp_atk_alignment* (an enum for C/C++ and a parameter for Fortran) and the trait value of 64 is specified in the *xy_traits* declaration. These declarations are followed by a call to the *omp_init_allocator()* function to combine the memory space (*xy_memspace*) and the traits (*xy_traits*) to form an allocator (*xy_alloc*).

In the C/C++ code the API *omp_allocate()* function is used to allocate space, similar to *malloc*, except that the allocator is specified as the second argument. In Fortran an **allocators** directive is used to specify an allocator for the following Fortran *allocate* statement. A variable list in the **allocate** clause may be supplied if the allocator is to be applied to a subset of variables in the Fortran allocate statement. Here, the *xy_alloc* allocator is specified in the modifier of the **allocator** clause, and the set of all variables used in the *allocate* statement is specified in the list.

―――――――――――――― C / C++ ――――――――――――――

Example allocators.1.c (`omp_5.0`)

```
#include    <omp.h>
#include  <stdio.h>
#include <stdlib.h>
#include <stdint.h>
#define N 1000

int main()
{
   float  *x, *y;
   float s=2.0;

   omp_memspace_handle_t   xy_memspace = omp_default_mem_space;
   omp_alloctrait_t        xy_traits[1]= {omp_atk_alignment, 64};
   omp_allocator_handle_t xy_alloc     =
                          omp_init_allocator(xy_memspace,1,xy_traits);


```

```
S-18        x=(float *)omp_alloc(N*sizeof(float), xy_alloc);
S-19        y=(float *)omp_alloc(N*sizeof(float), xy_alloc);
S-20
S-21        if( ((intptr_t)(y))%64 != 0 || ((intptr_t)(x))%64 != 0 )
S-22        { printf("ERROR: x|y not 64-Byte aligned\n"); exit(1); }
S-23
S-24        #pragma omp parallel
S-25        {
S-26           #pragma omp for simd simdlen(16) aligned(x,y:64)
S-27           for(int i=0; i<N; i++){ x[i]=i+1; y[i]=i+1; } // initialize
S-28
S-29           #pragma omp for simd simdlen(16) aligned(x,y:64)
S-30           for(int i=0; i<N; i++) y[i] = s*x[i] + y[i];
S-31         }
S-32
S-33        printf("y[0],y[N-1]: %5.0f %5.0f\n",y[0],y[N-1]);
S-34        // output y[0],y[N-1]: 3 3000
S-35
S-36        omp_free(x, xy_alloc);
S-37        omp_free(y, xy_alloc);
S-38        omp_destroy_allocator(xy_alloc);
S-39
S-40        return 0;
S-41    }
```

———————————————————— C / C++ ————————————————————
———————————————————— Fortran ————————————————————

1   *Example allocators.1.f90* (omp_5.2)

```
S-1     program main
S-2      use omp_lib
S-3
S-4      integer, parameter :: N=1000
S-5      real, allocatable  :: x(:),y(:)
S-6      real               :: s = 2.0e0
S-7      integer            :: i
S-8
S-9      integer(omp_memspace_handle_kind ) :: xy_memspace = omp_default_mem_space
S-10     type(   omp_alloctrait             ) :: xy_traits(1) = &
S-11                                    [omp_alloctrait(omp_atk_alignment,64)]
S-12     integer(omp_allocator_handle_kind) :: xy_alloc
S-13
S-14       xy_alloc   =   omp_init_allocator(   xy_memspace, 1, xy_traits)
S-15
S-16       !$omp allocators allocate(allocator(xy_alloc): x, y)
S-17       allocate(x(N),y(N))
S-18                              !! loc is non-standard, but found everywhere
```

```
S-19                                !! remove these lines if not available
S-20    if(modulo(loc(x),64) /= 0 .and. modulo(loc(y),64) /=0 ) then
S-21        print*,"ERROR: x|y not 64-byte aligned"; stop
S-22    endif
S-23
S-24    !$omp parallel
S-25
S-26        !$omp do simd simdlen(16) aligned(x,y: 64) !! 64B aligned
S-27        do i=1,N  !! initialize
S-28          x(i)=i
S-29          y(i)=i
S-30        end do
S-31
S-32        !$omp do simd simdlen(16) aligned(x,y: 64) !! 64B aligned
S-33        do i = 1,N
S-34            y(i) = s*x(i) + y(i)
S-35        end do
S-36
S-37    !$omp end parallel
S-38
S-39    write(*,'("y(1),y(N):",2f6.0)') y(1),y(N) !!output: y... 3. 3000.
S-40
S-41    deallocate(x,y)
S-42    call omp_destroy_allocator(xy_alloc)
S-43
S-44    end program
S-45
```

──────────────────────────── Fortran ────────────────────────────

When using the **allocators** construct with optional clauses in Fortran code, users should be aware of the behavior of a reallocation.

In the following example, the *a* variable is allocated with 64-byte alignment through the **align** clause of the **allocators** construct. The alignment of the newly allocated object, *a*, in the (reallocation) assignment $a = b$ will not be reallocated with the 64-byte alignment, but with the 32-byte alignment prescribed by the trait of the *my_alloctr* allocator. It is best to avoid this problem by constructing and using an allocator (not the **align** clause) with the required alignment in the **allocators** construct. Note that in the subsequent deallocation of *a* the deallocation must precede the destruction of the allocator used in the allocation of *a*.

—————————————————————— Fortran ——————————————————————

Example allocators.2.f90 (**omp_5.2**)

```fortran
S-1      program main
S-2         use omp_lib
S-3         implicit none
S-4
S-5         integer, parameter :: align_32=32
S-6         real, allocatable  :: a(:,:)
S-7         real               :: b(10,10)
S-8
S-9         integer(omp_memspace_handle_kind ) :: my_memspace
S-10        type(   omp_alloctrait        ) :: my_traits(1)
S-11        integer(omp_allocator_handle_kind) :: my_alloctr
S-12
S-13        my_memspace  =  omp_default_mem_space
S-14        my_traits    = [omp_alloctrait(omp_atk_alignment,align_32)]
S-15     !                                   allocator alignment ^^
S-16        my_alloctr   =  omp_init_allocator(my_memspace, 1, my_traits)
S-17
S-18        !$omp allocators allocate(allocator(my_alloctr), align(64): a)
S-19        allocate(a(5,5)) ! 64-byte aligned by clause <---------^^
S-20
S-21        a = b  ! reallocation occurs with 32-byte alignment
S-22             ! uses just my_alloctr (32-byte align from allocator)
S-23
S-24        deallocate(a)   ! Uses my_alloctr in deallocation.
S-25        call omp_destroy_allocator(my_alloctr)
S-26
S-27     end program main
```

—————————————————————— Fortran ——————————————————————

When creating and using an **allocators** construct within a Fortran procedure for allocating storage (and subsequently freeing the allocator storage with an **omp_destroy_allocator** construct), users should be aware of the necessity of using an explicit Fortran deallocation instead of relying on auto-deallocation.

In the following example, a user-defined allocator is used in the allocation of the *c* variable, and then the allocator is destroyed. Auto-deallocation at the end of the *broken_auto_deallocation* procedure will fail without the allocator, hence an explicit deallocation should be used (before the **omp_destroy_allocator** construct). Note that an allocator may be specified directly in the **allocate** clause without using the **allocator** complex modifier, so long as no other modifier is specified in the clause.

1   *Example allocators.3.f90* (**omp_5.2**)

```fortran
S-1     subroutine broken_auto_deallocation
S-2        use omp_lib
S-3        implicit none
S-4        integer, parameter :: align_32=32
S-5        real, allocatable  :: c(:)
S-6
S-7        integer(omp_memspace_handle_kind ) :: my_memspace
S-8        type(   omp_alloctrait           ) :: my_traits(1)
S-9        integer(omp_allocator_handle_kind) :: my_alloctr
S-10
S-11       my_memspace   =  omp_default_mem_space
S-12       my_traits     = [omp_alloctrait(omp_atk_alignment,align_32)]
S-13       my_alloctr    =  omp_init_allocator(my_memspace, 1, my_traits)
S-14
S-15       !$omp allocators allocate(my_alloctr: c)
S-16       allocate(c(100))
S-17
S-18       !...
S-19
S-20       call omp_destroy_allocator(my_alloctr)
S-21       ! Auto-deallocation of c fails,
S-22       ! because my_alloctr is no longer available.
S-23
S-24    end subroutine
```

2   The **allocate** directive is a convenient way to apply an OpenMP allocator to the allocation of
3   declared variables.

4   This example illustrates the allocation of specific types of storage in a program for use in libraries,
5   privatized variables, and with offloading.

6   Two groups of variables, {*v1*, *v2*} and {*v3*, *v4*}, are used with the **allocate** directive, and the
7   {*v5*, *v6*} pair is used with the **allocate** clause. Here we explicitly use predefined allocators
8   **omp_high_bw_mem_alloc** and **omp_default_mem_alloc** with the **allocate** directive
9   in CASE 1. Similar effects are achieved for private variables of a task by using the **allocate**
10   clause, as shown in CASE 2.

11   Note, when the **allocate** directive does not specify an **allocator** clause, an
12   implementation-defined default, stored in the *def-allocator-var* ICV, is used (not illustrated here).
13   Users can set and get the default allocator with the **omp_set_default_allocator** and
14   **omp_get_default_allocator** API routines.

1   *Example allocators.4.c* (`omp_5.1`)

```
S-1     #include <omp.h>
S-2     #include <stdio.h>
S-3
S-4     void my_init(double *,double *,int, double *,double *,int, \
S-5                  double *,double *,int);
S-6     void lib_saxpy(double *,double *,double,int);
S-7     void my_gather(double *,double *,int);
S-8
S-9     #pragma omp begin declare target
S-10    void my_gpu_vxv(double *, double *, int);
S-11    #pragma omp end  declare target
S-12
S-13    #define Nhb 1024*1024       // high bandwith
S-14    #define Nbg 1024*1024*64    // big memory, default
S-15    #define Nll 1024*1024       // low latency memory
S-16
S-17    void test_allocate() {
S-18
S-19      double  v1[Nhb], v2[Nhb];
S-20      double  v3[Nbg], v4[Nbg];
S-21      double  v5[Nll], v6[Nll];
S-22
S-23    /*** CASE 1: USING ALLOCATE DIRECTIVE ***/
S-24      #pragma omp allocate(v1,v2) allocator(omp_high_bw_mem_alloc)
S-25      #pragma omp allocate(v3,v4) allocator(omp_default_mem_alloc)
S-26
S-27      my_init(v1,v2,Nhb,  v3,v4,Nbg,  v5,v6,Nll);
S-28
S-29      lib_saxpy(v1,v2,5.0,Nhb);
S-30
S-31      #pragma omp target map(to: v3[0:Nbg], v4[0:Nbg]) map(from:v3[0:Nbg])
S-32      my_gpu_vxv(v3,v4,Nbg);
S-33
S-34    /*** CASE 2: USING ALLOCATE CLAUSE ***/
S-35      #pragma omp task private(v5,v6) \
S-36                       allocate(allocator(omp_low_lat_mem_alloc): v5,v6)
S-37      {
S-38        my_gather(v5,v6,Nll);
S-39      }
S-40
S-41    }
```

1   *Example allocators.4.f90* (`omp_5.1`)

```
S-1     subroutine test_allocate
S-2       use omp_lib
S-3
S-4       interface
S-5         subroutine my_gpu_vxv(va,vb,n)
S-6         !$omp declare target
S-7         integer :: n
S-8         double precision  :: va(n), vb(n)
S-9         end subroutine
S-10      end interface
S-11
S-12      integer,parameter :: Nhb=1024*1024,    & !! high bandwith
S-13                           Nbg=1024*1024*64,& !! big memory, default
S-14                           Nll=1024*1024        !! low latency memory
S-15
S-16      double precision  ::  v1(Nhb), v2(Nhb)
S-17      double precision  ::  v3(Nbg), v4(Nbg)
S-18      double precision  ::  v5(Nll), v6(Nll)
S-19
S-20    !*** CASE 1: USING ALLOCATE DIRECTIVE ***!
S-21      !$omp allocate(v1,v2) allocator(omp_high_bw_mem_alloc)
S-22      !$omp allocate(v3,v4) allocator(omp_default_mem_alloc)
S-23
S-24      call my_init(v1,v2,Nhb, v3,v4,Nbg, v5,v6,Nll)
S-25
S-26      call lib_saxpy(v1,v2,5.0,Nhb)
S-27
S-28      !$omp target map(to: v3, v4) map(from:v3)
S-29        call my_gpu_vxv(v3,v4,Nbg)
S-30      !$omp end target
S-31
S-32    !*** CASE 2: USING ALLOCATE CLAUSE ***!
S-33      !$omp task private(v5,v6) &
S-34      !$omp&        allocate(allocator(omp_low_lat_mem_alloc): v5,v6)
S-35        call my_gather(v5,v6,Nll)
S-36      !$omp end task
S-37
S-38    end subroutine test_allocate
```

11.3 Race Conditions Caused by Implied Copies of Shared Variables in Fortran

───────────────── Fortran ─────────────────

The following example contains a race condition, because the shared variable, which is an array section, is passed as an actual argument to a routine that has an assumed-size array as its dummy argument. The subroutine call passing an array section argument may cause the compiler to copy the argument into a temporary location prior to the call and copy from the temporary location into the original variable when the subroutine returns. This copying would cause races in the **parallel** region.

Example fort_race.1.f90

```fortran
SUBROUTINE SHARED_RACE

  INCLUDE "omp_lib.h"        ! or USE OMP_LIB

  REAL A(20)
  INTEGER MYTHREAD

!$OMP PARALLEL SHARED(A) PRIVATE(MYTHREAD)

  MYTHREAD = OMP_GET_THREAD_NUM()
  IF (MYTHREAD .EQ. 0) THEN
     CALL SUB(A(1:10)) ! compiler may introduce writes to A(6:10)
  ELSE
     A(6:10) = 12
  ENDIF

!$OMP END PARALLEL

END SUBROUTINE SHARED_RACE

SUBROUTINE SUB(X)
  REAL X(*)
  X(1:5) = 4
END SUBROUTINE SUB
```

───────────────── Fortran ─────────────────

12 Program Control

Basic concepts and mechanisms for directing and controlling a program compilation and execution are provided in this introduction and illustrated in subsequent examples.

CONDITIONAL COMPILATION and EXECUTION

Conditional compilation can be performed with conventional #ifdef directives in C, C++, and Fortran, and additionally with OpenMP sentinel (**!$**) in Fortran. The **if** clause on some directives can direct the runtime to ignore or alter the behavior of the construct. Of course, the base-language **if** statements can be used to control the execution of stand-alone directives (such as **flush**, **barrier**, **taskwait**, and **taskyield**). However, the directives must appear in a block structure, and not as a substatement. The **metadirective** and **declare variant** directives provide conditional selection of directives and routines for compilation (and use), respectively. The **assume** and **requires** directives provide invariants for optimizing compilation, and essential features for compilation and correct execution, respectively.

CANCELLATION

Cancellation (termination) of the normal sequence of execution for the threads in an OpenMP region can be accomplished with the **cancel** construct. The construct uses a *construct-type-clause* to set the region-type to activate for the cancellation. That is, inclusion of one of the *construct-type-clause* names **parallel**, **for**, **do**, **sections** or **taskgroup** on the directive line activates the corresponding region. The **cancel** construct is activated by the first encountering thread, and it continues execution at the end of the named region. The **cancel** construct is also a cancellation point for any other thread of the team to also continue execution at the end of the named region.

Also, once the specified region has been activated for cancellation any thread that encounnters a **cancellation point** construct with the same named region (*construct-type-clause*), continues execution at the end of the region.

For an activated **cancel taskgroup** construct, the tasks that belong to the taskgroup set of the innermost enclosing taskgroup region will be canceled.

A task that encounters a **cancel taskgroup** construct continues execution at the end of its task region. Any task of the taskgroup that has already begun execution will run to completion, unless it encounters a **cancellation point**; tasks that have not begun execution may be discarded as completed tasks.

CONTROL VARIABLES

Internal control variables (ICV) are used by implementations to hold values which control the execution of OpenMP regions. Control (and hence the ICVs) may be set as implementation defaults, or set and adjusted through environment variables, clauses, and API functions. Initial ICV values are reported by the runtime if the **OMP_DISPLAY_ENV** environment variable has been set to **TRUE** or **VERBOSE**.

NESTED CONSTRUCTS

Certain combinations of nested constructs are permitted, giving rise to *combined* constructs consisting of two or more directives. These can be used when the two (or several) constructs would be used immediately in succession (closely nested). A *combined* construct can use the clauses of the component constructs without restrictions. A *composite* construct is a combined construct which has one or more clauses with (an often obviously) modified or restricted meaning, relative to when the constructs are uncombined.

Certain nestings are forbidden, and often the reasoning is obvious. For example, worksharing constructs cannot be nested, and the **barrier** construct cannot be nested inside a worksharing construct, or a **critical** construct. Also, **target** constructs cannot be nested, unless the nested target is a reverse offload.

The **parallel** construct can be nested, as well as the **task** construct. The parallel execution in the nested parallel construct(s) is controlled by the **OMP_MAX_ACTIVE_LEVELS** environment variable, and the **omp_set_max_active_levels** routine. Use the **omp_get_max_active_levels** routine to determine the maximum levels provided by an implementation. As of OpenMP 5.0, use of the **OMP_NESTED** environment variable and the **omp_set_nested** routine has been deprecated.

More details on nesting can be found in the *Nesting of Regions* of the *Directives* chapter in the OpenMP Specifications document.

12.1 Conditional Compilation

1

──────────────────── C / C++ ────────────────────

The following example illustrates the use of conditional compilation using the OpenMP macro **_OPENMP**. With OpenMP compilation, the **_OPENMP** macro becomes defined.

Example cond_comp.1.c

```
S-1    #include <stdio.h>
S-2
S-3    int main()
S-4    {
S-5
S-6    # ifdef _OPENMP
S-7        printf("Compiled by an OpenMP-compliant implementation.\n");
S-8    # endif
S-9
S-10       return 0;
S-11   }
```

──────────────────── C / C++ ────────────────────
──────────────────── Fortran ────────────────────

The following example illustrates the use of the conditional compilation sentinel. With OpenMP compilation, the conditional compilation sentinel **!$** is recognized and treated as two spaces. In fixed form source, statements guarded by the sentinel must start after column 6.

Example cond_comp.1.f

```
S-1          PROGRAM EXAMPLE
S-2
S-3    C234567890
S-4    !$    PRINT *, "Compiled by an OpenMP-compliant implementation."
S-5
S-6          END PROGRAM EXAMPLE
```

──────────────────── Fortran ────────────────────

12.2 Internal Control Variables (ICVs)

According to Section 2.3 of the OpenMP 4.0 specification, an OpenMP implementation must act as if there are ICVs that control the behavior of the program. This example illustrates two ICVs, *nthreads-var* and *max-active-levels-var*. The *nthreads-var* ICV controls the number of threads requested for encountered parallel regions; there is one copy of this ICV per task. The *max-active-levels-var* ICV controls the maximum number of nested active parallel regions; there is one copy of this ICV for the whole program.

In the following example, the *nest-var*, *max-active-levels-var*, *dyn-var*, and *nthreads-var* ICVs are modified through calls to the runtime library routines `omp_set_nested`, `omp_set_max_active_levels`, `omp_set_dynamic`, and `omp_set_num_threads` respectively. These ICVs affect the operation of `parallel` regions. Each implicit task generated by a `parallel` region has its own copy of the *nest-var, dyn-var*, and *nthreads-var* ICVs.

In the following example, the new value of *nthreads-var* applies only to the implicit tasks that execute the call to `omp_set_num_threads`. There is one copy of the *max-active-levels-var* ICV for the whole program and its value is the same for all tasks. This example assumes that nested parallelism is supported.

The outer `parallel` region creates a team of two threads; each of the threads will execute one of the two implicit tasks generated by the outer `parallel` region.

Each implicit task generated by the outer `parallel` region calls `omp_set_num_threads(3)`, assigning the value 3 to its respective copy of *nthreads-var*. Then each implicit task encounters an inner `parallel` region that creates a team of three threads; each of the threads will execute one of the three implicit tasks generated by that inner `parallel` region.

Since the outer `parallel` region is executed by 2 threads, and the inner by 3, there will be a total of 6 implicit tasks generated by the two inner `parallel` regions.

Each implicit task generated by an inner `parallel` region will execute the call to `omp_set_num_threads(4)`, assigning the value 4 to its respective copy of *nthreads-var*.

The print statement in the outer `parallel` region is executed by only one of the threads in the team. So it will be executed only once.

The print statement in an inner `parallel` region is also executed by only one of the threads in the team. Since we have a total of two inner `parallel` regions, the print statement will be executed twice – once per inner `parallel` region.

1   *Example icv.1.c*

```
S-1    #include <stdio.h>
S-2    #include <omp.h>
S-3
S-4    int main (void)
S-5    {
S-6      omp_set_nested(1);
S-7      omp_set_max_active_levels(8);
S-8      omp_set_dynamic(0);
S-9      omp_set_num_threads(2);
S-10     #pragma omp parallel
S-11       {
S-12         omp_set_num_threads(3);
S-13
S-14         #pragma omp parallel
S-15           {
S-16             omp_set_num_threads(4);
S-17             #pragma omp single
S-18               {
S-19                   // The following should print:
S-20                   // Inner: max_act_lev=8, num_thds=3, max_thds=4
S-21                   // Inner: max_act_lev=8, num_thds=3, max_thds=4
S-22                 printf ("Inner: max_act_lev=%d, num_thds=%d, max_thds=%d\n",
S-23                 omp_get_max_active_levels(), omp_get_num_threads(),
S-24                 omp_get_max_threads());
S-25               }
S-26           }
S-27
S-28         #pragma omp barrier
S-29         #pragma omp single
S-30           {
S-31                   // The following should print:
S-32                   // Outer: max_act_lev=8, num_thds=2, max_thds=3
S-33             printf ("Outer: max_act_lev=%d, num_thds=%d, max_thds=%d\n",
S-34                     omp_get_max_active_levels(), omp_get_num_threads(),
S-35                     omp_get_max_threads());
S-36           }
S-37       }
S-38     return 0;
S-39   }
```

1   *Example icv.1.f*

```
S-1          program icv
S-2          use omp_lib
S-3
S-4          call omp_set_nested(.true.)
S-5          call omp_set_max_active_levels(8)
S-6          call omp_set_dynamic(.false.)
S-7          call omp_set_num_threads(2)
S-8
S-9    !$omp parallel
S-10         call omp_set_num_threads(3)
S-11
S-12   !$omp parallel
S-13         call omp_set_num_threads(4)
S-14   !$omp single
S-15   !     The following should print:
S-16   !     Inner: max_act_lev= 8 , num_thds= 3 , max_thds= 4
S-17   !     Inner: max_act_lev= 8 , num_thds= 3 , max_thds= 4
S-18         print *, "Inner: max_act_lev=", omp_get_max_active_levels(),
S-19       &             ", num_thds=", omp_get_num_threads(),
S-20       &             ", max_thds=", omp_get_max_threads()
S-21   !$omp end single
S-22   !$omp end parallel
S-23
S-24   !$omp barrier
S-25   !$omp single
S-26   !     The following should print:
S-27   !     Outer: max_act_lev= 8 , num_thds= 2 , max_thds= 3
S-28         print *, "Outer: max_act_lev=", omp_get_max_active_levels(),
S-29       &             ", num_thds=", omp_get_num_threads(),
S-30       &             ", max_thds=", omp_get_max_threads()
S-31   !$omp end single
S-32   !$omp end parallel
S-33         end
```

12.3 Placement of `flush`, `barrier`, `taskwait` and `taskyield` Directives

The following example is non-conforming, because the **flush**, **barrier**, **taskwait**, and **taskyield** directives are stand-alone directives and cannot be the immediate substatement of an **if** statement.

──────────────── C / C++ ────────────────

Example standalone.1.c (**omp_3.1**)

```
void standalone_wrong()
{
  int a = 1;

        if (a != 0)
  #pragma omp flush(a)
/* incorrect as flush cannot be immediate substatement
   of if statement */

        if (a != 0)
  #pragma omp barrier
/* incorrect as barrier cannot be immediate substatement
   of if statement */

        if (a!=0)
  #pragma omp taskyield
/* incorrect as taskyield cannot be immediate substatement of if statement
*/

        if (a != 0)
  #pragma omp taskwait
/* incorrect as taskwait cannot be immediate substatement
   of if statement */

}
```

──────────────── C / C++ ────────────────

The following example is non-conforming, because the **flush**, **barrier**, **taskwait**, and **taskyield** directives are stand-alone directives and cannot be the action statement of an **if** statement or a labeled branch target.

—————————————————————— Fortran ——————————————————————

Example standalone.1.f90 (`omp_3.1`)

```
S-1
S-2
S-3     SUBROUTINE STANDALONE_WRONG()
S-4
S-5       INTEGER  A
S-6
S-7       A = 1
S-8
S-9       ! the FLUSH directive must not be the action statement
S-10      ! in an IF statement
S-11      IF (A .NE. 0) !$OMP FLUSH(A)
S-12
S-13      ! the BARRIER directive must not be the action statement
S-14      ! in an IF statement
S-15      IF (A .NE. 0) !$OMP BARRIER
S-16
S-17      ! the TASKWAIT directive must not be the action statement
S-18      ! in an IF statement
S-19      IF (A .NE. 0) !$OMP TASKWAIT
S-20
S-21      ! the TASKYIELD directive must not be the action statement
S-22      ! in an IF statement
S-23      IF (A .NE. 0) !$OMP TASKYIELD
S-24
S-25      GOTO 100
S-26
S-27      ! the FLUSH directive must not be a labeled branch target
S-28      ! statement
S-29      100 !$OMP FLUSH(A)
S-30      GOTO 200
S-31
S-32      ! the BARRIER directive must not be a labeled branch target
S-33      ! statement
S-34      200 !$OMP BARRIER
S-35      GOTO 300
S-36
S-37      ! the TASKWAIT directive must not be a labeled branch target
S-38      ! statement
S-39      300 !$OMP TASKWAIT
S-40      GOTO 400
```

```
S-41
S-42      ! the TASKYIELD directive must not be a labeled branch target
S-43      ! statement
S-44      400 !$OMP TASKYIELD
S-45
S-46      END SUBROUTINE
```

———————————————————— Fortran ————————————————————

The following version of the above example is conforming because the **flush**, **barrier**, **taskwait**, and **taskyield** directives are enclosed in a compound statement.

———————————————————— C / C++ ————————————————————

Example standalone.2.c (**omp_3.1**)

```
S-1    void standalone_ok()
S-2    {
S-3      int a = 1;
S-4
S-5      #pragma omp parallel
S-6      {
S-7        if (a != 0) {
S-8    #pragma omp flush(a)
S-9        }
S-10       if (a != 0) {
S-11   #pragma omp barrier
S-12       }
S-13       if (a != 0) {
S-14   #pragma omp taskwait
S-15       }
S-16         if (a != 0) {
S-17   #pragma omp taskyield
S-18         }
S-19     }
S-20   }
```

———————————————————— C / C++ ————————————————————

The following example is conforming because the **flush**, **barrier**, **taskwait**, and **taskyield** directives are enclosed in an **if** construct or follow the labeled branch target.

-- Fortran --

Example standalone.2.f90 (`omp_3.1`)

```fortran
S-1     SUBROUTINE STANDALONE_OK()
S-2       INTEGER  A
S-3       A = 1
S-4       IF (A .NE. 0) THEN
S-5         !$OMP FLUSH(A)
S-6       ENDIF
S-7       IF (A .NE. 0) THEN
S-8         !$OMP BARRIER
S-9       ENDIF
S-10      IF (A .NE. 0) THEN
S-11        !$OMP TASKWAIT
S-12      ENDIF
S-13      IF (A .NE. 0) THEN
S-14        !$OMP TASKYIELD
S-15      ENDIF
S-16      GOTO 100
S-17      100 CONTINUE
S-18      !$OMP FLUSH(A)
S-19      GOTO 200
S-20      200 CONTINUE
S-21      !$OMP BARRIER
S-22      GOTO 300
S-23      300 CONTINUE
S-24      !$OMP TASKWAIT
S-25      GOTO 400
S-26      400 CONTINUE
S-27      !$OMP TASKYIELD
S-28    END SUBROUTINE
```

-- Fortran --

12.4 Cancellation Constructs

The following example shows how the **cancel** directive can be used to terminate an OpenMP region. Although the **cancel** construct terminates the OpenMP worksharing region, programmers must still track the exception through the pointer ex and issue a cancellation for the **parallel** region if an exception has been raised. The primary thread checks the exception pointer to make sure that the exception is properly handled in the sequential part. If cancellation of the **parallel** region has been requested, some threads might have executed **phase_1()**. However, it is guaranteed that none of the threads executed **phase_2()**.

— C++ —

Example cancellation.1.cpp (**omp_4.0**)

```
S-1     #include <iostream>
S-2     #include <exception>
S-3     #include <cstddef>
S-4
S-5     #define N 10000
S-6
S-7     extern void causes_an_exception();
S-8     extern void phase_1();
S-9     extern void phase_2();
S-10
S-11    void example() {
S-12        std::exception *ex = NULL;
S-13    #pragma omp parallel shared(ex)
S-14        {
S-15    #pragma omp for
S-16            for (int i = 0; i < N; i++) {
S-17                // no 'if' that prevents compiler optimizations
S-18                try {
S-19                    causes_an_exception();
S-20                }
S-21                catch (std::exception *e) {
S-22                    // still must remember exception for later handling
S-23    #pragma omp atomic write
S-24                    ex = e;
S-25                    // cancel worksharing construct
S-26    #pragma omp cancel for
S-27                }
S-28            }
S-29            // if an exception has been raised, cancel parallel region
S-30            if (ex) {
S-31    #pragma omp cancel parallel
S-32            }
S-33            phase_1();
S-34    #pragma omp barrier
```

```
S-35          phase_2();
S-36        }
S-37        // continue here if an exception has been thrown in
S-38        // the worksharing loop
S-39        if (ex) {
S-40            // handle exception stored in ex
S-41        }
S-42    }
```

————————————————————— C++ —————————————————————

The following example illustrates the use of the **cancel** construct in error handling. If there is an error condition from the **allocate** statement, the cancellation is activated. The encountering thread sets the shared variable **err** and other threads of the binding thread set proceed to the end of the worksharing construct after the cancellation has been activated.

————————————————————— Fortran —————————————————————

Example cancellation.1.f90 (**omp_4.0**)

```
S-1     subroutine example(n, dim)
S-2       integer, intent(in) :: n, dim(n)
S-3       integer :: i, s, err
S-4       real, allocatable :: B(:)
S-5       err = 0
S-6     !$omp parallel shared(err)
S-7     ! ...
S-8     !$omp do private(s, B)
S-9       do i=1, n
S-10    !$omp cancellation point do
S-11        allocate(B(dim(i)), stat=s)
S-12        if (s .gt. 0) then
S-13    !$omp atomic write
S-14            err = s
S-15    !$omp cancel do
S-16        endif
S-17    !    ...
S-18    ! deallocate private array B
S-19        if (allocated(B)) then
S-20            deallocate(B)
S-21        endif
S-22      enddo
S-23    !$omp end parallel
S-24    end subroutine
```

————————————————————— Fortran —————————————————————

The following example shows how to cancel a parallel search on a binary tree as soon as the search value has been detected. The code creates a task to descend into the child nodes of the current tree node. If the search value has been found, the code remembers the tree node with the found value through an **atomic** write to the result variable and then cancels execution of all search tasks. The function **search_tree_parallel** groups all search tasks into a single task group to control the effect of the **cancel taskgroup** directive. The *level* argument is used to create undeferred tasks after the first ten levels of the tree.

———————————————————— C / C++ ————————————————————

Example cancellation.2.c (**omp_5.1**)

```
#include <stddef.h>

typedef struct binary_tree_s {
    int value;
    struct binary_tree_s *left, *right;
} binary_tree_t;

binary_tree_t *search_tree(binary_tree_t *tree, int value, int level) {
    binary_tree_t *found = NULL;
    if (tree) {
        if (tree->value == value) {
            found = tree;
        }
        else {
#pragma omp task shared(found) if(level < 10)
            {
                binary_tree_t *found_left = NULL;
                found_left = search_tree(tree->left, value, level + 1);
                if (found_left) {
#pragma omp atomic write
                    found = found_left;
#pragma omp cancel taskgroup
                }
            }
#pragma omp task shared(found) if(level < 10)
            {
                binary_tree_t *found_right = NULL;
                found_right = search_tree(tree->right, value, level + 1);
                if (found_right) {
#pragma omp atomic write
                    found = found_right;
#pragma omp cancel taskgroup
                }
            }
#pragma omp taskwait
        }
```

```
S-37            }
S-38        return found;
S-39    }
S-40    binary_tree_t *search_tree_parallel(binary_tree_t *tree, int value) {
S-41        binary_tree_t *found = NULL;
S-42    #pragma omp parallel shared(found, tree, value)
S-43        {
S-44    #pragma omp masked
S-45            {
S-46    #pragma omp taskgroup
S-47                {
S-48                    found = search_tree(tree, value, 0);
S-49                }
S-50            }
S-51        }
S-52        return found;
S-53    }
```

─────────────────────────── C / C++ ───────────────────────────

The following is the equivalent parallel search example in Fortran.

▼────────────────────────── Fortran ──────────────────────────▼

Example cancellation.2.f90 (`omp_5.1`)

```
S-1     module parallel_search
S-2       type binary_tree
S-3         integer :: value
S-4         type(binary_tree), pointer :: right
S-5         type(binary_tree), pointer :: left
S-6       end type
S-7
S-8     contains
S-9       recursive subroutine search_tree(tree, value, level, found)
S-10        type(binary_tree), intent(in), pointer :: tree
S-11        integer, intent(in) :: value, level
S-12        type(binary_tree), pointer :: found
S-13        type(binary_tree), pointer :: found_left => NULL(), &
S-14                                       found_right => NULL()
S-15
S-16        if (associated(tree)) then
S-17          if (tree%value .eq. value) then
S-18            found => tree
S-19          else
S-20    !$omp task shared(found) if(level<10)
S-21            call search_tree(tree%left, value, level+1, found_left)
S-22            if (associated(found_left)) then
S-23    !$omp critical
```

```fortran
S-24                    found => found_left
S-25    !$omp end critical
S-26
S-27    !$omp cancel taskgroup
S-28            endif
S-29    !$omp end task
S-30
S-31    !$omp task shared(found) if(level<10)
S-32            call search_tree(tree%right, value, level+1, found_right)
S-33            if (associated(found_right)) then
S-34    !$omp critical
S-35                found => found_right
S-36    !$omp end critical
S-37
S-38    !$omp cancel taskgroup
S-39            endif
S-40    !$omp end task
S-41
S-42    !$omp taskwait
S-43        endif
S-44      endif
S-45    end subroutine
S-46
S-47    subroutine search_tree_parallel(tree, value, found)
S-48      type(binary_tree), intent(in), pointer :: tree
S-49      integer, intent(in) :: value
S-50      type(binary_tree), pointer :: found
S-51
S-52      found => NULL()
S-53    !$omp parallel shared(found, tree, value)
S-54    !$omp masked
S-55    !$omp taskgroup
S-56      call search_tree(tree, value, 0, found)
S-57    !$omp end taskgroup
S-58    !$omp end masked
S-59    !$omp end parallel
S-60    end subroutine
S-61
S-62    end module parallel_search
```

Fortran

12.5 `requires` Directive

The declarative **requires** directive can be used to specify features that an implementation must provide to compile and execute correctly.

In the following example the **unified_shared_memory** clause of the **requires** directive ensures that the host and all devices accessible through OpenMP provide a *unified address* space for memory that is shared by all devices.

The example illustrates the use of the **requires** directive specifying *unified shared memory* in file scope, before any device directives or device routines. No **map** clause is needed for the *p* structure on the device (and its address *&p*, for the C++ code, is the same address on the host and device). However, scalar variables referenced within the **target** construct still have a default data-sharing attribute of firstprivate. The *q* scalar is incremented on the device, and its change is not updated on the host.

--------------------- C++ ---------------------

Example requires.1.cpp (**omp_5.0**)

```cpp
#include <iostream>
using namespace std;

#pragma omp requires unified_shared_memory

typedef struct mypoints
{
   double res;
   double data[500];
} mypoints_t;

void do_something_with_p(mypoints_t *p, int q);

int main()
{
  mypoints_t p;
  int q=0;

  #pragma omp target // no map clauses needed
  {                     // q is firstprivate
     q++;
     do_something_with_p(&p,q);
  }
  cout<< p.res << " " << q << endl;   // output 1 0
  return 0;
}
void do_something_with_p(mypoints_t *p, int q)
{
```

```
S-30        p->res = q;
S-31        for(int i=0;i<sizeof(p->data)/sizeof(double);i++)
S-32            p->data[i]=q*i;
S-33    }
```

—————————————————————— C++ ——————————————————————

—————————————————————— Fortran ——————————————————————

Example requires.1.f90 (`omp_5.0`)

```
S-1
S-2    module data
S-3    !$omp requires unified_shared_memory
S-4      type,public :: mypoints
S-5          double precision :: res
S-6          double precision :: data(500)
S-7      end type
S-8    end module
S-9
S-10   program main
S-11     use data
S-12     type(mypoints) :: p
S-13     integer        :: q=0
S-14
S-15     !$omp target      !! no map clauses needed
S-16        q = q + 1      !! q is firstprivate
S-17        call do_something_with_p(p,q)
S-18     !$omp end target
S-19
S-20     write(*,'(f5.0,i5)') p%res, q     !! output 1.    0
S-21
S-22   end program
S-23
S-24   subroutine do_something_with_p(p,q)
S-25     use data
S-26     type(mypoints) :: p
S-27     integer        :: q
S-28
S-29     p%res = q;
S-30     do i=1,size(p%data)
S-31        p%data(i)=q*i
S-32     enddo
S-33
S-34   end subroutine
```

—————————————————————— Fortran ——————————————————————

12.6 `declare variant` Directive

A **declare variant** directive specifies an alternate function, *function variant*, to be used in place of the *base function* when the trait within the **match** clause matches the OpenMP context at a given call site. The base function follows the directive in the C and C++ languages. In Fortran, either a subroutine or function may be used as the *base function*, and the **declare variant** directive must be in the specification part of a subroutine or function (unless a *base-proc-name* modifier is used, as in the case of a procedure declaration statement). See the OpenMP 5.0 Specification for details on the modifier.

When multiple **declare variant** directives are used a function variant becomes a candidate for replacing the base function if the context at the base function call matches the traits of all selectors in the **match** clause. If there are multiple candidates, a score is assigned with rules for each of the selector traits. The scoring algorithm can be found in the OpenMP 5.0 Specification.

In the first example the *vxv()* function is called within a **parallel** region, a **target** region, and in a sequential part of the program. Two function variants, *p_vxv()* and *t_vxv()*, are defined for the first two regions by using *parallel* and *target* selectors (within the *construct* trait set) in a **match** clause. The *p_vxv()* function variant includes a **for** construct (**do** construct for Fortran) for the **parallel** region, while *t_vxv()* includes a **distribute simd** construct for the **target** region. The *t_vxv()* function is explicitly compiled for the device using a declare target directive.

Since the two **declare variant** directives have no selectors that match traits for the context of the base function call in the sequential part of the program, the base *vxv()* function is used there, as expected. (The vectors in the *p_vxv* and *t_vxv* functions have been multiplied by 3 and 2, respectively, for checking the validity of the replacement. Normally the purpose of a function variant is to produce the same results by a different method.)

C / C++

Example declare_variant.1.c (**omp_5.1**)

```
S-1
S-2    #define N 100
S-3    #include <stdio.h>
S-4    #include <omp.h>
S-5
S-6    void p_vxv(int *v1,int *v2,int *v3,int n);
S-7    void t_vxv(int *v1,int *v2,int *v3,int n);
S-8
S-9    #pragma omp declare variant( p_vxv ) match( construct={parallel} )
S-10   #pragma omp declare variant( t_vxv ) match( construct={target}   )
S-11   void vxv(int *v1,int *v2,int *v3,int n)      // base function
S-12   {
S-13      for (int i= 0; i< n; i++)  v3[i] = v1[i] * v2[i];
S-14   }
S-15
S-16   void p_vxv(int *v1,int *v2,int *v3,int n)     // function variant
```

```
S-17        {
S-18           #pragma omp for
S-19           for (int i= 0; i< n; i++)   v3[i] = v1[i] * v2[i]*3;
S-20        }
S-21
S-22     #pragma omp begin declare target
S-23     void t_vxv(int *v1,int *v2,int *v3,int n)   // function variant
S-24     {
S-25        #pragma omp distribute simd
S-26        for (int i= 0; i< n; i++)   v3[i] = v1[i] * v2[i]*2;
S-27     }
S-28     #pragma omp end declare target
S-29
S-30     int main()
S-31     {
S-32        int v1[N], v2[N], v3[N];
S-33        for(int i=0; i<N; i++){ v1[i]=(i+1); v2[i]=-(i+1); v3[i]=0; }    //init
S-34
S-35        #pragma omp parallel
S-36        {
S-37           vxv(v1,v2,v3,N);
S-38        }
S-39        printf(" %d  %d\n",v3[0],v3[N-1]); //from p_vxv --  output: -3  -30000
S-40
S-41        #pragma omp target teams map(to: v1[:N],v2[:N]) map(from: v3[:N])
S-42        {
S-43           vxv(v1,v2,v3,N);
S-44        }
S-45        printf(" %d  %d\n",v3[0],v3[N-1]); //from t_vxv --  output: -2  -20000
S-46
S-47        vxv(v1,v2,v3,N);
S-48        printf(" %d  %d\n",v3[0],v3[N-1]); //from   vxv --  output: -1  -10000
S-49
S-50        return 0;
S-51     }
```

———————————————— C / C++ ————————————————
———————————————— Fortran ————————————————

Example declare_variant.1.f90 (**omp_5.0**)

```
S-1
S-2      module subs
S-3        use omp_lib
S-4      contains
S-5        subroutine vxv(v1, v2, v3)                !! base function
S-6           integer,intent(in)  :: v1(:),v2(:)
S-7           integer,intent(out) :: v3(:)
```

```
S-8              integer                :: i,n
S-9              !$omp  declare variant( p_vxv ) match( construct={parallel} )
S-10             !$omp  declare variant( t_vxv ) match( construct={target}   )
S-11
S-12             n=size(v1)
S-13             do i = 1,n; v3(i) = v1(i) * v2(i); enddo
S-14
S-15          end subroutine
S-16
S-17          subroutine p_vxv(v1, v2, v3)              !! function variant
S-18             integer,intent(in)   :: v1(:),v2(:)
S-19             integer,intent(out) :: v3(:)
S-20             integer                :: i,n
S-21             n=size(v1)
S-22
S-23             !$omp do
S-24             do i = 1,n; v3(i) = v1(i) * v2(i) * 3; enddo
S-25
S-26          end subroutine
S-27
S-28          subroutine t_vxv(v1,  v2,  v3)            !! function variant
S-29             integer,intent(in)   :: v1(:),v2(:)
S-30             integer,intent(out) :: v3(:)
S-31             integer                :: i,n
S-32             !$omp declare target
S-33             n=size(v1)
S-34
S-35             !$omp distribute simd
S-36             do i = 1,n; v3(i) = v1(i) * v2(i) * 2; enddo
S-37
S-38          end subroutine
S-39
S-40       end module subs
S-41
S-42
S-43    program main
S-44       use omp_lib
S-45       use subs
S-46       integer,parameter :: N = 100
S-47       integer                :: v1(N), v2(N), v3(N)
S-48
S-49       do i= 1,N; v1(i)= i; v2(i)= -i; v3(i)= 0;   enddo  !! init
S-50
S-51       !$omp parallel
S-52          call vxv(v1,v2,v3)
S-53       !$omp end parallel
S-54       print *, v3(1),v3(N)     !! from p_vxv -- output: -3   -30000
```

```
S-55
S-56        !$omp target teams map(to: v1,v2) map(from: v3)
S-57            call vxv(v1,v2,v3)
S-58        !$omp end target teams
S-59        print *, v3(1),v3(N)        !! from t_vxv -- output: -2  -20000
S-60
S-61        call vxv(v1,v2,v3)
S-62        print *, v3(1),v3(N)        !! from    vxv -- output: -1  -10000
S-63
S-64    end program
```

─────────────────────────────── Fortran ───────────────────────────────

In this example, traits from the *device* set are used to select a function variant. In the
declare variant directive, an *isa* selector specifies that if the implementation of the
"*core-avx512*" instruction set is detected at compile time the *avx512_saxpy()* variant function is
used for the call to *base_saxpy()*.

A compilation of *avx512_saxpy()* is aware of the AVX-512 instruction set that supports 512-bit
vector extensions (for Xeon or Xeon Phi architectures). Within *avx512_saxpy()*, the
parallel for simd construct performs parallel execution, and takes advantage of 64-byte data
alignment. When the *avx512_saxpy()* function variant is not selected, the base *base_saxpy()*
function variant containing only a basic **parallel for** construct is used for the call to
base_saxpy().

─────────────────────────────── C / C++ ───────────────────────────────

Example declare_variant.2.c (**omp_5.0**)

```
S-1     #include <omp.h>
S-2
S-3     void   base_saxpy(int, float, float *, float *);
S-4     void avx512_saxpy(int, float, float *, float *);
S-5
S-6     #pragma omp declare variant( avx512_saxpy ) \
S-7                         match( device={isa("core-avx512")} )
S-8     void base_saxpy(int n, float s, float *x, float *y)   // base function
S-9     {
S-10        #pragma omp parallel for
S-11        for(int i=0; i<n; i++) y[i] = s*x[i] + y[i];
S-12    }
S-13
S-14    void avx512_saxpy(int n, float s, float *x, float *y) //function variant
S-15    {
S-16        //assume 64-byte alignment for AVX-512
S-17        #pragma omp parallel for simd simdlen(16) aligned(x,y:64)
S-18        for(int i=0; i<n; i++) y[i] = s*x[i] + y[i];
S-19    }
S-20
```

```
S-21    // Above may be in another file scope.
S-22
S-23    #include <stdio.h>
S-24    #include <stdlib.h>
S-25    #include <stdint.h>
S-26    #define N 1000
S-27
S-28    int main()
S-29    {
S-30        static float x[N],y[N] __attribute__ ((aligned(64)));
S-31        float s=2.0;
S-32                                // Check for 64-byte aligned
S-33        if( ((intptr_t)y)%64 != 0 || ((intptr_t)x)%64 != 0 )
S-34        { printf("ERROR: x|y not 64-Byte aligned\n"); exit(1); }
S-35
S-36        for(int i=0; i<N; i++){ x[i]=i+1; y[i]=i+1; } // initialize
S-37
S-38        base_saxpy(N,s,x,y);
S-39
S-40        printf("y[0],y[N-1]: %5.0f %5.0f\n",y[0],y[N-1]);
S-41        //output: y[0],y[N-1]: 3    3000
S-42
S-43        return 0;
S-44    }
```

———————————————————— C / C++ ————————————————————
———————————————————— Fortran ————————————————————

Example declare_variant.2.f90 (**omp_5.0**)

```
S-1
S-2     module subs
S-3       use omp_lib
S-4     contains
S-5
S-6       subroutine base_saxpy(s,x,y)                  !! base function
S-7          real,intent(inout) :: s,x(:),y(:)
S-8          !$omp  declare variant( avx512_saxpy ) &
S-9          !$omp&             match( device={isa("core-avx512")} )
S-10
S-11         y = s*x + y
S-12
S-13      end subroutine
S-14
S-15      subroutine avx512_saxpy(s,x,y)               !! function variant
S-16         real,intent(inout) :: s,x(:),y(:)
S-17         integer             :: i,n
S-18         n=size(x)
```

```
S-19                                   !!assume 64-byte alignment for AVX-512
S-20            !$omp parallel do simd simdlen(16) aligned(x,y: 64)
S-21            do i = 1,n
S-22               y(i) = s*x(i) + y(i)
S-23            end do
S-24
S-25        end subroutine
S-26
S-27    end module subs
S-28
S-29
S-30    program main
S-31       use omp_lib
S-32       use subs
S-33
S-34       integer, parameter :: N=1000, align=64
S-35       real, allocatable  :: x(:),y(:)
S-36       real               :: s = 2.0e0
S-37       integer            :: i
S-38
S-39       allocate(x(N),y(N))    !! Assumes allocation is 64-byte aligned
S-40                              !! (using compiler options, or another
S-41                              !! allocation method).
S-42
S-43                              !! loc is non-standard, but found everywhere
S-44                              !! remove these lines if not available
S-45       if(modulo(loc(x),align) /= 0 .and. modulo(loc(y),align) /=0 ) then
S-46          print*,"ERROR: x|y not 64-byte aligned"; stop
S-47       endif
S-48
S-49       do i=1,N  !! initialize
S-50         x(i)=i
S-51         y(i)=i
S-52       end do
S-53
S-54       call base_saxpy(s,x,y)
S-55
S-56       write(*,'("y(1),y(N):",2f6.0)') y(1),y(N) !!output: y... 3. 3000.
S-57
S-58       deallocate(x,y)
S-59
S-60    end program
```

—————————————————————— Fortran ——————————————————————

12.7 Metadirectives

A **metadirective** directive provides a mechanism to select a directive in a **when** clause to be used, depending upon one or more contexts: implementation, available devices and the present enclosing construct. The directive in an **otherwise** clause is used when a directive of the **when** clause is not selected.

In the **when** clause the *context selector* (or just *selector*) defines traits that are evaluated for selection of the directive that follows the selector. This "selectable" directive is called a *directive variant*. Traits are grouped by *construct*, *implementation* and *device sets* to be used by a selector of the same name.

In the first example the architecture trait *arch* of the *device* selector set specifies that if an *nvptx* architecture is active in the OpenMP context, then the **teams loop** *directive variant* is selected as the directive; otherwise, the **parallel loop** *directive variant* of the **otherwise** clause is selected as the directive. That is, if a *device* of *nvptx* architecture is supported by the implementation within the enclosing **target** construct, its *directive variant* is selected. The architecture names, such as *nvptx*, are implementation defined. Also, note that *device* as used in a **target** construct specifies a device number, while *device*, as used in the **metadirective** directive as selector set, has traits of *kind*, *isa* and *arch*.

─────────────────────── C / C++ ───────────────────────

Example metadirective.1.c (**omp_5.2**)

```
#define N 100
#include <stdio.h>

int main()
{
    int v1[N], v2[N], v3[N];
    for(int i=0; i<N; i++){ v1[i]=(i+1); v2[i]=-(i+1); }

    #pragma omp target map(to:v1,v2) map(from:v3) device(0)
    #pragma omp metadirective \
                  when(      device={arch("nvptx")}: teams loop) \
                  otherwise(                         parallel loop)
       for (int i= 0; i< N; i++)   v3[i] = v1[i] * v2[i];

    printf(" %d  %d\n",v3[0],v3[N-1]); //output: -1  -10000

    return 0;
}
```

─────────────────────── C / C++ ───────────────────────

1 *Example metadirective.1.f90* (`omp_5.2`)

```
S-1    program main
S-2       integer, parameter :: N= 100
S-3       integer ::  v1(N), v2(N), v3(N);
S-4
S-5       do i=1,N;  v1(i)=i; v2(i)=-i;  enddo    ! initialize
S-6
S-7       !$omp  target map(to:v1,v2) map(from:v3) device(0)
S-8       !$omp  metadirective &
S-9       !$omp&     when(     device={arch("nvptx")}: teams loop) &
S-10      !$omp&     otherwise(                         parallel loop)
S-11        do i= 1,N; v3(i) = v1(i) * v2(i); enddo
S-12      !$omp  end target
S-13
S-14      print *, v3(1),v3(N) !!output: -1  -10000
S-15   end program
```

2 In the second example, the *implementation* selector set is specified in the **when** clause to distinguish
3 between platforms. Additionally, specific architectures are specified with the *device* selector set.

4 In the code, different **teams** constructs are employed as determined by the **metadirective**
5 directive. The number of teams is restricted by a **num_teams** clause and a thread limit is also set
6 by a **thread_limit** clause for *vendor* platforms and specific architecture traits. Otherwise, just
7 the **teams** construct is used without any clauses, as prescribed by the **otherwise** clause.

8 *Example metadirective.2.c* (`omp_5.2`)

```
S-1    #define N 100
S-2    #include <stdio.h>
S-3    #include <omp.h>
S-4
S-5    void work_on_chunk(int idev, int i);
S-6
S-7    int main()                      //Driver
S-8    {
S-9       int i,idev;
S-10
S-11      for (idev=0; idev<omp_get_num_devices(); idev++)
S-12      {
S-13         #pragma omp target device(idev)
S-14         #pragma omp metadirective \
S-15                 when( implementation={vendor(nvidia)},          \
S-16                                        device={arch("kepler")}: \
```

```
S-17                          teams num_teams(512) thread_limit(32) )      \
S-18              when( implementation={vendor(amd)},                      \
S-19                                    device={arch("fiji"  )}:  \
S-20                          teams num_teams(512) thread_limit(64) )      \
S-21              otherwise(                                               \
S-22                          teams)
S-23          #pragma omp distribute parallel for
S-24          for (i=0; i<N; i++) work_on_chunk(idev,i);
S-25        }
S-26      return 0;
S-27    }
S-28
```

────────────────────────── C / C++ ──────────────────────────
────────────────────────── Fortran ──────────────────────────

1   *Example metadirective.2.f90* (**omp_5.2**)

```
S-1     program main                       !!Driver
S-2       use omp_lib
S-3       implicit none
S-4       integer, parameter :: N=1000
S-5       external           :: work_on_chunk
S-6       integer            :: i,idev
S-7
S-8       do idev=0,omp_get_num_devices()-1
S-9
S-10        !$omp target device(idev)
S-11        !$omp begin metadirective &
S-12        !$omp&   when( implementation={vendor(nvidia)},        &
S-13        !$omp&              device={arch("kepler")}:           &
S-14        !$omp&          teams num_teams(512) thread_limit(32) ) &
S-15        !$omp&   when( implementation={vendor(amd)},           &
S-16        !$omp&              device={arch("fiji"  )}:           &
S-17        !$omp&          teams num_teams(512) thread_limit(64) ) &
S-18        !$omp&   otherwise( teams )
S-19        !$omp distribute parallel do
S-20        do i=1,N
S-21           call work_on_chunk(idev,i)
S-22        end do
S-23        !$omp end metadirective
S-24        !$omp end target
S-25
S-26      end do
S-27
S-28    end program
```

────────────────────────── Fortran ──────────────────────────

In the third example, a *construct* selector set is specified in the **when** clause. Here, a **metadirective** directive is used within a function that is also compiled as a function for a target device as directed by a declare target directive. The *target* directive name of the **construct** selector ensures that the **distribute parallel for/do** construct is employed for the target compilation. Otherwise, for the host-compiled version the **parallel for/do simd** construct is used.

In the first call to the *exp_pi_diff()* routine the context is a **target teams** construct and the **distribute parallel for/do** construct version of the function is invoked, while in the second call the **parallel for/do simd** construct version is used.

This case illustrates an important point for users that may want to hoist the **target** directive out of a function that contains the usual **target teams distribute parallel for/do** construct (for providing alternate constructs through the **metadirective** directive as here). While this combined construct can be decomposed into a **target** and **teams distribute parallel for/do** constructs, the OpenMP 5.0 specification has the restriction: "If a **teams** construct is nested within a **target** construct, that **target** construct must contain no statements, declarations or directives outside of the **teams** construct". So, the **teams** construct must immediately follow the **target** construct without any intervening code statements (which includes function calls). Since the **target** construct alone cannot be hoisted out of a function, the **target teams** construct has been hoisted out of the function, and the **distribute parallel for/do** construct is used as the *variant* directive of the **metadirective** directive within the function.

———————————————————— C / C++ ————————————————————

Example metadirective.3.c (**omp_5.2**)

```
#include <stdio.h>
#include   <math.h>
#define      N 1000

#pragma omp begin declare target
void exp_pi_diff(double *d, double my_pi){
   #pragma omp metadirective \
              when(   construct={target}: distribute parallel for ) \
              otherwise(                   parallel for simd )
   for(int i = 0; i<N; i++) d[i] = exp( (M_PI-my_pi)*i );
}
#pragma omp end declare target

int main()
{
   //Calculates sequence of exponentials: (M_PI-my_pi) * index
   //M_PI is from math.h, and my_pi is user provided.

   double d[N];
   double my_pi=3.14159265358979e0;
```

```
S-22              #pragma omp target teams map(tofrom: d[0:N])
S-23              exp_pi_diff(d,my_pi);
S-24                                              // value should be near 1
S-25              printf("d[N-1] = %20.14f\n",d[N-1]); // ...= 1.00000000000311
S-26
S-27              exp_pi_diff(d,my_pi);            // value should be near 1
S-28              printf("d[N-1] = %20.14f\n",d[N-1]); // ...= 1.00000000000311
S-29      }
```

────────────────────────── C / C++ ──────────────────────────
────────────────────────── Fortran ──────────────────────────

1   *Example metadirective.3.f90* (omp_5.2)

```
S-1    module params
S-2       integer, parameter :: N=1000
S-3       DOUBLE PRECISION, PARAMETER::M_PI=4.0d0*DATAN(1.0d0)
S-4                                      ! 3.1415926535897932_8
S-5    end module
S-6
S-7
S-8    subroutine exp_pi_diff(d,    my_pi)
S-9      use params
S-10     implicit none
S-11     integer          ::  i
S-12     double precision ::  d(N), my_pi
S-13     !$omp declare target
S-14
S-15     !$omp    metadirective &
S-16     !$omp&        when( construct={target}: distribute parallel do )   &
S-17     !$omp&        otherwise(                parallel do simd )
S-18
S-19     do i = 1,size(d)
S-20        d(i) = exp( (M_PI-my_pi)*i )
S-21     end do
S-22
S-23   end subroutine
S-24
S-25   program main
S-26     ! Calculates sequence of exponentials: (M_PI-my_pi) * index
S-27     ! M_PI is from usual way, and my_pi is user provided.
S-28     ! Fortran Standard does not provide PI
S-29
S-30     use params
S-31     implicit none
S-32     double precision    :: d(N)
S-33     double precision    :: my_pi=3.14159265358979d0
S-34
```

```
S-35          !$omp target teams map(from: d)
S-36          call exp_pi_diff(d,my_pi)
S-37          !$omp end target teams
S-38                                        ! value should be near 1
S-39          print*, "d(N) = ",d(N)        ! 1.00000000000311
S-40
S-41          call exp_pi_diff(d,my_pi) ! value should be near 1
S-42          print*, "d(N) = ",d(N)        ! 1.00000000000311
S-43
S-44    end program
```

――――――――――――――――― Fortran ―――――――――――――――――

The **user** selector set can be used in a metadirective to select directives at execution time when the **condition(** *boolean-expr* **)** selector expression is not a constant expression. In this case it is a *dynamic* trait set, and the selection is made at run time, rather than at compile time.

In the following example the *foo* function employs the **condition** selector to choose a device for execution at run time. In the *bar* routine metadirectives are nested. At the outer level a selection between serial and parallel execution in performed at run time, followed by another run time selection on the schedule kind in the inner level when the active *construct* trait is **parallel**.

(Note, the variable *b* in two of the "selected" constructs is declared private for the sole purpose of detecting and reporting that the construct is used. Since the variable is private, its value is unchanged outside of the construct region, whereas it is changed if the "unselected" construct is used.)

――――――――――――――――― C / C++ ―――――――――――――――――

Example metadirective.4.c (**omp_5.2**)

```
S-1     #define N 100
S-2     #include <stdbool.h>
S-3     #include    <stdio.h>
S-4     #include       <omp.h>
S-5
S-6     void foo(int *a, int n, bool use_gpu)
S-7     {
S-8        int b=0;   //  use b to detect if run on gpu
S-9
S-10       #pragma omp metadirective \
S-11                 when( user={condition(use_gpu)}:            \
S-12                      target teams distribute parallel for \
S-13                      private(b) map(from:a[0:n]) )          \
S-14                 otherwise(                                  \
S-15                      parallel for )
S-16       for (int i=0; i<n; i++) {a[i]=i; if(i==n-1) b=1;}
S-17
S-18       if(b==0) printf("PASSED 1 of 3\n");
```

```
S-19        }
S-20
S-21        void bar (int *a, int n, bool run_parallel, bool unbalanced)
S-22        {
S-23           int b=0;
S-24           #pragma omp metadirective \
S-25                      when(user={condition(run_parallel)}: parallel)
S-26           {
S-27              if(omp_in_parallel() == 1 && omp_get_thread_num() == 0)
S-28              {printf("PASSED 2 of 3\n");}
S-29
S-30              #pragma omp metadirective \
S-31                  when( construct={parallel}, \
S-32                        user={condition(unbalanced)}: for schedule(guided) \
S-33                                                    private(b)) \
S-34                  when( construct={parallel}         : for schedule(static))
S-35              for (int i=0; i<n; i++) {a[i]=i; if(i==n-1) b=1;}
S-36           }
S-37           // if guided b=0, because b is private
S-38           if(b==0) printf("PASSED 3 of 3\n");
S-39        }
S-40
S-41        void foo(int *a, int n, bool use_gpu);
S-42        void bar(int *a, int n, bool run_parallel, bool unbalanced);
S-43
S-44        int main(){
S-45
S-46           int p[N];
S-47           // App normally sets these, dependent on input parameters
S-48           bool use_gpu=true, run_parallel=true, unbalanced=true;
S-49
S-50           // Testing: set Env Var MK_FAIL to anything to fail tests
S-51           if(getenv("MK_FAIL")!=NULL) {
S-52              use_gpu=false; run_parallel=false; unbalanced=false;
S-53           }
S-54
S-55           foo(p, N, use_gpu);
S-56           bar(p, N, run_parallel,unbalanced);
S-57
S-58        }
```

———————————————————————— C / C++ ————————————————————————

1

Example metadirective.4.f90 (`omp_5.2`)

```
S-1    subroutine foo(a, n, use_gpu)
S-2       integer :: n, a(n)
S-3       logical :: use_gpu
S-4
S-5       integer :: b=0   !! use b to detect if run on gpu
S-6
S-7       !$omp metadirective &
S-8       !$omp&            when(user={condition(use_gpu)}:          &
S-9       !$omp&                   target teams distribute parallel for &
S-10      !$omp&                   private(b) map(from:a(1:n)) )       &
S-11      !$omp&            otherwise(                                 &
S-12      !$omp&                   parallel do)
S-13      do i = 1,n; a(i)=i; if(i==n) b=1; end do
S-14
S-15      if(b==0) print *, "PASSED 1 of 3"  ! bc b is firstprivate for gpu run
S-16   end subroutine
S-17
S-18   subroutine bar (a, n, run_parallel, unbalanced)
S-19      use omp_lib, only : omp_get_thread_num
S-20      integer :: n, a(n)
S-21      logical :: run_parallel, unbalanced
S-22
S-23      integer :: b=0
S-24      !$omp begin metadirective when(user={condition(run_parallel)}: parallel)
S-25
S-26      if(omp_in_parallel() == 1 .and. omp_get_thread_num() == 0) &
S-27         print *,"PASSED 2 of 3"
S-28
S-29      !$omp metadirective &
S-30      !$omp&  when(construct={parallel}, user={condition(unbalanced)}: &
S-31      !$omp&           for schedule(guided) private(b)) &
S-32      !$omp&  when(construct={parallel}: for schedule(static))
S-33      do i = 1,n; a(i)=i; if(i==n) b=1; end do
S-34
S-35      !$omp end metadirective
S-36
S-37      if(b==0) print *, "PASSED 3 of 3"   !!if guided, b=0 since b is private
S-38   end subroutine
S-39
S-40   program meta
S-41      use omp_lib
S-42      integer, parameter :: N=100
S-43      integer :: p(N)
S-44      integer :: env_stat
```

```
S-45                        !! App normally sets these, dependent on input parameters
S-46         logical ::  use_gpu=.true., run_parallel=.true., unbalanced=.true.
S-47
S-48                        !! Testing: set Env Var MK_FAIL to anything to fail tests
S-49         call get_environment_variable('MK_FAIL',status=env_stat)
S-50         if(env_stat /= 1) then                  ! status =1 when not set!
S-51            use_gpu=.false.; run_parallel=.false.; unbalanced=.false.
S-52         endif
S-53
S-54
S-55         call foo(p, N, use_gpu)
S-56         call bar(p, N, run_parallel,unbalanced)
S-57
S-58    end program
```

────────────────────────── Fortran ──────────────────────────

Metadirectives can be used in conjunction with templates as shown in the C++ code below. Here
the template definition generates two versions of the Fibonacci function. The *tasking* boolean is
used in the **condition** selector to enable tasking. The true form implements a parallel version
with **task** and **taskwait** constructs as in the *tasking.4.c* code in Section 5.1. The false form
implements a serial version without any tasking constructs. Note that the serial version is used in
the parallel function for optimally processing numbers less than 8.

────────────────────────── C++ ──────────────────────────

Example metadirective.5.cpp (**omp_5.0**)

```
S-1     #include <stdio.h>
S-2
S-3     // revised Fibonacci from tasking.4.c example
S-4
S-5     template <bool tasking>
S-6     int fib(int n) {
S-7       int i, j;
S-8       if (n<2) {
S-9         return n;
S-10      } else if ( tasking && n<8 ) { // serial/taskless cutoff for n<8
S-11        return fib<false>(n);
S-12      } else {
S-13        #pragma omp metadirective \
S-14                    when(user={condition(tasking)}: task shared(i))
S-15        {
S-16          i=fib<tasking>(n-1);
S-17        }
S-18        #pragma omp metadirective \
S-19                    when(user={condition(tasking)}: task shared(j))
S-20        {
S-21          j=fib<tasking>(n-2);
```

```
S-22          }
S-23          #pragma omp metadirective \
S-24                      when(user={condition(tasking)}: taskwait)
S-25          return i+j;
S-26        }
S-27      }
S-28
S-29      int main(int argc, char** argv) {
S-30        int n = 15;
S-31        #pragma omp parallel
S-32        #pragma omp single
S-33        {
S-34          printf("fib(%i) = %i\n", n, fib<true>(n));
S-35        }
S-36        return 0;
S-37      }
S-38      // OUTPUT:
S-39      // fib(15) = 610
```

C++

12.8 Nested Loop Constructs

The following example of loop construct nesting is conforming because the inner and outer loop regions bind to different **parallel** regions:

───────────────────────────────── C / C++ ─────────────────────────────────

Example nested_loop.1.c

```
S-1   void work(int i, int j) {}
S-2
S-3   void good_nesting(int n)
S-4   {
S-5     int i, j;
S-6     #pragma omp parallel default(shared)
S-7     {
S-8       #pragma omp for
S-9       for (i=0; i<n; i++) {
S-10        #pragma omp parallel shared(i, n)
S-11        {
S-12          #pragma omp for
S-13          for (j=0; j < n; j++)
S-14            work(i, j);
S-15        }
S-16      }
S-17    }
S-18  }
```

───────────────────────────────── C / C++ ─────────────────────────────────
───────────────────────────────── Fortran ─────────────────────────────────

Example nested_loop.1.f

```
S-1         SUBROUTINE WORK(I, J)
S-2         INTEGER I, J
S-3         END SUBROUTINE WORK
S-4
S-5         SUBROUTINE GOOD_NESTING(N)
S-6         INTEGER N
S-7
S-8           INTEGER I
S-9   !$OMP   PARALLEL DEFAULT(SHARED)
S-10  !$OMP     DO
S-11            DO I = 1, N
S-12  !$OMP       PARALLEL SHARED(I,N)
S-13  !$OMP         DO
S-14              DO J = 1, N
S-15                CALL WORK(I,J)
S-16              END DO
```

```
S-17    !$OMP        END PARALLEL
S-18              END DO
S-19    !$OMP    END PARALLEL
S-20           END SUBROUTINE GOOD_NESTING
```

———————————————————————— Fortran ————————————————————————

The following variation of the preceding example is also conforming:

———————————————————————— C / C++ ————————————————————————

Example nested_loop.2.c

```
S-1     void work(int i, int j) {}
S-2
S-3
S-4     void work1(int i, int n)
S-5     {
S-6       int j;
S-7       #pragma omp parallel default(shared)
S-8       {
S-9         #pragma omp for
S-10        for (j=0; j<n; j++)
S-11          work(i, j);
S-12      }
S-13    }
S-14
S-15
S-16    void good_nesting2(int n)
S-17    {
S-18      int i;
S-19      #pragma omp parallel default(shared)
S-20      {
S-21        #pragma omp for
S-22        for (i=0; i<n; i++)
S-23          work1(i, n);
S-24      }
S-25    }
```

———————————————————————— C / C++ ————————————————————————

1   *Example nested_loop.2.f*

```
S-1          SUBROUTINE WORK(I, J)
S-2          INTEGER I, J
S-3          END SUBROUTINE WORK
S-4
S-5          SUBROUTINE WORK1(I, N)
S-6          INTEGER J
S-7   !$OMP PARALLEL DEFAULT(SHARED)
S-8   !$OMP DO
S-9          DO J = 1, N
S-10           CALL WORK(I,J)
S-11         END DO
S-12  !$OMP END PARALLEL
S-13         END SUBROUTINE WORK1
S-14
S-15         SUBROUTINE GOOD_NESTING2(N)
S-16         INTEGER N
S-17  !$OMP PARALLEL DEFAULT(SHARED)
S-18  !$OMP DO
S-19         DO I = 1, N
S-20           CALL WORK1(I, N)
S-21         END DO
S-22  !$OMP END PARALLEL
S-23         END SUBROUTINE GOOD_NESTING2
```

12.9 Restrictions on Nesting of Regions

The examples in this section illustrate the region nesting rules.

The following example is non-conforming because the inner and outer loop regions are closely nested:

--- C / C++ ---

Example nesting_restrict.1.c

```
S-1
S-2   void work(int i, int j) {}
S-3
S-4   void wrong1(int n)
S-5   {
S-6
S-7     #pragma omp parallel default(shared)
S-8     {
S-9       int i, j;
S-10      #pragma omp for
S-11      for (i=0; i<n; i++) {
S-12        /* incorrect nesting of loop regions */
S-13        #pragma omp for
S-14          for (j=0; j<n; j++)
S-15            work(i, j);
S-16      }
S-17    }
S-18
S-19  }
```

--- C / C++ ---
--- Fortran ---

Example nesting_restrict.1.f

```
S-1
S-2           SUBROUTINE WORK(I, J)
S-3           INTEGER I, J
S-4
S-5           END SUBROUTINE WORK
S-6
S-7           SUBROUTINE WRONG1(N)
S-8
S-9           INTEGER N
S-10          INTEGER I,J
S-11  !$OMP   PARALLEL DEFAULT(SHARED)
S-12  !$OMP     DO
S-13            DO I = 1, N
S-14  !$OMP       DO              ! incorrect nesting of loop regions
```

```
S-15                    DO J = 1, N
S-16                        CALL WORK(I,J)
S-17                    END DO
S-18                END DO
S-19    !$OMP    END PARALLEL
S-20
S-21        END SUBROUTINE WRONG1
```

———————————— Fortran ————————————

The following orphaned version of the preceding example is also non-conforming:

———————————— C / C++ ————————————

Example nesting_restrict.2.c

```
S-1     void work(int i, int j) {}
S-2     void work1(int i, int n)
S-3     {
S-4       int j;
S-5     /* incorrect nesting of loop regions */
S-6       #pragma omp for
S-7         for (j=0; j<n; j++)
S-8           work(i, j);
S-9     }
S-10
S-11    void wrong2(int n)
S-12    {
S-13      #pragma omp parallel default(shared)
S-14      {
S-15        int i;
S-16        #pragma omp for
S-17          for (i=0; i<n; i++)
S-18            work1(i, n);
S-19      }
S-20    }
```

———————————— C / C++ ————————————

1   *Example nesting_restrict.2.f*

```
S-1         SUBROUTINE WORK1(I,N)
S-2         INTEGER I, N
S-3         INTEGER J
S-4   !$OMP   DO        ! incorrect nesting of loop regions
S-5         DO J = 1, N
S-6           CALL WORK(I,J)
S-7         END DO
S-8         END SUBROUTINE WORK1
S-9         SUBROUTINE WRONG2(N)
S-10        INTEGER N
S-11        INTEGER I
S-12  !$OMP   PARALLEL DEFAULT(SHARED)
S-13  !$OMP     DO
S-14          DO I = 1, N
S-15            CALL WORK1(I,N)
S-16          END DO
S-17  !$OMP   END PARALLEL
S-18        END SUBROUTINE WRONG2
```

2   The following example is non-conforming because the loop and **single** regions are closely nested:

3   *Example nesting_restrict.3.c*

```
S-1   void work(int i, int j) {}
S-2   void wrong3(int n)
S-3   {
S-4     #pragma omp parallel default(shared)
S-5     {
S-6       int i;
S-7       #pragma omp for
S-8         for (i=0; i<n; i++) {
S-9   /* incorrect nesting of regions */
S-10          #pragma omp single
S-11            work(i, 0);
S-12        }
S-13    }
S-14  }
```

Fortran
---

1   *Example nesting_restrict.3.f*

```
S-1           SUBROUTINE WRONG3(N)
S-2           INTEGER N
S-3
S-4            INTEGER I
S-5    !$OMP   PARALLEL DEFAULT(SHARED)
S-6    !$OMP     DO
S-7              DO I = 1, N
S-8    !$OMP       SINGLE                ! incorrect nesting of regions
S-9                  CALL WORK(I, 1)
S-10   !$OMP       END SINGLE
S-11             END DO
S-12   !$OMP   END PARALLEL
S-13          END SUBROUTINE WRONG3
```

Fortran
---

2   The following example is non-conforming because a **barrier** region cannot be closely nested
3   inside a loop region:

C / C++
---

4   *Example nesting_restrict.4.c*

```
S-1    void work(int i, int j) {}
S-2    void wrong4(int n)
S-3    {
S-4
S-5      #pragma omp parallel default(shared)
S-6      {
S-7        int i;
S-8        #pragma omp for
S-9        for (i=0; i<n; i++) {
S-10         work(i, 0);
S-11   /* incorrect nesting of barrier region in a loop region */
S-12          #pragma omp barrier
S-13          work(i, 1);
S-14        }
S-15      }
S-16   }
```

C / C++
---

498   OpenMP Examples Version 5.2 - April 2022

1 *Example nesting_restrict.4.f*

```
S-1         SUBROUTINE WRONG4(N)
S-2         INTEGER N
S-3
S-4           INTEGER I
S-5   !$OMP   PARALLEL DEFAULT(SHARED)
S-6   !$OMP     DO
S-7             DO I = 1, N
S-8               CALL WORK(I, 1)
S-9   ! incorrect nesting of barrier region in a loop region
S-10  !$OMP         BARRIER
S-11              CALL WORK(I, 2)
S-12            END DO
S-13  !$OMP   END PARALLEL
S-14        END SUBROUTINE WRONG4
```

2
3
4

The following example is non-conforming because the **barrier** region cannot be closely nested inside the **critical** region. If this were permitted, it would result in deadlock due to the fact that only one thread at a time can enter the **critical** region:

5 *Example nesting_restrict.5.c*

```
S-1   void work(int i, int j) {}
S-2   void wrong5(int n)
S-3   {
S-4     #pragma omp parallel
S-5     {
S-6       #pragma omp critical
S-7       {
S-8         work(n, 0);
S-9   /* incorrect nesting of barrier region in a critical region */
S-10        #pragma omp barrier
S-11        work(n, 1);
S-12      }
S-13    }
S-14  }
```

1 *Example nesting_restrict.5.f*

```fortran
S-1             SUBROUTINE WRONG5(N)
S-2             INTEGER N
S-3
S-4    !$OMP    PARALLEL DEFAULT(SHARED)
S-5    !$OMP       CRITICAL
S-6                 CALL WORK(N,1)
S-7    ! incorrect nesting of barrier region in a critical region
S-8    !$OMP          BARRIER
S-9                 CALL WORK(N,2)
S-10   !$OMP       END CRITICAL
S-11   !$OMP    END PARALLEL
S-12            END SUBROUTINE WRONG5
```

2
3
4

The following example is non-conforming because the **barrier** region cannot be closely nested inside the **single** region. If this were permitted, it would result in deadlock due to the fact that only one thread executes the **single** region:

5 *Example nesting_restrict.6.c*

```c
S-1    void work(int i, int j) {}
S-2    void wrong6(int n)
S-3    {
S-4      #pragma omp parallel
S-5      {
S-6        #pragma omp single
S-7        {
S-8          work(n, 0);
S-9    /* incorrect nesting of barrier region in a single region */
S-10         #pragma omp barrier
S-11         work(n, 1);
S-12       }
S-13     }
S-14   }
```

1   *Example nesting_restrict.6.f*

```
S-1          SUBROUTINE WRONG6(N)
S-2          INTEGER N
S-3
S-4   !$OMP    PARALLEL DEFAULT(SHARED)
S-5   !$OMP      SINGLE
S-6              CALL WORK(N,1)
S-7   ! incorrect nesting of barrier region in a single region
S-8   !$OMP      BARRIER
S-9              CALL WORK(N,2)
S-10  !$OMP      END SINGLE
S-11  !$OMP    END PARALLEL
S-12         END SUBROUTINE WRONG6
```

12.10 Target Offload

In the OpenMP 5.0 implementation the **OMP_TARGET_OFFLOAD** environment variable was defined to change *default* offload behavior. By *default* the target code (region) is executed on the host if the target device does not exist or the implementation does not support the target device.

In an OpenMP 5.0 compliant implementation, setting the **OMP_TARGET_OFFLOAD** variable to **MANDATORY** will force the program to terminate execution when a **target** construct is encountered and the target device is not supported or is not available. With a value **DEFAULT** the target region will execute on a device if the device exists and is supported by the implementation, otherwise it will execute on the host. Support for the **DISABLED** value is optional; when it is supported the behavior is as if only the host device exists (other devices are considered non-existent to the runtime), and target regions are executed on the host.

The following example reports execution behavior for different values of the **OMP_TARGET_OFFLOAD** variable. A handy routine for extracting the **OMP_TARGET_OFFLOAD** environment variable value is deployed here, because the OpenMP API does not have a routine for obtaining the value.

Note: The example issues a warning when a pre-5.0 implementation is used, indicating that the **OMP_TARGET_OFFLOAD** is ignored. The value of the **OMP_TARGET_OFFLOAD** variable is reported when the **OMP_DISPLAY_ENV** environment variable is set to **TRUE** or **VERBOSE**.

─────────────────────────── C / C++ ───────────────────────────

Example target_offload_control.1.c (**omp_5.0**)

```
S-1     #include    <omp.h>
S-2     #include   <stdio.h>
S-3     #include   <ctype.h>
S-4     #include <stdlib.h>
S-5     #include <string.h>
S-6
S-7     typedef enum offload_policy
S-8     {MANDATORY, DISABLED, DEFAULT, UNKNOWN, NOTSET} offload_policy_t;
S-9
S-10
S-11    offload_policy_t get_offload_policy()
S-12    {
S-13       char *env, *end;
S-14       size_t n;
S-15
S-16       env = getenv("OMP_TARGET_OFFLOAD");
S-17       if(env  == NULL) return NOTSET;
S-18
S-19       end = env + strlen(env);                   //Find trimmed beginning/end
S-20       while (      *env && isspace(*(env  )) ) env++;
S-21       while (end != env && isspace(*(end-1)) ) end--;
```

```
S-22         n = (int)(end - env);
S-23
S-24                          //Find ONLY string -nothing more, case insensitive
S-25         if      (n == 9 && !strncasecmp(env, "MANDATORY",n)) return MANDATORY;
S-26         else if (n == 8 && !strncasecmp(env, "DISABLED" ,n)) return DISABLED ;
S-27         else if (n == 7 && !strncasecmp(env, "DEFAULT"  ,n)) return DEFAULT   ;
S-28         else                                                 return UNKNOWN   ;
S-29     }
S-30
S-31
S-32     int main()
S-33     {
S-34         int i;
S-35         int device_num, on_init_dev;
S-36
S-37         // get policy from OMP_TARGET_OFFLOAD variable
S-38         offload_policy_t policy = get_offload_policy();
S-39
S-40         if(_OPENMP< 201811)
S-41         {
S-42            printf("Warning: OMP_TARGET_OFFLOAD NOT supported, version %d\n",
S-43                   _OPENMP );
S-44            printf("           If OMP_TARGET_OFFLOAD is set, "
S-45                   "it will be ignored.\n");
S-46         }
S-47
S-48         // Set target device number to an unavailable
S-49         // device to test offload policy.
S-50         device_num = omp_get_num_devices() + 1;
S-51
S-52         // Policy:
S-53         printf("OMP_TARGET_OFFLOAD Policy:  ");
S-54         if      (policy==MANDATORY)
S-55            printf("MANDATORY-Terminate if dev. not avail\n");
S-56         else if(policy==DISABLED )
S-57            printf("DISABLED -(if supported) Only on Host\n");
S-58         else if(policy==DEFAULT  )
S-59            printf("DEFAULT  -On host if device not avail\n");
S-60         else if(policy==UNKNOWN  )
S-61            printf("OMP_TARGET_OFFLOAD has unknown value\n" );
S-62         else if(policy==NOTSET   )
S-63            printf("OMP_TARGET_OFFLOAD not set\n" );
S-64
S-65
S-66         on_init_dev = 1;
S-67         // device# out of range--not supported
S-68         #pragma omp target device(device_num) map(tofrom: on_init_dev)
```

```
S-69              on_init_dev=omp_is_initial_device();
S-70
S-71        if (policy == MANDATORY && _OPENMP >= 201811)
S-72           printf("ERROR: OpenMP implementation ignored MANDATORY policy.\n");
S-73
S-74        printf("Target region executed on init dev %s\n",
S-75               on_init_dev ? "TRUE":"FALSE");
S-76
S-77        return 0;
S-78     }
```

─────────────────────── C / C++ ───────────────────────
─────────────────────── Fortran ───────────────────────

1   *Example target_offload_control.1.f90* (**omp_5.0**)

```
S-1     module offload_policy
S-2        implicit none
S-3        integer, parameter :: LEN_POLICY=10
S-4     contains
S-5        character(LEN_POLICY) function get_offload_policy()
S-6           character(64) :: env
S-7           integer       :: length, i
S-8           env=repeat(' ',len(env))
S-9                                        !policy is blank if not found *
S-10          call get_environment_variable("OMP_TARGET_OFFLOAD",env,length)
S-11
S-12          do i = 1,len(env)              !Makes a-z upper case
S-13             if(iachar(env(i:i))>96) env(i:i)=achar(iachar(env(i:i))-32)
S-14          end do
S-15
S-16          get_offload_policy = trim(adjustl(env)) !remove peripheral spaces
S-17
S-18          if(length==0) get_offload_policy="NOTSET"
S-19
S-20          return
S-21
S-22       end function
S-23
S-24    end module
S-25
S-26    program policy_test
S-27
S-28       use omp_lib
S-29       use offload_policy
S-30
S-31       integer                 :: i, device_num
S-32       logical                 :: on_init_dev
```

```
S-33        character(LEN_POLICY)  :: policy
S-34
S-35        policy = get_offload_policy() !!Get OMP_TARGET_OFFLOAD value
S-36
S-37        if (OPENMP_VERSION < 201811) then
S-38           print*,"Warning: OMP_TARGET_OFFLOAD NOT supported by VER.", &
S-39                  OPENMP_VERSION
S-40           print*,"          If OMP_TARGET_OFFLOAD is set, it will be ignored."
S-41        endif
S-42
S-43           ! Set target device number to an unavailable device
S-44           ! to test offload policy.
S-45        device_num = omp_get_num_devices() + 1
S-46
S-47                            !! Report OMP_TARGET_OFFOAD value
S-48        select CASE (policy)
S-49           case("MANDATORY")
S-50              print*,"Policy:  MANDATORY-Terminate if dev. not avail."
S-51           case("DISABLED")
S-52              print*,"Policy:  DISABLED-(if supported) Only on Host."
S-53           case("DEFAULT")
S-54              print*,"Policy:  DEFAULT On host if device not avail."
S-55           case("NOTSET")
S-56              print*,"          OMP_TARGET_OFFLOAD is not set."
S-57           case DEFAULT
S-58              print*,"          OMP_TARGET_OFFLOAD has unknown value."
S-59              print*,"          UPPER CASE VALUE=",policy
S-60        end select
S-61
S-62
S-63        on_init_dev = .FALSE.
S-64                            !! device# out of range--not supported
S-65        !$omp target  device(device_num) map(tofrom: on_init_dev)
S-66           on_init_dev=omp_is_initial_device()
S-67        !$omp end target
S-68
S-69        if (policy=="MANDATORY" .and. OPENMP_VERSION>=201811) then
S-70           print*,"OMP ERROR: ", &
S-71                  "OpenMP 5.0 implementation ignored MANDATORY policy."
S-72           print*,"          Termination should have occurred", &
S-73                  " at target directive."
S-74        endif
S-75
S-76        print*, "Target executed on init dev (T|F): ", on_init_dev
S-77
S-78     end program policy_test
```
——————————————— Fortran ———————————————

12.11 Controlling Concurrency and Reproducibility with the `order` Clause

The **order** clause is used for controlling the parallel execution of loop iterations for one or more loops that are associated with a directive. It is specified with a clause argument and optional modifier. The only supported argument, introduced in OpenMP 5.0, is the keyword **concurrent** which indicates that the loop iterations may execute concurrently, including iterations in the same chunk per the loop schedule. Because of the relaxed execution permitted with an **order(concurrent)** clause, codes must not assume that any cross-iteration data dependences would be preserved or that any two iterations may execute on the same thread.

The following example in this section demonstrates the use of the **order(concurrent)** clause, without any modifiers, for controlling the parallel execution of loop iterations. The **order(concurrent)** clause cannot be used for the second and third **parallel for/do** constructs because of either having data dependences or accessing threadprivate variables.

C / C++

Example reproducible.1.c (**omp_5.0**)

```
#include <stdio.h>
#include <omp.h>

int main()
{
    const int n = 1000;
    int v[n], u[n];
    static int sum;
    #pragma omp threadprivate(sum)

    // no data dependences, so can execute concurrently
    #pragma omp parallel for order(concurrent)
    for (int i = 0; i < n; i++) {
        u[i] = i;
        v[i] = i;
        v[i] += u[i] * u[i];
    }

    // with data dependences, so cannot execute iterations
    // concurrently with the order(concurrent) clause
    #pragma omp parallel for ordered
    for (int i = 1; i < n; i++) {
        v[i] += u[i] * u[i];
        #pragma omp ordered
            v[i] += v[i-1];
    }
```

```
S-28        sum = 0;
S-29        // accessing a threadprivate variable, which would not be
S-30        // permitted if the order(concurrent) clause was present
S-31        #pragma omp parallel for copyin(sum)
S-32        for (int i = 0; i < n; i++) {
S-33           sum += v[i];
S-34        }
S-35
S-36        #pragma omp parallel
S-37        {
S-38           printf("sum = %d on thread %d\n", sum, omp_get_thread_num());
S-39        }
S-40
S-41        return 0;
S-42    }
```

C / C++

Fortran
---

1   *Example reproducible.1.f90* (**omp_5.0**)

```
S-1     program main
S-2        use omp_lib
S-3        implicit none
S-4        integer, parameter :: n = 1000
S-5        integer :: v(n), u(n)
S-6        integer :: i
S-7        integer, save :: sum
S-8        !$omp threadprivate(sum)
S-9
S-10       !! no data dependences, so can execute concurrently
S-11       !$omp parallel do order(concurrent)
S-12       do i = 1, n
S-13          u(i) = i
S-14          v(i) = i
S-15          v(i) = v(i) + u(i) * u(i)
S-16       end do
S-17
S-18       !! with data dependences, so cannot execute iterations
S-19       !! concurrently with the order(concurrent) clause
S-20       !$omp parallel do ordered
S-21       do i = 2, n
S-22          v(i) = v(i) + u(i) * u(i)
S-23          !$omp ordered
S-24             v(i) = v(i) + v(i-1)
S-25          !$omp end ordered
S-26       end do
S-27
```

```
S-28        sum = 0
S-29        !! accessing a threadprivate variable, which would not be
S-30        !! permitted if the order(concurrent) clause was present
S-31        !$omp parallel do copyin(sum)
S-32        do i = 2, n
S-33           sum = sum + v(i)
S-34        end do
S-35
S-36        !$omp parallel
S-37           print *,"sum = ",sum," on thread ", omp_get_thread_num()
S-38        !$omp end parallel
S-39
S-40    end program
```

———————————————————————— Fortran ————————————————————————

Modifiers to the **order** clause, introduced in OpenMP 5.1, may be specified to control the
reproducibility of the loop schedule for the associated loop(s). A reproducible loop schedule will
consistently yield the same mapping of iterations to threads (or SIMD lanes) if the directive name,
loop schedule, iteration space, and binding region remain the same. The **reproducible**
modifier indicates the loop schedule must be reproducible, while the **unconstrained** modifier
indicates that the loop schedule is not reproducible. If a modifier is not specified, then the **order**
clause does not affect the reproducibility of the loop schedule.

The next example demonstrates the use of the **order(concurrent)** clause with modifiers for
additionally controlling the reproducibility of a loop's schedule. The two worksharing-loop
constructs in the first **parallel** construct specify that the loops have reproducible schedules, thus
memory effects from iteration *i* from the first loop will be observable to iteration *i* in the second
loop. In the second **parallel** construct, the **order** clause does not control reproducibility for
the loop schedules. However, since both loops specify the same static schedules, the schedules are
reproducible and the data dependences between the loops are preserved by the execution. In the
third **parallel** construct, the **order** clause indicates that the loops are not reproducible,
overriding the default reproducibility prescribed by the specified static schedule. Consequentially,
the **nowait** clause on the first worksharing-loop construct should not be used to ensure that the
data dependences are preserved by the execution.

———————————————————————— C / C++ ————————————————————————

Example reproducible.2.c (**omp_5.1**)

```
S-1     #include <stdio.h>
S-2
S-3     int main()
S-4     {
S-5        const int n = 1000;
S-6        int v[n], u[n];
S-7
S-8        #pragma omp parallel
```

```
S-9         {
S-10            // reproducible schedules are used for the following two constructs
S-11            #pragma omp for order(reproducible: concurrent) nowait
S-12            for (int i = 0; i < n; i++) {
S-13                u[i] = i;
S-14                v[i] = i;
S-15            }
S-16            #pragma omp for order(reproducible: concurrent)
S-17            for (int i = 0; i < n; i++) {
S-18                v[i]  += u[i] * u[i];
S-19            }
S-20        }
S-21
S-22        #pragma omp parallel
S-23        {
S-24            // static schedules preserve data dependences between the loops
S-25            #pragma omp for schedule(static) order(concurrent) nowait
S-26            for (int i = 0; i < n; i++) {
S-27                u[i] = i;
S-28                v[i] = i;
S-29            }
S-30            #pragma omp for schedule(static) order(concurrent)
S-31            for (int i = 0; i < n; i++) {
S-32                v[i]  += u[i] * u[i];
S-33            }
S-34        }
S-35
S-36        #pragma omp parallel
S-37        {
S-38            // the default reproducibility by the static schedule is not
S-39            // preserved due to the unconstrained order clause.
S-40            // use of nowait here could result in data race.
S-41            #pragma omp for schedule(static) order(unconstrained: concurrent)
S-42            for (int i = 0; i < n; i++) {
S-43                u[i] = i;
S-44                v[i] = i;
S-45            }
S-46            #pragma omp for schedule(static) order(unconstrained: concurrent)
S-47            for (int i = 0; i < n; i++) {
S-48                v[i]  += u[i] * u[i];
S-49            }
S-50        }
S-51
S-52        return 0;
S-53    }
```

--- C / C++ ---

1   *Example reproducible.2.f90* (**omp_5.1**)

```fortran
program main
   implicit none
   integer, parameter :: n = 1000
   integer :: v(n), u(n)
   integer :: i

   !$omp parallel
      !! reproducible schedules are used the following two constructs
      !$omp do order(reproducible: concurrent) nowait
      do i = 1, n
         u(i) = i
         v(i) = i
      end do
      !$omp do order(reproducible: concurrent)
      do i = 1, n
         v(i) = v(i) + u(i) * u(i)
      end do
   !$omp end parallel

   !$omp parallel
      !! static schedules preserve data dependences between the loops
      !$omp do schedule(static) order(concurrent) nowait
      do i = 1, n
         u(i) = i
         v(i) = i
      end do
      !$omp do schedule(static) order(concurrent)
      do i = 1, n
         v(i) = v(i) + u(i) * u(i)
      end do
   !$omp end parallel

   !$omp parallel
      !! the default reproducibility by the static schedule is not
      !! preserved due to the unconstrained order clause.
      !! use of nowait here could result in data race.
      !$omp do schedule(static) order(unconstrained: concurrent)
      do i = 1, n
         u(i) = i
         v(i) = i
      end do
      !$omp do schedule(static) order(unconstrained: concurrent)
      do i = 1, n
         v(i) = v(i) + u(i) * u(i)
```

```
S-45            end do
S-46        !$omp end parallel
S-47
S-48    end program
```

12.12 `interop` Construct

The **interop** construct allows OpenMP to interoperate with foreign runtime environments. In the example below, asynchronous cuda memory copies and a *cublasDaxpy* routine are executed in a cuda stream. Also, an asynchronous target task execution (having a **nowait** clause) and two explicit tasks are executed through OpenMP directives. Scheduling dependences (synchronization) are imposed on the foreign stream and the OpenMP tasks through **depend** clauses.

First, an interop object, *obj*, is initialized for synchronization by including the **targetsync** *interop-type* in the interop **init** clause (**init (targetsync,obj)**). The object provides access to the foreign runtime. The **depend** clause provides a dependence behavior for foreign tasks associated with a valid object.

Next, the **omp_get_interop_int** routine is used to extract the foreign runtime id (**omp_ipr_fr_id**), and a test in the next statement ensures that the cuda runtime (**omp_ifr_cuda**) is available.

Within the block for executing the *cublasDaxpy* routine, a stream is acquired with the **omp_get_interop_ptr** routine, which returns a cuda stream (*s*). The stream is included in the cublas handle, and used directly in the asynchronous memory routines. The following **interop** construct, with the **destroy** clause, ensures that the foreign tasks have completed.

---------------------------------- C / C++ ----------------------------------

Example interop.1.c (**omp_5.1**)

```
#include <omp.h>
#include <stdio.h>
#include <stdlib.h>
#include <cublas_v2.h>
#include <cuda_runtime_api.h>

#define N 16384

void myVectorSet(int n, double s, double *x)
{
    for(int i=0; i<n; ++i) x[i] = s*(i+1);
}
void myDaxpy(int n, double s, double *x, double *y)
{
    for(int i=0; i<n; ++i) y[i] = s*x[i]+y[i];
}
void myDscal(int n, double s, double *x)
{
    for(int i=0; i<n; ++i) x[i] = s*x[i];
}

```

```
S-23    int main(){
S-24      const  double scalar=2.0;
S-25      double *x, *y, *d_x, *d_y;
S-26      int    dev;
S-27
S-28      omp_interop_t obj=omp_interop_none;
S-29      intptr_t  type;
S-30
S-31      // Async Memcpy requires pinned memory
S-32      cudaMallocHost( (void**)&x,   N*sizeof(double) );
S-33      cudaMallocHost( (void**)&y,   N*sizeof(double) );
S-34      cudaMalloc(     (void**)&d_x, N*sizeof(double) );
S-35      cudaMalloc(     (void**)&d_y, N*sizeof(double) );
S-36
S-37      dev = omp_get_default_device();
S-38      omp_target_associate_ptr(&x[0], d_x, sizeof(double)*N, 0, dev);
S-39      omp_target_associate_ptr(&y[0], d_y, sizeof(double)*N, 0, dev);
S-40
S-41      #pragma omp target nowait depend(out: x[0:N]) \
S-42                       map(from: x[0:N]) device(dev)
S-43      myVectorSet(N,  1.0, x);
S-44
S-45      #pragma omp task depend(out: y[0:N])
S-46      myVectorSet(N, -1.0, y);
S-47
S-48      // get obj for syncing
S-49      #pragma omp interop init(targetsync: obj) device(dev) \
S-50                    depend(in: x[0:N]) depend(inout: y[0:N])
S-51
S-52                                          //foreign rt id and string name
S-53      int       id = (int  )omp_get_interop_int(obj, omp_ipr_fr_id,   NULL);
S-54      char* rt_name = (char*)omp_get_interop_str(obj, omp_ipr_fr_name, NULL);
S-55
S-56      if(obj != omp_interop_none && id == omp_ifr_cuda) {
S-57
S-58        printf(" OpenMP working with %s runtime to execute cublas daxpy.\n",
S-59               rt_name);
S-60        cublasHandle_t handle;
S-61        int rc;
S-62        cublasCreate(&handle);
S-63
S-64        cudaStream_t s=
S-65            (cudaStream_t)omp_get_interop_ptr(obj, omp_ipr_targetsync, &rc);
S-66        if(rc != omp_irc_success) {
S-67          fprintf(stderr,"ERROR: Failed to get %s stream, rt error= %d.\n",
S-68                  rt_name, rc);
S-69          if(rc == omp_irc_no_value)
```

```
S-70                fprintf(stderr,
S-71                        "Parameters valid, no meaningful value available.");
S-72            exit(1);
S-73        }
S-74
S-75        cublasSetStream( handle,s );
S-76        cudaMemcpyAsync( d_x, x, N*sizeof(double),
S-77                         cudaMemcpyHostToDevice, s );
S-78        cudaMemcpyAsync( d_y, y, N*sizeof(double),
S-79                         cudaMemcpyHostToDevice, s );
S-80        cublasDaxpy(     handle, N, &scalar, &d_x[0], 1, &d_y[0], 1 ) ;
S-81        cudaMemcpyAsync( y, d_y, N*sizeof(double),
S-82                         cudaMemcpyDeviceToHost, s );
S-83
S-84    } else {      // Execute as OpenMP offload.
S-85
S-86        printf(" Notice: Offloading myDaxpy to perform daxpy calculation.\n");
S-87
S-88        #pragma omp target depend(inout: y[0:N]) depend(in: x[0:N]) nowait \
S-89                            map(to: x[0:N]) map(tofrom: y[0:N]) device(dev)
S-90        myDaxpy(N, scalar, x, y);
S-91
S-92    }
S-93
S-94     // This also ensures foreign tasks complete.
S-95    #pragma omp interop destroy(obj) nowait depend(out: y[0:N])
S-96
S-97    #pragma omp target depend(inout: x[0:N])
S-98    myDscal(N, scalar, x);
S-99
S-100   #pragma omp taskwait
S-101   printf("(-1:-16384) %f:%f\n", y[0], y[N-1]);
S-102   printf("(-2:-32768) %f:%f\n", x[0], x[N-1]);
S-103
S-104  }
```

———————————————————— C / C++ ————————————————————

12.13 Utilities

This section contains examples of utility routines and features.

12.13.1 Timing Routines

The **omp_get_wtime** routine can be used to measure the elapsed wall clock time (in seconds) of code execution in a program. The routine is thread safe and can be executed by multiple threads concurrently. The precision of the timer can be obtained by a call to the **omp_get_wtick** routine. The following example shows a use case.

──────────────── C / C++ ────────────────

Example get_wtime.1.c

```
#include <stdio.h>
#include <unistd.h>
#include <omp.h>

void work_to_be_timed()
{
  sleep(2);
}

int main()
{
  double start, end;

  start = omp_get_wtime();
  work_to_be_timed();     // any parallel or serial codes
  end = omp_get_wtime();

  printf("Work took %f seconds\n", end - start);
  printf("Precision of the timer is %f (sec)\n", omp_get_wtick());
  return 0;
}
```

──────────────── C / C++ ────────────────

1   *Example get_wtime.1.f90*

```fortran
S-1    subroutine work_to_be_timed
S-2      use, intrinsic :: iso_c_binding, only: c_int
S-3      interface
S-4         subroutine fsleep(sec) bind(C, name="sleep")
S-5            import c_int
S-6            integer(c_int), value :: sec
S-7         end subroutine
S-8      end interface
S-9      call fsleep(2)
S-10   end subroutine
S-11
S-12   program do_work
S-13     use omp_lib
S-14     implicit none
S-15     double precision :: start, end
S-16
S-17     start = omp_get_wtime()
S-18     call work_to_be_timed     ! any parallel or serial codes
S-19     end = omp_get_wtime()
S-20
S-21     print *, "Work took", end - start, "seconds"
S-22     print *, "Precision of the timer is", omp_get_wtick(), "(sec)"
S-23   end program
```

12.13.2 Environment Display

The OpenMP version number and the values of ICVs associated with the relevant environment variables can be displayed at runtime by setting the **OMP_DISPLAY_ENV** environment variable to either **TRUE** or **VERBOSE**. The information is displayed once by the runtime.

A more flexible or controllable approach is to call the **omp_display_env** API routine at any desired point of a code to display the same information. This OpenMP 5.1 API routine takes a single *verbose* argument. A value of 0 or .false. (for C/C++ or Fortran) indicates the required OpenMP ICVs associated with environment variables be displayed, and a value of 1 or .true. (for C/C++ or Fortran) will include vendor-specific ICVs that can be modified by environment variables.

The following example illustrates the conditional execution of the API **omp_display_env** routine. Typically it would be invoked in various debug modes of an application. An important use case is to have a single MPI process (e.g., rank = 0) of a hybrid (MPI+OpenMP) code execute the routine, instead of all MPI processes, as would be done by setting the **OMP_DISPLAY_ENV** to **TRUE** or **VERBOSE**.

1　*Example display_env.1.c* (**omp_5.1**)

```
S-1    #include <omp.h>
S-2
S-3    //implementers: customize debug routines for app debugging
S-4    int debug(){ return 1; }
S-5    int debug_omp_verbose(){ return 0; }
S-6
S-7    int main()
S-8    {
S-9       if( debug() ) omp_display_env( debug_omp_verbose() );
S-10      // ...
S-11      return 0;
S-12   }
```

2　*Example display_env.1.f90* (**omp_5.1**)

```
S-1    !implementers: customize debug routines for app debugging
S-2    function  debug()
S-3      logical :: debug
S-4      debug = .true.
S-5    end function
S-6
S-7    function debug_omp_verbose()
S-8      logical :: debug_omp_verbose
S-9      debug_omp_verbose = .false.
S-10   end function
S-11
S-12   program display_omp_environment
S-13     use omp_lib
S-14     logical :: debug, debug_omp_verbose
S-15
S-16     if( debug() ) call omp_display_env( debug_omp_verbose() )
S-17     !! ...
S-18   end program
S-19
```

A sample output from the execution of the code might look like:

```
OPENMP DISPLAY ENVIRONMENT BEGIN
   _OPENMP='202011'
  [host] OMP_AFFINITY_FORMAT='(null)'
  [host] OMP_ALLOCATOR='omp_default_mem_alloc'
  [host] OMP_CANCELLATION='FALSE'
  [host] OMP_DEFAULT_DEVICE='0'
  [host] OMP_DISPLAY_AFFINITY='FALSE'
  [host] OMP_DISPLAY_ENV='FALSE'
  [host] OMP_DYNAMIC='FALSE'
  [host] OMP_MAX_ACTIVE_LEVELS='1'
  [host] OMP_MAX_TASK_PRIORITY='0'
  [host] OMP_NESTED: deprecated; max-active-levels-var=1
  [host] OMP_NUM_THREADS: value is not defined
  [host] OMP_PLACES: value is not defined
  [host] OMP_PROC_BIND: value is not defined
  [host] OMP_SCHEDULE='static'
  [host] OMP_STACKSIZE='4M'
  [host] OMP_TARGET_OFFLOAD=DEFAULT
  [host] OMP_THREAD_LIMIT='0'
  [host] OMP_TOOL='enabled'
  [host] OMP_TOOL_LIBRARIES: value is not defined
OPENMP DISPLAY ENVIRONMENT END
```

12.13.3 `error` Directive

The **error** directive provides a consistent method for C, C++, and Fortran to emit a *fatal* or *warning* message at *compilation* or *execution* time, as determined by a **severity** or an **at** clause, respectively. When **severity(fatal)** is present, the compilation or execution is aborted. Without any clauses the default behavior is as if **at(compilation)** and **severity(fatal)** were specified.

The C, C++, and Fortran examples below show all the cases for reporting messages.

——————————————————————— C / C++ ———————————————————————

Example error.1.c (**omp_5.2**)

```
S-1   #include <stdio.h>
S-2   #include    <omp.h>
S-3
S-4   int main(){
S-5
S-6   #pragma omp metadirective \
S-7               when(implementation={vendor(gnu)}: nothing )    \
S-8               otherwise(error at(compilation) severity(fatal) \
```

```
S-9                         message("GNU compiler required."))
S-10
S-11    if( omp_get_num_procs() < 3 ){
S-12      #pragma omp error at(runtime) severity(fatal) \
S-13                       message("3 or more procs required.")
S-14    }
S-15
S-16    #pragma omp parallel master
S-17    {
S-18      // Give notice about master deprecation at compile time and run time.
S-19      #pragma omp error at(compilation) severity(warning) \
S-20                       message("Notice: master is deprecated.")
S-21      #pragma omp error at(runtime) severity(warning) \
S-22                       message("Notice: masked used next release.")
S-23
S-24       printf(" Hello from thread number 0.\n");
S-25    }
S-26
S-27    }
```

———————————————— C / C++ ————————————————
———————————————— Fortran ————————————————

1   *Example error.1.f90* (omp_5.2)

```
S-1     program main
S-2     use omp_lib
S-3
S-4     !$omp   metadirective &
S-5     !$omp&      when( implementation={vendor(gnu)}: nothing     ) &
S-6     !$omp&      otherwise( error at(compilation) severity(fatal) &
S-7     !$omp&               message( "GNU compiler required." ) ) )
S-8
S-9
S-10    if( omp_get_num_procs() < 3 ) then
S-11      !$omp  error at(runtime) severity(fatal) &
S-12      !$omp&        message("3 or more procs required.")
S-13    endif
S-14
S-15      !$omp parallel master
S-16
S-17    !! Give notice about master deprecation at compile time and run time.
S-18      !$omp  error at(compilation) severity(warning) &
S-19      !$omp&        message("Notice: master is deprecated.")
S-20      !$omp  error at(runtime) severity(warning) &
S-21      !$omp&        message("Notice: masked to be used in next release.")
S-22
S-23      print*," Hello from thread number 0."
```

```
S-24
S-25        !$omp end parallel master
S-26
S-27    end program
```

-- Fortran --

13 OMPT Interface

OMPT defines mechanisms and an API for interfacing with tools in the OpenMP program.

The OMPT API provides the following functionality:

- examines the state associated with an OpenMP thread
- interprets the call stack of an OpenMP thread
- receives notification about OpenMP events
- traces activity on OpenMP target devices
- assesses implementation-dependent details
- controls a tool from an OpenMP application

The following sections will illustrate basic mechanisms and operations of the OMPT API.

521

13.1 OMPT Start

There are three steps an OpenMP implementation takes to activate a tool. This section explains how the tool and an OpenMP implementation interact to accomplish tool activation.

Step 1. *Determine Whether to Initialize*

> A tool is activated by the OMPT interface when it returns a non-NULL pointer to an **ompt_start_tool_result_t** structure on a call to **ompt_start_tool** by the OpenMP implementation. There are three ways that a tool can provide a definition of **ompt_start_tool** to an OpenMP implementation: (1) Statically linking the tool's definition of **ompt_start_tool** into an OpenMP application. (2) Introducing a dynamically linked library that includes the tool's definition of **ompt_start_tool** into the application's address space. (3) Providing the name of a dynamically linked library appropriate for the architecture and operating system used by the application in the *tool-libraries-var* ICV.

Step 2. *Initializing a First-Party tool*

> If a tool-provided implementation of **ompt_start_tool** returns a non-NULL pointer to an **ompt_start_tool_result_t** structure, the OpenMP implementation will invoke the tool initializer specified in this structure prior to the occurrence of any OpenMP event.

Step 3. *Monitoring Activity on the Host*

> To monitor execution of an OpenMP program on the host device, a tool's initializer must register to receive notification of events that occur as an OpenMP program executes. A tool can register callbacks for OpenMP events using the runtime entry point known as **ompt_set_callback**, which has the following possible return codes: **ompt_set_error**, **ompt_set_never**, **ompt_set_impossible**, **ompt_set_sometimes**, **ompt_set_sometimes_paired**, **ompt_set_always**.

> If the **ompt_set_callback** runtime entry point is called outside a tool's initializer, registration of supported callbacks may fail with a return code of **ompt_set_error**. All callbacks registered with **ompt_set_callback** or returned by **ompt_get_callback** use the dummy type signature **ompt_callback_t**. While this is a compromise, it is better than providing unique runtime entry points with precise type signatures to set and get the callback for each unique runtime entry point type signature.

To use the OMPT interface a tool must provide a globally-visible implementation of the **ompt_start_tool** function. The function returns a pointer to an **ompt_start_tool_result_t** structure that contains callback pointers for tool initialization and finalization as well as a data word, *tool_data*, that is to be passed by reference to these callbacks. A **NULL** return indicates the tool will not use the OMPT interface. The runtime execution of **ompt_start_tool** is triggered by the first OpenMP directive or OpenMP API routine call.

In the example below, the user-provided **ompt_start_tool** function performs a check to make sure the runtime OpenMP version that OMPT supports (provided by the omp_version argument) is identical to the OpenMP implementation (compile-time) version. Also, a **NULL** is returned to indicate that the OMPT interface is not used (no callbacks and tool data are specified).

Note: The omp-tools.h file is included.

────────────────────────── C / C++ ──────────────────────────

Example ompt_start.1.c (**omp_5.0**)

```
#include <stdio.h>
#include <omp.h>
#include <omp-tools.h>

ompt_start_tool_result_t *ompt_start_tool(
unsigned int omp_version,
const char *runtime_version
){
  if(omp_version != _OPENMP)
    printf("Warning: OpenMP runtime version (%i) "
            "does not match the compile time version (%i)"
            " for runtime identifying as %s\n",
            omp_version, _OPENMP, runtime_version);
  // Returning NULL will disable this as an OMPT tool,
  // allowing other tools to be loaded
  return NULL;
}

int main(void){
  printf("Running with %i threads\n", omp_get_max_threads());
  return 0;
}
```

────────────────────────── C / C++ ──────────────────────────

This page intentionally left blank

A Feature Deprecations and Updates in Examples

Deprecation of features began in OpenMP 5.0. Examples that use a deprecated feature have been updated with an equivalent replacement feature.

Table A.1 summarizes deprecated features and their replacements in each version. Affected examples are updated accordingly and listed in Section A.1.

TABLE A.1: Deprecated Features and Their Replacements

Version	Deprecated Feature	Replacement
5.2	**default** clause on metadirectives	**otherwise** clause
5.2	delimited **declare target** directive for C/C++	**begin declare target** directive
5.2	**to** clause on **declare target** directive	**enter** clause
5.2	non-argument **destroy** clause on **depobj** construct	**destroy** (*argument*)
5.2	**allocate** construct for Fortran **ALLOCATE** statements	**allocators** construct
5.2	**depend** clause on **ordered** construct	**doacross** clause
5.2	**linear** (*modifier(list): linear-step*) clause	**linear** (*list:* **step** (*linear-step*), *modifier*) clause
5.1	**master** construct	**masked** construct
5.1	**master** affinity policy	**primary** affinity policy
5.0	**omp_lock_hint_*** constants	**omp_sync_hint_*** constants

These replacements appear in examples that illustrate, otherwise, earlier features. When using a compiler that is compliant with a version prior to the indicated version, the earlier form of an example for a previous version is listed as a reference.

A.1 Updated Examples for Different Versions

The following tables list the updated examples for different versions as a result of feature deprecation. The *Earlier Version* column of the tables shows the version tag of the earlier version. It also shows the prior name of an example when it has been renamed.

Table A.2 lists the updated examples for OpenMP 5.2 in the Examples Document Version 5.2. The *Earlier Version* column of the table lists the earlier version tags of the examples that can be found in the Examples Document Version 5.1.

TABLE A.2: Updated Examples for Version 5.2

Example Name	Earlier Version	Feature Updated
error.1.c, f90	5.1	**default** clause on metadirectives
metadirective.1.c, f90	5.0	replaced with **otherwise** clause
metadirective.2.c, f90	5.0	
metadirective.3.c, f90	5.0	
metadirective.4.c, f90	5.1	
target_ptr_map.4.c	5.1	
target_ptr_map.5.c, f90	5.1	
array_shaping.1.f90	5.0	**to** clause on **declare target**
target_reverse_offload.7.c	5.0	directive replaced with **enter** clause
target_task_reduction.1.c, f90	5.1	
target_task_reduction.2a.c, f90	5.0	
target_task_reduction.2b.c, f90	5.1	
array_shaping.1.c	5.0	delimited **declare target**
async_target.1.c	4.0	directive replaced with
async_target.2.c	4.0	**begin declare target**
declare_target.1.c	4.0	directive for C/C++
declare_target.2c.cpp	4.0	
declare_target.3.c	4.0	
declare_target.4.c	4.0	
declare_target.5.c	4.0	
declare_target.6.c	4.0	
declare_variant.1.c	5.0	
device.1.c	4.0	
metadirective.3.c	5.0	
target_ptr_map.2.c	5.0	
target_ptr_map.3a.c	5.0	
target_ptr_map.3b.c	5.0	
target_struct_map.1.c	5.0	

table continued on next page

table continued from previous page

Example Name	Earlier Version	Feature Updated
target_struct_map.2.cpp	5.0	
target_struct_map.3.c	5.0	
target_struct_map.4.c	5.0	
doacross.1.c, f90	4.5	**depend** clause on **ordered**
doacross.2.c, f90	4.5	construct replaced with **doacross**
doacross.3.c, f90	4.5	clause
doacross.4.c, f90	4.5	
linear_modifier.1.cpp, f90	4.5	modifier syntax change for **linear**
linear_modifier.2.cpp, f90	4.5	clause on **declare simd** directive
linear_modifier.3.c, f90	4.5	
allocators.1.f90	5.0	**allocate** construct replaced with **allocators** construct for Fortran allocate statements
depobj.1.c, f90	5.0	argument added to **destroy** clause on **depobj** construct

Table A.3 lists the updated examples for OpenMP 5.1 in the Examples Document Version 5.1. The *Earlier Version* column of the table lists the earlier version tags and prior names of the examples that can be found in the Examples Document Version 5.0.1.

TABLE A.3: Updated Examples for Version 5.1

Example Name	Earlier Version	Feature Updated
affinity.5.c, f	4.0	**master** affinity policy replaced with **primary** policy
async_target.3.c, f90	5.0	**master** construct replaced with **masked** construct
cancellation.2.c, f90	4.0	
copyprivate.2.c, f	3.0	
fort_sa_private.5.f	3.0	
lock_owner.1.c, f	3.0	
masked.1.c, f	3.0: *master.1.c, f*	
parallel_masked_taskloop.1.c, f90	5.0: *parallel_master_taskloop.1.c, f90*	
reduction.6.c, f	3.0	
target_task_reduction.1.c, f90	5.0	
target_task_reduction.2b.c, f90	5.0	
taskloop_simd_reduction.1.c, f90	5.0	

table continued on next page

table continued from previous page

Example Name	Earlier Version	Feature Updated
task_detach.1.c, f90	5.0	

Table A.4 lists the updated examples for OpenMP 5.0 in the Examples Document Version 5.1. The *Earlier Version* column of the table lists the earlier version tags of the examples that can be found in the Examples Document Version 5.0.1.

TABLE A.4: Updated Examples for Version 5.0

Example Name	Earlier Version	Feature Updated
critical.2.c, f	4.5	`omp_lock_hint_*` constants
init_lock_with_hint.1.cpp, f	4.5	replaced with `omp_sync_hint_*` constants

B Document Revision History

B.1 Changes from 5.1 to 5.2

- General changes:
  - Included a description of the semantics for OpenMP directive syntax (see Section 2 on page 3)
  - Reorganized the Introduction Chapter and moved the Feature Deprecation Chapter to Appendix A
  - Included a list of examples that were updated for feature deprecation and replacement in each version (see Appendix A.1)
  - Added Index entries
- Updated the examples for feature deprecation and replacement in OpenMP 5.2. See Table A.1 and Table A.2 for details.
- Added the following examples for the 5.2 features:
  - Mapping class objects with virtual functions (Section 6.7 on page 184)
  - **allocators** construct for Fortran **allocate** statement (Section 11.2 on page 451)
  - Behavior of reallocation of variables through OpenMP allocator in Fortran (Section 11.2 on page 451)
- Added the following examples for the 5.1 features:
  - Clarification of optional **end** directive for strictly structured block in Fortran (Section 2.4 on page 9)
  - **filter** clause on **masked** construct (Section 3.14 on page 49)
  - **omp_all_memory** reserved locator for specifying task dependences (Section 5.3.9 on page 122)
  - Behavior of Fortran allocatable variables in **target** regions (Section 6.5 on page 176)
  - Device memory routines in Fortran (Section 6.17.5 on page 258)
  - Partial tiles from **tile** construct (Section 8.3 on page 299)
  - Fortran associate names and selectors in **target** region (Section 10.14 on page 436)
  - **allocate** directive for variable declarations and **allocate** clause on **task** constructs (Section 11.2 on page 451)

1   – Controlling concurrency and reproducibility with **order** clause (Section 12.11 on page 506)

2   • Added other examples:

3   – Using lambda expressions with **target** constructs (Section 6.14 on page 230)

4   – Target memory and device pointer routines (Section 6.17.5 on page 258)

5   – Examples to illustrate the ordering properties of the *flush* operation (Section 11.1 on page 440)

6   – User selector in the **metadirective** directive (Section 12.7 on page 482)

B.2 Changes from 5.0.1 to 5.1

8   • General changes:

9   – Replaced **master** construct example with equivalent **masked** construct example
10   (Section 3.14 on page 49)

11   – Primary thread is now used to describe thread number 0 in the current team

12   – **primary** thread affinity policy is now used to specify that every thread in the team is
13   assigned to the same place as the primary thread (Section 4.1.3 on page 65)

14   – The **omp_lock_hint_*** constants have been renamed **omp_sync_hint_*** (Section 9.1
15   on page 309, Section 9.11 on page 350)

16   • Added the following new chapters:

17   – Deprecated Features (on page 525)

18   – Directive Syntax (Section 2 on page 3)

19   – Loop Transformations (Section 8 on page 285)

20   – OMPT Interface (Section 13 on page 521)

21   • Added the following examples for the 5.1 features:

22   – OpenMP directives in C++ *attribute* specifiers (Section 2.2 on page 5)

23   – Directive syntax adjustment to allow Fortran **BLOCK ... END BLOCK** as a structured block
24   (Section 2.4 on page 9)

25   – **omp_target_is_accessible** API routine (Section 6.3 on page 160)

26   – Fortran allocatable array mapping in **target** regions (Section 6.5 on page 176)

27   – **begin declare target** (with **end declare target**) directive (Section 6.13.2 on
28   page 218)

29   – **tile** construct (Section 8.1 on page 285)

1   – **unroll** construct (Section 8.2 on page 289)

2   – Reduction with the **scope** construct (Section 10.9.6 on page 412)

3   – **metadirective** directive with dynamic **condition** selector (Section 12.7 on page 482)

4   – **interop** construct (Section 12.12 on page 512)

5   – Environment display with the **omp_display_env** routine (Section 12.13.2 on page 516)

6   – **error** directive (Section 12.13.3 on page 518)

7   • Included additional examples for the 5.0 features:

8   – **collapse** clause for non-rectangular loop nest (Section 3.8 on page 32)

9   – **detach** clause for tasks (Section 5.4 on page 126)

10   – Pointer attachment for a structure member (Section 6.4 on page 169)

11   – Host and device pointer association with the **omp_target_associate_ptr** routine
12   (Section 6.17.4 on page 255)

13   – Sample code on activating the tool interface (Section 13.1 on page 522)

14   • Added other examples:

15   – The **omp_get_wtime** routine (Section 12.13.1 on page 515)

B.3 Changes from 5.0.0 to 5.0.1

17   • Added version tags (**omp**_*x.y*) in example labels and the corresponding source codes for all
18   examples that feature OpenMP 3.0 and later.

19   • Included additional examples for the 5.0 features:

20   – Extension to the **defaultmap** clause (Section 6.2 on page 155)

21   – Transferring noncontiguous data with the **target update** directive in Fortran (Section 6.8
22   on page 185)

23   – **conditional** modifier for the **lastprivate** clause (Section 10.8 on page 382)

24   – **task** modifier for the **reduction** clause (Section 10.9.2 on page 391)

25   – Reduction on combined target constructs (Section 10.9.3 on page 396)

26   – Task reduction with **target** constructs (Section 10.9.4 on page 400)

27   – **scan** directive for returning the *prefix sum* of a reduction (Section 10.10 on page 425)

28   • Included additional examples for the 4.x features:

- Dependence for undeferred tasks (Section 5.3.9 on page 122)
- **ref**, **val**, **uval** modifiers for **linear** clause (Section 7.4 on page 277)
- Clarified the description of pointer mapping and pointer attachment in Section 6.3 on page 160.
- Clarified the description of memory model examples in Section 11.1 on page 440.

B.4 Changes from 4.5.0 to 5.0.0

- Added the following examples for the 5.0 features:
  - Extended **teams** construct for host execution (Section 3.3 on page 18)
  - **loop** and **teams loop** constructs specify loop iterations that can execute concurrently (Section 3.15 on page 52)
  - Task data affinity is indicated by **affinity** clause of **task** construct (Section 4.2 on page 66)
  - Display thread affinity with **OMP_DISPLAY_AFFINITY** environment variable or **omp_display_affinity()** API routine (Section 4.3 on page 68)
  - **taskwait** with dependences (Section 5.3.6 on page 110)
  - **mutexinoutset** task dependences (Section 5.3.7 on page 117)
  - Multidependence Iterators (in **depend** clauses) (Section 5.3.8 on page 120)
  - Combined constructs: **parallel master taskloop** and **parallel master taskloop simd** (Section 5.8 on page 140)
  - Reverse Offload through *ancestor* modifier of **device** clause. (Section 6.1.6 on page 152)
  - Pointer Mapping - behavior of mapped pointers (Section 6.3 on page 160)
  - Structure Mapping - behavior of mapped structures (Section 6.4 on page 169)
  - Array Shaping with the *shape-operator* (Section 6.8 on page 185)
  - The **declare mapper** directive (Section 6.9 on page 189)
  - Acquire and Release Semantics Synchronization: Memory ordering clauses **acquire**, **release**, and **acq_rel** were added to flush and atomic constructs (Section 9.7 on page 328)
  - **depobj** construct provides dependence objects for subsequent use in **depend** clauses (Section 9.9 on page 340)
  - **reduction** clause for **task** construct (Section 10.9.2 on page 391)
  - **reduction** clause for **taskloop** construct (Section 10.9.5 on page 405)

1 – **reduction** clause for **taskloop simd** construct (Section 10.9.5 on page 405)

2 – Memory Allocators for making OpenMP memory requests with traits (Section 11.2 on
3 page 451)

4 – **requires** directive specifies required features of implementation (Section 12.5 on page 474)

5 – **declare variant** directive - for function variants (Section 12.6 on page 476)

6 – **metadirective** directive - for directive variants (Section 12.7 on page 482)

7 – **OMP_TARGET_OFFLOAD** Environment Variable - controls offload behavior (Section 12.10
8 on page 502)

9 • Included the following additional examples for the 4.x features:

10 – more taskloop examples (Section 5.7 on page 136)

11 – user-defined reduction (UDR) (Section 10.9.7 on page 414)

B.5 Changes from 4.0.2 to 4.5.0

13 • Reorganized into chapters of major topics

14 • Included file extensions in example labels to indicate source type

15 • Applied the explicit **map(tofrom)** for scalar variables in a number of examples to comply
16 with the change of the default behavior for scalar variables from **map(tofrom)** to
17 **firstprivate** in the 4.5 specification

18 • Added the following new examples:

19 – **linear** clause in loop constructs (Section 3.9 on page 38)

20 – **priority** clause for **task** construct (Section 5.2 on page 103)

21 – **taskloop** construct (Section 5.7 on page 136)

22 – *directive-name* modifier in multiple **if** clauses on a combined construct (Section 6.1.5 on
23 page 149)

24 – unstructured data mapping (Section 6.11 on page 209)

25 – **link** clause for **declare target** directive (Section 6.13.5 on page 227)

26 – asynchronous target execution with **nowait** clause (Section 6.16 on page 242)

27 – device memory routines and device pointers (Section 6.17.5 on page 258)

28 – doacross loop nest (Section 9.10 on page 344)

29 – locks with hints (Section 9.11 on page 350)

- C/C++ array reduction (Section 10.9.1 on page 384)

- C++ reference types in data sharing clauses (Section 10.13 on page 434)

B.6 Changes from 4.0.1 to 4.0.2

- Names of examples were changed from numbers to mnemonics

- Added SIMD examples (Section 7.1 on page 263)

- Applied miscellaneous fixes in several source codes

- Added the revision history

B.7 Changes from 4.0 to 4.0.1

Added the following new examples:

- the `proc_bind` clause (Section 4.1 on page 60)

- the `taskgroup` construct (Section 5.5 on page 131)

B.8 Changes from 3.1 to 4.0

- Beginning with OpenMP 4.0, examples were placed in a separate document from the specification document.

- Version 4.0 added the following new examples:

  - task dependences (Section 5.3 on page 105)

  - `target` construct (Section 6.1 on page 144)

  - array sections in device constructs (Section 6.6 on page 180)

  - `target data` construct (Section 6.10 on page 196)

  - `target update` construct (Section 6.12 on page 212)

  - `declare target` directive (Section 6.13 on page 216)

  - `teams` constructs (Section 6.15 on page 233)

  - asynchronous execution of a `target` region using tasks (Section 6.16.1 on page 242)

  - device runtime routines (Section 6.17 on page 251)

  - Fortran ASSOCIATE construct (Section 10.14 on page 435)

  - cancellation constructs (Section 12.4 on page 469)

Index

Printed in Great Britain
by Amazon

27922097R00309